The Last Ranch

Sam Bingham

The Last Ranch

A Colorado Community and the Coming Desert

Pantheon Books New York

 Published in the United States by Pantheon Books, a division of Random House, Inc., New York, and simultaneously in Canada by Random House of Canada Limited, Toronto.

Grateful acknowledgment is made to the following for permission to reprint previously published material: *Curtis Brown:* Excerpt from "The Land" by Vita Sackville-West. Copyright © 1927 by Vita Sackville-West. Reprinted by permission of Curtis Brown, London. · *Peggy Godfrey:* Excerpts from "Hey, Cowboy," "Cattle Work," "Time-Honored Ways," and "Vigil of 559," from *Write'em Cowboy* by Peggy Godfrey. Copyright © 1993 by Peggy Godfrey. Reprinted by permission of Peggy Godfrey, 19157 Country Road 60, Moffat, CO 81143. · *Henry Holt and Company, Inc.:* Excerpt from "West Running Brook" by Robert Frost, from *The Poetry of Robert Frost,* edited by Edward Connery Lathem. Copyright © 1956 by Robert Frost. Copyright © 1928, 1969 by Henry Holt and Company, Inc. · *Howlin' Dog Records:* Excerpt from "The Land of Little Rain" by Don Richmond. Copyright © 1991 by Don Richmond. Reprinted by permission of Don Richmond and Howlin' Dog Records, P.O. Box 825, Alamosa, CO 81101. · *Bud and Eunice Williams:* Transcript excerpts from *The Stockman Grass Farmer Grazing Conference,* filmed and recorded by Bud and Eunice Williams. Copyright © 1990 by Bud and Eunice Williams. Reprinted by permission of Bud and Eunice Williams, P.O. Box 2220, Lloydminster, Alberta, T9V 1R6, CANADA.

Library of Congress Cataloging-in-Publication Data

Bingham, Sam.
The last ranch / Sam Bingham.
p. cm.
Includes index.
ISBN 0-679-42283-8
1. Ranches—Colorado—Saguache County.
2. Desertification—Colorado—Saguache County.
3. Ranch life—Colorado—Saguache County.
4. Ranchers—Colorado—Saguache County. 5. Saguache County (Colo.)—Biography. I. Title.
SF196.U5B55 1996
333.74'137'0978849—dc20 96-6175
CIP

Book design by M. Kristen Bearse
Map by General Cartography, Inc.

Manufactured in the United States of America
First Edition
2 4 6 8 9 7 5 3 1

To the memory of my aunt Kathleen Raoul. When I was six, she changed my life forever by reading *The Secret Garden* aloud and teaching me the word *ecology*. Then, after a joyful spinsterhood teaching other children to find delight in things that creep and grow while spending nothing on herself, she left me the wherewithal to write this book.

Ecological processes are not only more complex than we think. They are more complex than we can *ever* think.

—MICHAEL CROFOOT,
American soil scientist

Contents

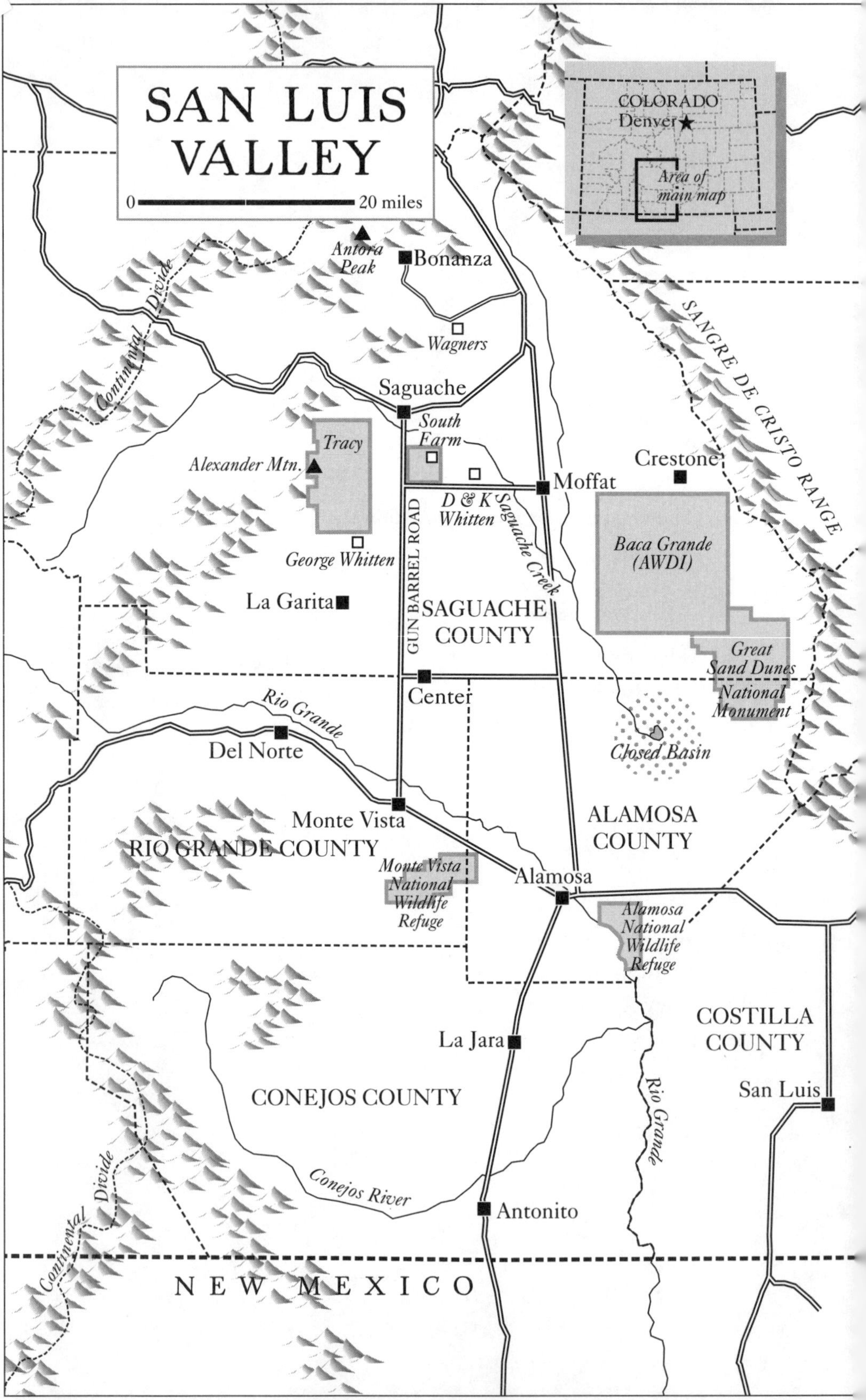
SAN LUIS VALLEY
0 20 miles
COLORADO
Denver
Area of main map
Antora Peak
Bonanza
Wagners
Continental Divide
SANGRE DE CRISTO RANGE
Saguache
South Farm
Tracy
Alexander Mtn.
Crestone
Moffat
D & K Whitten
Saguache Creek
Baca Grande (AWDI)
George Whitten
GUN BARREL ROAD
La Garita
SAGUACHE COUNTY
Great Sand Dunes National Monument
Center
Rio Grande
Closed Basin
Del Norte
Monte Vista
ALAMOSA COUNTY
RIO GRANDE COUNTY
Monte Vista National Wildlife Refuge
Alamosa
Alamosa National Wildlife Refuge
COSTILLA COUNTY
La Jara
Rio Grande
CONEJOS COUNTY
San Luis
Conejos River
Antonito
Continental Divide
NEW MEXICO

Preface

I have written this book to say something about the remorseless advance of deserts, which, according to studies commissioned by the United Nations and other concerned institutions, affects nearly a billion people and almost 30 percent of the Earth's all-too-finite stock of land. The book itself evolved as a series of anecdotes and meditations loosely organized around the working year of a Colorado ranch family, but the writing of it was for me a personal voyage of discovery among larger questions of life on Earth and our human role in it.

I first encountered desert in 1971 when my wife and I accepted teaching positions at Rock Point Community School in the middle of the Navajo Indian Reservation in northeast Arizona. We approached our new home along a road we'd just seen in the movie *Easy Rider*, starring Dennis Hopper. The red bastions of Monument Valley crenellated the horizon. Coming from the leafy Appalachians, it was the most fantastic landscape I'd ever seen, the art of Creation at its most extravagant and most elemental.

We lived there several years before a ninety-year-old Navajo lady first shook this Kodak understanding of deserts. We had asked her to demonstrate the preparation of traditional wild foods to our students.

"How kind of you to ask, young man," she said. "I myself would by all means oblige. The problem lies with the plants. They don't grow here anymore. They've lost interest."

Seeing that she had caught mine, she gestured toward a local landmark called Sheep Shit Spring across land as barren as a tennis court except for a scattering of salt bushes. "In my youth at this time of year

I could take a basket out there and by noon when the sheep got to the spring, I would have collected enough seed from the sacaton grass to feed my family for a day."

Sacaton seeds are hardly bigger than dust particles, and she had had a large family.

"Now the grass is gone, so we collect food stamps. Your students have grown up eating paper." The idea made her laugh.

"And what killed the grass?" I asked.

"I already told you. Nothing killed it. It lost interest. When the government forced us to cut back our sheep, the grasses saw no reason to grow there, so they left. Then the sky had no reason to trouble himself with sending down rain, so we settled into drought, and a lot of other plants left. Some people argue that the sky became disgusted first over the sheep and let the grass die, but I think the grass went first. Either way, grass or sky, I understand how they felt. When they took the sheep, a lot of Navajos lost interest in life and left us, too."

For some years after that, I repeated the old woman's account often to illustrate the difference between "science" and "myth." Records showed that the rainfall pattern, though always erratic, had not changed measurably in her lifetime and certainly not in the thirty-five years since the Bureau of Indian Affairs' Stock Reduction Program had slaughtered and cremated several hundred thousand Navajo sheep before the eyes of their uncomprehending owners.

I taught a vocational agriculture course and had just won a federal grant to direct a small research and education program called the Rock Point Range Management Project after the name of the community where we lived. I had it from world-class range scientists that the waist-high grassland described by the old woman's generation had probably never covered a tenth of the land they claimed to remember. The environment was simply too harsh. Furthermore, the only problem with the stock reduction program was that it had come seventy-five years too late. The extreme desertification we faced now resulted without question from the fact that the old woman and her clansmen had systematically cheated on their livestock quotas and probably would continue to do so as long as they held to the primitive Navajo attitude that more animals meant more prestige, even if they were nothing but bones.

The future of Navajo Country depended on my beating it into the heads of the paper-fed generation that prestige was a function of cash return, and they could get more of that with fewer, fatter animals. Also, I had to convince them that the land would have to be plowed and reseeded. Earthworks must be thrown up to stop erosion. It might require fertilizer at the start, and maybe half a dozen years of complete rest from livestock. Since "treatment" of even so small an area as the way to Sheep Shit Spring would cost more than the fattest livestock could pay back in a century, the land, too, would have to go on welfare.

Neither my students nor their parents took much pleasure in this message, but they bought it because I was the College Trained Expert, and this was "science," and Grandma was an illiterate who talked to plants as if they were people.

I stayed in Navajo Country thirteen years, long enough to see or take part in every kind of range land welfare—plowing, seeding hybrid grasses, seeding native grasses, seeding by aircraft, green belts, weed control by poison, weed control by fire, clearing brush, planting better brush, tree planting, fenced pastures, well drilling, emergency feed programs, enforced rest, exotic breeds, and much much more.

Most of these measures made matters instantly worse. None promised a sustainable, affordable, belly-filling solution.

About that time, however, I ran into an anthropologist who had just come back from a research project in the Sahel region of western Africa, which had just suffered the first really murderous drought ever recorded on TV. She first surprised me by pointing out that the Sahel did not look much worse than Navajo Country, except that African governments could not give people paper to eat. Then she recounted how the range scientists on her team had insisted that the problem was too much livestock and would continue as long as the people held to the primitive native attitude that more animals meant more prestige, even if they were nothing but bones.

"We anthropologists disagreed," she said, "because old people told us that herd sizes had fluctuated greatly in the past and droughts come and gone, but the consequences hadn't been nearly so catastrophic when people lived in the 'Old Way,' by which they meant before secured borders, fences, roads, cash, farming, drilled wells, regulations, wage work, and the rest of it. We came to the conclusion that the desertification had nothing to do with numbers of animals and primitive values, but with the way socioeconomic developments had forced changes in the way people managed their farms and flocks. I suspect something similar happened in Navajo Country."

I thought afresh about that statement: "The plants lost interest."

A short time later I encountered another scientist fresh out of Africa who made those words more than just a colorful metaphor. A Rhodesian wildlife biologist named Allan Savory had just come to North America with the astonishing thesis that in arid environments grass and large grazing animals had evolved a symbiotic relationship so that removing herds would cause grass to stagnate and even die. Furthermore, he pointed out that when soil is laid bare to bake and crust over, rain may run off and evaporate so fast that a landscape becomes drought-stricken in the wettest of years.

Really?!!

"Check out the 'most progressive' ranch bordering the Navajo Reservation," Savory advised. "I can tell you without looking that it, too, looks like the Sahel, but the rancher will remember his great-grandfather saying he lost calves in the sacaton. The only reason people aren't starving there now is that no one lives there anymore but the rancher and his wife. Their kids have split, because they know they'll never pay the mortgage on the place."

He was right.

For many years now I have remained close to Savory as his theories have continued to develop at right angles to the standard version, slowly winning acceptance in the teeth of often vehement derision. As my own thinking about the workings of the world has progressed and broadened, the desert question—through which my smug assurance of knowing-anything-for-certain was shattered forever—remains for me a metaphor for all the life we destroy because our habit of thought blinds us.

It was tempting to set this book in Navajo Country where my experience began, but I did not, for several reasons. First, thirteen years as an Anglo on the Reservation is no license to play around with Navajo metaphors when your former students will read your work. More important, I want the heros of my tale to stand as far from the Third World as possible. Desertification is already too easy to dismiss as a problem urbanized, industrialized societies have risen above, and this discounts the benefit of doing something about it or learning from it.

Interspersed throughout are also many asides on Africa, because I could not ignore the continent where the very term "desertification" originated. *And* not to mention it would again imply a difference between life there and life here. In significant ways rural Colorado has more in common with rural Burkina Faso than with Denver, which in turn shares more with Ouagadougou than with the principal town of Saguache County.

This is not a common thesis, but I did not invent it. Robert Kaplan, writing in the February 1994 issue of *The Atlantic Monthly* about the compounding disasters consuming Africa and many other places in the Third World, said:

> When the Berlin Wall was falling, in November of 1989, I happened to be in Kosovo, covering a riot between Serbs and Albanians. The future was in Kosovo, I told myself that night, not in Berlin. The same day that Yitzhak Rabin and Yaser Arafat clasped hands on the White House lawn, my Air Afrique plane was approaching Bamako, Mali, revealing corrugated-zinc shacks at the edge of an expanding desert. The real news wasn't at the White House, I realized. It was right below.

This viewpoint may appear no less odd than the Navajo woman's opinion that the plants had "lost interest" but perhaps will prove no less true if we find a way to understand it.

A few months after reading Kaplan I found myself in Paris. The newspapers on Saturday, June 18, 1994, had a lot to say about the latest collapse of the dollar on world markets, the crisis of ruling political parties throughout Europe and Japan, stalled Bosnian peace talks, the knife murder of American ex-football star O. J. Simpson's ex-wife, the machete murder of 250,000 Tutsi tribespeople in Rwanda, the possibility of nuclear war with North Korea, and the opening matches of the World Cup Soccer Tournament.

With such headlines, French editors did not mention that in their own capital the Intergovernmental Negotiating Committee for the

Elaboration of an International Convention to Combat Desertification in those Countries Experiencing Serious Drought and/or Desertification, Particularly in Africa had agreed on a text after an all-night session in the UNESCO building. No current famine, locust plague, or other crisis lent drama to the event, and the committee itself had wrangled for nearly two years since a United Nations Conference on Environment and Development in Rio de Janeiro had commissioned its work.

The Convention to Combat Desertification would take its place beside recently concluded blueprints for worldwide campaigns against climate change and the loss of biodiversity, which are perhaps only other manifestations of the same crisis. Despite the competing headlines it still might have made the evening news if it had bound anyone to spend money or actually do much. Unfortunately, the negotiators had worked in shifts around the clock and made sure it didn't. When their mandate expired without an accord on financial arrangements, they had even pushed on into surreality and created a thirty-two-hour day, recording their adjournment time of 8 A.M. Saturday as midnight Friday. In the windowless conference rooms and corridors of diplomacy, however, redefining the revolution of the planet is no big deal.

Actually combatting deserts, which has to do with keeping the planet alive, is a lot harder. If the 299 committee delegates from 100 countries and the hundreds of attending observers, technicians, legal experts, advocacy groups, economists, and analysts of many kinds who contributed to the convention on desertification often looked like characters out of the Humpty Dumpty story, they could blame the scale of the challenge.

"Particularly in Africa," as the official title of the convention reflected, the misery caused by desertification, the degradation of productive land through human impact and fickle weather, has reached levels that have linked the very word to some dark list of horrors peculiar to that continent. The threat, however, is truly global.

According to UN statistics oft cited at plenary sessions of the Negotiating Committee, more than 40 percent of all land qualifies as desert or dry land, and is thus vulnerable to desertification, and 70 percent of that has been degraded already, affecting the lives of 900 million people. The resulting starvation, forced migration, poverty, and warfare defies measure.

I believe it also defies common habits of thought, which explains why the International Convention to Combat Desertification in those Countries Experiencing Serious Drought and/or Desertification, Particularly in Africa turned out the way it did.

Despite its stubbornly ambiguous language and avoidance of financial commitment, the resulting report is not an irrelevant document, and the people who cobbled it together deserve considerable credit. Apart from a few, like the Saudi who protested all reference to "alternative energy sources" as a greater threat to Saudi well-being than the sands of Araby, most negotiators kept their self-interest enlightened. Surprisingly for such a forum, they officially recognized that solutions would require much more sophisticated forms of regional cooperation than the patchwork of project grants and development programs common in the past. They accepted the need for local participation in all decisions, including the voices of women and previously disenfranchised minorities. They outlined a creative response to the double corruption of governments that steal aid money and donor nations that featherbed their own institutions through useless projects with high overhead. But I do not believe that they got to the real heart of deserts.

Coming out of the Paris Metro on the morning before the Intergovernmental Negotiating Committee for the Elaboration of the International Convention to Combat Desertification in those Countries Experiencing Serious Drought and/or Desertification, Particularly in Africa declared the thirty-two-hour day and issued its twenty-seven-page text and four regional annexes, I chanced to meet His Excellency Mr. Abdoulaye Bathily, minister of the environment and the protection of nature of Senegal, and asked him how he viewed the proceedings.

"Well," he said, "there isn't going to be any money. We've cut out all reference to nomadic peoples, grazing, and livestock, which everybody knows is central to any solution. In fact we've deleted reference to anything specific, but we are told that this is necessary because otherwise there would be no agreement at all. We are going to produce a document by diplomats and for diplomats. That is to say, it is in the language of diplomats in which words are chosen that mean what people want them to mean. I doubt they mean to your government what they mean to me or what they might mean to your next government or mine, so I cannot tell *you* what they mean. They mean we've met, and we talked, and will do so again."

Maybe this is all we can expect, and maybe it is even healthy. Nevertheless, it made me aware of one more reason I wrote this book, though I could not have articulated it before.

Subliminally I had hoped that as I labored through the choice of words and fine metaphors, I would discover a language through which the rancher, the scientist, the anthropologist, the African nomad, the urban land developer, the environmental activist, and I could meet and talk to one another with sharpness of meaning and revolutionary significance about our little planet.

I guess I'm still embarrassed about laughing at an old woman who said "the plants lost interest," but I want to put the Tower of Babel behind us. If the Almighty divided us to keep us from dominating His creation, perhaps He'll let us come back together to save what's left.

The Last Ranch

1

Welcome to the Desert

The year is 1992. The double-wide trailer house out on the flats southeast of Saguache, Colorado, is as good a place as any to start saving the world, not that Donnie and Karen Whitten would ever express it that way. To raise cattle, sheep, and three children named Clint, Nathan, and Sarah there is vocation enough, but maybe it's the same thing.

When regarded from an address like 52,495 County Road T, the tender lonesomeness of the planet is hard to ignore. The Whittens get a kind of astronaut's perspective on it out there, and when Donnie says, "Anybody who's been here a long time can see that things can't keep going the way they have been," he isn't just talking about Saguache County.

An axiom of biology holds that changes in the health of an organism show up first at the margins, and this spot in the San Luis Valley of south-central Colorado is a margin. Why should someone living there, then, not suspect that maybe he, not the denizens of great cities and well-watered heartlands, lives on the cutting edge of the future, and why should he not take this responsibility seriously?

Donnie and Karen met as kids in 4-H and married soon after high school with a vision of doing exactly what they are in fact doing. Not long ago they actually wrote down what they want from life. Karen says it took them hours and hours of discussion to distill into words desires that they admit might have been expressed by almost anyone at any place in any age. And yet, says Donnie, "When you're caught up with making a living, you don't stop to think much about what you're really after. We still have to go back and look at it from time to time just to keep it in mind. Otherwise you forget why you're here."

The statement reads:

> We want to live in and be a part of a healthy and vital rural community. We want to maintain our individuality. Our family, neighbors, and friends are important to us, as is a healthy environment. We want to stay in touch with current events and be able to continue to learn about all our world through education, travel, and other contacts with people and ideas. We feel we need to have good communication between ourselves, our children, our neighbors, and our community. We enjoy the outdoors, working with livestock and wildlife, and our tie to the land. We would like to be able to live comfortably yet be able to maintain our budget. We like a nice home, and it is important to be able to maintain it as well as all the outbuildings, etc. We would like to see each of us continue to grow as individuals with the love and support of all our family. We feel there must be a balance between time we commit to work and personal, family, and couple time.

There could be other goals to shoot for, but probably easier places to do it.

The San Luis Valley is flat, stark country, and it's easy to imagine some young Jacob pausing there on a blind flight from the drudgery of an Iowa farm toward a dream of fortune and looking straight up into heaven and digging a well, which is more or less what Donnie's granddad, William Eugene Whitten, did in 1898, but unlike Jacob, he didn't move on. He stayed.

He sought ranch work and eventually acquired a piece of land, a foothold on which he'd build, and sheep at a time when the grass grew belly high in the foothills, springs were abundant, chico brush held less dominion over the plain, and the mountains teemed with miners who paid dearly for meat. When he died, his three children, one of them Donnie's father, George, split the land, even though by then it produced less than it had as virgin ground. When Donnie and his brother, George, Jr., finished high school and against all logic wanted to stay in the valley and raise families, their father opened a liquor store down the valley in the town of Center to lighten the burden on the ranch. When he retired, however, the two brothers split the land again. Each now has 2,500 acres plus a summer grazing permit on federal land in the western foothills on which to realize his goals. This pushes the bottom limit of what the agricultural economists at Colorado State University consider a viable resource base in that kind of country.

The valley is high desert. From the 14,000-foot wall of the Sangre de Cristo range to the east to the less abrupt but equally powerful rise of the Continental Divide to the west, it stretches 50 miles wide and 75 miles long and is level as a tennis court. Eight inches of precipitation bless it in an average year, but no gambler would bet on the average. Somewhat more reliable mountain snows feed such plentiful acquifers beneath the plain, however, that they outcrop in marshes that occasionally still teem with waterfowl. The Rio Grande rises there and escapes into New Mexico by a mighty crack in the mountains, dropping 7,500 feet through even brittler land to Texas, Mexico, and the sea.

Changes in the valley itself began with European settlement not 200 years ago. San Luis, the oldest town in Colorado, was incorporated in 1854. The graying fence rails in the Whittens' corral, according to Donnie, were cut by his grandfather around 1900. That in itself is another symptom of desert life. The record stays. Nothing rots. The fence rails will last forever. So will the ruins of the homesteaders' cabins, abandoned by the dozens during the Depression. So will the sky-raking skeletons of willows that the homesteaders transplanted for shade and that, like their transplanted planters, grew more ambitiously than the alkali soil could support and died at the height of their grandeur. Except, being willows, they never quite died, so green shoots still sprout here and there on the huge blanched trunks.

Now, because the soil proved so hostile to cultivation, ranching dominates the north half of the valley, but in the south end the groundwater feeds one of the world's greatest concentrations of center pivot irrigation. There, solemnly rotating aluminum booms sprinkle more than 2,000 quarter-mile circles of potatoes and malt barley (Colorado brews more beer than any other state), as well as carrots, lettuce, alfalfa, and anything else that can make a crop in 100 frost-free days.

Nevertheless, even the most prosperous farmers there know that from nature's point of view this is cosmetology. The place is still a desert, harsher yet for their efforts than the one their ancestors settled. If the water table drops, if credit dries up, if prices fall, if soil salinity increases, if fuel and chemical costs rise, if exotic pests multiply, the green makeup will crack right off the hard dry face of it.

Similar fears haunt the whole length of the Rio Grande. Despite international treaties and compacts guaranteeing its life, now only a salty trickle of the Great River reaches the Gulf of Mexico, thanks to the dry winds and flash floods that rip the water off land made barren by exploitation and neglect. And because the San Luis Valley is marginal in comparison to the economies of New Mexico, West Texas, Chihuahua, Coahuila, and Nuevo Leon that depend on the river, the federal government has arranged by means of electric pumps, 170 wells, 115 miles of pipe, and a 42-mile canal to put an extra 100,000 acre feet a year of San Luis Valley groundwater into the Rio Grande to keep the flow legal according to multiple compacts and treaties.

Higher up the valley, a group of private investors that calls itself American Water Development, Inc., hoped to pump a similar amount of groundwater and *sell* it downstream to Albuquerque or El Paso or pump it over the mountains and sell it to metropolitan Denver. According to the engineers they employed, hugely sophisticated computer programs derived from infallible equations prove that neither project will make life in the valley even the slightest bit more marginal.

Natives like the Whittens mainly find the export of groundwater symbolic of the value the outside world sets on their home country. In the West, they say, water flows uphill toward money. The San Luis Valley would not be the first place, even in Colorado, to be sucked dry and laid to waste by this phenomenon, but precedent points to the likelihood of other more chthonian forces as well.

The fact is that no place even remotely as arid as the San Luis Valley has ever come into the orbit of any civilization and escaped reduction into howling desert. Nor, it must be pointed out, have the civilizations—Mede, Persian, Nabatean, Anasazi—survived either, although to be sure this extraordinarily dismal record was achieved before the advent of modern science and technology.

On a bright Saturday morning in February, however, the practical business of ranch work banishes such abstract worries. The Whittens' neighbor, Marty Shellebarger, who happens also to be a vet, is at the corral testing bulls. The process is simple. The animals, already confined in a chute, are prodded one by one into a steel crush that holds them fast. Then Donnie, dressed in coveralls and work boots, lubricates an object resembling a 90-mm artillery shell with grease from a tube and eases it up the rectum of each prospective father of his calf crop.

On his knees beside the crush, Marty holds in his right hand what amounts to a condom stretched open over a small frame. He maneuvers that into position under his subject and with his left hand turns a dial on a black box, which is connected by one set of wires to the artillery shell and by another to the battery of his truck. The bull's penis shoots out and in a spasm of what in other circumstances might be ecstasy ejaculates into the condom. A few more twirls of the dial for good measure, and the specimen is ready for the microscope on the front seat of the pickup. The first test, for motility, under relatively low magnification shows the sperm as a shimmering mass, fairly glittering with life. A more powerful lens checks the sperms' morphology. Are the cells round and smooth? Are the tails straight and strong? Donnie and Marty squint into the eyepiece at 7,000 years of genetics. Somewhere in each of those translucent tadpoles are the quantum fragments of the bulls of Cretan murals, Egyptian friezes, Camargue bogs, English hill farms, and the vast plateaux of Spain. Not all of this will survive, however. An occasional sample shows up less than vigorous, the heads of the tadpoles lopsided, the tails broken and bent. Donnie jots down the donor's number. Therewith his line is ended. His impact on world hunger will come soon, as hamburger.

The selection of bulls each year is a moment for creativity in a herd and in coming to terms with a desert. It's one of several points where Darwin, aesthetics, economics, and prejudice all come together. When Karen Whitten, remarking on a newcomer to the ranching business, said, "He doesn't identify much with his cows yet. To him they're just cows," she wasn't implying that she views Whitten cows as pets. She meant that they, like her children, Nathan, Clinton, and Sarah, were genetically Whittens. For nearly a century Whittens have annually selected which genes to add to their bovine family and, through culling and selling, which would leave it. If the third-grade teacher in Saguache could guess Clint's surname from the shape of his ears, his family's cattle were also Whittens in much more than brand.

In Tuareg tents, Australian cattle stations, and the coffee shop in Saguache, livestock people endlessly discuss how applied human brainpower can make creation better. The trick, of course, is to define "better," to breed a race of animals that thrives on your land in your climate under your style of management, sells in your markets, and fits your finances. This is a much more complex task than implied in most lay descriptions of what modern genetic engineering can do for the livestock business. A championship bull of a recognized breed may sell for $100,000 and his semen produce offspring that show terrific rates of growth, great weight by the time they wean, excellent "cutability" as the butcher's phrase goes, and consistent color. But, for the price, will these progeny calve on the open range? Will they fight off predators? Will they handle gently? Can they breathe at high altitude? Will the calves be too big for my cows? Are they disease resistant? Will they thrive on desert forage?

This selection of the best for the place and need has given rise to hundreds of cattle breeds, among them, although not officially registered, the Whittens' black Hereford-Angus cross cattle. This year's bulls, however, break with Whitten tradition. They will spice the gene pool with a touch of French blood. Red Tarentaise cattle, first imported in 1972 from an Alpine valley that feeds the Rhône, are one of many "exotic" breeds promoted in the United States in recent years as American cattle people have scrambled to react to changing conditions—consumer flight to lean cuts; rising capital, land, and labor costs; competition from poultry and pork; and advances in the science of cattle feeding.

The Whittens' criteria are specific.

"We want small, hardy cattle," Donnie says, "because, to be honest, we lose a few out here, and having your life savings tied up in more little ones rather than fewer big ones is less risky. We like little calves, because we can't afford calving problems. And of course, we do want them to grow fast and be heavy when they wean. It's also important that our cows handle easy but be extremely protective mothers."

He can thank a few centuries of Savoyard herdsmen for sharing this point of view. The Tarentaise are one of the few continental European breeds that are fairly small, and yet because they have also been selected for dairy production, breeders claim 1,000-pound cows produce enough milk to grow a steer calf to 600 pounds by sale time, which beats the best Herefords by about 70 pounds and the Whittens' smaller race by even more. The American Tarentaise Association advertises well-formed teats that do not balloon with age, early puberty, an excellent mothering instinct, and lean meat. They also claim that Tarentaise-cross cattle in North Africa have performed wonderfully in an arid environment. Most intriguing of all, to the Whittens, is the promise of a mystical phenomenon called heterosis, hybrid vigor, the likelihood that the issue of diversity will be better in all traits than either of the parents. The Tarentaise are real exotics whose mountain homeland kept them apart from other breeds.

Their electrified sexual activity over, Donnie turns his bulls, doomed and fertile alike, back out to pasture, and Marty packs away his equipment. As any vigorous male fraternity would, before settling down to graze the bulls butt and cavort a bit in familiar rehearsal for the time in June when they will compete at a ratio of thirty females to the bull to demonstrate their own ability to decide whose traits will prevail. Having assured himself that his bulls can do their part, Whitten will abet Darwin to the extent that any cow that fails, *for any reason,* to conceive and raise a calf to weaning time goes to the packinghouse before the next season, if not immediately.

Since ancient times, herdsmen have used similar selective breeding and culling criteria to improve production by adapting their animals to fit the environment, but this goal is not as obvious as it might seem, especially given the options afforded by modern science. Often in response to market opportunities, stock growers have adapted their herds to exploit rather than harmonize with their habitat. In Colorado, in the era of Donnie's grandfather, this led to open warfare between cattle and sheep raisers. The cattlemen, who argued that sheep destroyed their ranges, simply did not see that in fact their own animals had destroyed the heavy fibrous grasses on which cows thrive better than sheep and created an environment in which sheep (dainty nibblers they) were more profitable. In areas where destructive sheep grazing has further reduced the range to brush, goats, which can browse standing on their hind legs, often still thrive, thus earning an ill-deserved reputation as the world's most destructive grazers, when in fact their niche is often merely the last to go. They cannot compete with cows on lusher grass.

Now we have the further option of creating animals that produce prodigiously and then adapting the environment to them rather than vice versa. Thus we have super dairy cows that even before getting extra lactation hormones can't physically consume grass fast enough to keep a super udder in business. If they don't get a highly concentrated, scientifically formulated diet, the demand of their outrageous organ will actually cause them to starve. Similarly, the beef industry has achieved remarkable production levels by turning a grazing animal into one that can convert grain into meat almost as efficiently as a hog or chicken, but this occurs best in a feedlot well supplied with surplus soybeans and corn.

Both strategies exist side by side in the San Luis Valley, even on the Whittens' land, to the extent that they don't rely totally on open rangeland. They mitigate the demands of winter by raising hay on irrigated meadows. They buy alfalfa in winter emergencies. And their calves do fatten in a feedlot. But they talk less about producing meat than "harvesting sunlight," turning the energy God sheds on their land into something useful.

In fact, Donnie and Karen pin their hopes on a more positive extension of the adaptation theory. They like to think that the land adapts to their animals as actively as vice versa and consequently can change positively as well as negatively if they can just learn how to make it happen.

"We've got elk, mule deer, and pronghorn antelope here," Donnie points out, "which really aren't that much different in terms of how they eat than cattle, sheep, and goats, although the niches overlap a little differently. There must have been thousands of wild grazers here once. Against the south slope of any little hill where the snow melts in winter you can find enough old arrowheads and bones to indicate that big bunches of Indians spent the winter here and lived off the game. Every once in a while over at the Great Sand Dunes National Monument southeast of here a dune moves and uncovers the remains of big encampments. Nobody knows exactly what condition the land was in, but at least it must have been pretty stable. That's what I'd like to shoot for with our livestock."

Not too far away from the corrals, where the new bulls are showing their stuff, 250 Whitten cows, still mostly black with white faces, their bodies wide in the last days of pregnancy, munch the remains of last year's grass and wait for spring. The scene violates ancient Western custom, however, because dispersed among the cattle are 200 sheep, also swollen with unborn lambs.

"There're a lot of folks in the valley would tell you that's absolutely impossible, but I think having both sheep and cattle uses the range better, and the extra diversity is some kind of insurance, like not putting all your eggs in one basket. They've learned to get along just fine," says Donnie, as one of the sheep separates from the bunch and challenges us with a warning bark and bared fangs. It is actually Ralph, a shaggy white Great Pyrenees dog who was raised with lambs and learned to consider them family. He stays out with his ruminant harem day and night, eating dry kibbled dog food from an automatic dispenser and watching for coyotes.

"I wish I'd had my camera the other evening," Whitten went on. "I noticed Ralph sitting on a little rise just off to one side of the sheep, and there facing him not fifty yards away sat two coyotes. They stayed there for a long time, and you could just imagine the conversation going on, but in the end those coyotes just got up and went away. They've learned to get along."

It was the second time he had used the phrase. Do competing species learn to get along with each other? Did Ralph actually teach the coyotes a lesson or merely catch them in the act for the umpteenth time? Can you really expect to negotiate getting along with a wild creature that competes with you at the top of the food chain? And further down the food chain, can sheep and cattle learn to get along with the plants they eat, as Donnie would like to believe on the evidence of their wild cousins? Can a modern family actually achieve the quality of life the Whittens envision by learning to get along rather than merely to get? These are all radical ideas that cowboy tradition long ago answered in the negative, but what use is youth and ownership if not to raise questions?

In Indian tradition, coyotes personify creative devilment and a flair for sophistry quite sufficient for debating with a European sheepdog, but with some notable exceptions, communications have broken down in recent times. To the average rancher now, coyotes incarnate nothing but evil. By law and policy in all Western states today the only really good coyote is a dead one.

"Like everyone else around here, I was raised to shoot a coyote on sight," explains Donnie. "In our spare time we'd go out in the brush somewhere with coyote callers that scream like wounded rabbits and shoot them for the hell of it. It didn't make much difference. They really are crafty, and when food is plentiful, they multiply like rabbits. This, combined with the fact that they will move in from great distances to reoccupy any vacant territory, means you don't ever get rid of them. Before Ralph, they'd take a few thousand dollars in lambs a year no matter what we did. Now they don't take any, and we don't shoot any."

Off in the direction of the foothills to the west one could hear the hum of a small plane punctuated by an occasional pop of rifle fire.

"That's the air war," Whitten chuckled.

ADC (for Animal Damage Control) officers from the U.S. Department of Agriculture were cruising the hinterland pursuing the final solution from the open door of a Piper Supercub and apparently finding a lot of targets.

"They'll get hundreds. They're supposed to get permission to shoot on private land, so they won't come here, but a lot of folks do invite them in. By and large it's a typical government program. Since they can't shoot around livestock, they don't get the ones that have learned to live on livestock, so we don't see much effect from it, which means they can justify doing it forever. The skins used to be worth so much that on a good day they could easily get enough to pay for the air time and make a little profit, but the animal rights campaign has pretty much killed the fur market."

Ralph has dealt with the coyotes on a more sophisticated level. A continuing interest in his lambs notwithstanding, he has largely taught them to apply their wit elsewhere, and to his advantage. They have apparently agreed to pay in kind for the privilege of staying in a place where no one shoots or poisons them. During calving time, they have learned to hang around and snatch the afterbirths without risking the wrath of the mothers by threatening the calves. They keep ground squirrels, prairie dogs, and rabbits down to reasonable numbers without bullets or poison. They snack on dung beetles and also eat carrion, including stillborn calves. In any case, they sing about their good fortune every night, very likely to keep others out.

If the relationship between predator and prey is thus subtler than it seems, so too, perhaps, is the relationship between the grass and the stock.

The amount of grass standing or stored as hay at the onset of frost represents the total winter feed for whatever animals must live on it, unless the Whittens buy more. Growth stops and the summer's leaves, stems, and seeds die and cure. In the valley, as in most other snow-prone places, ranchers habitually raise hay on their irrigated land and cut and stack as much as possible against those winter days when grass is covered. Unlike sheep, goats, and bison, cattle won't dig through snow, so the rancher must haul a ration out from the pile on a sledge and scatter it around every day. It's backbreaking work, and Donnie and Karen don't do it anymore.

"I got the idea from a ranch in Utah," explains Donnie. "They probably get more snow than we do, but they just rake the hay into little piles scattered here and there and leave it. I saw it when the snow had crusted over so hard you could stand on it, but they had used portable electric fence to concentrate animals to the point where they couldn't help but break through and trample out the snow until they exposed the hay. Once they could see and smell it, they began to eat and uncovered the piles. They wore the hair off their noses reaching up under the ice, but they were all fat, and of course the more they exposed the dark hay, the quicker the sun went to work and melted the snow. Moving the fence was a whole lot easier than stacking and hauling hay, and I couldn't see any waste at all."

In fact, Whitten deduced that except in very deep snow, the concentrated herd would probably open up the ground even if he didn't cut and rake hay at all, but he would lose a lot of it to the weight of the snow, dampness, and trampling. Anything that didn't get eaten remained on the ground as a good mulch. Patches of hard, barren, alkaline ground dating back to Grandfather Whitten's time began to heal where Donnie raked up hay over them and cattle tramped in the fallen seeds and mulch. The coyotes had no complaints. Rodents nesting in the little haystacks made handy snacks.

Then there was the matter of the manure. Cattle and sheep, messy as they are, like clean food and don't enjoy grazing near their own dung and urine. When scattered widely over a pasture, their scattered manure quickly makes large areas unappetizing to them. When the Whittens move their electric fence, the cattle leave yesterday's fouled ground at once and fall to in a concentrated way on today's fresh rations. They don't go back, which means only moving one fence to take in the new ground. They also eat more of what is there and seem to be healthier.

When they hear the sound of Donnie's truck, the cows and sheep move toward the fence and look expectantly. "It isn't just that they anticipate what I'm going to do. They've learned that if they look hungry enough and bawl, I'll do it whether they need it or not. They'll lie to you. In fact, they're very good at training ranchers to do what they want."

On this mild day, moving the fence takes little time. The wire isn't really wire. The stout barbed wired that tamed the West has given way to just a thread of electrified foil woven into two strands of a plastic string (one high enough to shock a cow going over and one low enough to touch a sheep going under) and looped along some wopsy plastic posts spiked into the ground by hand. The stock could go through it if they felt like it, and one of the sheep does but comes back when she discovers herself apart from the herd.

The learning all seems so simple in the middle of winter. You get good stock. Train a sheepdog. Lay off the coyotes. Lay the hay in this new way. Your land improves. Your margins improve. A few new techniques and you gain a stride or two on the desert. You learn to beat the system. But of course this is only February, agricultural dreamtime, when everything seems possible, predictable, and even mechanical. Inevitably the season will turn. The 150 ewes will spill out 300 lambs. Calves by the score will hit the ground and stagger into life, and none of this young life will have learned anything. The irrigation water will come pouring down from the mountain snowfields. Plants will begin to grow, as the fickle weather allows it. And these momentous events, however foreseeable, are not mechanical. They are all pieces of life, as undetermined and pregnant with possibility as the lives of unborn children, the fruitfulness or sterility of which no formula can ensure no matter how much money, or science, or love goes into their care.

"Perhaps that is why we get so hung up on tradition and technological answers to our problems," says Donnie on the drive back to his house. "We ranchers have a reputation for being ornery and independent-minded, and we like to think we are, but really we are about the most cautious, fatalistic group of people you can find. When everything you deal with, whether it's the weather, or the growth rate of your forage, or the health of your animals, or the futures market, is so complex and changeable, your first instinct is to do things like Grandpa did and say, 'That's how it's done, and that's how I did it, and ain't it bad luck that we didn't quite make it this year.' It's only a short step from there to putting your trust in some other authority that supposedly knows *scientifically* how it's done and tells you some new breed or system or machine will save your ass because still, if you fail, it's not your fault. We're trying to learn to think things through for ourselves, but it comes hard.

"It's hard to imagine how scary it was to go into a winter without putting up hay in the traditional way, even though I'd seen that Utah ranch. At first I didn't know what to say when neighbors would ask me, 'What are you going to do when we get three feet of snow and it all freezes over?' Finally, I realized I could just ask them, 'What are *you* going to do?' because in fact that would be a big crisis for everybody and probably no worse for me. I know on one level that you've got to think everything through from the beginning and try to really figure out what's going on, but things like that make you feel pretty lonesome."

Nothing in the atmosphere at 52,495 County Road T on the threshold of an uncharted adventure into spring gives much excuse for brooding, however. The three children, Sarah, six, Clint, eight, and Nathan, ten, having been released from homework by Karen, are kicking soccer balls and chasing loose chickens around outbuildings and relics of a century of survival that still quake with life. There are hutches of rabbits of various kinds, and pens of Spanish and Nubian goats, and a horse and a motorcycle for riding the range. There are stock trailers and broken harrows, and a maybe workable horse-drawn potato planter, and a hierarchy of old trucks to serve as organ donors for one another, and a boxcar from the days when the San Luis Valley Central still made a profit shipping livestock from Moffat to the main line of the Denver and Rio Grande Western at Alamosa.

A shed, where a lot of Whittens were born when it used to be Granddad Whitten's cabin, still stands near a towering willow, and nearby rests the wagon that hauled from the mountains the immortal aspen poles to build it. And in the double-wide mobile home that has taken over from the old cabin there is a party line and the number of the prayer circle from the Methodist Church, an IBM computer with the latest accounting software, and enough cow and sheep in the freezer for unlimited hospitality.

2

Calves

By late March, snow has gone out of the north end of the valley. Water is everywhere. Ducks float in all the ditches and paddle around in the half-flooded meadows. The meadows flood because left-over ice and occasional beaver dams choke Saguache Creek and its spiderweb of attached irrigation and drainage ditches. Ranchers in fits of rage over bogged-down trucks and soaked haystacks tend to shoot beavers for their part in this and dynamite their work, but the furry engineers, even more provoked than their counterparts in the Bureau of Reclamation by the sound of running water, keep doing their best to eliminate it.

Bald eagles, as many as a dozen in a bunch, perch in the old willow and cottonwood skeletons waiting for the wind to bring them news of a free lunch. They know calving season is under way, and somewhere a carcass is bloating to perfection. Gray sandhill cranes on their way north stop in the valley in large numbers to refuel on things they hunt in cow dung and old grain stubble like so many stilted chickens. They hang around for a few weeks, then all at once launch in a jumble of air-borne jackstraws, sort themselves into magnificent skeins, and their wild rippling voices swell and fade until they circle up into shimmering nothingness. Like a musical daytime Pleiades, their formations arc toward Montana above the highest peaks.

If we have a niche in the natural order, perhaps it is simply to take responsibility for life and death where it touches us. As Saint-Exupéry's Little Prince said, "It is the time that you have lost for your rose that makes your rose so important." The labor of care makes bonds, not love but not unlike it either and maybe stronger. This is calving season, the moment when the care and the bond and the wild and the domestic lose distinction. The rancher lives, of course, by raising animals to be bashed on the head, gutted, and eaten. He must succeed at fostering life, knowing that the measure of his success is death. That's working both ends of the food chain simultaneously. That is really wild, for wildness is not a fight to the death of tooth and claw. Victory in that game is the definition of desert—starving victors. It is a dance of life and death that must be kept going, and to go through calving is to get yanked into the middle of it with the terrible knowledge of what would happen if the music stopped.

Today frost gleams in the early sun, but the cold is not painful as Donnie and Karen set out to look for signs of troubled labor. This is almost April, and winter has definitely broken. Calving time is a tradeoff between economics and nature. Calve early and you have heavier animals to sell at the end of the season, and you can sell sooner. Calve late to cut the risk of weather and the expense of feeding lactating mothers until the grass turns green. Calve too late and warm weather increases infections and the calves aren't stout enough when they must move to summer range. The Whittens waited until after the equinox and despite the danger of a late spring ice storm have let the mature cows give birth on their own out on the range.

Donnie and Karen have charge of 850 pregnant mother cows, 250 of their own and 600 that belong to a neighbor, and this flood tide of life leaves no doubt about their connection to nature. A couple of weeks into the calving, the Whittens have lost three calves, the neighbors sixteen, about even, given the relative herd sizes, but as the season gets under way the signs point to a host of problems.

"This comes," says Donnie, "because to get into the game fast our neighbor bought 'trader cows' that were already bred, and many of them were for sale because they were not doing well somewhere else. Some don't have enough milk or can't handle the altitude or lack enough mothering instinct to protect a calf. Some are just plain old and have weak hearts."

The winter in the valley, despite fears of global warming elsewhere, was in fact the longest, coldest, and snowiest on record. A sturdy calf can make it in a 10 degree night if his mother licks him off right away and he gets a drink, but there is not much margin. A touch of scours—strength and warmth gushing out in white diarrhea—and he won't see daybreak.

"It struck a neighbor a while back," said Donnie. "Carcasses stacked up in the pickups and cows groaning and dying all around and everything steaming in the cold. They were tubing medicine into calves in the middle of the night with all the lights turned on and a dozen people around. Probably they hadn't slept for days. Next year I think we'll wait until April."

"When it's so cold and you have to calve in a corral with all the cattle standing on top of each other in the snow and the filth, you're just guaranteed to get scours, and then it runs through the whole lot," said Karen. "At twenty or twenty-five degrees below zero, everything just freezes anyway." She said one arctic week in early February had cost another neighbor 140 calves. At $400 a pop, that wiped out more than his margin.

This morning, however, things look not so bad. In the rising sun of the equinox, healthy new calves cavort among the chico bushes on the level range. Only it would have been better if it were April. The winter was so terrible that the grass isn't green, and almost everyone in the valley has had to buy hay, an expense that a normal season, if there is such a thing, would have spared them.

A cow and calf, both frozen to the ground, lie in one of the corrals. The calf died on its own. Donnie shot the cow yesterday. "Once they go down and won't get up, there's really no hope. I've never seen one come back. It was probably age plus altitude or a weak heart. After all the strain of calving, there's just not enough left to go on."

With a tractor, he would haul the two carcasses out to some obscure brush patch for the coyotes.

"Interesting though," he says. "A month ago they would pretty much clean it up in a week. The calf would disappear in a day, but now they don't seem as interested. I've noticed prairie dogs looking up here and there, so I guess they've got another food source, another reason for not calving early when they might not wait for a calf to die."

He checks another cow for engorged teats. The night before he had to milk them down so the calf could get his mouth around them at all. For his trouble the cow kicked his arm and nearly broke it. Today, the two back quarters are still engorged, but the calf is apparently staying ahead of the front two. By the time Donnie and Karen get the hay wagon hitched and out to where the bales are piled in a great loaf, the sun has burned off the frost, and flinging down a hundred bales breaks a sweat. The presence of rabbit pellets twenty feet up on the top of the stack attest to the severity of the winter and a nest of rabbit kits tucked between the bales to its end.

Donnie and Karen ride around the field on a flatbed throwing down hay in flakes as the tractor grinds along in low gear by itself. Larks sing from the fence posts, and a marsh hawk flaps around in the distance, but reminders of how dicey life can be keep turning up. The last bales go to outlier cows who have stayed by their calves. They have an informal baby-sitting system. When most of the mothers wander off after the hay wagon or to get a drink, always a few stay back. One, however, is lying down beside her dead calf, snot streaming from her nose and festooned on the chico bushes where she had flung her head around in despair. Her calf died yesterday, and she, although lively enough, had been roaming around crazily, staggering and charging the tractor. Donnie figures she was pretty clearly a goner now but might as well have a last meal if she wants it.

An hour later she hasn't touched it. Donnie takes a big folding pocketknife and jams it into the base of her neck. She groans and eyes him suspiciously as he rummages about for the jugular. Eventually he finds something that bleeds fairly strongly, but though she gazes about with a slightly dazed expression, she shows no obvious signs of weakening. Donnie rummages again and strikes something major. The blood gushes and in about 30 seconds her head wobbles and droops. It sags lower and lower until it rests on the ground. Then, in a kind of "oh shit, what the hell" gesture she flings her head back, rolls over on her side, heaves a bored sigh, and dies.

A rider appears, all buckskin under a battered felt hat, which, when pushed back, reveals the wind-burned smile of a middle-aged woman. Peggy Godfrey, cowboy poet and midwife of large animals, has a few sheep and cows of her own. She grew up in Louisiana, but after escaping the life of a dentist's wife and several other false starts, she wound up in Saguache County and hires out as a cowhand.

My days are long and busy
'Cause I'm livin' from the land.
Clothes don't make ya 'cowboy,'
It's the work that makes the hand.

But she wears more leather than Donnie ever owned.

I curled my hair by the brandin' fire,
'Twas there I thickened my lashes.
My job was to stoke, now I smell like smoke,
It's the height of the ranchin' fashion.

She also would never dream of checking cattle by truck or motorbike as Donnie would for the sake of efficiency.

I love to ease through the cattle,
Hear 'em breathe, watch 'em move, hear 'em chew,
Stuff I can't do from a warm pickup truck,
When I'm hurryin', rushin' to get through.

"Oh darn," she says looking at the gore on the grass. "There's too much death around here. Here I am trying to give all these little darlin's a good start in the world, and every time I get all excited and happy about it, I find another dead one under a chico bush. There are two over there by the irrigation ditch and another two by the road, and there's a cow over there by the rise. The calf is half out of her, and you can see her feet sticking up."

Cows struggling to give birth not infrequently roll themselves into some depression or against a bush and wind up on their backs. Then they just bloat and die.

"I think," says Peggy, "that the eagles must have killed the calves. I know you don't want to believe it, but that's their style, you know. They don't kill them right off. They tear at them and then wait around for them to die later. These little guys have gashes all around their eyes."

Donnie shrugs. It could have happened, but he'd rather think not, or if so that better mothering would have stopped it. Even as they talk, a coyote materializes out of the bushes at the far corner of the field and trots in and out among the cows. They move closer to their calves. One even nudges a sleeping youngster to its feet, but the coyote trots on. Then he pauses, crouches, makes an enormous leap, and comes up with a very live mouse by the tail. This interests the cows. Their ears come forward and the coyote senses an audience. He dances about, flinging his mouse high in the air—10, 15, 20 feet up—and every time makes a stupendous catch. Then he simply swallows it and vanishes again into the bushes.

"Now," says Peggy when the show is over, "there is an old baldy cow that's been trying to have her calf since last night and not gettin' anywhere, and I think she needs some help. There's one I'm going to save."

They find her standing by herself looking tired and worried, strings of gunk hanging out her back end. She doesn't want to go anywhere, but they haze her into a nearby corral and into a steel crush that holds her fast.

"Will you need the jack?" asks Donnie. The jack is a large steel contraption with levers, hooks, and chains that fits into the bars of the crush for pulling out calves.

"I hope not," says Peggy. "You can pull a calf to pieces with that thing, and that bothers me. Find me some baling string." She eases her arm full length into the cow. "Aha. A live one. With at least three feet, but I can't tell right off where they belong. Get me some baling string. It's a trick I learned from James Herriot."

They laugh. This place is so far from Yorkshire, but the cows and the questions are the same, and everybody has read the book. She takes off her wedding ring, soaps her arm in a bucket of ditch water, and eases it into the cow again.

A nose and a foot
Come out the slot.
The other danged leg
Has definitely not.

She has to struggle as hard as Herriot ever did. The cow strains. Her eyes bug out. Peggy finds the hoof. The cow farts in her face. "Oh dear." Then at last the foot comes out, and in a sudden slimy rush the whole calf lands on the ground like a sack of potatoes. It blinks, coughs, and raises its head. Peggy drags it by the hind legs around in front of its mother, throws open the crush, grabs her tools, and clears out. "You've got to leave mama alone with her baby. After all that, there's a chance they won't recognize each other."

Mama sniffs the ground, then the calf, then walks halfway around it and sniffs again. Then looks sharply at the people watching from the fence and sniffs again. Then she begins to lick it dry. Peggy cheers. The calf staggers to his feet and starts looking for breakfast. In the fall, Donnie may well send the mother to the packer for failing to deliver on her own, but that is months and a world of eagles and coyotes away. For now, both man and beast can rejoice a bit and smile at a flight of cranes overhead.

It was after such a day that Peggy went home and wrote:

One solitary black baldy
Stands among the chico thorns,
Mooing softly to her white-faced calf
Whose eye sockets are dark and sightless.
No response to the cow's lowing,
It lies sprawled and lifeless
Beneath the chico, mouth agape.
Large pressed patches of soft earth
Show where mama spends the nights.
Tracks toward the water hole and back,
Out to the feed ground and back,
Out and back,
Day after day.
A once-bright white face
Grows more dull by the day
As death works
Nature's own version of recycling.
Piles of manure attest
To the futile efforts of life
To draw some response
From the mystery

Of the sleeping calf
Who once bawled and sucked,
Who stood in response
To the mama's gentle urging.
Each day she paws
One hoof-full of soft earth
To her chest.
Not the gesture of anger
Nor fear
But a motion of despair
As in the wearing
of sackcloth and ashes
I, too, #559, stand helpless
in the emptiness
of death.

3

The Real Life or Death Question

The bitter and sweet dramas of calving season open the cycle of the ranching year, but the cycle itself is a drama of bookkeeping, which is much more serious and often as thrilling. The fiscal and physical accounting of gain and loss even has its own poetry:

> Under the double spell of night and frost,
> Within the yeoman's kitchen scheme
> The year revolves its immemorial prose.
> He reckons labour, reckons too the cost;
> Mates up his beasts, and sees his calf-run teem. . .

as Vita Sackville-West put it. Donnie and Karen, looking forward into 1992, could do it even better and in color with Lotus 1,2,3 running on the PC in their bedroom. They could almost count sitting close together before the bright rows and columns on the monitor as "couple time" when it went well, which it sometimes did, because the program specialized in the "what if" questions of dreams as well as those of nightmares.

What if the price of feeder steers goes to $1.10? What happens if we don't sell them right after weaning in October but finish them in the feedlot at our expense and sell them in February? How fast will our herd grow if we retain all of our heifers instead of just those we need for replacements? What happens if we do that five years running? Can we buy a motorcycle for Nathan, so he can help move cattle with it in the summer?

Put in the number, hit return, and the silicon oracle would ripple one scenario after another over the screen.

What if feeders drop to 85 cents, diesel goes to $1.40, and only 75 percent of the calves survive to sale? How could they even think of justifying money for Donnie to take flying lessons? How much did Karen spend traveling around the state to livestock shows with the little band of prize La Mancha goats she kept as a hobby? Those questions weren't so much fun. Like any couple, they constructed elaborate arguments over contrasting printouts and occasionally shut off the machine and went to bed without reconciling them.

Beneath the software, however, lay a deeper problem, the land itself. Not only was their share of it smaller than what Grandpa Whitten had accumulated, it was also not necessarily as fruitful, and in the end their chances depended on whether they could reverse this decline or were doomed to ride it down to ruin. The losses had occurred slowly over many years and not everywhere or continually, but the trend was undeniable throughout the valley. The rich mix of grass species that had flourished in Saguache County at the turn of the century had changed. Some, in fact, were hard to find at all now. Artesian wells that once shot 20 feet in the air now required pumping. Saguache Creek hardly ever made it to the valley floor. Chico brush grew where old-timers once cut hay, and here and there bare alkali ground outcropped as hard as cement.

"If we could increase the yield of this pasture by ten cattle days per acre, then what?"

"We got good precipitation in 1991? What did it yield in 1990?"

The specter of decreases accumulating implacably down the years sent little trickles of adrenalin into the late-night computer sessions and charged them with a significance that went beyond the statistics of calving success, rainfall, pounds of beef per acre, and discounted cash flow. The real capital of the Whitten ranch resided in the soil itself, in its capacity to absorb water, support life, and withstand wind and drought. That the rippling columns on the computer screen ultimately reflected the health of this endowment was not a source of comfort.

The San Luis Valley is not a desert on the order of Death Valley, the Atacama, or the central Sahara, where life has never amounted to much more than a sharp, scaly, furtive experiment, but people who have tried to live there know how easily it could simply refuse to put up with them anymore, stop feeding their livestock, throw up dust storms, cook away yet more moisture, and become truly useless. Scarier still, this threat of barrenness, latent, coiled within and waiting to avenge any offense, is worldwide.

Recently, some large areas of Africa have carried it out on a scale that killed enough people to attract passing notice from those living in less volatile zones. Public comment has ranged from, "How could this happen in the twentieth century, when we have food surpluses elsewhere!" to "Isn't it barbaric that emergency food distribution is foiled by politics and civil war!" to simply, "Sure sounds like Africa." Seldom mentioned is the fact that roughly 15 percent of the world's landmass, most of it not in Africa, is in similar shape for reasons not clearly understood. A big piece of the southwestern United States, for example, would routinely yield the same harvest of corpses if people had to subsist from it in anything like the same density that prevails in most of the affected parts of Africa. That assumes they had no oil income, welfare, footloose industry, or cities to flee to.

The first international conference on desertification, held in Nairobi in 1977, determined that a third of the world's arable land could easily go out of production within the next fifty years. Their conjectures for grazing land ranged far beyond that. True, these were rough statistics, extrapolated over wide areas and stretches of time with simple formulas. Also, coming as it did in the go-go decade of the Green Revolution and grain surpluses, many scientists and economists tended to discount the report's warning of a food crisis. Yet, however crude, the evidence pointed to a worldwide degradation of arid land every bit as drastic as the destruction of rain forests or the rise of greenhouse gases.

The Nairobi conference first brought the word "desertification" into common speech. It was a direct response to a drought that between 1969 and 1973 devastated a region called the Sahel, which borders the southern Sahara from the Atlantic coast of Mauritania eastward into Sudan. This was the first drought catastrophe to draw serious interest from scientists outside the field of meteorology, largely because the return of rain to the Sahel did not immediately restore the land as it always had before.

From Europe and the United States, teams of soil scientists, entomologists, botanists, zoologists, agronomists, anthropologists, hydrologists, and civil engineers prowled the Sahel trying to describe the situation in precise scientific detail and determine causes and solutions. Recent breakthroughs in meteorology sparked by computer models and satellite images even suggested that a massive loss of ground cover such as had occurred in the Sahel could upset continental weather patterns and thus perpetuate itself or cause problems elsewhere.

One of the most extensive studies, involving interdisciplinary teams from the Center for Agrobiological Research in Wageningen, Holland, and supported by the most advanced testing equipment, concluded in the euphemistic language of scientific reports that the condition of the Sahel was hopeless and not a matter of the Sahara creeping south but of death from within. The problem, they concluded, started in the savannah just short of the rain forest, where precipitation averaged 20–30 inches a year (three times the rainfall on the Whitten ranch) and was spreading north *toward* the Sahara. Except where economic development programs had recently drilled wells, the most arid areas had suffered least because drought had early on driven nomadic herders out. In the settled areas, however, and around new water points, the combination of cultivating marginal land, overgrazing, firewood gathering, and drought so denuded the land that rainfall hardly mattered. Ninety percent of it almost instantly dried up or ran off into gullies and flash floods. Worse, even the 10 percent that did stay in the soil had become nearly irrelevant because the soil had lost so much nitrogen and phosphorus that struggling new seedlings died of malnutrition, not thirst.

The causes, identified after many lengthy monographs compiled from extremely detailed data, confirmed everyone's initial hypothesis: too many people, too much livestock, communal land tenure, too little education, technology, and capital. It didn't immediately register that, ecologically speaking, the semi-arid region along the Rio Grande in the United States had come to strongly resemble the Sahel, in spite of a small rural population, comparatively little livestock, private ownership, and no end of education, technology, and capital. The research team could not now have found anything in Chad much more barren than the Rio Puerco Valley west of Albuquerque, where grass grew so thick in the nineteenth century that people mowed it for hay.

Predictably, the solutions reflected the specialties of the researchers. A reforestation specialist suggested planting trees. Grasslands experts thought that foolish because even in the best of times trees occupied only 5 percent of the land. Soil scientists offered three ideas for keeping the starving populations in business: increase the productivity of livestock herds with better breeds, which would advance the destruction and require imported feed supplements; reduce herds for some at the expense of others, which would be politically impossible; or apply nitro-phosphate fertilizer to 800,000 square miles, which not even the richest government could afford.

An agronomist suggested ways to intensify production from the usable crop land that remained, but it involved inputs that required a cash flow and promised little cash. The engineers suggested myriad ways to salvage runoff and to irrigate an extra crop in the dry season, but most of these ideas demanded capital, labor, and maintenance far beyond local capacity.

By the time people began starving in large numbers in neighboring Sudan and Ethiopia, the most practical response was still to raise emergency food support through rock music concerts.

African famines became just one more messy problem that evoked lots of hand wringing and cries that we *could* do something if only we had the will to spend the money. Quite possibly, however, no amount of money and will would help because truly messy problems, and all those involving living organisms, confound our accustomed approaches to problem solving. In this, desertification in Africa differs little from street crime in America. Desertification technicians don't commonly discuss how forces such as population growth, economic trends, or tribal politics that lie outside their discipline could overwhelm their recommendations any more than law enforcement experts ever suggest that economic and social conditions might produce more criminals than police forces can ever hope to catch.

"Virtual deserts" such as urban slums, surburban strips, acid dead lakes, and charred rain forests resemble much of what we now consider "real desert" of the barren, sandy variety in bearing witness to the same grim entropy of human endeavor, of intense economic advance never quite offsetting a bleeding away of elemental vitality. Even Thomas Robert Malthus, the great pessimist who predicted that population would outrun the productivity of land, did not factor in the active and evidently permanent destruction of its underlying fertility, but that destruction has occurred so uniformly in so many otherwise unrelated situations that one might suspect that desertification is the dark companion of all human progress.

Much of the rich history of the Mediterranean was bought at the price of desert, from the vanished cedars of Lebanon to the long-barren fields of Carthage and the naked Illyrian coast, whence came, once upon a time, the masts of Venetian ships. The legendary Timbuktu, the vanished myrrh-rich forests of Arabia and Yemen, the bitter shriveled Aral Sea, the lost gardens of Babylon, the scorched plains of Sind, the scoured fringes of the Gobi, the once teeming veldt of southern Africa, and of course the vanished cattle and sheep empires of the American West all testify to the amazing diligence of humankind.

According to the common wisdom about desertification, the original bad idea was the domestication of livestock. Anthropologists date the onset of serious desertification to the appearance of herding cultures about 7,000 years ago. They tell us that from then on cattle, horses, camels, and particularly sheep and goats have systematically stripped the semi-arid areas of the world. This, combined with a tendency of nomads to enjoy rapine and pillage, has buried a long succession of otherwise healthy civilizations under erosion and silt.

The Sahel researchers certainly recognized domestic livestock as major agents of doom. John Muir called cattle "hooved locusts." The English scientist James Lovelock, whose "Gaia Hypothesis" treats the Earth as a single living organism, regards livestock as a potentially terminal disease. The burning of ranges and forest, the ground laid bare by overgrazing, the dust, and the silt, he says, have already reached a level bound to upset the world's climate as much as the burning of fossil fuel, and the pace is picking up.

The straight livestock theory doesn't hold. Domestic animals undeniably have reduced a lot of land to desert, but the rate of this destruction parallels exactly the sophistication of the prevailing civilization. Truly "primitive" (and self-sufficient) nomads have maintained themselves and their herds in very stable niches on very fragile land as they once did in the Sahel. But wherever fixed housing, schools, bureaucrats, taxes, coined money, art, science, and industry took root nearby, the same animals destroyed fragile ecosystems as surely in antiquity as they do today, although not nearly as quickly. According to an *Atlas of Desertification* published by the International Center for Arid and Semi-Arid Land Studies at Texas Tech University in 1992, in less than a century the United States has achieved a degree of degradation that took many centuries or even millennia in Asia and Africa and in some cases did not even begin until modern times.

Continuous documentation of this extraordinary correlation between civilization and destruction runs back to antiquity. One of the more widely circulated recent versions, "Conquest of the Land Through 7,000 Years," came out of the U.S. Soil Conservation Service. Although the study laid some of the blame on crop farmers, the researchers failed to find a single example in the history of the world of a high civilization developing on arid land without devastating it. Not one. Most bloomed and collapsed rather quickly, a unique exception being Egypt, thanks to the regenerative floods of the Nile. The SCS report appeared in 1953, just as American agriculture was setting off on the most conquistadorial era of development the world has ever seen. The SCS reissued it in 1975, after the Sahel disaster.

The deeper question facing Donnie and Karen on their computer screen was, of course, not whether animals or farm crops were good or bad but whether or not the human brain, relative to the challenge of survival, was any better than a lemming's. Did it inevitably create crises it then tried to solve with fantastic but fatally dysfunctional mental accomplishments of which domestication of animals was only a prelude to inventing nuclear weapons and chlorofluorocarbons? Whatever destructive potential a herd of goats might have, they don't destroy anything independently of markets, trade, property rights, politics, and all the rest of society's inventions, including greed and prejudice.

On the other hand, maybe people are not merely lemmings with advanced degrees but free intelligent creatures living in a creation that is not mechanical or predetermined but itself intelligent. Intelligent beings communicate, negotiate, argue, fight, make choices, improvise, make mistakes, learn from them, and (this is the leap of faith) ultimately create things wholly new.

In *So Human an Animal*, microbiologist René Dubos eloquently describes how such a view of life can radically change how we understand what we see:

> If scientists elect to study man only by physicochemical methods, they will naturally discover only the physicochemical determinants of his life and find that his body is a machinery of atoms. But they will overlook other human characteristics that are at least as interesting and important. One of them is that man hardly ever reacts passively to external forces. The most characteristic aspect of his behavior is that he responds not only actively but often unexpectedly and creatively. He is the more human the more vigorously he converts passive reactions into creative responses. The mechanical definition of human life misses the point because what is human in man is precisely that which is not mechanical.
>
> In fact, it is not likely that the orthodox mechanical definition of life applies to animals either. According to the Harvard biologist George Wald, the unpredictability of animal behavior led an exasperated physiologist to state what has come to be known as the Harvard Law of Animal Behavior:
>
> "Under precisely controlled conditions, an animal does as he damn pleases."

So, Dubos might have added, does the weather, the vegetation, the water, and the soil, not to mention the animals and the people, in the San Luis Valley, and if there, so also in the Sahel and other deserts, virtual and sandy, around the world.

Out at 52,495 Country Road T, when the wild mountain wind whips the soil from plowed out potato fields and obscures the corral, when the coyote stalks the mouse in the hay, when the cattle bawl at the gate, when the grass seeds sense the warmth of spring and ponder the worth of sprouting, when Bureau of Reclamation engineers compute how much groundwater to pump to Texas, when Karen Whitten listens to commodity prices while washing dishes, when Donnie broods over his aviation magazines, they're all doing what they damn please. If they could do it harmoniously they would have less desert, but that takes as much diplomacy as science.

So Donnie and Karen think, plan, enter the numbers, and dispute. What if they keep all the heifers? What if this year they don't graze spring growth in the pasture where the herd started last spring? What if they move their calving period to late April, when the grass is greener? Will the range get better? Will their costs fall? Will their cash flow improve?

Late in February, as under the double spell of night and frost they schemed, they heard a thunderclap and a spatter of rain against the window, a reminder that spring would come, as it damn pleased, whether planned for or not.

4

The Big Idea

In about 1982, Donnie Whitten and his brother George had to face the hopelessness of their situation. The land that had supported their grandfather and, after division among his three heirs, barely supported their father, would definitely not support them and their new families. George, Jr., as the elder son, laid first claim to a theoretical niche helping his father, George, Sr. When Donnie came back from military school in New Mexico and got married, he had to settle for driving the county road grader.

To make room for both sons, George, Sr. bought a liquor store in the town of Center, where binging migrant laborers, unemployed cowboys, and a lot of other people who hadn't even managed to get on with the county roads department made alcohol distribution the town's most conspicuous retail function. But no independent rancher could take much pleasure in that, and he thoroughly hated it.

The Whittens didn't recognize this situation as a question of ecology. If they had thought abstractly about their situation at all, they would have given the jaws of the vise closing in on them the more familiar name of progress. They accepted that despite occasional boomlets, rural communities in general declined as the greater economy grew more sophisticated and urbanized. In the treacherous world of Western ranching, the grand prize was simply to survive and get buried, as Grandpa Whitten had been, on your own land. The 8,000 acres that he had cobbled together from sweat, credit, and the failure of some neighbors had made his family feel modestly wealthy in a five-room log cabin without plumbing, and he had passed it on debt free.

In the hundred years since Grandpa Whitten came to Saguache County from Iowa, however, the formula for the carrying capacity of the land had changed. Crops and cattle now returned about 8 percent on the value of land in the valley, which you couldn't mortgage at less than 12 percent, and a pickup truck cost $15,000. This explained well enough why young people left the county, why three quarters of the town of Saguache was boarded up, and why a good share of the remaining population existed on welfare.

Sometimes Donnie or Karen or George or his wife Jane or George, Sr. would sneak a private moment at the kitchen table and multiply the cattle prices by the calves they expected to wean and stare for long periods at the resulting figure. Had they come to this impasse a few years earlier, they might have taken the easy answer and bought land. As late as 1978, any local boy who had grown up in 4-H and whose parents had land could spend twenty minutes in the Federal Land Bank in Monte Vista and come away with enough capital, say half a million at 16 percent interest, to become a bona fide member of the gentry, as long as his father signed the note. What happened next didn't matter much. For decades the value of land had grown like fungus. You didn't even really have to ship calves or raise a crop, except for form's sake. Every year you could just roll over the loan and borrow the payment against the appreciation. Fortunately for them, the Whittens had missed this train, and probably wouldn't have taken it anyway. As Donnie's Aunt Virginia often liked to say, "The secret to survival in agriculture is 'Don't borrow!' " She had vivid enough memories of her father's endless notes and of playing with other children in the cheerful door yards of smallholders who simply vanished from one day to the next into the maw of lapsed credit.

By 1984 the bubble had burst anyway, taking the Federal Land Bank and the rest of the quasi-federal Farm Credit System with it and putting several of the private banks active in the San Luis Valley on the ropes, too. But even though half the valley went up for sale at distress prices, the land still couldn't grow any crop short of marijuana worth enough to pay interest on a loan big enough to buy it—if you could find a lender. Economists had many theories about this, none of which considered the possibility of an ecological factor.

"We were pretty well stuck," recalls Donnie, "when George and I went down to Colorado Springs to the Colorado Cattlemen's Association's 1984 midwinter convention and heard a panel discussion on something called Holistic Resource Managment. There was this guy from Africa named Allan Savory who supposedly had developed a management technique that would allow you to double your herd without wrecking your land. It sounded too good to be true, but these men on the panel were convinced there was something to it."

Not long after that Allan Savory himself came to Colorado to lead a tour on one of these ranches, and both George and Donnie attended.

A ranch tour is typically about 90 percent society function. A proud rancher leads a convoy of pickups around his property to view some new state-of-the-art investment or prizewinning livestock, arriving at headquarters in time for a buffet during which men in white Stetsons and jeans sit around on hay bales balancing soggy paper plates of barbecue and beans on their knees and bemoan cattle prices, the weather, and government stupidity. This expedition followed the pattern, except that Savory paid no attention to the script. He stopped the caravan at random turnouts and spent most of the morning on all fours in the middle of what appeared to be an adult Easter egg hunt. He had his audience poking at the soil crust with their pocket knives, looking at plant seedlings, stolons, and old cow pies. He commented on ants, stink bugs, clusters of knapweed, the shapes of overgrazed bushes and tussocks of gray prairie bluestem, left ungrazed from years past. He said a lot about "plawnts," and very little about cattle.

At the buffet, more than one rancher ended a conversation with the comment, "Well, he's sure different," which in a profession that prides itself on being independent, eccentric, and conservative all at once can express either high praise or extreme suspicion.

Allan Savory was without question the most different person George and Donnie had ever met.

"We still had no idea what we were getting into," George would say later. "He used words like 'holistic' and 'desertification' that we had never heard. In fact, it never occurred to us that we lived in a desert. We merely wanted to raise beef, and here comes this fellow who starts out telling us about the ecosystem and the 'plawnts' and the 'grawss' and how we weren't really in the beef business at all. We were harvesting solar energy. He said, among other things, that he'd never seen an overstocked range, and that overrest had caused more damage than overgrazing ever did. We'd never heard anyone say that restoring rangeland usually required *more* livestock. When we thought about it, though, it made sense, so after that field day, we decided to go for it and put up $3,000 for a week-long course in Albuquerque."

In the spring of 1985, Allan Savory was a lithe, dark-haired man of fifty whose colonial accent hadn't yielded a bit to six years of living in Texas and New Mexico. He claimed to have launched a revolution of Copernican scale that would redefine not only range science but *all* institutional science in modern society, although he freely admitted that few people accepted this yet. If the nervous clucking his opinions had already set off in the established pecking order of rangeland specialists and desertification scholars was any precedent, however, his boast could not be dismissed out of hand.

In America, most range experts fall into only two categories. The kind you meet on Colorado ranch tours wear boots and tooled leather belts fastened by rodeo buckles from wilder days. They grew up in the country and like to hunt and fish, and many became academics because they found no other way to stay close to the land as family farms were divided and sold. They work for land grant colleges, spend as much time in the field as possible, and publish papers with titles like "Survival and Growth of Blue Grama Seedlings in Competition with Western Wheatgrass." Those who find the tenure track too stuffy wind up in the state extension services, the Forest Service, the Bureau of Land Management, or The U.S. Agency for International Development. It is they who set up the breeding programs in sub-Saharan Africa and oversee grazing permits in the Rio Grande National Forest.

The second group wear running shoes, narrow belts, and often khaki pants. They came out of the suburbs and the environmental movement, and for outdoor sport they climb rocks, backpack, and telemark ski. They like big subjects like exotic crops, global warming, and the relationship between El Niño and thunderstorm activity in Arizona. They graduated from the earth science departments of non–land grant universities and drift toward abstract and technical jobs in the U.S. Geological Survey, the Department of Agriculture's Research Service, or the National Center for Atmospheric Research. Some join the

Peace Corps, where they set up computer data banks in Third World capitals.

Individuals transcend these stereotypes, of course, but members of both groups early on began to refer to Allan Savory derisively as the Guru of Grazing, especially after he started using the word "holism," but this was disingenuous. People who presume to counsel on the use of God's creation assume the mantle of a kind of ministry in relationship to the land. Most take pride in being pastors of pastures. Erosion, noxious weeds, dust storms, and locust plagues burden them like the backsliding of a sinner. They aren't cynics, but they don't like heretics. This did not deter Savory because his vocation was to be not a guru but Luther. His epiphany had withstood greater trials.

In speech, bearing, and turn of mind, Savory was the distilled essence of British colonial history, his roots in southern Africa running back three generations to the glory days of Zulu armies, diamond strikes, and the Boer War. His father, an engineer, helped build the railroads and irrigation works that tamed Rhodesia. He himself grew up in Bulawayo amid more pith helmets and khaki than one could find in a shelf of Kipling. By 1955, at the age of twenty, he had cleared Natal University in South Africa with a degree in botany and zoology and signed on as the youngest ranger in the history of the Northern Rhodesian Game Department. "I had always dreamed of the Army, even of Sandhurst," he recalls, "but at that moment I could only look ahead to twenty years mouldering away as a peacetime soldier, so I followed my other calling, the bush."

The choice turned out to be academic. By 1959, he had seen the first shots fired in the Rhodesian civil war, which would last twenty years, and like many territorials, as native-born whites were called, he would drift constantly from the civilian to the military, to the civil service domain and back. Over the next two decades he held down various Game Department posts in both northern and southern Rhodesia. He freed settlements from the ravages of rogue elephants. He spent a year simply slaughtering wild animals in a quixotic government campaign to starve out the tsetse fly and make the land safe for cattle. He filed for a homestead on virgin land and grew sugarcane in the bush, then swapped the land for yet wilder country for his own game preserve. He promoted game ranching. He hired out as a ranch and farm consultant. He took up skydiving. He got married. In 1968 he won a seat in Parliament. Later on, guerrillas or political opponents, he never knew which, lobbed a Molotov cocktail into his house and burned it to the ground.

Also, by the age of thirty-three he was not just Allan Savory, M.P., he was Captain Savory, M.P. Drafted into the reserves, he had organized, trained, and led an elite band of military trackers whose exploits deep into Mozambique and Zambia gained him an international reputation in the netherworld of unconventional warfare and made him a household word at home. It would be hard to find another territorial who ever lived out so many of the ideals of his birthright so dramatically in so short a time.

Later he would say that his education as a tracker first gave him doubts about his own track, but in a deeper way they grew out of the bush itself. He had always sought more in it than the mystique of the White Hunter common to his class. He apprenticed himself to African trackers and learned to speak two native languages. As a game ranger he hunted poachers, but those who could give him a new tip on stalking or some other bit of bush lore found opportunities to escape. "I learned a lot from poachers," he recalls now. Eventually he arrived at the threshold of an insight that radicalized him.

"Tracking," he says now, "is a matter of taking in a huge and immensely diverse amount of data, any isolated piece of which is meaningless and thus often overlooked by the untrained eye. These signs that have no meaning at all apart from their context and relationship to other signs form an almost photographic picture when taken together." If this applied in finding a wounded lion or an armed poacher, then why not generally? If events, people, and even ideas leave subtle trails, then with the eyes of a tracker one should be able to see to a deeper level of reality. If one could learn to see detail in context that is invisible and meaningless out of context, one could see a lot.

Good trackers aren't psychic. "The craft requires practice and discipline," Savory says of it, "but it rests on very simple principles, such as, 'Don't go beyond the last point where you have evidence,' or 'Think through where the quarry would most likely go.' 'Look broadly as well as in detail.' One bent blade of grass says nothing. A dozen, a score, turned eccentrically in the sunlight mark a highway. 'Seek more than one kind of evidence.'" Trackers had to notice even negative evidence, such as the silence of insects.

By following the rules you could see what others could not, but only if you could accept what you saw without prejudice. The dominance of convention and the narrow perspective amazed him. Most people simply did not approach life with their eyes open, stopping to look when the trail grew dim. To the contrary, they commonly denied evidence that didn't fit. They crashed ahead as they had been programmed. He made the tracker unit go barefoot because Africans "knew" Europeans wore boots.

The destruction of the bush affected him worse than the war. "I used to sit on the banks of the Limpopo River and weep at the sight of my country being carried away. After a few good rains up-country, you could hear pieces of the bank crashing into the current." In this destruction he saw the institutionalized blindness of government land policies, including several he himself had originated. Irrigation, his father's passion, had consumed vast capital, affected only a small area, and was rapidly succumbing to silt from eroding watersheds. The tsetse fly campaign had slaughtered thousands of wild animals, uprooted native villages, and soaked the land in DDT while the fly prospered. Programs to save the overgrazed hill country by compelling native villagers to run fewer, but supposedly better, animals, had only turned the herders into guerrillas.

After forcing tribal hunters out of national parks to save the game, park officials now shot elephants, whole families at a time, to keep them from destroying trees, but the trees got battered to death anyway. The homestead scheme had lured settlers (white, of course) into impossible ventures on marginal land and broken everyone who failed to recognize the futility of it in time. Wells drilled to stop overgrazing by spreading livestock more evenly across the rangeland became growing chancres of desert. Spraying to control ticks had wiped out so many tick birds that wild animals were eaten alive, and cattle *by law* now had to be dipped every five days. Drought relief had become an annual ritual in areas notorious otherwise for flash floods.

"I really believed," says Savory, "that given good land policies, conditions would improve, and if we could only get the land itself healthy, the basic goodwill of people would let us put the civil war behind us. But no one was more ignorant about politics than I. When I got to Parliament I first spoke out only on conservation issues and joined as many parliamentary committees as I could, but the questions as I saw them never involved fewer than two ministries, which could only cooperate on negative decisions. And over all this gridlock loomed the racialism question."

His peers did not "see" the evidence quite as he did. When he finally stood up in the Rhodesian Parliament and declared himself a dissenting bloc of one, it cost him his army command, most of his friends, his land, and his marriage, but he stood fast, organized an opposition party, and lobbied in Washington and London against his government. He contacted Robert Mugabe and Joshua Nkomo, the black rebel leaders whose men he had once stalked. He remarried. When the headline "Try Savory for Treason" appeared in the Rhodesian press and a pair of burly agents of the Special Branch showed up in the night to interrogate him, he fled to exile in the Cayman Islands.

Even before graduating from university in Natal, he had noticed that wild land behaved differently from tame land. Particularly the raising of livestock made life dull over vast areas. With the possible exception of traditional nomads, few of whom still managed to practice their ancient ways, it didn't matter who owned the stock. Old-line territorials, Shona villagers, and big British land development syndicates did the same damage. It wasn't just that a bush fanatic like himself found cattle ranges boring. They were documentably monotonous. He had seen land lush with scores of different grasses and trees where wildebeest, buffalo, lions, leopards, elephants, and half a dozen kinds of antelope grazed and stalked and stampeded together in vast numbers. Then a few years later he had returned to find a scattering of cattle subsisting on near monocultures of one or two plants. Even when these ranges produced enough forage to delight the stockmen, the land felt sick.

A good tracker could sense the vitality of truly wild land. It was written there by the passage of stampeding buffalo, even as they pounded the grass to powder in a way that would have left any agricultural extension agent in shock had a domestic herd done the same thing. It vibrated in the charge of an elephant anticipating a hunter's attack and in the dung beetles that could reduce a 30-pound pile of elephant dung to nothing in a day. Savory could tell when land was dying long before he could explain why or what to do about it. Ever since his early Game Department days, he had struggled to find the science behind this intuition.

Elsewhere at the time, the science of grazing had begun to entertain some new ideas, too. In France, André Voisin had come to the remarkable conclusion that the number of animals in a pasture at any given moment had relatively little connection to the problem of overgrazing. The length of time individual animals grazed there mattered a lot more. Voisin found that a single sheep in a large field would probably hang around in the same area biting down the same plants again and again as they struggled to regrow, thus weakening them to the point of death, whereas a thousand animals in the pasture for a day might chew off every single plant, but if then the herd left, all plants would recover quickly. There would be no overgrazing. Voisin had proven his theory by successfully doubling or even tripling production from the soft green pastures of France, but the African environment seemed to play by its own rules.

Quite unrelated to Voisin's work, however, a South African named John Acocks was concentrating big herds of sheep in small paddocks for short periods to force them to eat more of the available forage instead of selecting only the best. Then he moved them on and let the grazed areas rest for substantial periods. Even though Acock's animals did not fatten as quickly from forced membership in the clean plate club, they benefited indirectly because the land improved significantly. On the best of it, Savory found much of the vitality of his wild veld.

Voisin, Acock, and other experimenters approached the subject with an eye to improving cattle production, but Savory hated cattle. He wanted the keys to wildness. But clearly Voisin's insight about overgrazing applied to any grazing animal, and just as clearly, wild and domestic herds differed far more in their mobility than in the construction of their mouth parts or even their appetites. Also, if the signs that normally accompanied domesticated land—hard, crusted soil, lack of seedlings, scarcity of small life, and absence of the organic litter that could slow down a rain drop, shelter a sprout, or block the noon sun—did not show up so drastically on Acock's experiment, then livestock per se were not the problem. None of these signs of underlying health even had much direct relationship to grazing. They derived from everything else the animals did—pissing, shitting, rutting, slobbering, and trampling around. However, these activities, especially the trampling, were indeed functions of wildness.

When a few thousand gnus huddled together against the prospect of a lion attack and grazed up to a water hole, they left enough dung behind to attract a million dung beetles and long-billed birds. In fact, they fouled the ground so thoroughly they themselves wouldn't graze there again for a long time. When the lions did attack, they hammered the grass, dung, and dirt into a dusty mess that looked like hell but at the touch of rain bloomed like Eden. If you could use Voisin's insight to stop overgrazing and somehow command the benefits of wildness at the same time, perhaps you could save the land. In crude form, Savory had at least three keys to his problem.

First, overgrazing was indeed a function of time, not numbers, just as Voisin had said. This did not mean that the land would carry unlimited numbers, only that running too many animals was not what caused long-term damage to the range. This explained the resilience of wild areas. Under primeval conditions, droughts might cause great die-offs of wildlife, but the range would bounce back when the rains returned because constantly moving herds migrating over long distances did not stay in one place long enough to regraze plants as they struggled to regrow. Where a few ranch animals were allowed to overgraze and weaken plants one at a time, however, the whole ecosystem went downhill and stayed there.

Second, so-called brittle environments characterized by erratic or seasonal rainfall and dry air did not respond to rest the way humid, static, nonbrittle environments did. They *required* grazing animals to complete the decay part of the life cycle. In the nonbrittle environments where textbooks, including Voisin's, were written, everything organic rotted down into the mold whether you wanted it to or not. Even on a plate of glass this rapid recycling would cause life to progress from mildew right through to forest in no time at all. The semi-arid veld did not support enough microbial activity to return ungrazed plants to the soil, and fire did so only at a terrific cost in seedlings and soil condition. But when something ate the grass, whether cow or gemsbok, what came out the other end went right back to the soil and fueled the whole second half of the food chain. Grazing herds were therefore not just a convenient by-product of range land. It would stagnate without them. Grassland plants and grass-eating animals had coevolved and could not thrive separately.

Third, "herd effect" or "animal impact" played as big a role as grazing. The trampling and stampeding, which had always inspired hand-wringing denunciations from range scientists, were the only thing that could break down invasions of brush and old grass that had become too stale to eat. Although the burning of ranges to "revitalize" them had a long tradition and a good deal of scientific support, setting fires every year, as was widely done in Africa and elsewhere, killed seedlings and soil organisms, often stimulated many of the plants it was meant to kill, and did not break soil crusts, plant seeds, or grind in the tilth as well as a pounding hoof.

Until Voisin, research on grazing had hardly looked at the behavior of animals. Only numbers mattered. Too many animals would destroy the range. Now Savory could see that, given proper timing, increasing numbers could benefit land, especially if they got excited enough to kick up dust. Cutting them could harm it. Everyone "knew" that to heal damaged land you rested it; now Savory argued that this worked only in damp, stable climates where the usual result was forest. On brittle land, rest led to stagnation, and salvation came in the form of animals that would chew up the best forage, shit on the remains, and trample down anything too brittle to eat.

The arguments got pretty arcane and set off controversy probably destined to bubble over into the next millennium, particularly Savory's claims for the benefits of hoof action. Like many other sources of dispute, this one fell into the curious category of counterintuitive propositions that contradict all evidence and common sense as the situation appears but might change the situation if you dared apply them.

Promoting "herd effect" among people worried about desertification was like telling old Rhodesian colonials that they wouldn't see peace until they called off their peacekeeping forces. Promoting both ideas at the same time was in fact not altogether coincidence. It represented Savory's growing suspicion that he belonged to a culture that habitually approached things backward.

Overnight he dropped his campaign against the livestock industry. He also reversed his position on "game ranching," the heart of his consulting business, when he realized that wild animals under normal ranch managment quickly learned to behave like cattle and did the same damage for half the profit. Because roads, fences, and human settlement had already carved up the home ranges of naturally functioning wild herds over much of his country, his campaign to save eroding watersheds and fragments of habitat would have to depend on managing domestic animals according to his three keys. If this could be done, at least the soil and the habitat would survive. He shouted his discovery around southern Africa with all the naked enthusiasm of an Archimedes while a majority of agricultural experts denounced him as a heretic. A public test that involved moving a fairly dense herd through a series of small paddocks settled nothing. Articles in the *Rhodesian Journal of Agriculture* found it totally inconclusive. By his own criteria, however, it succeeded, and his consulting business continued to attract clients, including a 1.3 million-acre spread controlled by the British agribusiness giant Liebig.

On the other hand, as he reflected on his past triumphs and failures from his Caymanian beach, he had to admit that even his grazing theories seemed to carry the same disaster virus as his other endeavors. Few of his commercial clients had proven able to make his methods work on their own, and of scientists hardly any. They somehow failed to see a piece of land as a dynamic living thing that changed from day to day. Particularly scientists, devotees of rigorous experiments, suppressed flexibility as a sacred duty. They liked clean data from a strict schedule of moving cattle from one paddock to the next, from one season to the next, oblivious to changing context. Then, when the system collapsed, they blamed him. Not long after Savory's departure, Liebig's management fell into a routine and failed to change their timing when drought stretched out the time grazed plants needed to recover. Their huge concentrations of cattle then hit every single subdivision of land at the worst possible phase of regrowth, stripping practically every single perennial grass plant out of the whole project in a matter of months.

There had to be a fourth key that would help people think or at least ask the right questions—the question of carrying capacity, for example. The whole structure of arid lands research and management rested on quantifying carrying capacity. It seemed so obvious that a given piece of land could feed a limited number of creatures, so if you knew the number, you could avoid screwing up. But in practice the number was as elusive as the weight of the stone that God cannot lift or the precise value of *pi.* If a denser herd over a shorter time and behaving differently could increase carrying capacity, then you had an open-ended and extremely complicated feedback loop quite apart from other variables like the weather and the market. The more rigorously you applied the scientific method to this problem, the less you could hope to solve it, because controlling any variable distorted the reality you wanted to test.

On the other hand, time was straightforward. If Liebig had realized that in order to rest plants longer they would have to hold the herd longer on each piece of ground, they would have discovered as soon as the first paddock ran out of grass and before any of it was overgrazed by a fatal second bite how much carrying capacity the drought had cost them. Noticing when plant growth slowed down and when a plant had had enough recovery time required something of the tracker's sensitivity, and there had to be a system of thought to it.

For a long time Savory had chided clients to "think holistically" without knowing how to articulate the concept very well himself. He knew the word only because it had been coined by the Afrikaaner general and statesman Jan Smuts, whom he had admired since childhood for his military leadership and diplomacy. Eventually, however, he read his hero's philosophical tome, *Holism and Evolution,* and found that it really did address his problem. According to Smuts, life was not a mechanical assemblage of inert parts but a hierarchy of wholes, each more significant than the sum of its parts and with characteristics that transcended them. Just as expert knowledge of hydrogen and oxygen didn't give you much useful information about water, so knowing a lot about animals or plants or soil or economics didn't guarantee that you would see what mattered in a piece of land. A truly holistic thinker would never address a problem through his knowledge of its parts. He would try to understand the whole as a thing in itself first and from there determine which parts to mess with and how. Nevertheless, if all wholes connected to other greater, lesser, and equal wholes in the hierarchy, this could get tough.

One had to find a way to apply such a grand concept systematically to real problems in the way the scientific method offered a practical and systematic way to tackle simple mechanical relationships or the trackers' rules applied to the bush. This, as soon as he could work out the details, would be Savory's fourth key. Some years later a friend discovered an expression of this challenge that Savory used in his book *Holistic Resource Management:*

> In the early 1800s the German writer Heinrich von Kleist interviewed a famous puppeteer. How, Kleist wanted to know, can a normal person possibly manage the body and each individual limb of a marionette so that it moves harmoniously like a real person instead of like a robot? How does the puppeteer learn that when he moves the puppet's leg forward, he also has to tilt its head slightly, bend the torso, and shift both arms in opposite directions?
>
> The puppeteer answered that von Kleist had not understood the actual challenge, which was both simpler and more elegant. Of course no human could produce natural gestures by pulling any number of individual strings. No matter how skilled the puppeteer, the result would still look mechanical. On the other hand a skillfully designed marionette had a center of gravity, and simply moving that would bring about all the other gestures automatically, just as a human, when taking a step, automatically moves all the other parts of his body to stay in balance.

All Savory had to do was define the center of gravity and attach strings that would move it in all dimensions.

For the present, however, he had to make a living. Within six months he left the Caymans and with an associate from Rhodesia hung out a shingle in San Angelo, Texas, as a ranch consultant. In Africa and elsewhere, an idea that bore the cachet of American science had clout. If one meant to foment revolution, what better place to start than Texas? The ads for SGM (Savory Grazing Method) read:

> Double Production or Fees Returned
>
> One week school on the Savory Grazing Method taught by Allan Savory.
>
> If you attend this school and then apply SGM, as I teach it to you, you will:
>
> - Increase your range carrying capacity to at least double the conventional or Soil Conservation Service rate. Furthermore you will achieve this result:
> - Regardless of how low or high a rainfall area you are ranching in.
> - Regardless of how good or poor your range condition is currently.
> - Without any brush clearing, reseeding, or any other costly range reclamation aid and within one year of first applying SGM.
>
> If you do not achieve such results after applying what I teach you, either on a trial area of your ranch or on your whole ranch, then I shall willingly return the fees you have paid me.

If Savory had made SGM sound a bit less like patent medicine, he might have spared himself some of the harsh reaction of his peers, but the move was pure Savory—thoroughly radical and irreverent, right down to the mention of the Soil Conservation Service by name. But even though very few of his students actually did double production in one year, none asked for their money back, and he never retreated from his claims. Even his associate didn't appreciate, however, that this unalloyed appeal to the pocketbooks of American ranchers was just the first step in a grand design to save Africa, and not for cattle ranching either, but for the peaceful wildness of his dreams.

Savory's experience in southern Africa had convinced him that the academic institutions that ruled on such matters would never take his "four keys" seriously unless forced to by their own clientele. If enough American ranchers could demonstrate the power of his four keys, the institutions that served them would have to take notice. Then, for all the places of the world where life had dried up and blown away, for veld and steppe where the wild herds had thinned out and the people starved into glum migration into the slums of exile, there would be a remedy in the very domestic animals that had set the disaster in motion. He had a tool that, in theory at least, any peasant shepherd could apply, a tool that moreover paid for itself.

By the time Donnie and George Whitten shook Savory's hand in Colorado Springs six years later and decided to sign up for his course, it looked as if his strategy might prove itself. Epic hard times in the cattle industry had opened a window for new ideas just as Savory realized that his biological insights would never take hold unless he took on the whole manner in which people and institutions approached the management of land. He changed SGM (Savory Grazing Method) to HRM, for Holistic Resource Management, and founded the nonprofit Center for Holistic Resource Management with help from some of the deepest pockets in the Texas oil patch. He found experts to give courses in personal relations, estate planning, family businesses, and financial management and sought to incorporate their ideas into his "holistic model." Members of the center became known for their tendency to pull out a membership card in any conversation that touched on the state of the natural world and deliver a little homily built around unorthodox jargon that cemented the guru epithet to Savory forever. The back of the card carried a step-by-step guide to holistic decision making.

All the elements in this document were familiar to the Whittens. Only the order ran backward. This caused them to recognize that, like most people, they had done very little thinking at all except in response to problems. Right at the top, the holistic model reminded them to define the "whole" they expected to deal with, and then to list, not problems, but what they wanted. In recent times, "mission statements" and "goal setting" have become the tired jargon of a management consultant industry, but they were fresher then, and Savory defined them in a unique way. A goal, he said, must have three parts. It should define a quality of life and a general kind of activity to support it and describe a landscape that will sustain it.

This seemed obvious enough, although describing the ideal life took longer for the Whitten family than they anticipated. They also had no problem writing down (although they had never written it before) that they wanted to live from production off the land itself—livestock and perhaps some farming if it seemed to fit. In thinking about the landscape, however, the model pushed them into deeper water. Just saying they needed better grass would not do. They had to describe the land in terms of basic ecosystem processes—the cycling of water and minerals, the flow of solar energy, and the irrepressible characteristic of all living things to build ever more complex communities, which science recognizes as "natural succession." These phenomena, known to every schoolchild, were in fact the center of gravity of the ecosystem puppet. They defined all interactions at all levels.

"We knew we needed better forage," said Donnie, "but we had never thought about whether minerals, like old manure and dead grass, were recycling. It never occurred to us that rainfall could be effective or not depending on the way we managed the soil. Energy flow was also a new concept, but it is pretty obvious that if your grass has wider leaves, and you have species that start growing earlier and go further into the fall, you capture more energy. As to succession, that was entirely new. To us, plants were just plants. We never thought about them developing complex communities on their own. But we found we could describe our land by how well these processes were going on, and it made us see how far we had to go."

The statements were simple: "We would like high successional grassland with great diversity of species including some bushes for browse and cover. We need higher organic activity in soils to recycle dead material, etc." Pretty mundane stuff, but the exact reverse of what they would have said before: "Eradicate thistle infestations. Increase weight of weaned calves."

The three-part goal had the appeal of a moral position. It affirmed the value of acting on principle where complexity and lack of data made objective decisions impossible. If you had a pest outbreak, for example, you might not know why, but you'd say, "This is a successional thing. We've got a community that allows these bugs to explode," and you'd look for ways to affect succession instead of attacking the problem any old way.

The model also listed the strings on the puppet—rest, grazing, animal impact, fire, living organisms, technology—and a reminder that applying any of them involved creativity plus money, labor, or both. Finally, the model listed key words relating to guidelines to proper use of these tools, including six tests for whether to use a particular one at all. Any tool should: honor the ecosystem as a whole, strengthen the weak link in the operation, address causes not symptoms, give the best marginal reaction per dollar, represent a conscientious use of energy and nonrenewable wealth, and respect society and culture.

Across the bottom, the card said PLANMONITORCONTROL REPLAN as a mode of operation. In other words, don't try something and wait until it fails. Plan it and then watch closely enough to notice before it does fail so you can change course. Savory would later replace this twenty-four–letter warning with the more graphic:

Whenever skeptics, particularly academics who had "disproved" Savory's grazing theories, cited tests and cases, he would throw this PLANMONITORCONTROLREPLAN line at them in the form of a tautology that many found infuriating. "If it failed, it wasn't holistic management," he would say. "If you had followed the model, you would have noticed getting off course and kept changing tactics until you did succeed. There is no such thing as a holistic *system,* only a holistic *method* for finding the best course from moment to moment."

This was, as ranchers say, "sure different." But really not. It had plenty to do with earth and sky, steaming beasts and small critters, weeds and flowers, money and time, the Limpopo and the Rio Grande, water and fire, sex and death—things the Whittens had known since birth but hadn't ever thought of as their partners in a dance greater than the dancers.

5

Tracy

From Donnie and Karen Whitten's place out on the chico flats that dominate the north end of the great level San Luis Valley, County Road T runs west along the section line past a few abandoned houses and their accumulations of old cars and tattered tar paper to Swede's Corners, where the willow plantings of an immigrant homesteader named August Johnson now dance in the wind like fat old widows in a prayer meeting. There it crosses the Gun Barrel, the local name for two lanes of pavement that shoot 40 miles without a micron of bend or rise from Saguache, county seat of Saguache County, in the north end of the San Luis Valley, to Monte Vista, the administrative center of Rio Grande County to the south. West of the Gun Barrel, County Road T climbs imperceptibly to the Rio Grande Canal, which, for the 50 miles of its sinuous run from the Great River, marks the western edge of the valley floor before dispersing itself into a series of hopeful ditches just north of the Whittens' that flow only in the rare year when the canal runs full.

West yet of the canal and its accompanying fence and cattle guard begins the North Tracy Common Allotment, which is to say, 38,370 acres of public land administered by the U.S. Bureau of Land Management. There, County Road T sheds the rulered discipline of the General Survey grid and relaxes onto the contour of an arroyo called Tracy Creek that winds out of the foothills of the San Juan Mountains. The chico bushes that know how to exploit the shallow water table of the flat valley floor give way here to gray-green rabbit brush, which grazing animals avoid, and the occasional salt bush, which they love. Farther up the rising land, these yield to vast expanses of pale grama grass broken by darker shades of green along outwashes from the hills. Outriders of the mountains to the west lift and fold the grama sod carpet like knees under a blanket to form a landscape of interconnecting rooms open to the sky. The grama climbs the sides of these chambers like a wainscot to a line of piñon and juniper trees and outcrops of black volcanic basalt.

In past years, Donnie and Karen often sought out some sheltered cove and camped there for weeks at a time to look after the cattle they summered "on Tracy," and Nathan, Clint, and Sarah spent their days chasing ground squirrels and rabbits around rocks until the three of them became nearly indistinguishable from their quarry. Throughout the summer, small herds of pronghorn antelope ghost from one quiet pocket to the next, and in winter the elk come down from the high country.

But this fine and beautiful place is also a battleground of greed, need, and good intentions, and its condition tells a story almost universally common to public resources exploited for private gain. The Europeans drove out the Ute Indians, then almost at once fought the same battles all over again among themselves as bigger operators muscled squatters and small holders out of the picture. By the 1920s, conflict seldom flared beyond the occasional fistfight, and livestock management settled down to a routine, the object of which was to harvest as much as possible of a bounty that everyone knew would return every spring as surely as grass grew and rivers flowed. A few families ran cattle in the Tracy drainage all summer long, but large and small bands of sheep used the country almost year round. It was hell on herders, but sheep could harvest in winter any feed left standing after forage plants stopped growing in the fall. Unlike cattle, the woolies eat snow for water and thus can range over areas inaccessible to any domestic stock in summer. In 1935, a Forest Service report on the unrelenting grazing pressure on the upper end of the drainage remarked that "the range has been grubbed into the ground."

That was a year after passage of the Taylor Grazing Act, which gave federal agencies authority to control the size of herds and the time they spent on public land by issuing permits to stockmen who could prove a history of customary use. For a few years a political consensus promised to make the permit system a powerful instrument of conservation. Thanks to the Dust Bowl, soil erosion had become a national issue. When some engineering studies predicted that silt washing off denuded rangeland might rapidly fill the recently constructed Lake Mead, even Western politicians accepted the need to regulate grazing. They could yield that point for the promise of grand New Deal water projects—Grand Coulee Dam on the Columbia and the irrigation of California's Central Valley and a host of others, some of which were not built until the 1970s. When the headlines faded, however, the political power of the livestock industry asserted itself and the permit system lost its connection to stewardship. It evolved into an instrument for regulating relationships between established ranchers and provided a legal way to keep out the small fry. Out on the Tracy Common, however, environmental questions asserted themselves without government help.

"In the 1950s it just hardly rained at all for five or six years," remembered one of the present permittees, Jim Coleman, whose family had used the land since the 1870s. "We thought the grass had flat out died and we never would see it again."

It got so bad that in 1956 the BLM did cut the Tracy allotment permits back 53 percent, from 7,164 animal unit months to 3,367, of which over half were winter sheep numbers. To sustain even that, the agency had to install pipes and storage tanks at a number of springs and seeps because the streams had vanished. They chained off 550 acres of piñon and juniper trees and planted crested wheatgrass, a Mediterranean species considered "grazing resistant" because it tends to survive enormous grazing pressure, in part because it becomes nearly inedible in hot weather. The new pipes and tanks allowed many of the sheep permits, including those belonging to the Whittens, to be converted to summer cattle. Now the cattle permits add up to 2,540 animal unit months through the summer, which means about 40 acres have to feed a cow and calf for about three months. No one winters sheep there anymore because the wildness of the country demands a full-time herder and none of the current permits would allow a herd big enough to pay one a modern wage. Although a communal herder might pay, such a thing has never been done in that part of the valley.

After the 1956 reduction, the BLM also reasserted its right to determine every year when the range is ready for livestock and when it has had enough, even if that means the permittees can't harvest their limit of AUMs. That has cut the total amount of grazing substantially. Since the late 1980s, most permittees have not filled their limits anyway, and some have not turned out at all because calves did not gain weight fast enough to make the $1.92 per AUM grazing fee worth the hassle.

None of this has answered the ancient question of how to manage a common resource. For all the world's fixation on socialism, the seminal theoretical paper on communal rangeland did not appear until 1968, when the Tracy allotment had already run out of water. In that year, biologist Garrett Hardin published a paper, "The Tragedy of the Commons," in *Science* magazine. He pointed out that by putting an extra cow on a common range, a private owner would profit to nearly the full potential of the cow while paying only his small share of the common cost. Because all users of the common ground had reason to make the same calculation, they would surely add stock until they destroyed the grass utterly and lost everything in one common disaster. Appealing to conscience, said Hardin, would never work, because it would reward those who, for lack of it, defied the common good and put out more cows, while punishing those who cut back. Hardin did not limit his conclusions to livestock. He used the pasture case to illustrate the necessity of strong government policies and even compulsion to restrict people's "right to breed." The survival of the whole planet, as the Ultimate Common, demanded no less. Out on Tracy, the problem seemed real enough but not quite so simple.

Nearly dictatorial power over the allotment resided nominally in the hands of a career civil servant named Royce Wheeler, the chief range conservationist at the BLM's district headquarters in the south valley town of Alamosa. In practice, however, Royce had to work through an entity called the Tracy Common Grazing Association, in which nine permittees voted and their spouses and relatives participated vigorously. Nearly all of them had roots in the last century and at the drop of a hat could invoke history and precedent for purposes more complex than Hardin's perfectly rational and self-interested peasants ever imagined.

Donnie and Karen were coming into the house for coffee on the spring morning when the mailman put Royce's letter in their box out on Road T. Like the rest of their routines, the Whitten coffee ritual gets straight to the point. Two or three times a year, Karen soaks a few pounds of grounds in cold water to make an evil black syrup that she stores in the back of the icebox. Pour boiling water onto a dash of that, and presto, a hot hit that will really focus your mind, and they needed it. They had taken shifts through the night checking the first calf heifers corralled out back, fed a half dozen orphaned calves, tended the goats and chickens, and spent a hectic hour getting Nathan, Clint, and Sarah breakfasted, connected with their homework and mittens, and out to the bus.

The letter, which they read together at the kitchen table, announced a meeting of the Tracy association to discuss the summer turnout. It followed a familiar format. The meeting would take place the following Thursday at the house of member Bill Strickland down at Swede's Corners. This time, however, Royce had allowed himself a couple of extra paragraphs of bland prose referring to "reviewing our goals," "developing a comprehensive plan," and "improving the resource."

Karen groaned. "It looks as if this year Royce finally means to start pushing to get some change," she said when she had read to the end. At past meetings he had earnestly pled the case for trying some new ideas but never made the matter an agenda item. "Some of these guys aren't going to like that," said Karen.

Donnie rather sympathized with Royce but knew what he was up against. "I'd rather not turn out at all than get caught between the BLM and everybody else," he said. "We've got enough pasture so if it rains at all we could just keep our cows down here on our own land and the hell with Tracy. We've done it before."

"Of course," Karen added, "if we expect to do the land any good up there, we've got to participate, but. . . . There's too much family, too many neighbors, too many relationships. It might be a lot smoother if we didn't have to deal with that."

"Royce can. He's not from here. The worst part is we're going to wind up working our butts off just to make a point that no one's interested in."

They agreed. They would best keep their cows at home, be holistic on their own private 2,500 acres, and stay neutral on association politics. Royce could fend without them.

Nevertheless, on the following Thursday, Donnie drove down to the meeting at Swede's Corners to work out plans for turning out their cows on the North Tracy Common Allotment come June and not incidently to discuss "improving the resource."

Turning into Bill Strickland's driveway, he could see the pickups of the others already nuzzled up to the house—his brother George, George's brother-in-law Eric Davey, Eric's father John and uncle Earl, whose grandfather was an English blacksmith who came west to escape the Civil War draft and sold steel arrowheads to the Utes, Glen Alexander from whose grandfather the highest of the hills on the allotment, which they just called Alexander, got its name, and old Kenneth Schmittel, whose father-in-law, Bill Hagan, had developed one of the major springs on Tracy before the Taylor Grazing Act and managed to get private title to a patch of land around it. And there was Denise Temple and her husband Danny from Cheyenne Wells out on the plains. He would still have fire in his eyes because of a dispute that grew more complicated every year over the conversion of sheep permits and a lease on a patch of state land within the allotment.

Out in front, still waiting for late arrivals, Bill Strickland could be identified by his animated gestures. He would be elaborating his latest production strategy to the man beside him in the sweat-stained felt hat—Jim Coleman of Coleman Natural Beef, whose ancestor drove a bunch of shaggy Galway cattle all the way from New York to Saguache in the 1870s.

The BLM's green Dodge pickup also had taken its place among the others, and the bureau's two range conservationists, Royce Wheeler and Fran Ackley, were already inside setting up chairs around the Stricklands' long dining room table and unfolding their easel and maps. All the way down the Gun Barrel they had discussed their agenda. For four years they had preached and cajoled in the ardent faith that the Tracy Common Grazing Association couldn't fail to recognize the slow stagnation of the allotment and rouse themselves to do something about it. Perhaps the time had come to flex the bureaucratic muscle a bit and move things along. After surviving nearly two decades of turmoil within the BLM itself, Royce felt he finally had a mandate to act.

In 1974, the bureau had been blindsided by a lawsuit filed by an outfit few ranchers or agency officials had ever heard of and initially dismissed as meddlesome upstarts. However, when the Natural Resources Defense Council actually prevailed in its claim that the 1969 National Environmental Policy Act required the agency to file environmental impact statements for individual grazing districts, it threw livestock interests and their civil service friends into deep shock. This turned to outrage two years later when the NRDC and some other national environmental organizations successfully secured passage of the Federal Land Policy and Management Act, which required that all public land be managed for "multiple use," which, besides grazing, included wildlife, fishing, and recreation.

The immediate result was the so-called Sagebrush Rebellion of 1979, when the Nevada legislature voted to seize 49 million acres of BLM land for the undeclared purpose of privatizing it. That same year, Senator Orin Hatch of Utah sponsored a bill to turn all BLM and Forest Service land west of the 100th meridian over to the states. These moves, like similar ones since, failed, in part because organized environmentalism was already too strong and in part because pragmatic ranchers realized that in any scramble for privatized lands, they would lose out to speculators, mining and petroleum companies, and even environmental organizations like the Nature Conservancy.

Beginning in the mid-1980s, a panoply of groups, from the tree spikers and eco-saboteurs (Monkey Wrenchers, they called themselves) of Earth First! to the gentlemen of Trout Unlimited in their Orvis waders, had laid siege to all the federal land agencies, the BLM, the Forest Service, and the National Parks Service, and made the desertification of the West by grazing into a national issue. Every year now, in curious coalition with cattlemen from states that had no public land, they shoved a bill a few votes further through Congress that would raise grazing fees above what most permit holders thought they could pay. For all the pain this attention inflicted in the Department of Interior, it gave its work a significance it hadn't enjoyed since the days when Harold Ickes headed Franklin Roosevelt's Interior Department in the 1930s.

Word filtered through the hierarchy that anybody who demonstrated an ability to rehabilitate a significant piece of ground would win a lot of points, especially if it included one of the streamside "riparian" habitats that across much of the West had changed since the turn of the century from willow-shaded oases to dead gullies. Idealists like Royce and Fran responded like buried larvae in the spring sun. Since the first Reagan administration, when a sagebrush rebel named James Watt had headed the Department of Interior and a Colorado rancher named Bob Burford directed the BLM, field staffers who mentioned the word "ecology" had risked spending the rest of their careers sorting oil lease applications in some windowless office in Denver.

But novel ideas had never quite ceased to filter through the cracks. Even during the Burford years, both Fran and Royce had taken a short holistic management course at a Best Western motel in Colorado Springs sponsored by the bureau itself. Savory was, after all, friendly to livestock, and even some hard-liners had begun to look for ways to reconcile the competing lobbies, if not actually fix something. These were also the years when the gospel of "collaborative decision making" began to seep into the bureaucratic consciousness. This notion, long promoted under various names in the business world by such management gurus as Peter Drucker and Tom Peters as a way to beat the Japanese, emphasized trust and consensus. Get all the players to buy into a common goal and build a team driven more by its own esprit de corps than petty ambitions and you could overcome red tape and prejudice and sell Fords on Hokkaido.

By the time this rage swept through the Department of Interior, every school board and church committee was already busy drafting mission statements and setting goals, so getting a room full of ornery Saguache County ranchers to agree on a three-part holistic goal no longer seemed very radical. It didn't come naturally to them, however, nor to the BLM, nor to Royce himself. "If you look at our successes," he often said, "you find that one person at the field level put his career on the line by ignoring his superiors and made things happen on the ground—and made enemies in both places."

As the BLM pickup truck hummed along the Gun Barrel, Fran went over the list of goals that had emerged from a goal setting-session back in the fall. In the spirit of holism, the two range conservationists had invited the local game warden from the Colorado Division of Wildlife, the representative of the state land board, and members of the Tracy Common Grazing Association. Royce had scrawled goals on giant sheets of newsprint as the group brainstormed one idea after another: profit from livestock; increase revenue for Saguache County through tourism, hunting, and firewood collecting; protect wildlife; increase living organisms, including invertebrates. The landscape goals called for increasing ground cover generally and the number and extent of cool season grasses in particular. The association agreed to slow the advance of erosion gullies and increase diversity and area of riparian zones.

Both Fran and Royce had found the goal-setting experience exhilarating. It validated their calling. It linked to the greater picture what others might have seen as lives of exile in the backwash of American culture. But Royce at least had been around long enough to wonder where it would lead. Now in his early fifties, he had about reached the only career horizon he had been able to see from his youth. He grew up in the farm town of Rocky Ford, where, before a Denver suburb bought the water rights and dried the place up, the Arkansas River had irrigated fields of sugar beets and cantaloupes on the barren plains of eastern Colorado. Although his father was a baker, Royce grew up in 4-H and worked on farms and ranches, which were the heart of life in Rocky Ford. At eighteen he went off to Colorado State to study animal and range science. Then, because his family moved, he transferred to Texas Tech, in Lubbock, where two of the grand old men of range management were then teaching. Laurance Stoddart and Thadis Box literally wrote the book on range science in the United States. Although their basic text, *Range Management,* contradicts absolutely and fundamentally everything Allan Savory would later conclude about management, as teachers Box and Stoddart communicated the same sense of mission and wonder for their subject. So Royce joined the BLM, glad to work outside, live in small towns, and traffic in elements like snakeweed and grama grass, but often in doubt as to whether he could make much difference.

Fran Ackley's early exposure to grassland management was mowing 500 square feet of backyard in Palos Heights, Illinois, which anyone from elsewhere would call South Chicago. He still apologizes for this. One summer in the early 1970s, after freshman year at Northern Illinois University, he hitchhiked west, and on the second morning out, when he saw the Rockies rising out of the plains at the end of Interstate 76, he realized that he had been raised as an illegitimate foundling in an alien home. He swore never to go back. He joined the Forest Service, and after a few years of hauling rocks on trail crews enrolled at Colorado State thinking a little science might make his efforts count a little more. In CSU's Department of Range and Forest Management, they taught him about "range improvements"—how to chain off, burn, plow, and seed degraded rangeland, how to match lethal chemicals to pests and weeds he might need to kill, how to run a cost/benefit analysis through a computer and write up a basic environmental impact statement.

"Out of the whole thing, three courses have really helped me," he would explain later, "grass systematics, plant taxonomy, and range ecogeography [why various plants choose to grow where they do]. I learned to identify hundreds of different plants backwards and forwards and competed in intercollegiate plant identification contests. I got pretty good at observing minute details, and I started to notice small changes in the Whittens' land that were really interesting and weren't explained by anything I'd been taught. They had perennial cool season grass sprouts around water points where you almost never see them, because as the first species to green up in the spring they usually get wiped out. Spots that I saw badly trampled out on one visit, I'd find fully recovered by the next, and I knew no precedent for that degree of resilience." That hooked Fran, too, on Savory's ideas.

Fran Ackley and Royce Wheeler talked often about the changes they could wreak on Tracy—for the Bureau, for the permittees, for environmental politics, for the planet.

At nearly 40,000 acres, Tracy was big enough to permit an extremely flexible management plan that could take advantage of anomalous events such as a thunderstorm crossing one end while the other remained dry. If they ran together, the nearly 600 cow-calf pairs that the nine permittees could turn out could deliver the kind of animal impact that Savory recommended, and the size of the allotment would allow them to move that herd so after every dose of grazing, every plant got ninety days or even more to recover. By controlling when and where the herd hit Tracy Creek (for years now only a dry arroyo), they could assure that vegetation of some kind covered the bottom and trapped silt during spring runoff and the August thunderstorm season. In time, they could heal the deep gash the water course had made of its bed.

Most of all, they would demonstrate the power of community action. If the permittees worked together toward goals that had the blessing of wildlifers, conservationists, and the local public, then they could build a case for far more radical moves. They might amalgamate myriad individual allotments into bigger communal ones that made ecological sense. They could argue for shifting permits around the valley to deliver impact and rest to riparian zones far worse than Tracy Creek. If they could make something of Tracy, they could argue generally for stepping beyond numbers, permits, regulations, and boundaries and managing for the need of the land as nature and enlightened minds must see it. They could hold tours. The BLM would publish four-color pamphlets about it, as they did when a holistic district range conservationist in Prineville, Oregon, revived a single trout stream.

When the metal gray road shot them on beyond the cultivated land into the ragged zone of chico bushes and cows and they saw the slopes of the allotment rising to the west, the sight had sobered them. They had, after all, spent four years talking about their vision without inspiring more than the faintest echo, except from the Whitten brothers, who had inspired *them*, but, as it was often said in the bureau, "These things take time."

The site of the meeting, Bill Strickland's place at Swede's Corners, shares a luxuriant willow grove with the somewhat larger two-story white clapboard farmhouse where the Swede Johnson once lived. Strickland's smaller replica is not clapboard, though, but dazzling white vinyl that looks like it, and a glance inside confirms the hypothesis that it is in fact a dream house, built fresh to fulfill a desire that had had to wait until children were grown and portfolios matured. Thirty years an engineer for a large manufacturer of industrial pumps and a careful investor, he had always aimed to live on the land and leave behind his split-level suburban house and its shelves of Value-line reports and photos of the country, but he was finding the simple life the most elusive goal he'd ever set.

As soon as representatives of all nine Tracy permits arrived, thirteen people, including relatives and allies, the association filed into the Strickland dining room and took up places around the table, and Royce adjusted his easel to catch the light pouring in through the picture window. Had it opened to the west, they could have seen Tracy Canyon, but the view was east across a jumble of corrals and the misty level of the valley to the 14,000-foot wall of the Sangre de Cristo range. The sight is so awesome, no one can look at it without wondering whether the palaver of a baker's dozen of mere humans matters at all.

Royce's easel supported a map of the allotment overlaid with lines indicating fences, pipes, and water tanks. It was his shot at a plan for eliminating overgrazing in a holistic way. If the association put all its animals together, they could move from one paddock to another and never graze a plant twice before it had a chance to recharge. It was an ambitious plan that would require everyone spending a week or more stringing wire and laying pipe, if indeed the BLM could come up with supplies. And someone would have to move the herd every three or four days.

Fran Ackley opened the meeting, alternately bending over his notes and glancing from face to face to gauge the response. "I think we all decided that we have to have some plan," he began, "in case the Sierra Club or some other environmental group challenges our grazing practices. In twenty years I'd like to still see cattle on the allotment, healthy plants and soil, and profit for you guys. I want people coming up here to see that cattle can be a benefit to the land. Our riparian areas could be a lot better. They tell me that once so much water ran up there, they didn't have to pipe water to the cattle and they actually irrigated potatoes on some of the flat land. I'd like to see that much water in those creeks again. If we could do that, I think we'd see better community relations. I'd like us to share our feelings about our goals."

In a thin voice that the others bent forward to hear, John Davey began. It would have been presumptuous to say anything about desertification to him. Eight decades of sun and weather had twisted him down to the size of his boyhood and spot-welded all his joints. All the motion of his thoughts had to come out in his eyes, which rolled right and left as he scanned the faces and said, "There's been a lot of change since before the BLM came in. Way back, sheep came on in the spring and grazed until fall. The cows came on the first of July, if there was still feed, and went to wherever they could get it first. You could push the cows up when there was grass on the high places, but some would always drift down to the ditch and stay there all summer. There were no fences, and the cows could choose what suited them."

Jim Coleman, although high in his fifties himself, gave John the respect of a moment's silence, but he was a partner in a somewhat radical enterprise, Coleman Natural Beef. "If the environmentalists come in," he said, "if we don't have a plan, if we can't say what we're doing to benefit the country, then we're in trouble. But if we can show the country what we're doing, we have some chance. But in advance we've got to do a lot of things, mainly water. If we could get better water, we could do a lot."

But then George Whitten, compact and intense like his brother but more headstrong, interrupted. "I'd like to see more ground covered, *and* more grazing. I'm not as old as John and some of you others, but I've seen a lot of deterioration even over the time I've been going up there. One of the biggest things holding us up is lack of trust, both in the government and in ourselves. I'd like to do what I can to get that back."

Donnie picked up on that. "It puzzles me," he said. "We've had a lot of wet years, but back in the past there were creeks where they raised potatoes. Now it doesn't seem to matter how much it rains. There's something wrong out there that's not the weather. I'd like to see the place better for my kids than it is—not worse."

George's contemporary, Eric Davey, six feet, five inches of lanky vitality towering over his father and his Uncle Earl, reared back in his chair and looked at the ceiling. "Well," he said, "I guess I'd just like to get back together again like we used to be. We need to do something about the water, but if we pipe it from one canyon to another, I expect we could dry up areas below." This was full of code. "Get back together" indicated an already serious division between reformers and conservatives. "Dry up areas below" meant that however much they might all want water, the main issue would come out in how they developed it.

Then it was Bill Strickland's turn. Although Eric handled a lot of his day-to-day management for him, Tracy raised questions that intrigued him. "Whatever we do must be long term," he said, "and we need very detailed plans and objectives. If we say we're going to increase ground cover, and we don't, then we have to change and do something else. It might mean moving cattle every day or every week, but a lot of these are political objectives. If they raise grazing fees, then I'm off the range, as simple as that. It's just the same economically as a drought. We've got to be aware of what the environmentalists are saying and educate them about what we are doing."

As the how-do-you-feel session progressed through the membership, Denise Temple took notes so vigorously that the table vibrated as if it might blow up at any moment. Her husband Danny was really wired. One look at his eyes and the tense muscle under his shirt collar and you knew you had better speak diplomatically or remove your glasses and false teeth and step back. His was the anger of a man at the height of his youth and ambition who sees all the mindless forces of law and convention drawn up against him. It went back, of course, to the festering old sore that neither the association nor the BLM desired to discuss, but the technicalities of the case hardly mattered anymore.

Over the past century, hundreds of Danny Temples have come into that country and thought the same thoughts, and everyone around the table knew it. "Here I am, tough and strong and ready to work, willing to strike out in a country so big hardly anybody wants to live here. You better let me have at it. It's my right." So thought all the homesteaders and prospectors whose ruined houses dotted the countryside. In fact, the family history of everyone around the table owed something to that spirit, except perhaps Bill Strickland's, and he wouldn't have minded if it did.

"If I have to put in work out on Tracy, I will," he said finally. "But I can't be playing games out there. I think all this fencing is a bunch of beans. The cross fencing to keep the cattle from drifting down on the low country worked okay, but all these little plots you want to do, and moving the stock every day—well, we might as well hire a herder, and we'd need four or five of them. Hell, I got payments to make."

"Moving every day is a misconception," countered Fran. "It would only be every two or three days."

Kenneth Schmittel, the old cowboy whose authority came from his wife's private spring in the middle of Tracy, coughed loudly and muttered to no one in particular, "Every time the government gets a new idea, it seems like it ends up that they cut us back in number or time. As for all these fences, I won't have it. The more work we do, the less we have."

"I'd like to say that I'm not here to do that," Fran pleaded. Schmittel never did think much of the government, but unbeknownst to Fran, the State Division of Wildlife had just annexed for a game refuge 700 acres of a state lease that his wife's cattle had grazed since there was a state. They had told him that even when the grass built up and began to choke itself he couldn't use it. They would burn it off, because letting private cows back on a state refuge would be political dynamite. "I ran wild through that country, and so did my kids, and so did my grandkids, then here comes the damned government, and they know everything," Schmittel grumbled on.

Royce had flipped over a new page on his easel, and he scrawled whenever a comment sounded hopeful: "increase ground cover, continue grazing, develop plan, help wildlife, reverse decline, develop trust and respect, improve for future generations, change but cautiously, have long-term objectives."

Bill Strickland squinted at the list. "Now probably all of those are good things," he said, "but some, like wildlife, is a social issue, not a business issue. I can't make a profit on wildlife. I can on cows. I need to sort out my personal objectives from the general ones. I would like to learn better ways to run cows in a brittle environment."

Donnie: "Well, is our whole purpose to put these things in to satisfy outside politics? Maybe some of them are good for us, too. If the land looked better, you might want to start a photo club or something."

Kenneth: "I'd like to say we got along a lot better before the BLM had an office in Alamosa. I'm against all this ecology stuff. Once we didn't turn out stock up there for three years because they told us the range wasn't 'ready,' and it didn't do a damn bit of good."

Fran: "Let's look at the production goal. Increased tourism, protection of wildlife. Increase in living organisms, including invertebrates."

Bill: "On that profit from livestock. I don't think we can measure that. If the market falls, so does our profit. I'd say our objective is heavier calves and more numbers."

Fran: (pushing ahead) ". . . provide increased revenue to Saguache County through tourism, hunting, firewood cutting, etc. These things are in there because people in Saguache County and the Division of Wildlife would like to see them, and it would be good to have them in there."

Jim Coleman took off his hat, looked long at some detail of its battered crown, then said affably, "I myself don't care much about elk or invertebrates, but if the Sierra Club or someone else wants it in there, okay."

Fran: "Okay, listen to the landscape description. Increase ground cover, increase cool season grasses like Indian rice grass, reduce piñon/juniper trees, attack gullies on the streams, preserve elk habitat, and improve deer and antelope. Increase mosaic of brush areas."

Kenneth shook his head sadly. "Now you're not going to do anything with those gullies. That's a thing of nature. Once I was driving some cattle down when a big storm caught up with us. It washed out great big boulders, stripped some land right down to the rock. You can make reservoirs, but the water just runs right on through. You ain't stopping that."

The conversation went back and forth over the hope or futility of controlling nature. Could you do anything about grass if it didn't rain? The older men cited the dismal example of the "range improvements" implemented on Tracy in the 1950s—the pulling down of vast numbers of piñon and juniper trees, the seeding of exotic grass species, and the reduction of the grazing permits.

If deforestation had become an international issue, and governments spent millions trying to establish green belts of trees to hold back the Sahara, why did they cut trees on Tracy? This was the theory as practiced in the 1950s and Royce Wheeler studied it in the 1960s and Fran Ackley in the 1980s and is still widely taught in the 1990s. It rested on strong circumstantial evidence that woody plants, including some trees, invade stressed rangeland and, once established, consume water and nutrients in such vast amounts that grasses disappear altogether. Nearly every region has its invader tree—piñon pine and juniper in high deserts like Colorado, mesquite in Texas and Mexico, acacia in southern Africa—and in areas too harsh for trees, invader bushes—sage, salt bush, chico, snakeweed, and a host of others.

Where water and mineral cycles become totally dysfunctional or where people desperate for firewood or browse for their stock cut them down, as happens in Africa and Asia, the invaders, too, get wiped out. Nevertheless, around the world and within historic memory, enormous areas of once productive grassland now support nearly inedible shrubs and trees under which the ground remains absolutely bare.

The obvious remedy was to destroy the invaders by fire, poison, or a large yellow machine, replant grass, and give it a few years of rest to take hold. Old-timers had seen it done on a piece of Tracy and were not impressed. The new grass did grow, but the reinvasion began almost at once, as it had on virtually all the millions of acres worldwide where the practice had been applied. Nor did the grass flourish well beyond the first few years. It was still there all right, vestiges of the same plants in the rows where the seed drill had put them, but they had scarcely propagated at all beyond that in thirty-four years.

The discussion went on and on, and Fran got nowhere in trying to convince Kenneth Schmittel why Allan Savory, too, might consider cutting piñons a waste of money, or that he, Fran, had anything useful to say about water and mineral cycles and the debilitating effects of resting land. What could this boy from Chicago possibly know about addressing the causes of the invasion through clever management of the cattle? He'd never grown a blade of grass or raised a pound of beef. Besides that, he was a BLM agent, and where could he point to a government project that hadn't ultimately screwed up?

Through all this, Eric Davey's long body slouched lower and lower in his chair, but all at once he straightened to his full height and said, "Hey, you folks, I'm finding it a little hard to concentrate. We're in the middle of calving. It's been damn cold at night, and we've had a lot of problems like toxemia and all kinds of infections. Can we make some decisions and get out of here?"

After that, it didn't take the group long to get down to brass tacks. Royce insisted that before the BLM would contribute any water pipe or fencing material, he had to have a long-term commitment to work toward holistic management. In the end, this came easy, because the BLM had only enough money and the association could contemplate only enough labor to develop one 10,000-acre demonstration area in the north end of the allotment, instead of the whole 40,000 acres, that they would subdivide into five paddocks with temporary electric fences.

George and Donnie Whitten and Jim Coleman would put about 250 cow-calf pairs through all of them in succession during July. They would all spend another short week on a patch of private land the Whittens owned and finish up on the open range outside the demonstration area. Glen Alexander, who up to now had sat aloof with a bemused grin on his leathery face, said he'd think about joining, but he worried that his bulls would fight with the others.

Then Bill Strickland confessed that, despite his sincere interest, he couldn't use his permit this year at all. On the strength of some studies he'd made, he had recently bought a large number of cheap yearling heifers with the idea of spaying them. Death losses and the cost of the operation had quickly proven the plan unprofitable, however, so now he was stuck with libidinous heifers that he could not run with other people's bulls and bred cows.

Danny Temple wouldn't budge. "I don't see any sense in giving cows all they can eat and then holding them until they starve. That's what this thing is about, isn't it?"

"Well, Danny, you just don't understand holistic resource management," countered Royce.

Danny: "Well, it ain't going to work because it costs too much. And you want us to 'measure the grass.' We can just look at the grass. You want us to put out rain gauges. Are you going to go out there and read them? We don't need anyone to tell us when it rains."

Fran: "I'd like to point out that if we grew just one half-ounce more of forage per square yard, that would be 8,000 extra animal unit months over the whole allotment."

"Well, I'm going to keep my cattle out of this mess altogether," said Kenneth. "If I have to watch them starve, it'll be on my land, not government land."

When the meeting finally broke, they agreed on dates to gather on the land itself to build the 5 miles of fence and lay out the 3 miles of plastic pipe required for the new holistic demonstration area. Royce reminded them that workdays on a common allotment required the participation of all members, even though it would run as two parts. The Whittens, Jim Coleman, and maybe Glen Alexander would try out holism in the north. The others in the south would use existing fences to make their animals use the higher country instead of hanging out all summer on the bottom land.

All of them young enough to shoulder a shovel, including Royce and Danny Temple, would turn up on the appointed May mornings to lay the waterline and build the fence for the demonstration area, and not because the BLM could have given them trouble if they didn't or even out of gratitude that it put up about $7,000 in PVC pipe, wire, and a solar-powered fence charger from New Zealand that could send a 6,000-volt jolt through 50 miles of fence. They came mostly because they were in fact neighbors, and they enjoyed that kind of work.

In the way of things in small communities, the association members more or less turned back into neighbors after the meeting. Bill Strickland, Eric, and Royce lingered a while. As they picked up the Styrofoam cups and doughnut crumbs that mark the small steps of so much human progress, they reflected on the unspoken matter of time, not grazing time or work time, but the theme of a human life.

Eric said his uncle Earl had no heirs who wanted to ranch. His own brothers and sisters could not say how long their interest in the Tracy permit would continue when John passed it on to them. Ken Schmittel had a son and daughter-in-law who could pick up for him, but they had a thriving business taking tourists on pack trips. Would they have the time to mess with moving cattle? Danny Temple? For all his fire, his stock would probably always be a sideline. He made his real living selling piñon and juniper trees that the Forest Service and BLM licensed him to dig and occasionally some that they did not. Jim Coleman? He had an interest, but the Coleman enterprises had gotten caught with too much debt in the farm crisis of the mid-1980s, and were still digging out. They hoped to survive but had to think short term.

Bill Strickland? He had an intellectual interest in proving that he could turn a profit in his new profession without harming anything. "It would be worth it to me to forgo a little profit to learn how to run cattle in a brittle environment," he said several times during the meeting. On the other hand, he could not count himself in the succession of generations on Tracy.

And, of course, Fran Ackley and Royce Wheeler, representatives of the true owners of the land, the American people, would not stay there forever. Fran, in fact, already had his transfer papers to the office in Canon City, where he would take charge of putting wild horses up for adoption. They, too, were turning the West into desert, but the animal rights lobby didn't want horses turned into dog food and glue.

The three men, Eric the young heir, Bill the newcomer, and Royce the bureaucrat, lamented this fickleness of the human presence and so articulated the deeper tragedy of the commons. Garrett Hardin's original thesis described quite well the original burst of exploitation that hit Tracy following European invasion, but it also spelled out pretty well why, as the Declaration of Independence put it, governments are instituted among men. The members of the Tracy association, ornery as they were, weren't fools. They knew the range had limits and at the end of the day accepted responsibility for them. They weren't always the same limits as expressed by that other government, represented by the Bureau of Land Management, which they suspected of being seriously infiltrated by wilderness freaks and vegetarians, but they recognized the process.

The real tragedy was the loss of memory and with it the loss of vision. Even the old men, Ken Schmittel and John Davey, who had followed cows around Tracy Common in the 1920s, had only seen it on the cusp of its decline, when they were too young to know the context of what they saw. Natural communities seldom collapse as dramatically as Hardin's model described. They change like the face of a friend growing old before your own aging eyes, too close to be clearly recalled in childhood. Even the old men, if they felt the loss at all, felt it like the weight of their own years as the immutable entropy of all good things.

"Yes," said John Davey, when asked to reflect, "my father did tell about not being able to see a calf lying down out there in the summertime for all the grass, but I couldn't tell you if it was always like that. I guess I've seen grass out there, too, but it wasn't every year. When it rained we had grass, but I remember some awful dry years, too. It was true that the streams used to run much more, but probably the pumping out in the valley affected them. That happened about the same time, but they say the climate might be changing, too."

Ken Schmittel would always blame the government. "Oh sure, it was better. There were dry years, but we did all right until the government got the idea in the 1950s that they could improve it. When they dragged down all those piñon and juniper trees, they said we'd get more grass. What we really got was people coming in in wagons to get firewood. They made ruts that started all this erosion and gullies. It washed out the streams and left us with what we have today. When it rains now, the water just pours through, and it's gone."

The Whitten brothers found the ambiguity maddening. "I can remember riding in a wagon," said George as he and Donnie held postmortems on the meeting. "We were crossing open country with hills to the west. It must have been Tracy or maybe just south because we used to trail sheep through there, but ecologically it would have been the same. I remember feeling very small sitting on the wagon in all that open country, but all around the wind waves moved over the grass like they do across a wheat field. It was so beautiful, and I know I saw it, but I don't know when."

When they reckoned it out, it had to have been in the mid-1950s, when the Forest Service said the nearby range was "grubbed into the ground" and Jim Coleman worried about seeing grass again, ever. But maybe for one brief moment of one spring there was grass.

The BLM had records on the North Tracy Common Allotment, but when Royce retrieved the bulging folder from the gray steel archives in the back of the headquarters garage, he found it contained copious correspondence from Danny Temple but gave not even such record of the land as a casual diarist might keep that told what the land actually looked like, no mention of fat cattle or lean cattle, grasshoppers, cool season grasses, drought, or flash floods. Just isolated remarks without any context whatever. Some years passed without comment. None gave a detailed picture. A 1959 note remarks on "poor stand of grass due to overgrazing," but doesn't say how poor, what kind of grass, or after how much grazing. A range inventory in 1963 found 6,730 acres in good condition and the rest only fair. Some 5,956 acres were improving, and the rest were static.

In 1972, the area manager wrote that by late July the turnout was delayed because the allotment could stand only 30 percent of normal use, and they would probably have to come in early also. In 1975, he didn't allow turnout until mid-August.

Whatever happened after that happened off the record. The vision of calves hidden in the grass beside flowing streams, of irrigated potato fields and wind waves flashing in the sun, had receded so far out of memory as to have become mere legend. In the world's most scientifically aware country, and in a place where the same families had raised animals continuously for over a century (half of it under the eye of a concerned government), the ecological story of Tracy and its meaning left more room for conjecture than the courtship rites of Martians. That made a strong case for assuming that elsewhere in the world, too, such knowledge was likely to be very thin, indeed. It also meant that the demonstration idea was very much a voyage into the unknown.

Not too long after the meeting, on his way back from one of the workdays, Royce stopped at a curious little monument on the eastern edge of the allotment, a bit south of the demonstration area. Inside a square of twisted old juniper posts and rusty barbed wire lay a piece of ground about 10 yards on a side that nothing larger than a rabbit had grazed for about sixty years. Such "exclosures" dated back to the era of the Taylor Grazing Act and were designed to demonstrate to a resistant ranching community what bounty they could expect if they stopped piling animals on the common land.

Driving along the dusty eastern boundary of Tracy, Royce could see the plot from a long way off. Its darker color and higher profile stood out against the pale grama turf, which spread unbroken into the sunset. The professional rangeland specialist might go there as to the steppe equivalent of a sacred grove to reflect on the past and divine the future. Unfortunately, as an oracle, the exclosure dispensed nothing but Delphic riddles.

Inside the sagging picket gate, Royce walked back and forth a few times with bent head, staring at the ground. To be sure, even this grass wouldn't have hidden a jack rabbit, not to mention a calf, but a square yard of it easily bore the half-ounce of extra leaf that Fran, tapping at his calculator, had multiplied by 4,840 square yards per acre times 38,370 acres divided by 32 half-ounces per pound and 2,000 pounds per ton to come up with 2,901.7312 extra *tons* of forage for the allotment. At 25 pounds per day, that would come close to feeding 8,000 extra cow-calf pairs for a month. That would mean running four times what the allotment carried now.

No wonder the old-timers who came into the country in its prime could not imagine a limit to its abundance. Even if they did manage to harvest all that grew in one season, at first it always came back in the spring. The land did not collapse all at once, and in dry years they forgave it the shortfalls, so no one could remember a moment when it actually failed or saw the connection to what they did. There again was the real tragedy of the commons, the failure of memory and thus imagination. Those who had never seen half an ounce extra per square yard could not dream of it. But, of course, a vision meant nothing if you couldn't harvest it without killing the grass.

Now, no layman would have guessed that the grama grass on both sides of the fence belonged to the same race. Those within the exclosure stood erect like society dowagers and flaunted their foliage over the beaten masses outside. The problem was that the exclosure grass was decadent in its nobility. If anything, the bare spots between the patches where the wind had scoured the earth from under an armor of pebbles were larger inside the fence. And despite no end of seed heads and stolons, evident now as stiff gray stalks from past years, no young plants had joined the ranks for years. Sex in general had become an irrelevant hobby. In the northeast corner of the exclosure, two or three lusty green bunches rose even above the grama, but they had an even less hopeful story to tell. They were all that remained of strip plantings put in thirty years ago to test various species for a role in a grand rehabilitation of the allotment. For a brief period after they had been planted, the grama had momentarily roused itself and moved in on them, and that was that. The relics, with their fantastic Latin names, stood there still in the seed rows where they began. A couple of shocks of *Oryzopsis hymenoides*, Indian rice grass, its lacy white panicles still full of seed; then from Eurasia one big *Psathrostachys juncea*, Russian wild rye, and an *Agropyron desertorum*, crested wheat grass; and last a couple of North American cousins, *Agropyron spicatum*, bluebunch wheat grass, and *Andropogon scoparius*, little bluestem. All beautiful, but without a conquering spirit.

Two years prior, after hearing Savory talk about how land bloomed after a thundering herd tore it up, Royce had driven out to the exclosure with a rototiller and churned up yard-wide strips inside and outside the fence to see what would happen. Out of nowhere, a low, ground-hugging European purslane colonized every square inch. It was an annual, and when it first appeared he had hoped that it would be, as Savory had predicted, the first step in a robust succession. The next year, which was dry, some annual cheat grass had sprouted. Now, at the beginning of the third season, purslane again, no perennial plants, not even grama. Something was going on, but now he simply could not say what. Neither Savory's theories nor any textbook he could recall could explain fully the apparently random complexity of even this small patch.

Royce stopped short in the middle of his reverie, closed the gate on the exclosure, got back in the pickup, and headed for home. Every time he looked at the place, he left with more questions than he brought. Was the soil too far gone to come back? What was the impact of the bands of sheep in times past? What were the first signs of decline, if anyone had cared to notice? Was the condition of the exclosure really as static as it seemed or merely building to a critical moment when change would break loose? How could you really know, if the time scale outdistanced your life?

Not long after that, Jim Coleman had a chance for similar, if less scientific, reflection. He had land and some corrals not far from the Saguache cemetery, an exclosure running back to well before 1900, where most of those old stockmen of legend, including his New York ancestor of the Galway cattle, lay buried. Although not actually on the Tracy allotment, the land was similarly elevated above the flood plain. Why, he had reason to wonder, did the grama turf stop at the cemetery fence? Inside, the grass was hardly rich, but it was almost all Indian rice grass, and thickest around the older graves, the Colemans, Daveys, Hagans, and others. That, too, was something different.

6

Water

May came and with it the water off the hills and hints of green in the warmer crannies of the Tracy. Royce had sent notes and even telephoned members of the association to remind them that on the 5th they had agreed to meet at the cattle guard on the Tracy road west of Swede's Corners. They would spend the day replacing the old North Tracy waterline and install a tank for the new demonstration area.

Royce and the Whitten brothers hoped the demonstration area would show once and for all that they could compel the conjunction of natural forces that they believed had once made the Tracy Common a lush and vibrant place. Jim Coleman had joined the experiment as a passive participant with a small contingent of heifers that had either lost their calves or not born any and thus depended less on good feed. After much stroking of his chin, Glen Alexander had decided to keep his cattle out and watch for a season. Bill Strickland, because he had bought heifers that he could't afford to spay, and Ken Schmittel, because he was fed up with the government, weren't turning out any animals at all, even though they would sacrifice much of their winter hay reserve to do this. And the others, the Daveys and Danny Temple, had rejected the idea from the start.

The present plan called for an electric boundary fence around 8,000 acres and a storage tank big enough to water 300 cow-calf pairs. During July and part of August, they would move through twelve roughly equal subdivisions of the demonstration area. These would be defined by portable electric fence that would be moved by hand every four or five days. Over time, this treatment would wreak profound changes in plants, water, and soil—or so Royce and the Whittens hoped—but it distressed them to think of how much more flexibly they could have planned and how much more dramatic an impact they could have had on the land if they had had all 38,000 acres and 700 cattle to play with.

Environmentalists concerned about returning the land to its primeval state might have found it odd that the demonstration would involve the installation of so much hardware, but if Allan Savory's holistic analysis was correct, the end would justify the means. The wire, pipe, and tank were minor intrusions anyway compared to the "range improvements" of the past on Tracy, and they would not be just another techno-fix. They would create conditions for a revolution like the one that occurs when water reaches 212° Fahrenheit and, having remained pretty bland for the last 180°, suddenly becomes the stuff for hauling freight trains and lighting cities. The land would come to life.

The cattle guard at the North Tracy Common Allotment fence is out on the level, half a mile or more before the foothills rise, so as Royce paced by his pale green BLM pickup, hands pocketed against the morning nip, he could see the dust plumes of the association members' trucks converging from the east and south. Along the Rio Grande Canal, flocks of ravens launched, black-suited, from their roosts in willow and cottonwood for their morning commute down the Gun Barrel in search of rabbits squashed by eighteen-wheelers in the night, and a couple of tweedy Swainson's hawks found enough heat rising off basalt brows of the foothills to lift them away for an inventory of prairie dog towns.

No hint of the rancor and doubt of the planning sessions at Bill Strickland's house spilled over into the freshness of the spring morning. Everyone except Royce had grumbled the night before about putting off some pressing private matter, but by nine o'clock both Whitten men, Danny Temple, Glen Alexander, Jim Coleman, and Bill Strickland had all showed up. Just being away from routines and in strong company promised to make something of a party of this day. Besides, an act of care affirms ties, not just between people but between people and land and perhaps even between people and a federal land agency.

Many historical, hydrological, and biological threads came together in the North Tracy waterline project. The pipeline itself dated back to the early 1960s, when the BLM built it to compensate for the dwindling over the years of naturally flowing water that had become increasingly vital given the shift of grazing away from winter sheep (which ate snow) to summer cattle, which drank 20 gallons of water apiece per day. It carried water down onto the level eastern side of the allotment from a spring about 2 miles back and 500 feet up in the foothills, supplying a series of drinking troughs along the way. Being for summer use only, it was not buried very deep and surfaced wherever it crossed ledges of limestone or small gullies. The original steel pipe did not drain well and had rusted, frozen, and burst so frequently that in the early 1980s the BLM replaced it with black plastic guaranteed to last forever.

In Saguache County, however, the elements had treated exotic polymers as carelessly as they had the steel. In hardly a decade, the plastic had become sclerotic and prone to split. Now the line consisted largely of rusty hose clamps and fountaining splices. Alongside it, failed sections 10 yards long lay twisted on the sand where various association members had yanked them out of the ground amid the bawling of thirsty cattle. The summer before, everybody who had cattle in North Tracy had fixed a leak every other day at great expense in time, tires, gas, and patience. That the BLM had finally found a way to supply a couple of miles of new and improved plastic pipe was another incentive to pitch in. Now in black coils that weighed Royce's pickup down to the blocks, it glistened in the sun like new money.

Another historical twist on the North Tracy pipe was the fact that, like much of the rest of the perennial water on Tracy, the flow in this public artery was technically private. In the American Southwest, as in arid country worldwide, the control of rangeland was traditionally exercised not through fences and the county deed registry but by control of water. Back in the glory days of the Homestead Act, when land was parceled out in 160-acre squares, a family that could "prove up" on such a patch surrounding a spring acquired effective power over all the land as far in every direction as grazing depended on that water. A good bit of the water for the southern half of Tracy came through a BLM pipe from a spring on a private patch in the middle of the allotment acquired in this way and now belonging to Ken Schmittel. Up here in North Tracy, the checkered land status map showed the water coming from a small white square belonging to the Whittens, which Grandpa Whitten had bought to guarantee his grazing rights in the days before the BLM asserted government authority on the surrounding public land. Because Tracy Creek had flowed more then and sheep did not require a water source through much of the winter, the spring had never conferred an absolute right, but the idea of an absolute property right over grazing land is virtually unknown in herding cultures that haven't acquired barbed wire. Water was owned. Crop land was owned. Livestock was owned. But rangeland, like the open sea, was always subject to opportunity and negotiation.

Despite the obvious potential for conflict in such an ambiguous system, a traditional Masai or Tuareg or Navajo would defend it as essential because it also rewards cooperation, at least within the tribe. When drought overtakes the land near your water, you migrate toward some friend or kinsman whose country is green and make a deal. This might require networking on a grand scale plus a little muscle, but it permits a flexibility in response to crisis that a thoroughly seized, patented, and fenced landscape denies. And arid lands fall into crisis *continually*.

Even Grandpa Whitten, who as a child of Iowa felt driven to buy and fence as much land as he could, understood the custom of open range perfectly. The Bureau of Land Management has since done its best to civilize the ancient nonsystem of semi-tenure through its fenced allotments, permits, and drilled wells but has never quite superseded the logic of it.

As long as the BLM could control their grazing permits, Donnie and George, of course, had no reason to withold their water. Doing so would only have forced the agency to assess the grazing association for the expense of drilling a well. So, for the nine and a half months when no livestock ran on Tracy, the Whitten spring water ran freely out of a cluster of wild currant bushes and disappeared into the limestone gravel, but from July through mid-September it went into the BLM pipe. At 4.5 gallons a minute it could quench the thirst of 300 cows a day—about right for the demonstration. Other springs might have served, but like the people and animals that used them, they all had personalities.

Onion Spring, nearer to the dry eastern side of the allotment, had euchred the group into digging it out and cleaning it only the year before with a promise of 8 gallons a minute, then out of pure malice it went practically dry in midsummer. Another private source, Iron Spring, had the perverse ability to clog pipes and float valves and cutoffs with gobs of red oxide. The Whitten spring was "good water."

The seven members of the work crew gathered around the topographical map that Royce unfolded on the hood of his pickup and reviewed the plan. Donnie, driving an antique road grader that he had picked up for salvage after his days of driving one for the county road crew, would scour a new ditch alongside the old line with the lowered corner of his blade. Royce would follow with his pickup, playing off the pipe from a trailer-mounted reel he had welded out of scraps in the BLM shop. The rest would guide the pipe into the ditch, weight it down with stones, and stand ready to hoist new rolls of pipe onto the spindle whenever necessary. Then Donnie would take the grader back down the hill and cover the pipe.

Along the way, the men talked about water. Near its lower end, the pipe ran across the back side of an old dam that intercepted the dry bed of Tracy Creek where it left the foothills. The BLM had built the dam in the 1950s in response to the half-century metamorphosis of Tracy Creek from a steady trickle through swales of green into a scoured raceway for flash floods. It resembled tens of thousands of similar "erosion structures" thrown up across the West by big yellow machines in the age of cheap diesel and was supposed to catch the flood water and hold it for beneficial use.

In fact, the dam had held water so briefly and so unpredictably that its record wasn't worth remembering. One of the men remarked that it had probably cost about as much as a good water lawyer billed in a year and produced less water.

Jim Coleman pointed east to a pattern of 120-acre green polka dots clustered on the plain near Swede's Corners. Spray from the center pivot irrigation booms flashed white in the sun. "It's that South Farm," he said. "That's where the water is going. When they turn on the pumps, everything down there sure goes dry, and the recharge for that deep aquifer is probably up here somewhere. That could explain a whole lot."

Whatever the reason, the big dam may have kept a flash flood from cutting a channel down to the plain, but it never provided reliable stock water on Tracy. That would only happen when the ground oozed enough water to allow the creek to run again, and frankly, no one knew whether or how that was possible. Meanwhile, the pipe could at least supply the cows.

Thanks to Donnie's arthritic old road scraper, the work went quickly. Danny walked behind the squeaking reel, peeling the stiff black coil into the open ground, the others following to pin it down with chunks of limestone until Donnie's blade pushed the dirt back over it. Somewhere along the way, Glen, kicking dirt over the trench with the toe of his boot, remarked that for all the long snowy winter, the soil an inch down was damn dry, powdery in fact. Hard to imagine moisture oozing from that, ever, if not now.

The comment sparked no conversation because anyone growing up in Saguache County had learned to expect the unexpected from water. Among many reasons is a condition desertification techies refer to as the P/PET (Pee-Pet) ratio: precipitation divided by potential evaporation-transpiration. In practice, the value is usually extrapolated by standard formulas from average temperatures, wind speeds, and humidity. It relates the water that falls (P) to what the air would suck back up (PET) from puddles, soil, and plants under hypothetically maximized conditions. Although evaporation-transpiration may seldom approach its theoretical potential, and variation in rates from various plants and soils is large, one can imagine in a climate with a P/PET of 1.0 a swimming pool left open to the sun for a year might rise and fall a bit with the seasons but would break even overall. Any land with a P/PET of under .45 qualifies as semi-arid. A swimming pool in the San Luis Valley would lose about 6 feet of water to the heat and dryness against 8 inches recharge from snow and rain, a P/PET of .11, square in the middle of the arid range.

Due to its elevation, Tracy is probably somewhat better than the valley floor but low enough on the scale for its groundwater to behave strangely. Under the influence of a low P/PET, it acquires, for example, an alarming tendency to defy gravity. In any soil much finer than coarse sand, dry air will wick water up from astonishing depths, the way a flame draws oil out of a lamp or the sun can suck water to the top of the tallest redwood. Put a shovel into a spot of bare desert right after a downpour and you may find it wet to the depth of the blade, if the soil is not crusted over and sealed. A day or so later, though, you may find the top millimeter bone dry, then an inch or two of damp, and below that dry again, as in the Tracy pipe ditch. Little if any of the rain falling on such a place will ever reach the water table, no matter how shallow. And not only that. On its way out, the ungrateful water will carry all kinds of nasty salts up to the surface and leave them there as it evaporates. This explains how on the valley floor sheets of toxic alkali can alternate with swamp and why from California's San Joaquin Valley to the Aral Basin of Central Asia salination has forced hundreds of thousands of acres of irrigated land out of production.

Wherever water flows down rather than up, it creates a radically different environment. It recharges the water table, keeps the ground wet, and carries minerals down. Extreme downward flow can leach nutrients below the root zone of plants and deplete buffering minerals such as calcium until the soil becomes as destructively acid as desert soils become alkali. Thus, where rain forests are cleared of the deep-rooted trees that recycled nutrients to the surface, the soil rapidly loses its fertility. Downward flow is axiomatic wherever the P/PET is greater than 1.0, but in arid climates it only happens in remarkably delicate circumstances. Melting snow can recharge soil until the sun dries out the surface. After that, a mulch cover of dead grass and other plant litter can drastically reduce evaporation, but gravel and sand will also serve. Desert Indians in the Southwest still exploit this principle to raise corn in what look like sterile dunes.

The dynamics become further complicated by the apparant tendency of land to protect itself when all else fails. Left to their own devices, most desert soils will form a crust of minerals and opportunistic algae that effectively keeps water from going in *or* out. A crust also defends them against wind and rain erosion, but it contributes mightily to runoff and flooding in a downpour and inhibits the germination of seeds and the accumulation of litter.

The threshold point between water in and water out is fiendishly critical in all senses of the word. Wherever it depends on plants, relatively minor changes can make the flow go negative over vast areas. Then the land will dry out despite almost any amount of rain, water tables fall, and plant communities shift toward the thornier, more narrow-leaved species although the effects may not show up for years. This is why plowing up the Great Plains for wheat has always been a dicey proposition. Long before they exhaust the fertility of the soil, sod busters continue to go broke from drought, even when it rains, because on plowed ground the P/PET can suck all the water out of the root zone in a couple of years. Shift conditions even the smallest amount to the positive side by covering the soil with a bit of mulch or organic litter, however, and the whole picture changes radically. Even a small dose of rain travels down until plants put it to use or it winds up stored in an aquifer. This is a kind of ecological boiling point.

A few weeks after the last snow had left Tracy, the water bank had stopped accepting deposits, but of course that was why the men were laying pipe.

About noon, not far below the spring itself, the brown paper bags and green stainless steel Thermos bottles came out, and the men took lunch in the shadow of Donnie's grader. As they ate, a handsome pronghorn buck materialized on the sunny slope of Tracy Canyon across from them and cocked his ears as if to eavesdrop. Donnie Whitten mentioned that he had entered the drawing for an antelope license for so many years that he was bound to get one this year and that maybe this buck had his name on it. The buck looked back at him unafraid.

The men talked about hunting and sports and women, and because Glen Alexander's domestic life had fallen under the enthusiastic management of a highly intelligent girl named Penny, who was half as old and twice as ornery, they made him retell the story of the sheepdog showdown. It had happened the previous fall, while gathering cattle on a neighboring allotment, that Penny's young Australian heeler had gotten overenthusiastic about chasing another man's cows, and he had offered to shoot it. "She warned him, 'Don't you think of it, you sonofabitch,' " said Glen, "and if he'd known her like I do he wouldn't have turned his back when he reached for that .30-06 on his gun rack." There was some discussion over whether Penny had actually knocked him out. "Without his hat, though, that shovel probably would have killed him," said Eric.

From there, story followed story until they ended where they always did, on water. In arcane language laced with jargon about senior rights, historic flows, confined and unconfined aquifers, artesian pressure, impermeable substrata, and the like, the various plots flowed and blended like the dark lines and blotches on the plain that spread out vastly below them and beyond the mouth of Tracy Canyon and that were of course not metaphors but the real stories.

Far across the valley, where the buff landscape turned up to meet the mountain wall, lay the 100,000-acre Baca Grande land grant. It belonged, or used to belong, if one takes a long series of asset swaps among corporations of interlocking substance at face value, to Maurice Strong. Strong himself happened at that moment to be in Geneva, Switzerland, getting ready to chair the U.N. Conference on Environment and Development that would open the following month in Rio de Janeiro. As undersecretary of the United Nations, Strong had conceived and organized the conference with all the zeal and genius he had once applied to making several billion dollars in Canadian oil, gas, and real estate, and he billed it as the greatest international convocation in the history of the world in terms of the number of delegates and nations represented.

Strong and his Danish wife, Hanne, had wound up owning the Baca in 1978 as a mere by-product of aggressive investing, but they had found its beauty divine—so divine that Hanne decided to make it a spiritual center. Through her largesse and influence, she soon attracted a Carmelite Catholic monastery, a refugee Tibetan Buddhist monastery, two Hindu ashrams, a New Age center, a Native American center, and enough independent meditators and seekers to nearly levitate the adjacent hamlet of Crestone and provide older valley residents with a source of both inspiration and astonishment for the rest of time. It was Hanne's husband, however, who brought them face to face with higher powers.

Strong often described the Baca as his favorite place on Earth, but no oil tycoon could limit his appreciation of such dramatic geology to aesthetic and spiritual plains. The realization that the alluvial plain of San Luis lay atop an aquifer 6,000 feet deep moved him profoundly. The corporation he formed to exploit the cash value of this dirt-filled fold between the Sangre de Cristos and the Continental Divide, American Water Development, Inc., promised profits that would make a Saudi prince gasp. In 1986, AWDI applied to the Colorado State Engineer for the right to pump from under the Baca 200,000 acre feet of water annually, which, considering some Western cities were paying from $6,000 to $10,000 an acre foot, worked out to gross cash flows approaching $2 *trillion* a year. Reality would doubtless cut the take to some fraction of that, but Strong had no trouble leveraging this information with backing from a number of luminaries, including a former director of the U.S. Environmental Protection Agency, William Ruckleshouse, and a notorious corporate raider named Sam Belzberg from his native Canada.

In its whole turbulent history, the valley had never seen a bid to grab water on that scale. News of the application set off an equally unprecedented explosion of protest. It didn't require a lesson in old pastoral custom for local people to realize that mere greedy capitalism was not the issue. Transferring 200,000 acre feet of water out of the valley could quite possibly have the virtual effect of hauling actual acres to another place, if land permanently went out of production as a result. That amounted to a fundamental redefinition of geography by whatever society did it, capitalist, socialist, or other.

By the spring of 1992, perhaps because his moral position among environmentalists at Rio required no less, perhaps because he realized the seriousness of legal challenges raised against his plan, Strong had distanced himself from AWDI. Claiming that he had lost the control he needed to assert his own environmental standards for it, he said he sold his interest. The AWDI corporate structure, however, remained so insanely complex and secretive nearly everyone in the valley continued to hold him personally responsible.

George Whitten sat on the board of the Rio Grande Water Conservancy District, which was one of the main litigants against AWDI, but even he did not know who AWDI was by name. "It seems they have investors lined up from all over the world," he said. Would they make a more political push to acquire groundwater rights? Were they going broke? Did they have new capital? Would they file for bankruptcy and reconstitute themselves under a new name? Would they simply buy up ranches and farms that already had water rights? George could say only that another big legal battle would utterly break the conservancy district and no doubt the rest of the valley as well. Maurice Strong notwithstanding, AWDI had no face. It was the terrible power of the cities against the country, money against nature, the gnomes of Zurich against men of the soil.

"I don't think it's going to change before the whole system ends up in a wreck," said George.

Danny Temple grumbled, "The damn cities take everything."

Glen Alexander, although he said nothing, had cause to reflect on that. There he sat under the very shadow of the peak named after his grandfather, Alexander, looking to any observer like an almost post-card old-timer: crooked teeth, day-old stubble, and faded jeans. Yet he had not chosen this life. When word came that his father had died with his cows scattered all over the public land and no hay stored for the winter, Glen had been living in relative comfort in St. Louis overseeing the selling of specialized castings for a large steel company. He had had no intention at all of going back to calving heifers on winter nights and worrying himself sick over the fickleness of rain. Yes, he was a rancher now and he would not contradict the company line, but he wasn't sentimental about it. A living was a living however you came by it. He said that if the valley got sucked dry, he hoped he got paid for it.

Of more immediate concern was what had already gone dry—Saguache Creek, for example. From where the men sat, it appeared only as a wisp of imperfection in the plain where smudges of darker sedge and the borders of fields as subtly different in hue as wet and dry paint marked the sinuous line of a water course. It was hard to imagine that 30 miles to the west, where it gathered out of the national forest, rapids big enough to knock down a man boiled with trout and poured through vast meadows and banks of willows. Here, Saguache Creek was dry most of the time, which was indeed the issue. Most of the men present, including the Whitten brothers, had water rights in Saguache Creek that they could never exercise because water hardly ever got that far.

"Now that's the kind of right you should sell to AWDI," said George, "but they'd probably find a way to get the water."

No one laughed. The dryness of Saguache Creek sprang from twin sources. One of them was the infamous South Farm that Glen had sworn at earlier, but it was difficult to attack because its right to pump was well adjudicated. This meant that although water in Saguache

Creek disappeared whenever the South Farm turned on its pumps, the law did not recognized any causal relationship. Any argument against this was complicated by the second problem. A lot less water got even as far as the South Farm than legally should have anyway. This, too, was measurable and no doubt actionable, but *sociopolitical* factors made this problem difficult to acknowledge, too.

The State Department of Natural Resources paid a "Water Commissioner" named Tim Lovato to patrol Saguache Creek for illegal diversions. Referred to locally as the "ditch rider," Lovato aroused remarkably predictable reactions among his constituents. People farming upstream from Lovato's land found him wise and conscientious. Those below often failed to find adjectives they could repeat in public. The previous summer, which had been very dry, members of the latter group made jokes about the verdure and productivity of his hay field, which was clearly visible from the Gun Barrel. It was even alleged, and vigorously denied, that people who hired Lovato as manager or overseer got a pretty good hay crop, too, but no abuse was ever proved or even scientifically investigated, thanks in part to the beavers. They dammed the creek and flooded meadows anywhere landowners let them get away with it. An effective organization of rights holders could have given Lovato a budget to buy the dynamite and ordered him to blow up beaver dams himself, but the political gap between Lovato's supporters and detractors made the subject difficult to raise.

Lovato's Spanish ancestry added a tribal element to the controversy because the complainers on lower Saguache Creek were all Anglo. Anglo–Spanish relations had a somewhat rocky history everywhere in the valley, including Saguache, and one didn't aggravate them unnecessarily. All things considered, maybe the county could do without a battle over Saguache Creek.

"Some people have been talking about organizing a new water district to take control of it," said Donnie, "but I wonder if we could get it done or if we could run it if we did. People are so ornery."

So there it sat. Water was politics, and politics was a lot more complicated than hydrology, whether it involved Maurice Strong and the United Nations or Saguache County. But both politics and hydrology turned on small things like a bit of organic litter or a petty argument. Dryness could spread like a disease or bad feelings and infect a place for centuries. Water in or water out did matter, and it could in time overwhelm the other questions. It could dry up cities. It could create international crises. It was even imaginable that under certain conditions the P/PET could put enough draught on the Great San Luis Aquifer to make serious pumping, even the existing irrigation, unsustainable. According to some engineering studies, the aquifer held 65 billion acre feet, a bit over twice the capacity stored by Hoover Dam in Lake Mead, but a lot of it lay far too deep to use, and no one really did know how fast it could recharge. The groundwater equation was no doubt part, too, of what ailed Saguache Creek. On the other hand, a long snowy winter or a run of economic good luck could make a lot of problems forgettable.

Lunch ended and the final length of pipe was laid up to the spring. A trace of solemnity crept into the act of hooking it up. The others stood back as George and Donnie rummaged in the muck for the connection. It was their spring, and they went about it with the familiar care of ownership. Royce snapped his propane torch to life to vulcanize the joint, and the thing was done.

The next job, installing a storage tank on a branch of the new pipe to the new demonstration area, took up the rest of the afternoon. The tank itself was a 6,000-gallon monster 15 feet high and 9 feet across coated with old tar and patches of rust.

The tank was another accommodation to the needs of the demonstration area. According to the practice applied in North Tracy for years, the herd would disperse over the whole area, and after some shuffling about, small groups would gather about lesser springs and the water troughs that drew off the main pipe. Traditional reasoning favored this as a way to distribute grazing pressure lightly, but animals, being unconscientious about the environment, tend to hang around water holes and destroy what grows there, especially if competition for water is keen or the source as unreliable as it had been the year before, when the pipe kept breaking. The habit doesn't develop under wilder conditions because predators psyche out the system and set ambushes near water, and even domestic animals learn to drink fast and clear out. Throughout the tame American West, however, the pandemic destruction of stream bank habitat by lounging cattle has become the biggest rallying point for environmentalists in their attacks on the ranching industry.

In the demonstration area, as many as 300 head in concentration would have to drink from one place, and the small divisions of land that narrowed near the water would not give them much place to graze while waiting for the trough to fill. If they could trust that they could drink their fill whenever they felt like it, in theory at least, they would not stand around on their own dung but would drink and leave. This could only happen by saving the flow from the Whittens' spring around the clock. A glorified toilet float valve on a trough made out of a surplus missile container would mete out water for the cows while protecting it from the P/PET.

The day had grown old by the time the big tank came to rest in a little glade that peeked out of the foothills. The ravens had begun their homeward commute, and the sky took on a Wedgewood blue that set off the white of a waxing half-moon that had risen unnoticed in the light of noon.

George headed south on the dirt road along the eastern boundary fence of Tracy. Small rabbits, enlivened by the dusk, exploded out of the weeds to left and right, and now and then a meadowlark flashed off a post and swooped alongside the truck before veering away. The exuberance of such vulnerable creatures impressed him more than it used to, perhaps because he had begun to take himself much more seriously. His recent appointment to the Water Conservancy District Board by the county commissioners had surprised him because he had not realized that others took him seriously. It had amazed him to think that an old guard, which he knew considered his holism and his ecology rhetoric heretical, had chosen him simply for his ardor, as if somehow even they knew that the future would demand passion they lacked.

A more important self-revelation had followed. As a new member of the board that oversaw the valley's vital water, he visited all the canals, drains, well fields, and diversions in the valley. His tour included the new Bureau of Land Reclamation project that pumped valley groundwater into the Rio Grande in order to satisfy an interstate compact and a Mexican treaty based on overly optimistic flow data.

"The Closed Basin Project, as they call it, is a controversial deal,"

George would say, "like anything here involving water, but my ears sure burned when I visited their gauge house by the road to Alamosa. The highway side was so shot to pieces they'd had to install military strength armor plate. I wondered if they knew I once did my target practice like that. Now, here I was with a voice in what happened to all this water, really for the health of the whole place. It made me think."

More delicate birds rising. Horned larks this time. Nighthawks ripping around against the slate of heaven on jackknife wings.

Donnie detoured into Saguache on his way home for a cup of coffee at a cinderblock pit stop called Shay's Eat 'n Run. Shay had tried his hand at living off the land up Saguache Creek a ways and rediscovered the impossibility of doing it without superhuman energy and abundant capital, so now he hung onto the rural life by selling chili, coffee, and shakes and renting videos. The heads of pronghorn, mule deer, and elk that looked down from the walls made the Eat 'n Run a homey place to the hunters who stopped there in fall and the stock haulers, Forest Service crews, and locals that kept it, and Shay, going the rest of the year.

Donnie had just flung himself down in a booth and stretched out his legs when in walked Tim Lovato and a buddy showing all the same signs of a long day's work. They strode in at the swinging pace of outdoor men who don't adjust to confined spaces until after they've about run into something. When they spotted Donnie, they came up short. Then they greeted each other without any sign that anything divided them. Politics mostly stay hidden, like groundwater.

7

Education

Donnie and Karen Whitten thought a great deal about education. They thought about it partly because they felt chiefly responsible for the education of their children, Nathan, Clint, and Sarah. They held all three to high standards on their homework, forbade daytime television, and served on committees at the public schools in Moffat and Saguache. In addition, Karen ran a chapter of 4-H in which she did her best to ensure that all kids in the community made the connection between book learning and the life of the land.

Their seriousness, however, came in part from the fact that in the things that had become most important to them they had both had to educate themselves pretty much and figure out on their own what "needed learned," as San Luis Valley grammar put it. Along with the shock of taking real responsibility for land and family, their encounter with Savory had made them take stock of their own powers of mind. He had given them a backdoor glimpse of science not as a forbidden temple from which priests in white coats dispensed truth to the unanointed but as a muddy arena where fallible mortals wrestled to make sense of the world. If that were so, then they could jump in and wrestle, too.

This insight gave Donnie in particular some reason to think better of his own formal education, which had been largely a specialized course in hell raising and physical confrontation. He and his older brother George had entered high school in the half-Spanish town of Center on the southern edge of Saguache County in the early 1970s, about the same time Cesar Chavez of the United Farm Workers' Union arrived from California to organize the valley's lettuce cutters and potato packers. High-minded talk about civil rights, equal opportunity, and economic development ran headlong into equally sanctimonious rhetoric about communism and law and order. At Center High School, this boiled down to license for one gang of juvenile delinquents to catch a member of the other alone in the boy's room and beat the shit out of him. The situation eventually got so bad that Donnie was packed off to a military school in New Mexico, where the harsh discipline merely deflected his genius for mayhem into riding bulls for the school rodeo team.

Later he would conclude that the confusion and instability of Center High and the wiles of good rodeo bucking stock were not completely irrelevant background for the challenges of his chosen career. Nature, like life, respected no division between a classroom and the world outside, and a good bull could educate even the toughest rider against the lunacy of trying to dominate wildness by sheer force. No man's physical strength meant anything to a bull, as even champions held on for only 8 seconds. A desert rancher did well to remember such lessons.

Donnie had brought back to the valley not only his ranching ambition and a rodeo buckle or two but also a slightly brash conviction that he would have to learn whatever he needed to on his own and a healthy suspicion that nothing ever happened quite the way people said it should—attitudes he shared with Karen. Perhaps she saw some of the same challenge in Donnie, whom she had met in 4-H and married fresh out of high school despite the considerable skepticism of her parents.

In any case, the unorthodoxy of Savory and his theories had intrigued both of them at once. The example of someone who had dared approach a complex riddle, the riddle of brittle environments, from the bush end added to their own working lives the challenge of real science. It licensed them to engage land without embarrassment as a living, intelligent (although often ornery and unpredictable) being, not as an anesthetized object for dissection. They no longer had to discount restroom fights, financial crises, water rights abuses, and droughts as distracting problems. They could see them as part of the job itself, which science had to tackle even as it tackled "scientific" questions like plant physiology and soil chemistry.

They began to read books and subscribed to scientific magazines, organic and traditional agriculture journals. They supplemented the Center *Post Dispatch* with the *Christian Science Monitor.* They learned about computer spreadsheets, futures markets, and world trade issues. But from what crossed their kitchen table, it was not hard for them to infer that, at least in the case of deserts, conventional academic approaches were floundering seriously in the face of maddeningly messy situations. Africa was a good example, and both Donnie and Karen paid some attention to it because Savory came from there and frequently drew parallels to it, and also because from where they stood it seemed only a bit farther out on the margin, and they could relate to that.

During the time the Tracy Common Grazing Association was haggling over the demonstration area, news out of the Dark Continent got so dark that starving Somalis began showing up in even the Center *Post Dispatch.* The media usually spotlighted only one crisis at a time, but footnotes about simultaneous disasters embroidered a seamless tapestry of crisis. The stories were often interchangeable except for the proper nouns.

> Abidjan, Ivory Coast (AP)—Armed Sahara nomads mounted on camels attacked the ancient city of Timbuktu in Mali earlier this month, looting shops of silver and gold, Mali state radio said yesterday. At least 12 people died.
>
> The radio said the attack Dec. 5 was an attempt to sabotage talks between the Tuareg desert warriors and the governments of Mali and Niger. There have been frequent clashes between the black-led governments and the lighter-skinned warriors who once enslaved them.
>
> There long has been hatred between desert nomads and the black Africans. Both Mali and Niger have accused Libya of inciting the Tuaregs to attack.
>
> Tensions between nomads and farmers have increased as the Sahara Desert increasingly encroaches on once-fertile land in the Sahel, which has suffered a succession of disastrous droughts.

Nothing quite so extreme had occurred in the San Luis Valley for at least a century, but anyone growing up there could read a lot between the lines.

The Tuaregs and the blacks were divided not only by race and religion. Those "tensions between nomads and farmers" no doubt got down to familiar questions of land and water overlaid with the politics of numbers, urbanization, financial power, and global economic forces.

"Why do the media almost never treat agriculture in any serious way?" Karen observed. "It's always just a matter of getting relief supplies to people or which armed faction is attacking which other armed faction. The condition of the land, the water situation, the things that are going on with the land, have got to make a difference. I don't believe it's all drought or global warming either."

Didn't the lead questions of Savory's holistic model apply just as they did in Saguache County? Could the varied peoples on the southern edge of the Sahara have articulated a quality of life that all could aspire to without annihilating someone else as a precondition? What could they raise from the land that would support this life? What kind of landscape would sustain it?

Press accounts reported the symptoms of imbalance in scattered bytes—a sweeping statement about the encroaching desert, a drought, the massive "thinning" of an elephant herd, the devastation of forests by slash-and-burn farming and firewood cutting, the population explosion, a flux of refugees. But of course these things were related.

"When I read those stories," said Donnie, "what really bothers me is that I can bet the people over there are getting the same advice we have heard here for years. There really aren't many new ideas. We aren't even sure we have the right questions, not to mention the answers. Savory's better, but even he is just a start."

The situation of the people who tried to make a living from livestock in Saguache County was not so different or much better understood than that facing the Kalmuks, Kirghiz, Fulani, Masai, Berbers, Bedouins, Turkana, Navajos, or any number of now-unemployed livestock people from the semi-deserts of the world, "idled by restructuring of the ecosystem," in the jargon of industrial economics—grassland counterparts to the rust belt refugees of Eastern Europe, Youngstown, Ohio, and the ghettos of Detroit.

Of course, the camel raiders of Timbuktu weren't really so awesome anymore. Nor were their kinsmen or the other nomads starved out of the desert who now swelled the slums of West African cities.

The capital of Mauritania, Nouakchott, alone had grown from a village of 5,000 into a refugee camp of 600,000 in the twenty years since the first big postcolonial drought struck in the early 1970s. The displaced Moors had not hesitated to butcher a few thousand black farmers along the Senegal River as they retreated from the desert.

Even since the return of some rain to the southern Sahara, thousands of Tuaregs remain stranded in destitution in and around cities and bore holes, their dry season pastures along the Niger gone to sand or plowed up by those farmers who themselves were pushed to extremes. Their warriors, bitter but high on racial disdain, still make news, but women carry on the real struggle. They do the begging, scraping, and prostitution while their men either raise hell with weapons gleefully supplied by Libya or head for the coast hoping for a wage.

Nor was Donnie wrong to sense the frustration of the people trying to give advice. The U.S. Agency for International Development (USAID) had recently begun a program called SARSA for the Sahel region of Africa, that band of grassland where the Tuaregs and other nomadic tribes wandered between the Sahara and the region of stable rainfall to the south. The program had once had a comprehensible acronym, but various refinements of policy had expanded the full title to "Systems Approach to Regional Income and Sustainable Resource Assistance," SARSA.

The director of SARSA, Larry Abel, described a personal education that could indeed have landed him in the agricultural extension office in Center had fate blinked along the way. He came out of upstate New York—cold winters but beautiful nonbrittle farm country. When he graduated from Cornell in the mid-1960s with a degree in animal science, he went right into the Peace Corps. The Vietnam War gave him the choice either to help people or to kill them.

The Peace Corps put him in charge of 3,000 dairy cows that the government of Kenya had bought from Europeans who had fled black power. The animals, of all ages and states of health, were consuming enormous amounts of feed and producing practically nothing, and Abel quickly figured out that any cow not pregnant or producing at least a gallon of milk a day would not pay. His specialty was artificial insemination, which had recently revolutionized livestock breeding in developed countries. In five months he made A1 technicians out of his workers and had half the herd in calf. In another three months half of the rest were pregnant. Next they gave him 7,000 nationalized Corydale sheep and a 160,000-acre government ranch.

In that Cold War era, the superpowers courted Third World governments by backing dramatic government projects that advertised technological prowess. By 1978, when Abel came back to Kenya as a USAID officer with the Kenyan National Ranch and Range Development Project, the Carter administration reigned in Washington and foreign aid philosophy had shifted from support of large government enterprises, which too often suffered from corruption, mismanagement, and technological overreach, to a new slogan, "The Poorest of the Poor." The end of colonialism had left Africa with what had long existed in Latin America: powerful elites who used the government apparatus to put as much distance as possible between themselves and the wretched of the outback. How could a modern economy or state develop unless people on the bottom could at least start the long march toward the middle class?

The Kenya project had a little bit of everything. It supported a "group ranching project" among the Masai, some cooperative ranch companies where private individuals had ownership in both the stock and land, and a project for nomads in the northeast, which had always been communal land. One of the ranches prospered under a zealous manager. The others suffered from predictable management and political lapses. The Masai groups never developed self-government, and a classic Tragedy of the Commons developed at once. Without traditional community restraints, individuals increased their private stock until the land collapsed. A booming market in wheat and barley lured people with capital, including some of the Masai leadership, to plow out some of the best pasture, even though it had no future as crop land. Finally, when the stressed herds began dying from a malignant catarrh, allegedly carried by wildlife but exacerbated by malnutrition, the government decided that tourism took precedence over the Masai and sided with the wildebeest.

"We had high hopes for the northeast, though," said Abel. "We had read the anthropology and accepted the idea that their migrations were probably more efficient than they'd gotten credit for in the past.

So we set up management blocks of one million acres each for various groups, with the idea that they would stay within those. There was an administrative rationale for this, and it seemed plausible to think they could operate within an area that large [about 40 miles square]. We figured each group would feel some responsibility for that. We put in wells and pumps and built check dams to assure water, but these did not work very well.

"We were wrong in several ways. The three classes of livestock that the people found essential—cattle, goats, and camels—frequently could not satisfy all their needs in one block, big as they were. Camels simply did not thrive in the lusher south. The Somalis in the north were migrating into Ethiopia's Ogaden, and they typically covered 15 million acres.

"We had also figured that since the people in each group were closely associated, they would keep others out, but this, too, was not the case. The nomadic code did not exclude other clans. Land was free, like air. The old mechanism based on the scarcity of water broke down, too. I remember flying over the area when people were burning off the old grass hoping to revitalize the range [satellite observations document seasonal smog banks derived from this practice that rival the soft coal pollution covering Eastern Europe], and it suddenly occurred to me that the plumes of smoke were evenly distributed as if by a mathematical formula as far as I could see. The wells were all fifteen–twenty miles apart. There was no longer any rational migration. People were competing by exploiting as much forage as they could in one place before someone else got to it. When drought did occur, everybody came crowding into one area."

This has been the story all over Africa to the point that no one wants to back a livestock project anymore. They destroy careers. Widespread failure of farming projects based on fertilizer eventually forced agronomists to promote mixed farms that included animals as a way to use crop residues and produce manure, but no one really wanted to talk about nomads.

During the 1980s, as food production in Africa dropped steadily, the USAID Africa Bureau actually cut its agriculture staff from forty-six to twenty-five because they simply couldn't show that they could help much. They went for several years without any livestock specialist at all after Abel moved over to SARSA. An anthropologist who has studied both the giving and receiving moieties of development aid culture observed, "When the development experts realized they had no technical package to offer pastoral people, they proceeded almost as if they had ceased to exist. Projects pretty much boiled down to veterinary services. Doctors deliver. Everybody likes that, but it doesn't get to the root of any problem."

But U.S. politics changed during the 1980s, too. When Ronald Reagan came to the White House, development agencies respectfully reached for the invisible hand of Adam Smith. "Unleash market forces [including multinational corporations]" replaced "Poorest of the Poor" as the operative maxim. In many ways, this made good sense. Post-colonial socialism, supported by the careless largesse of competing superpowers, had grotesquely distorted many national economies, and there was a lot of international capital sloshing around in search of cheap labor and commodities.

The same kind of cerebral energy that once went into reorganizing farms and ranches on a scientific basis now went into trying to bring Ayn Rand and Milton Friedman to the bush, often with parallel results. For example, without any aid at all, hugely elaborate free market networks developed all over Africa to supply firewood to the bursting cities. However, these also efficiently wrecked countless reforestation projects while stripping every combustible twig out of miles of country. The ideologues rationalized the disaster by pointing out that the urbanization that drove the fuel market resulted from impure policies in the past, but they still found themselves pawing through the dogma for ways to save the trees. That meant more bullying, tinkering, incentives, and dislocations not unlike those of the past. Nor did they fit into a neat "technical package."

"USAID undertook a marketing project in Mali," said Abel. "The idea was that, if the stock raisers up on the Niger could get a fair price for their animals, they would figure out the most efficient way to produce them. They would have a strong incentive not to overload the range with unproductive stock, and it would become worthwhile to keep marginal land in pasture rather than plow it. The market would thus address both the ecological and the economic problem. The idea may work, and it may help, but it is not simple.

"There isn't a lot of surplus anyway. There is theoretical access to a cash market for meat in Ivory Coast, which is relatively prosperous, and the Saudis will buy live animals if you can get them to a port, but getting livestock to those markets in good health across two international borders with all the bribes and breakdowns is awfully hard. Subsidized surplus meat from the European Community costs less in all the urban markets."

So now the slogan "systems approach" has appeared. It recognizes that there may be no answer but assumes there is a system. SARSA engages experts of many different kinds, including a brace of scholars from the Institute of Developmental Anthropology, their job being to dope out the system so at least development programs won't screw it up more.

"SARSA is an impossible name, but we know what we're trying to do," said Michael Horowitz, director of the institute and a friend of the Tuaregs who has spent time in their desert. "We'd like to find a way for the people themselves to take part in both deciding what they want and getting it."

Well, of course. But that is in fact always the missing, the unsystematic, element in every noble failure, from Saguache County to the black wool tents of the Tuaregs by the vanishing waters of Lake Faquibine outside Timbuktu. Now, ironically, although Abel worked in an office as airless as the rumen of a camel, the horizon of his responsibility had been flung back to a terrifying distance. The SARSA system embraced everything—the Tuaregs, the blacks, the bureaucrats, the bankers, the women, the men, the warrior, the peacemaker, the rich, the poor, the weak, the strong, the climate, the camel, the goat, the specialist, the scholar, the eland, the elephant, the grass, the brush, the exotic neem tree, the local acacia, the soil, and the sand.

It was hard to know where to begin, and not long after the Tuaregs raided Timbuktu, Donnie had his own taste of just how hard. He had to go to Center for a meeting of the Saguache County Soil Conservation Board. The bulk of their business was signing off on land management plans so that private farmers could participate in federal programs such as crop insurance and price supports, but there was something else.

Every year the soil conservation districts in the valley sponsored a teacher workshop at the state college in Alamosa. Elementary schoolteachers from around the state would come to burnish their certificates at the feet of biology professors and extension agents. They would talk about teaching conservation and learn how to demonstrate soil erosion by pouring cups of water on kitty litter boxes full of sand.

Like the other board members, Donnie voted for the Saguache district to contribute the usual amount, but as he drove north toward home a thought grew in his mind. It was one of those late May afternoons, pregnant with promise, when smallish rabbits come out at dusk to listen to grass grow and people see that the equinox has kept its promise. Sunlight would linger beyond the day's work, tomorrow morning's chores would not require a flashlight, and larks would sing from every fence post. The school bus, too, would come back before dark, and the kids would break for the open country in anticipation of the real freedom of summer.

By the time he passed out of the zone of wakening barley and potato fields around Center, the idea had taken shape. By the time he passed the bison ranch out on the chico flats south of his own land, he could see the outline of the presentation he himself would volunteer to make at the college. Talking to ranchers about holistic management never gave him much pleasure because many didn't really want advice from one of their own, but teachers, they could use some practical information.

Karen agreed. "A bunch of teachers won't give you any trouble," she said. As a 4-H leader she knew something about kids who swarmed around full of eagerness, squealing, "Mrs. Whitten, what are we doing today?"

"They're probably desperate for ideas, and you'll sure be different."

Clint, Nathan, and Sarah exchanged glances as they forked up the meat that last year was a steer with a broken leg. They were proud of their father, but both he and they knew that his enthusiasm for animal impact, succession, and holism could get a little long-winded. They enjoyed seeing him a little self-conscious about it now and squirmed deliciously at the thought of seeing him in front of a class that they were not part of.

"I'll think of something," he said. "It's an opportunity to help people see what ecology is really all about." That was a good line, but the real point that teachers of all people needed to get was that the standard way of going at things was almost always backward. He would not talk about halting erosion or the need to save soil or even about soil fertility and its importance. He would talk about looking at the landscape and trying to see in it what it could become and *had* to become to support the life people wanted. He would not talk about fixing problems at all but how to decide what *was* a problem and then how it might be induced to fix itself.

However, when the day came and Donnie found himself, former high school hellion, standing exposed on the cold vinyl tile of an Adams State College classroom in front of thirty teachers, mostly older than himself, the difficulty of his mission nearly left him speechless. In the end, he fell back on Savory's model and talked briefly about the need to have goals for the land before even looking at its condition. Even kids could relate to that. Did they want from it crops or wildlife or livestock or houses or a little bit of everything? Even kids could design landscapes, couldn't they? They could start talking about what kind of landscape would satisfy the needs of different people, not just those in the valley, but elsewhere.

Then they could go out to any roadside and check the health of water and mineral cycles, count the diversity of plants, and speculate about the energy going into the food chain. With those ideas, kids could make up tests and experiments. They could pour cans of water on the ground in different places and see how fast it ran off or sank in and how long it took to dry. They could count the seedlings of new plants, ask old-timers what used to grow there, and try to find where these plants grew now.

Donnie talked, too, about tools for changing things and how to choose them. He talked about numbers and time. A teacher could use doughnuts to demonstrate the subtle relationship between grazing animals and grass. Bring a dozen to class every morning and they all get eaten. Is that overgrazing? If you think so, "reduce the herd." Bring a dozen doughnuts but let only six kids choose a doughnut each and replace only those they eat. In a few days you'll have six stale doughnuts that no one will touch and six still get "overgrazed." So, too, with grass. If overrested it goes stale and dies. You can see it by the highway. How about having students grow grass in no. 10 cans under uniform conditions and compete to harvest as much as they can by dry weight? They can clip every day, cut it short, or let it grow long. They will discover the importance of time.

Out by U.S. 160 east of Alamosa, teachers found lots they had to stretch to explain. Why did nearly every chico bush have a shock of grass growing out of it? What accounted for the peculiar fertility of abandoned anthills? What ate yucca? Why did weeds grow where they did? Could one not see in such marvels opportunities instead of problems?

Donnie's two sessions were oversubscribed, and except for one man who ranched on the side and bogged down in cow talk, the teachers lapped it up. When he came home, Karen asked Donnie how it went.

"I enjoyed myself," he said. "It was different."

8

The Rio Summit

The questions that bothered Donnie and Karen Whitten—How do you make a living off fragile land without degrading it? How do you know when you're failing in time to do something about it? What do you do? How do you pay for it?—were neither simple nor merely local concerns, as the record of development assistance in Africa clearly showed. More than that. In only slightly different words the same questions applied to the oceans, the atmosphere, the forests, and the fresh water supplies of the world.

If Donnie illustrated this to elementary schoolteachers through experiments with doughnuts and no. 10 cans, his neighbor Maurice Strong, owner of the 100,000-acre Baca grant, both thought and acted globally. Strong's ventures in trying to sell the water out from under the valley might brand him as a quintessential capitalist yahoo among local environmentalists, but his pronouncements on the matter gave the impression of someone who saw "development" as an irresistible historical current. Launching one's own canoe into it was therefore an amoral act. Uncharacteristically for someone riding comfortably among the lead boats, however, he foresaw the great river of prosperity pouring out into a desert of environmental disaster and drying up. To resolve this terrible contradiction between trend and fate, he had set in motion and organized the U.N. Conference on Environment and Development (UNCED), scheduled to convene in Rio de Janeiro later in the summer.

Strong's background gave him a unique perspective. He was probably one of the last tycoons of the second millennium to have bootstrapped himself out of poverty, at age fifteen, trading furs. According to legend, while working as a clerk at a Hudson's Bay Company outpost, he had befriended Eskimos who helped him prospect for minerals. At twenty-five he was a millionaire. Thereupon followed an investment career, mostly in energy resources and real estate, that earned him a reputation as master of the art of sensing a bubble and getting his money out at the top of the market. That was a by-product, perhaps, of his global vision. He had also run Canada's foreign aid program and in 1972 organized the U.N. Conference on the Human Environment, the most important recognition of environmental issues by an international body up to that time.

"UNCED isn't about any one of these things, but about all of them," Strong told a *New Yorker* reporter who questioned the encyclopedia of crises his conference meant to address. "They're all linked."

The plenitude of heads of state who gathered in Rio that summer ultimately signed off on a thick document titled "Agenda 21," which vaguely committed them to take action in a host of areas. Alongside energy, biodiversity, rain forests, oceans, poverty, and some others, desertification took up an entire chapter and subsequently became the subject of four more conferences that spread over the next two years as experts and diplomats haggled over a treaty committing the nations of the world to a more detailed plan of action.

The precedents were not auspicious. In Nairobi in 1977, following the extended drought in the Sahel, the first U.N. convention on desertification had hammered out a Plan of Action to Combat Desertification. This had spawned an alphabet soup of organizations to study and monitor the problem and some enormously lucrative contracts for satellite photography and technical surveys but only disjointed response at the national level. After spending several billion dollars, the U.N. Environmental Program issued a report on the program a few months before Strong's environmental summit opened in Rio. The concluding paragraph read:

> Major efforts in implementing the Plan of Action to Combat Desertification were directed to supporting measures rather than to concrete corrective field operations. As the present assessment shows, the area of lands affected by desertification is not decreasing, although some trees were planted throughout

> the world and some areas of shifting sands were stabilized. Neither a major improvement of degraded irrigated crop lands nor control of soil erosion in rain-fed cropland nor substantial improvement of range lands were achieved. The entire rural environment in the drylands of the world continues to deteriorate, adversely affecting the socioeconomic conditions of their inhabitants.

The Rio convention thus faced anew much the same old riddle as members of the Tracy Common Grazing Association had in organizing their holistic demonstration area or Donnie had in working out a lesson plan for his teachers. Of course, the committee that gathered that spring at U.N. headquarters in New York to draft chapter 12 of Agenda 21 for signature at Rio had the advantage of including world-class scientists, economists, environmentalists, and politicians.

Up front their text implied that drought and desertification could be effectively eliminated by throwing money at it. Pay the money. Fix the problem. At that moment, local and international sources were putting about $850 million a year into 184 small anti-desertification projects in Africa. In fact, it would take $12.25 billion a year over twenty years or so to do the trick, but what was that on a continent where drought had killed at least 3 million people outright in the 1980s alone?

On close reading, however, the document offered few actual solutions. "It is by no means clear what needs to be done to halt this slow degradation of the world's land," admitted a U.N. Environmental Program analysis later. Chapter 12 was in fact a shopping list of unanswered questions requiring expensive research and objectives that no one had yet found a way to reach. Its six sections were a pretty good summary of the rough state of the art:

> A. Strengthening the knowledge base and developing information and monitoring systems of regions prone to desertification and drought as well as the economic and social aspects of these systems—$350 million.

The opening paragraph of this section admits to "insufficient basic knowledge of human-induced desertification processes and their interaction between climate fluctuations and recurrent droughts in world drylands."

After years of satellite surveys, botanical studies, and anthropology that had generated mountains of data, scientists did not yet have a firm grip on the processes that linked everything together. Their work remained more descriptive than analytic, and they needed more data yet. Part of the knowledge gap reflected the fact that in recent years the very definition of desertification as an objective physical process had become blurred. Maybe it was only 10 percent drought and destructive practices and 90 percent social screw-up. In its extreme form, this line of reasoning argued that what really mattered was how much people actually suffered, which in practice had less to do with the state of the ecosystem and swings of climate than how many people got caught in down cycles without a way to cope.

Since drought in the San Luis Valley did not kill people, desertification could not be as bad there as in Mali. And if people did not die in Saguache County because they had welfare, a continental job market, paved roads for long commutes, insurance, credit, and children pulling salaries in Denver, these things might serve as weapons in the fight against desertification. Even in Africa, evidence showed that a country with a stable government, functioning services, and a moderately diverse economy could get through even a quite severe drought without terrible consequences.

The so-called desertifying regions had gone through wet and dry cycles since way back in geological time, but crisis only ensued when too many people came to depend on a wet cycle. They plowed so much ground, grazed so many sheep, and cut so many trees that the next dry cycle cruelly but inevitably wiped them out just as surely as next year's typhoon would drown the land-hungry Bengalis who resettled the delta of the Ganges after last year's storm destroyed the previous lot.

If so, wasn't the best course to adapt human activity? How much emphasis should go to greater understanding of sand dunes, plant communities, and weather as opposed to studying population dynamics and the social economy? Would land degrade more or less if you tried to beat the cycle by subsidizing people in the lean years or created an economy big enough to absorb periodic migrations gracefully?

Did adaptation imply figuring out the "carrying capacity" of the bottom of the cycle and somehow forcing whole communities to stay within that so no one got hurt by overexpanding in the wet years? Or were there modern options that could handle a wildly varying carrying capacity?

Was the terrible depletion of trees and desert bushes that once contributed so much to the ecological stability of savannah and steppe a function of the urban firewood market, overpopulation in the countryside, the price of alternate fuels like butane, the inefficiency of traditional stoves, or was it an indirect result of some other damage?

Many of the new questions came out of the much larger speculation about whether the global climate was changing. If it was changing, was the human impact significant in relation to the natural progression of ice ages and sun? Should we try to counter the change or adapt? The sociopolitical dimension confused the range experts, meteorologists, and soil scientists, who had long defined problems in physical terms only. Often the new social point of view struck at the roots of their work.

A spate of papers, including some in the U.N.'s own *Bulletin of Desertification* and the *Journal of Range Management,* had suggested that old nomadic systems actually outperformed the American ranching model because they had more flexibility. The practice of moving large bands of animals long distances allowed them to avoid localized drought and take advantage of diverse opportunities such as grazing crop stubble after farmers had harvested their millet and sorghum, which the farmers welcomed because of the manure they left behind. There might even be advantages to the habit of favoring large herds of skeletal animals over smaller herds of fat ones, a prejudice that experts previously wrote off as "a dysfunctional cultural equation of big herds and prestige." It allowed them to expand quickly when good times came. This line of scholarship concluded that nomads could shrink, expand, respond to dire circumstances, and survive far better by ignoring the expert advice. Unfortunately, since the beginning of colonial time, settling or destroying nomadic cultures in the name of progress had been a bedrock of policy, and there was no expert opinion on how to resurrect them.

Altogether, given the vacuum of proven knowledge about a situation that Chapter 12's introduction said affected a sixth of the world's population and over a quarter of its total land area, a $350 million research budget was small potatoes. It about equaled the annual budget of the Denver public schools. By the end of 1992, the world community was spending considerably more than that on relief supplies for Somalia alone, not to mention untold millions to defend them.

> B. Combatting land degradation through, inter alia, intensifying soil conservation, aforestation, and reforestation activities—$6 billion.

This was the big-ticket item in support of the perhaps simplistic theory that direct action would help most. To put it in perspective, however, the cost was only $1 billion less than Exxon spent in 1992 just looking for new oil. Certainly a lot of useful knowledge could be put to work for that price, but the gaps in basic knowledge left a ragged picture. The paper talked of "an increasing vegetation cover that would promote and stabilize the hydrological balance." This was the same "water in–water out" P/PET issue at work on Tracy, and no one could guarantee to solve it even there for double $6 billion.

The money would also encourage governments to introduce "appropriate, environmentally sound and economically feasible agricultural and pastoral technologies" as if they were waiting on the shelf and grateful peasants and nomads stood ready to act as soon as the local Royce Wheeler told them what to do.

Reforestation of areas that woodcutters had devastated and planting new greenbelts of trees were the only specific recommendations in the draft that went to Rio. It ignored numerous working papers on the overwhelming problem of rangeland because the papers offered so little promise in return for the expense and political dangers. Little could be done to actually improve the productivity of range land, they concluded, with the possible exception of vast plantings of exotic varieties of the genus *Atriplex,* cousins to the very same salt bush that for all its benefits had increased on Tracy as the grass declined. Barring that, they could only reduce erosion and stabilize vegetation by enforced reduction of livestock to carrying capacity and raising more fodder on cultivated land and tree farms. Some land would require complete prohibition of use, but wildlife might be introduced as a management option. Almost certainly the "soil conservation" referred to in passing included the same catchments and check dams installed on Tracy thirty years before.

Chapter 12 admitted that degraded rangeland, defined as land best suited only for grazing livestock, accounted for 12.7 million square miles, roughly 22 percent of all global land. By comparison, the U.N. Environmental Program estimated that only 13 percent of land considered "sub-humid to arid [leaving out hyper-arid]" was farmed at all, and much of that more out of desperation than good sense. Only 3 percent was irrigated. Yet the range question was dismissed with a recommendation for promoting "participatory management of natural resources, including rangelands, to meet both the needs of the rural populations and conservation purposes, based on innovative or adapted indigenous technologies."

Of course, no innovative or adapted indigenous technologies were on the professional shelf yet. Despite the recent credit accorded nomadic traditions, understanding of how they worked was still very rudimentary, and experience in adapting them to modern borders, markets, settlement changes, and politics virtually nil. The tone of the preliminary papers from which this section derived left little doubt but that most of any $6 billion would go toward the old standard remedies on the small portion of possibly arable land.

Even farming technologies, however, were really only a footnote in this section of the proposal. The centerpiece of the campaign against desertification would not be the grass, shrubs, and other plants that give arid land its character, but trees, including the development and promotion of fast-growing, drought-resistant exotics.

Trees are certainly important as windbreaks and habitat, as providers of fuel, food, and fodder, as enrichers of the soil and havens of beauty and shade for smoking pipes and gossiping about foreign development workers. Plenty of research has shown the value of planting and protecting trees. And, true, land-hungry farmers, firewood cutters, and hard-pressed herdsmen have cut down everything higher than a man's head over vast areas of scrub and once parklike savannah. Here again, however, the history of major assaults on desertification through tree-planting projects is consistently awful, despite scattered success in encouraging farmers to maintain windbreaks and backyard shade trees. Almost all the enthusiastic literature cites two special cases in Niger, the 1,200-acre Guesselbodi National Forest Reserve just outside the capital, and an impressive 12-mile stretch of multiple windbreaks along the Majjia Valley 300 miles further east. Whether either can survive long without subsidy, and, at Guesselbodi, salaried guards, has not had a real test. Also, at Majjia, massive flash flooding from degraded rangeland above the project has deepened gullies and dropped the water table in the valley far enough to threaten the trees, requiring construction of enormously expensive (and high-maintenance) terraces, check dams, and other earthworks. Throughout the 1980s, dozens of ambitious and well-funded experiments in "aforestation" with plantations of high-yielding, intensively managed trees collapsed instantly when development aid subsidies ended. Of course, many of these projects should have worked according to all the best analysis, and who could say that $6 billion couldn't overwhelm the lack of social, economic, or ecological understanding that did them in? It could certainly buy a lot of cooperation from villagers and herders, for whom the temptation to poach firewood and graze off a piece of ground before their neighbors get to it is very strong.

> C. Developing and strengthening integrated programmes for eradication of poverty and promotion of alternative livelihood systems in areas prone to desertification—$3 billion.

Two lines of reasoning supported this. First was the theory that degradation of the land, if it existed at all outside natural cycles, would not produce crisis if people could make a living in a variety of ways. Droughts would come and go, but a prosperous community would feel less pressure to plow fragile land, graze the range down to bare soil, or strip the forests; and they would have something to live on whenever the rain didn't come.

On the positive side, perhaps if people could capture more profit from their labor on the land through complementary endeavors, they would actively try to improve it instead of just wearing it out and hitting the road for the city. Furthermore, the convention promised to affirm property rights for women and nomads on the tried and true capitalist logic that people took care of what they owned.

San Luis Valley people could recognize the whole program. In the century since the first white settlers began promoting land developments, they had probably established as many local chambers of commerce and planning commissions and launched as many investment promotions per acre as the United Nations ever would. In the end, they had always had to face the fact that their prosperity came out of the ground. Not only farms and ranches but also scenic tourism, free-spending hunting parties, and timber from surrounding mountains depended on healthy land first. Rural credit, marketing programs, and downstream industries were wonderful but ultimately meant nothing if underlying productivity dropped. New enterprises might keep some young people from going to the city, but there was plenty of evidence that prosperity could turn people to plunder as well as stewardship. Nor was it obvious that political forces favored a shift of enterprise to the country.

"The damn cities take everything," Danny Temple had cursed at the thought of valley water going to Denver or Los Angeles, but he could have been commenting on a couple of centuries of scholarship about farm policy.

City dwellers like cheap food, and city politicians know they must deliver it, whether as food stamps in Harlem or imported millet in Timbuktu. In Africa, especially, the shrug of an urban mob can topple a government, so it had better be kept happy. Subsidizing cities, however, makes for unhappy country people, who can't get a price for their goods and can't eat the cash crops they are forced to grow to pay for food imports. The smartest of them bail out and join that urban mob. It would be hard to say whether the syndrome in Senegal or Burkina Faso is more or less irrational than the network of subsidies and supports common in industrialized countries, but again, no off-the-shelf solutions come to mind.

Attracting industry that was not land based to rural areas sounded like a good way to reverse urban migration, but no government could afford a serious attempt when city slums were *already* full of unemployed migrants ready to explode tomorrow. Certainly rural Colorado had never generated much employment in this way. Almost the only exception was prison construction. Urban crime rates, which generally parallel mass migration from the land, had recently turned jail building into something of a rural development policy in its own right. Prisons represented about the only pump-priming investment the law-and-order legislature would discuss, and rural counties lobbied for them shamelessly. But the San Luis Valley had lost in that competition, too. It was hard to imagine that people in the deserts of underdeveloped countries could escape this treadmill any more easily.

> D. Developing comprehensive anti-desertification programmes and integrating them into national development plans and national environmental planning.

This made a lot of sense, and it would only cost $180 million a year to enlarge ministries, establish new ones along with liaison mechanisms, and train officials.

> E. Developing comprehensive drought preparedness and drought relief schemes, including self-help arrangements, for drought-prone areas and designing programmes to cope with environmental refugees.

This was the big Band-aid section, the institutionalization of crisis management so that when disaster struck next so many people wouldn't die on camera or pour over borders and destabilize the neighbors. No one could contest the need for this, even though it would do nothing for the condition of the land itself. It might even make things worse. If people knew that a vast international machine was going to spring into action to mitigate for dry years, would they have much reason to worry about the resilience of the land? Even if governments had contingency plans, would they believe and act on early warning if they had that?

Nevertheless, international agencies have a lot of experience in disaster relief. Put money into that, and you can see it work. The draft asked for $200 million. In Rio, with owl-eyed Somali children staring at them on CNN every night, the negotiators tacked on an extra billion to the request.

The nasty little truth about all this was that, although the idea of a convention on desertification would continue to spawn working groups, panels of experts, meetings in Geneva, Nairobi, and Paris, and delicate negotiations over whether Bulgarians or Peruvians would chair committees, who could say that the United Nations could deliver anything?

The billions portioned out in Agenda 21 existed in the same reality as Bosnian peacekeeping. Chapter 12 itself was only one mushy promise sandwiched between "Deforestation" and "Mountain Development," among forty chapters of urgent needs. Even though the Central African delegations in Rio had managed to force this one onto the agenda of follow-up meetings ahead of many others, they couldn't hope for much. They knew that Somalia, Zaire, Liberia, and maybe others could slip into absolute chaos within the next year, that emergencies and peacekeeping would likely soak up any loose development aid money in the two years that would pass before any commission on desertification could work out its plan.

No one pointed out that, alongside all the other ironies of wealth and poverty, Maurice Strong theoretically could have financed the whole program out of his own pocket with the sale of San Luis Valley water alone, had his project gone through.

Even people whose work was reflected in the proposal were cynical. "The whole thing is meaningless," said Michael Glanz, director of the Society and Environment study group at the National Center for Atmospheric Research in Boulder, Colorado. "The world is too poor. IBM is losing $5 billion a year. The U.S. doesn't even pay its dues to the U.N. Forget the rhetoric. There won't be any new bucks going into the environment, not in Africa, and especially not to fix up problems that are just symptoms of forces we're not about to control." For all its improbability as a promise of action, however, Chapter 12 did describe what the world thought *ought* to be done. It also had one more section.

The last section, F, was interesting because it was the only one that arose directly out of political pressure from African governments as opposed to the expert advice of the various research and monitoring institutions that had thrived on the desertification issue since the first U.N. conference on the subject in 1977. It was tacked on at the last minute:

> F. Encourage and promote popular participation and environmental education, focusing on desertification control and managing the effects of drought—$2.5 billion.

The wording of this section recognized that the dismal record of past land improvement schemes resulted mostly from the lack of local support and participation despite a lot of holy rhetoric about the need for it. Now the better heads in the countries such as Mali and Niger that had actually suffered most wanted drought and desertification consciousness drummed into children in their primary and secondary school curricula. They wanted teacher workshops like the one Donnie conducted at the college in Alamosa. They wanted experts trained at the village level, public awareness, open dialogue among all the levels of all the hierarchies, small loan programs, participation of women and indigenous people, and support of local initiatives—all the hot buzzwords of institutional reformers from the United Nations right down to Center High School, which was still tied in knots by ethnic politics twenty years after Donnie left.

This was the democracy section, acknowledgment of the vision of people learning to think globally and being allowed to act locally, of communities coming together in trust to carry out a common plan. It was perhaps the most distant and romantic vision of all, but if achieved it probably would make the trees grow on the reforestation projects, reorganize the grazing to let the grass grow back, and provide support to people in crisis. Maybe $2.5 billion could buy all that, assuming the world decided to spend any money at all on Chapter 12. Before the negotiators left Rio, however, they cut the number back to a round billion.

9

Antora

Former counterinsurgent leader Allan Savory talks fervently about planning in his courses on holistic thinking. "If one of my officers ever said he had no plan because ambushes, supply glitches, stupid orders, or any other unpredictable emergencies made planning impossible, I'd have his ass before he got himself and his men killed. It's exactly in the most chaotic and unpredictable situations that planning counts most. You must always have a plan, but the really hard part is that you must always assume it's wrong. Otherwise the plan will become dogma, and that does more harm than having no plan at all. Assume you're wrong and you will stay alert and watch for signs. Without a plan you will see nothing."

In their own operations, Donnie and Karen paid less attention to planning now than Savory might have approved, but even though they had made radical changes and undertook experiments like the Tracy demonstration, a broad current of tradition, experience, and history bore them safely around many obstacles that might have looked chaotic to others. They had a sense, for instance, for what cattle would do in a storm or when a quirk in the weather might produce a flush of poisonous plants.

This was not the case for their neighbors and clients John and Carol Wagner, who in the mid-1980s had bought the Woodard place and its brand, the Double Bar V, from one of the original Woodards. The property amounted to a beautiful string of meadows along Kerber Creek, which entered the valley from behind a substantial ridge at its north end. They had bought it sight unseen through a broker in Colorado Springs. Then, when they found it was too small to support a paying cattle operation, they bought two more historic ranches, the Hensen and the Ashley, out on the valley floor near the Whittens. These had long since passed from the pioneering families that named them to a Louisiana businessman named Gould, who had a cash flow problem at the time John Wagner found him. The Wagners subsequently also acquired another ranch up Kerber Creek called the Slash LD, after its brand. Like many Western ranches, including the Whittens', these parcels came with renewable leases for rights to a certain number of animal unit months of summer grazing on the public land administered by either the Forest Service or the Bureau of Land Management.

The Wagners had overseen the initial stages of this growing empire as absentee landlords, writing an astonishing stream of checks to a succession of on-site managers. Then one day in the offices of J.H. Wagner in Philadelphia, John caught his principal partner, who happened to be Carol, outside the elevator and suggested that they move to Colorado permanently within the week. Carol Wagner's disciplined business sense and flair for timing had contributed much to the partnership's success in the buying, selling, and brokering of municipal bonds, but she knew, if that were possible, even less about ranching than John. However, conventional wisdom had never provided a total strategy for her life or even for the bond business and little at all for dealing with John. She knew him well enough to know that by the time he made a "suggestion" he had already gunned his mind so far down the road that, were she to make chase on a Harley, butterfly net at the ready, she wouldn't catch it. So, falling back on her own flair for fast corners, she went home, told their kids, Chuck and Lee, and started packing.

Given the steady stream of luminaries and mystics drawn to the valley by its stupendous scenery and the spiritual communities that grew up under the patronage of Maurice Strong's wife in the town of Crestone, the Wagners did not stand out as particularly remarkable, but they were. John was mainline Philadelphia. His ancestors had walked with William Penn himself in the seventeenth century. Carol's ancestors were Armenian and had walked with Saint Bartholomew in the first century, which was reason enough for her relatives to vow to spill John's barbarian blood for courting her, but he had prevailed. He was at the time a middle-aged divorcé and director of the bank. She was working her way through Drexel University as a teller. They were both short, lively, wry, and extremely quick.

John was also more than just another well-cut suit. Animals liked him. He had spent a good deal of his childhood surrounded by owls and ravens and a friendly bat that dangled upside down all day from the headboard of his bed. He had been deadly on street lights with a slingshot at 100 yards. Later, dinner guests from the self-important world of finance were occasionally surprised by a six-foot black snake that liked to show off by disappearing into the Wagners' upstairs toilet bowl and emerging from the one downstairs. Moreover, John had the grace and genius to make a lot of money and spend it generously. Carol had reason to hope that her people would eventually find it difficult to murder such a man, and when she named Chuck after her father, they forgot all about it.

The Whittens first met John and Carol in the summer of 1988, not long after they moved to Kerber Creek. The occasion was a public tour of a ranch near Colorado Springs owned by a famous baseball pitcher, and the two Wagners ate the barbecue and admired the fence and water tanks and handsome Hereford cross cattle according to custom, but they looked a little too L.L. Bean to pass unnoticed.

Afterward another tour guest named Betsy Brown had said with some sympathy, "I sure hope they make out all right." She and her husband, Reeves, whose families had both ranched in South Texas since before the Alamo, had not too long before yanked up stakes and moved to Colorado themselves. For all their savvy, they were still struggling with the shift from heat and screw flies to snow and brisket disease.

"They seem to have pretty unlimited resources," Reeves had replied.

And Donnie, reflecting on the high turnover of ranchland in the valley, had said, "In this business you can pretty quick find that unlimited means a whole lot more than you thought," figuring that the Saguache grapevine would carry the usual bulletins that attended so-called tax code ranchers, who cared more about writing off losses than raising meat.

But the Wagners were serious, and they had enough business sense to realize quickly that even if they had been born to the cattle business they would have needed local knowledge and support that they couldn't buy and couldn't spend a generation discovering. Small things like an honest relationship with a plumber or a tractor mechanic or knowing whom to trust in a cattle sale could make the difference between respect and public humiliation, not to mention profit and loss.

So it happened that when Donnie and George split the Whitten ranch, thus turning their energies outward, a nascent friendship between Donnie and Karen and John and Carol developed into a lively partnership. Nominally, the Wagners hired Donnie as their manager, but that did not fully describe the relationship. From the Wagners' point of view, Donnie was less employee than consultant or even instructor. A lot of his job was telling them what they had to do. For his part, he got the chance to try his ideas on a far grander scale than his own resources allowed and to learn something from the Wagners' world besides. John Wagner had goals for his enterprise that were not always comprehensible to Donnie and Karen or even to Carol, but the creative tension that caused was for the most part indeed creative.

In early spring, when John got a call from the Forest Service office in Saguache to come in and present a plan for his summer grazing allotments, he and Donnie met to work out the details. The Double Bar V's amalgamated grazing rights now spread over nearly 100 square miles of public land, mostly national forest, but augmented by a swath of piñon-juniper country administered by the Bureau of Land Management.

It was a new arrangement. Originally the Wagners had run their herd on the largest of the allotments acquired with their various ranches, where they had been minority rights holders on a common allotment. The place was far, however, and they had had reason to believe their stock had suffered considerably at the hands of the dominant outfit. Since as newcomers they lacked the local clout to assert themselves, John had undertaken a series of purchases and swaps and succeeded in consolidating all his grazing rights as sole lessor of a chain of contiguous allotments in the Kerber Creek drainage and along the ridge that separated it from the San Luis Valley proper. In theory, the area would more than support the 425 cow-calf pairs, plus bulls, that they intended to put out. Unfortunately, neither John nor anyone else had ever managed a herd that size on that configuration of land before, so local knowledge about how to do it lacked altogether.

Because the Wagner outfit was the only permittee, there would be no politics among stockmen; however, the relevant Forest Service authorities, Jim Krugman and Jim Jaminet, did not share Royce Wheeler's enthusiasm for holistic management. Even more than the Bureau of Land Management, the Forest Service had become a battleground in the national struggle for control of environmental policy. Ardent environmentalists had fixed on the livestock permittee as symbol of the rape of a sacred heritage, while an equally vocal agglomeration of economic interests saw the cattleman as archetype of the "wise user" of the national wealth.

The "Klondyke," as the Wagner's giant allotment was called, was no marginal piece of steppe like the Tracy. It was a beautiful alpine watershed with 13,000-foot Antora Peak at one end of it and the famous ghost town of Bonanza in the middle. It already had environmental problems thanks to old mine workings, but the forest had nearly recovered from an era of uncontrolled cutting for mine props and railroad ties. Jaminet and Krugman could not afford a grazing wreck there.

The meeting took place in a windowless room over Styrofoam coffee cups. District Chief Krugman, his second in command Jaminet, Head Ranger Darol Cox, and Range Conservationist Michelle Bisbee, all in pressed uniforms, faced John Wagner, eighteen-year-old Chuck Wagner, and Donnie across a long conference table. The Saguache District of the Rio Grande National Forest rendered in topographic contour lines and green ink covered the wall beyond one end of the table.

The plan involved something over 425 cows plus their calves and bulls. Donnie presented it standing before the chart like a military briefer. They would split the battalion-size force into two companies. One would start from the Wagners' private land in the valley proper and move in stages across Bureau of Land Management land, up Findlay Gulch, onto Forest Service land, through Ute Pass at nearly 10,000 feet, and down through Graveyard Gulch into the Kerber

Creek Valley and the Wagners' private land. The other would be trucked to Kerber Creek and graze the Forest Service land in Cottonwood Canyon and Cody Gulch just north of Kerber Creek. In early July, the two forces would join and move up Kerber Creek right onto the shoulder of Antora Peak, back along the top of the ridge separating the great San Luis Valley from Kerber Creek, dropping down again on the valley side to make use of two big fenced areas that the Forest Service had rested the year before. Donnie had numbers and dates for how many would be where and when. "Finally, we'll cross back and come down Little Kerber Creek to finish up back in the Wagners' meadows on September 9," Donnie concluded.

There was a long silence as the green uniforms shifted in their chairs. Jim Krugman pointed with his pencil to several places, including Cody and Cottonwood gulches. "You'll run out of water there," he said. Donnie allowed as how he might, but the Wagners' meadows were rich enough to carry the numbers, if that happened. It would only cost them a little of the hay crop.

"We don't want a lot of cows out on the road," said Jaminet, looking sharply at John Wagner.

"There won't be," said Donnie.

John Wagner watched this performance with an expression of admiration salted with amusement. He constitutionally hated meetings of any kind and inwardly thanked God that Donnie was up there talking on precisely the Forest Service frequency. The sterility and presumption of charts and dates galled him. Although his iron gray hair and easy manner fit the local image of the successful financier who had retired with his pile, that didn't do him justice.

He had not retired. He had merely walked away from the municipal bond business when, in his words, it ceased to be fun—too purged of human give and take, too mindlessly cutthroat, too unprincipled, and hence too regulated, too rigid, too sterile, too lacking in character and diversity—in a word, too desertified.

"When I started, you could do hundred million dollar deals with a phone call, and you never had to check up," he liked to say. "When I left, there were guys in the business who would kill you if you didn't have a lawyer covering your backside. The livestock business couldn't be worse."

Getting nearly 900 animals up to 12,000 feet and back wouldn't be.

The plan was ambitious to say the least, but it was a plan, and many operators would turn up without one. Furthermore, there was that minority to whom the Forest Service would forever be the "dad gummed guvermint" whom they would have to watch like hawks. They could trust Donnie. After that, they discussed only details like the condition of fences and the times and places for counting the stock.

"Okay," said Jim Krugman. "We'll be interested to see how it works." And that was that.

Outside, Donnie and John laughed some over the matter of finding cows, not to mention herding them through the thicker parts of the forest. The lower elevations of the Klondyke were what is known throughout the West as PJ country, for the open stands of piñon pine and juniper trees that populate the shifting boundary land between grass and forest. Although controversy has raged for decades over the nature of this boundary and the wisdom of pushing back the trees with bulldozers, fire, and chains (as was done on parts of Tracy), PJ country is definitely rangeland, as is the open grassland above the timberline. In between, however, from the tall plate-armored Ponderosa pines up into the dark-needled Douglas fir and beyond, to where the arctic wind finally whips the pricklier spruce and the alpine fir down to nothing but bonsais, lies a zone of trouble.

Willow thickets, beaver dams, and the jumble of great trunks that the little devils chew down but can't haul off choke the hollows, and on the thigh-numbing slopes, low branches and spiky dead falls make passage hell for man and horse, not to mention the modern cowpoke's motorcycle. Grass does grow in this zone in swales cleared by fire, men, or beavers, and the speckled sun that filters through the aspen breaks supports a fragile green, but it isn't the sort of place where large, herding ruminants evolved or particularly thrive. Also, as John pointed out, you can't see them very well in there. Critics of the Forest Service who worry about what they would do to this complicated habitat and who don't like stepping in cow pies when they go hiking there question the wisdom of allowing cattle into it at all.

But as usual, the question had several sides to it. In strict ecological terms it could be argued that if cattle moved through the woods fairly quickly and did not hang out all summer in the few good places, they would have little impact. It was not what Savory would call a brittle environment. The fact that the town of Bonanza, once a teeming camp of 40,000 environmentally incorrect miners, had vanished with hardly a trace outside the mine sites proper testified to its resilience.

As to the open country above timberline and the PJ country, that depended on one's reading of the Theory of Limiting Habitat. Elk also grazed above treeline, but the elk herd was limited by the land they could graze in winter, consisting mostly of south-facing slopes in the PJ area. According to the theory, far more grass grew in the high country than the number of elk supported by the less abundant winter range could eat. Therefore, cattle should be able to harvest the balance without upsetting the elk account in the least.

This raised other issues, including the high duty of the Forest Service and the BLM to protect winter elk range. Once again, no real base line existed. Early travelers recorded huge herds of elk, bison, and antelope all over the valley floor, and of course, if they once had used more winter range, many more elk could have grazed the high country in summer. On the other hand, some argued that even elk didn't graze the mountains much at all before human activity pushed them there.

However, the very question was now academic. The elk weren't of the native stock anyway. As happened widely in the West, miners, meat hunters, and perhaps a succession of harsh winters had completely exterminated that before 1890. Local old-timers called today's animals "Roosevelt elk," not because they belonged to the subspecies of *Cervus elaphus* named for Teddy but because his administration popularized the idea of shipping Rocky Mountain elk out of Yellowstone to restart the herds. It had been eighty years since their ancestors leapt out of box cars 60 miles away in the town of Creede, and the Saguache County elk were still perfecting their survival strategy.

Also, for what it was worth, there was the question of nutrition. Alpine grasses grew lavishly but, due to the leaching of the soil by snow, lacked the mineral content of steppe and desert plants. Mineral deficiencies could affect health and weight gain and seemingly made genetically unadapted animals more prone to fatal altitude illness. Ranchers tend to go heavy on mineral supplements everywhere, just in case, but up high supplements can really count, and supply houses promote special mixes that come in 50-pound bags and look a lot like highway salt. The Wagners would have to truck dozens up there.

From out on the level south of Saguache, Donnie could look back over his shoulder at the ragged bulk of Antora, enormous even in the distance. Winter would bide there until well into June. He shivered and wondered abstractly what pushing nearly a thousand animals up there would take. The calves could come off the mountain stringy parodies of marketable animals. Some of them *could* wind up 50 miles away in Gunnison, or be shot by elk hunters in November. They could die. A wreck would foul up not only the Wagners' and the Forest Service's plans but the Whittens' as well. Well, by then at least Antora would be green and flower-clad when everything below had gone dry and dusty. If everything worked out, he would camp out there with the boys and fish the beaver ponds and sloughs left by ancient glaciers.

The move up began on July 13. Up to then, the plan had worked without much complication. The Forest Service's doubts about the water in Cody and Cottonwood gulches had proven correct. The cows hadn't found enough in the springs and seeps there. They had come down onto the road and looked mournfully over the fences at Kerber Creek until John let them into his meadows. Now the whole herd was gathered in the pastures on the high end of the Wagners' land waiting for the big push to the foot of Antora.

The Wagners' modest ranch house enjoyed a common room that embraced the broad scope of their lives from the kitchen and the line of Wellington boots by the door to bits of expensive art on the walls. The aroma of Carol's breakfast still hung in the air when John-and-his-dogs began welcoming the crew. John-and-his-dogs were a single concept, the canine part of which consisted of Benny the enormous Akita, Star the black Siberian husky, a huge shag rug called Rachael, who ate cats in spite of exotic French ancestry, and a mournful basset named Rufus. From ankle to jugular they delivered easily 500 pounds of welcome that tended to weed out the fainthearted at the threshold. Today's valiants were not the sort who posed for cigarette ads, but they were as plucky as any modern ranch help.

Peggy Godfrey, the freelance cowhand and poet, and the only person who actually looked like a cowboy, wheeled into the yard in her big-tired four-wheel-drive pickup pulling a gooseneck trailer with her horse inside and two dogs named Dingo and Katy—foxy gray Australian heelers with black spots. Then Donnie rolled up in a smaller truck with his mother-in-law and Karen on the front seat. Sarah and Nathan rode in back with Donnie's Yamaha 500 dirt bike and Nathan's 150 and lunch. A couple of neighbor kids showed up bareback on a pair of pinto ponies. Two or three others, including Carol, would go on foot.

The telephone rang. This time it was the Forest Service. John and Donnie had planned to move the herd in two stages over two days, but now the ranger, Darol Cox, was telling them that they would have to cover the whole distance in one move, over 8 miles, a lot for calves. By the terms of the lease he had to count them through a gate on the Bonanza road near the national forest boundary, and he couldn't be there tomorrow.

They began. From the last pasture on the Slash LD, the cattle surged up onto the Bonanza Road, and the drovers took up position at the sides and rear. Donnie counted slightly fewer than 400 cows, all with their calves. It was slightly fewer than he expected, but all 36 bulls were present, so there would be no large group that had escaped. For a couple of miles, all went swimmingly. The morning, sparkling and damp enough to settle the dust, promised warmth and cobalt skies. Above the bawling din of mothers and calves rose the yips of the herders, the brumming of the motorbikes, and the frantic whinnies that broke out whenever the two ponies got separated.

Some distance to the left of the road and below it, Kerber Creek ran willow-banked through a succession of meadows whose fences kept the herd on the road. Thus, most of the herders ranged along the bottom of the embankment on the other side, where a succession of gulches and coves tempted the occasional cow and her calf. Sometimes a bull, having carefully positioned himself ahead of the opportunity, would veer right and push a selection of his favorites out of the line of march. Then the ponies would dash about to haze them back or Peggy would shout, "Katy, Dingo, get that bull!" and the little dogs would rip snarling into action and a ton of annoyed beefsteak would trot humbly back into line.

Suddenly, however, the troops on the right flank noticed a weakening of pressure, in fact, a thinning of the whole bellowing column. When they climbed the embankment they discovered that little rivulets of animals were slipping through a series of open gates to join in a mighty torrent already pouring into the yard of a three-story log cabin set into the edge of a grove of trees.

An old man in eared hunting cap lay as if dead on the hood of a truly dead Chevy in the yard as the thunder of hooves and whine of revved out motorcycle engines bore down upon him.

Dutch Kempner had wandered up Kerber Creek many years before looking for cowhand work and married the widow of that house, an Ashley, in fact, of the original Ashleys' of Saguache County, a cultured woman who had published books of local history. Now he lived there alone, half deaf and three quarters blind, and spent his days dreaming of the past on the warm hood of the Chevy.

He sat up when John Wagner skidded to a halt just short of the Chevy's bumper.

"Are you moving a herd through here, young fella?" said Dutch to the unfocused shape in front of him.

John apologized with his usual grace and moved on, but the bellowing and dust, the shouts of boys, the crashing of willow thickets, great bodies plunging about, yapping dogs, the reek of dung, had given Dutch back his youth. His face radiant, he began to explain that in all the times he'd been on Antora, he'd never worn enough clothes, "but by golly there was one time. . . ." Once started, he could go on like that by the hour, but his blurry audience didn't care. They were only cows.

They stayed around for quite a while because while Donnie, John, Nathan, and some others frantically tried to drive the herd back up to the road, those behind it realized the battle was lost and sought to force them on through Dutch's wood lot into the meadow beyond, so for a while the two forces drove the confused herd back and forth through the old man's yard and empty corrals. In the middle of it all a coyote was seen to trot, tongue lolling, looking for rodents thrown into panic by the cows.

The confusion lasted for a good twenty minutes before the human contingent finally got together on pushing the cattle on through the wood lot and finally to the cattle guard and gate where Darol Cox waited to make his tally. Counting cattle pouring through a gate is a demanding and not altogether exact art at best, but his count of 392 adult cows and bulls was lower yet than Donnie had counted at the outset. Some were still hiding in the willows.

Not far after the count, where the hills squeeze down on Kerber Creek, are three washed-out settling ponds left over from the mining days—great slimy gray basins of sterile spoil now gashed 30 feet deep by the creek. Evil ocher-colored puddles stood in the sumps behind the ruptured dikes. The people drove the animals out onto one of these little deserts, hoping they would agree to rest there. At first, while the herders unlimbered picnic supplies on the tailgate of Karen's pickup, the cows stayed put. The din of bawling calves and mothers died down as they sorted themselves into pairs. Many of them actually lay down.

"The problem with this bunch," said Donnie as he pitched into a rasher of one of his wife's mutton sausages, "is that they don't have any idea where they are going. If we had even one cow that knew this country, it would go a whole lot easier. Next year they will take one look at this road, and they will start imagining all the waterholes and pastures up there, and just head for them. They never forget that stuff."

Like other animals, cattle do in fact have terrific geographical sense. Cows and calves, if they can't find each other after a long drive, for example, will both find their way back over long distances to the place where the calf last sucked. The old drovers on the Chisolm Trail used to hold a steer or two back to lead next year's herd to Abilene.

These cows remembered where they'd been, too. A bit before everyone got a sandwich, a sort of twitch ran through cows, a rotation of ears, a realignment of attention. A few bulls and a cow or two began to wander almost randomly back in the direction of the morning's start. Heads turned, and now half a dozen, then a dozen animals began to shamble about, aimlessly at first but gradually acquiring direction from the others until at a critical point those on the move began to coalesce into a direction. A small rivulet of cows appeared out of the static bulk and launched out across the dead tailings. A few lying cows sprang to their feet, and the leaders drew from this a vote of confidence and picked up speed. The alarm went up, and ponies and motorcycles raced down the embankment to turn the tide just as it breached the crest of the dam and began to pour down the face of it.

Two bites into the next sandwich, the same thing happened again. The third time, the herd was pushed back up on the road to continue the march, past Greenback Gulch, Greyback Gulch, Euclid Gulch, Eagle Gulch, Skunk Creek, Sawmill Gulch, past two abandoned grave sites and the gray timber bones of Little Bonanza Mill, to where Brewery Creek (no trace now of what had slaked the thirst of 40,000 Bonanza miners) entered Kerber Creek. Here the drive turned aside from the half-fenced road up the grassy valley toward Antora itself, whose snow-flecked flanks rose imperious above the quilting of evergreens and aspens drawn up over its loins.

At first, the herd surged willingly through the grassy valley, but certain individuals soon began to question the logic of this. Every once in a while a cow would simply cut from the moving ranks and set off in a new direction, sometimes leading a few friends and calves with her.

The bulls, too, increased their agitation, cutting out little bunches of cows or simply turning around and moving slowly against the flow, pulling the most ready dissenters with them. The herders on foot first noticed a new trace of surliness in their manner. "Yip, yip, hiyaah, move it!" didn't produce the same gratifying step-'n-fetchit response it had in the morning. The very suggestion of insubordination outraged Peggy's dogs, Dingo and Katy. They hurled themselves at suspected rebels, but gradually a note of frenzy began to creep into their barking.

The Forest Service fence at the end of the drive now lay only a mile or so ahead in the woods, just beyond a wide grassy meadow belonging also to Dutch Kempner. Instinctively, the herders fell in behind the cattle to give them a concentrated push toward the gate, but as the herd streamed across the open spring grass they began to slow down perceptibly.

The far end of the field dissolved into a succession of aspen and willow groves that melded into pure forest where the valley floor narrowed between steep hills. The ubiquitous beavers had also chosen this point to construct a great marsh choked with briars and alder brush and fortified everywhere by mighty deadfalls. Only one narrow way, cleared previously by chainsaw, lay open to the gate. Now Chuck stood there to one side triumphantly blowing a whistle. Through long conditioning in their winter pastures, the cattle knew that the sound of a whistle meant a move to fresh pasture, and Chuck had reason to believe that the herd would recognize his call as just reward for all their trouble. But just then the herd came to its own decision.

Suddenly, the herders coming up from behind realized that for the first time that day, the whole herd had come to a dead stop. For the next 20 minutes a running battle raged through thicket and bog. The cavalry, both horse and motorized, had to dismount in the tangle and, as at Dutch's, broke into contingents that could no longer see each other or communicate above the din. Secondary engagements like the side skirmishes of some epic civil war battle broke out where separate platoons of cattle took up defensive positions in the underbrush.

Soon, however, the tide turned, and the human side began to fall back before an increasingly single-minded attack. All of the nearly 400 cows and their calves now faced downhill. Rocks and sticks, not to mention shouts and barks, did not faze them now. Singly and in groups they began to move, picking up speed as the people fell back before them.

The cattle did this without flourish. They turned around and began to walk, as a *herd,* the simplest of acts. But all the other creatures standing in their path, from Donnie Whitten down to Dingo and Katy, found it profoundly and precipitously enlightening. Within 30 seconds, they understood how Gandhi freed India. They knew how Erich Honecker felt when the Berlin Wall fell, and what King Canute thought about the flood tide. They knew why Pharaoh gave in to Moses and why the Spartans died at Thermopolae, why democracy is fragile but hopeful and tyranny strong but doomed. They understood instantly how empires can crumble before drought and pestilence and realized that one can spend a day, a lifetime, or even a whole chapter of history doing something that seems sensible, right, and productive without noticing the rise of forces that in one instant can show it up as foolish, wrong, and disastrous.

Most of all, they saw that all the proud authority they had exercised all day was no authority at all. They didn't really control anything. Not the cattle, or the mountain, or the grass, or the weather, or the beavers, or a lot of other things they were too tired to think of just then, and ultimately they would get no further that day, or perhaps in life itself, than they were allowed to get.

Sarah Whitten, all seven years and 75 pounds of her, reached her tethered horse at the edge of the wood just ahead of an enormous bull and his cohort. Adults watching from a distance lost sight of her, but they could see Misty, ears laid back and ready to bolt, still standing fast in the shelter of a tree. Then Sarah's right foot appeared over the saddle, then her left hand on the saddle horn, then the top of her head, and in a minute she was away at a gallop. Not far away, one of the ponies came face to face with a bull five times his weight and went straight up in the air, bloodying his rider's nose before joining the flight down the meadow.

The riders and the motorcycle corps reached the bottom of the meadow barely in time to form a defensive line and stop the rout. They only succeeded because by then mothers and calves had become so scrambled that they slowed down to sort themselves out. The human side, emboldened by this success, began to advance again and within another hour of shouting and hazing managed to again push the herd well into the trees before the cattle again turned. This time most of the people yielded quickly, but morale began to crack. From their reformed line at the foot of the meadow the less valiant of the defenders had the glorious vision of Chuck Wagner against the evening sky, legs apart, whacking out a cannonade with his writhing bullwhip, and calling plaintively, "*Stop cows!*" as the beef flowed past him on both sides quoting Longfellow under their ruminous breath: ". . . be not like dumb driven cattle, be a hero in the strife . . . *ha!*"

Donnie surveyed his troops. Peggy slumped like the beaten Indian that Remington immortalized in bronze in *The End of the Trail*, her dogs collapsed on the grass. The pony soldiers lay back exhausted on the rumps of their steeds, and Nathan rested his forehead on the handlebars of his bike. Carol and the foot troops staggered like Germans retreating from the Marne.

"They're as tired as we are," said Donnie. "I can rig a temporary electric fence, and we can just leave them here. I think they'll stay until morning."

No one dissented, but just then John Wagner zoomed up in his four-wheeler, the flush of action beaming from his face. "I've got an idea," he said. "There's another gate just around the toe of that hill. It's not so far, and the woods aren't so thick. It wouldn't take us fifteen minutes."

Long silence. Where did this man get the energy even to consider such a thing? As he continued to talk, his enthusiasm seemed to grow. The troops looked from one to the other of their two commanders, then shuffled forward to the front.

The offensive lasted another hour, but the result was never in doubt. John had, in fact, found two gates, and at one point actually got cattle pouring through one of them only to come pouring back out the other. Even stoic Donnie cracked, and long after the bulk of the herd had trotted back to the meadow was seen madly leaping about in the woods trying to turn a single cow who paid him not the slightest attention despite the barrage of rocks, sticks, and obscenities he flung at her.

The herd, now absolutely unshakable in its resolve, gathered in the meadow, and the din subsided as mothers and calves found each other and fell to nursing. The herders slumped to the ground and began talking about cold beer and dinner. But the day had not quite ended.

Out of the woods came a single gray cow, moving fast at a brisk trot, horns high and eyes ahead, right through her resting comrades and on toward the foot of the pasture. And behind her came John, his four-wheeler airborne from rock to rock, shouting, "Stop that cow!" The humans leaped to their feet and waved their arms like jumping jacks, then jumped quickly aside as mother, man, and machine rocketed past and disappeared.

John reappeared a moment later, still radiating good humor and vitality. "She obviously had something on her mind," he said. "She wasn't going to listen to me."

The next morning the rested herd went through the gate without hesitation. True, Donnie, Peggy, John, and several of the others would keep discovering little lost bunches of cows over the next few weeks. But in the end all but the gray cow did reach the high shoulder of Antora in good order.

The gray cow mourned her loss alone. On their way home, the

herders passed her, still trotting fiercely along only a mile or two from where the day started, bawling for her calf, but she would not find him.

Weak from some disease or deficiency, he had fallen behind the main drive and been taken back to the Wagners in a horse trailer in a state of collapse. There, he recovered enough to escape and take up the search for his mother. He did not notice, however, that the trailer had already carried him past the place he last sucked, so he set off in the wrong direction. Three days later, 10 miles and four fences farther down Kerber Creek, a neighboring rancher found him exhausted and near death. They shot him and fed him to the ravens and coyotes.

10

AWDI

The defining moment of the Great Move to Antora, when the herd turned around and proved everyone not only helpless but foolish, supplied food for thought.

In the end things did work out, but it was close, and stories of similar endeavors that ended in catastrophe abounded. Systems might be unspeakably complex, amorphous, intelligent, and even creative (as in bulls that plotted to escape the driven herd), but embedded in the fluid dynamics of the whole thing were some hard limits, critical thresholds, and points of no return beyond which the system would break down altogether into nothing but desert, metaphorical or real. The challenge, as Savory continually reminded, was to catch the signs and replan in time.

There was simply no way to plan objectively, scientifically, if you will, in a way guaranteed to work without a glitch, because—and this was only too true—plans don't appear by immaculate conception. They are born out of the imperfect intercourse of ideas, desires, and prejudices going on in the head of the planner. The hard limits they might encounter often as not grow from forces sired by the plan itself. The dialectic. Make a plan and it will bring to life myriad counterplans that then must be planned for.

To its credit, the "holistic thought model" tried to deal with this up front by requiring some consideration of the whole to be planned for—a ranch, a valley, a nation—and of the stated goals—quality of life, production, landscape. A planner would then at least know what to seek when standing before the four Delphic eco-powers—the hot flux of solar energy, the cycling of water and of minerals, and the most inscrutable of all, succession. If you couldn't state your plan on their terms, then you'd better stop right there and think of something else or you could expect to wind up with desert, virtual or real. Savory argued this on the grounds that these eco-forces operated always and everywhere and were therefore as predictable as gravity. Down the road, they could also provide the only objective yardstick of success.

Among other difficulties, this reasoning couldn't eliminate the fact that even the most holistic plans often depended tactically on people who didn't bow so worshipfully to eco-powers.

Savory himself rather relished this challenge. He believed that even seemingly irreconcilable conflicts would resolve themselves in the holistic hierarchy of lesser wholes combining into ever greater ones with ever more transcendent qualities. Get the principles right in your lesser whole and it would harmonize with the whole structure. He didn't believe in trade-offs.

Besides his eco-principles, he carried like a flag into battle his faith that human desires, too, were universal, when one got right down to man and nature. Some said he had to believe this to rationalize his hope for a peaceful, fruitful, and heterogeneous Africa. On the other hand, the point could be argued on the basis of deep ecology. If humanity was indeed bound to the same wheel as the rest of creation, it must know it instinctively. It would only take a little consciousness raising, then, for people to embrace this truth intelligently and discover common ground. Savory often lamented that few institutions of modern society seemed to reinforce this notion.

But Savory could indeed face a group containing vegetarian socialist lesbians, feedlot operators, oil tycoons, and medicine men and at least plant the idea that they shared universal goals. He would tell them of a similar group from Africa, California, or the Upper Midwest and say with a certain light in his eyes, "And after hearing all their arguments and complaints about each other, I just had them write three sentences about the kind of life they wanted, and you know, when we looked at the papers, you couldn't tell who had written which. They all wanted healthy air and water, the chance to enjoy wildlife with their children, a supportive and stable community, a good living, and time for learning and perhaps some spiritual life. Things we all want.

"Then we took that warm feeling"—(a tinge of foreboding in his voice now)—"and went for a look at the land, and *this*"—flashing a slide on the screen—"is what we saw."

His heterogeneous listeners would gasp in unison at the low end of an apparently lush wheat field that had vomited forth a gout of sediment like the delta of the Nile.

"Community? Spiritual life? Good living? What future? When that's happening to the topsoil?"

It worked every time. No one could answer him. And when the time came to describe their dream lives, sure enough, the vegetarian socialist lesbians, the oil patch crowd, and the cattlemen all listed healthy air and water, wildlife, community, a living, a spiritual life, etc. On the strength of that revelation, they could lay aside their petty bigotries and counsel together, objectively, about healing wheat fields—for a few bright moments at least.

Nobody dared say, "Forget topsoil, the free market will handle it," or "The government will handle it," or "The scientists will find something else," or "I'd run a harrow over that, and you wouldn't know it happened. Just gimme the money now, okay?" A "make my day" glee would flicker across Savory's face, and everyone knew that one burst of his Brittanic irony would vaporize the argument, to the delight of his audience.

Nobody shook his head and said, "Hey, that stuff's not my problem. Gimme shopping malls, cheap gas, and an exciting real estate market." Before they could marshal an argument, Savory would heap overwhelming logic on his point that if wheat fields weren't healthy, tumbleweed would soon blow unrestricted through all the shopping malls of this world.

Neither George nor Donnie Whitten needed much convincing, but they had plenty of reason to see the future more in terms of apocalyptic struggle than growing unity. Nothing raised this prospect more poignantly than Maurice Strong's water project, a plan infinitely riskier than driving cows to Antora.

George in particular saw behind the plan the implacable forces of darkness. His position on the board of the Rio Grande Water Conservation District, which oversaw the exercise of rights to the water of river—as far as the New Mexico line—had made him acutely aware of the extreme demands on the whole system and the power of the interests behind them—Albuquerque, Mexico, Texas, all the way from El Paso to the Gulf. Thanks to a recent tunnel under the Continental Divide, the bottomless thirst of Phoenix and Los Angeles even came into play. "It's like a horror show," he would say. "They come at you from all directions, and nothing you can do fazes them. You can't talk with them about values and goals. You can't reason with them. You can't even see them. They're just out there."

He felt this way partly because even Strong himself seemed less in control of his fate than merely sensitive to it and perhaps in possession of a better model than Savory's for planning and replanning to reach his goals. Unique among the faceless forces, he at least had character. Strong was perhaps the most remarkable of the personalities to swarm out of the ant hole of history onto the Baca Grande Ranch, but he was not different in type. Beginning in 1863, when the U.S. government gave a 100,000-acre chunk of public land to the heirs of Don Luis Maria Cabeza de Baca as partial settlement of a disputed Spanish land grant, high-powered entrepreneurs had traded it like a poker chip.

The Bacas themselves used the deed to pay their lawyer, who let it go in a tax sale to former territorial governor and railroad promoter Alexander Hunt, who transferred it to David Moffat, another famous railroad builder, who passed it to a real estate promoter named Waddingham, who sold it to another speculator and ex-governor named Gilpin, who sold it to a cattleman named Adams, who sold it to a Mr. Shaw, who lost it back to Adams. Eventually it came into the hands of one Alfred Collins, who actually made it pay for a few years as a cattle ranch but had no heirs, so it sold again in 1950 and wound up in the hands of the California land development giant Newhall Land and Farming Co. (developer, coincidently, of the infamous South Farm), which sold it to the Arizona-Colorado Land Company when the assessed value failed to outpace the negative cash flow.

Strong discovered it accidentally among the assets of a successor land and mineral speculation outfit called AZL Resources, Inc., which he had bought through his Swiss investment company, Credit Immobilier, a name suspiciously close to the Credit Mobilier that starred in the railroad mega-scandals of the nineteenth century. This he later merged for a consideration in cash and stock into an oil refining company called Tosco Oil. That apparently helped Tosco fight off a furious attack by two notorious corporate pirates, Ken Good and fellow Canadian Sam Belzberg. The scandalous collapse of Good's Denver-based Silverado Savings and Loan soon took him out of action, but Belzberg joined Strong and a new brace of developers in establishing First Colorado Corporation, which later became the Baca Corporation, which whelped AWDI, which bought the Baca from its mother and filed for water rights.

In the beginning, Strong personally stumped the valley selling his idea, but when opposition began to organize in earnest, he actually sold his interest, most of it at least, to Belzberg and another partner, Alexander Crutchfield, citing disagreement over their goals. The $2.25 million profit went to a charitable foundation, but in the popular mind AWDI would always bear Strong's name. Crutchfield had virtually no public face at all. In 1991 he was forty-six, son of a Phoenix, Arizona, developer. He had begun speculating in resource properties after getting an MBA from Columbia in 1984. He had incorporated himself in Denver as Alexander Crutchfield and Co., Inc., as which he had established financial relationships of such astounding complexity that days of depositions taken later would fail to unravel them.

Were the forces behind such people the same as, independent of, superior to, or limited by the eco-forces?

The Rio Grande Water Conservation District itself led the legal opposition to AWDI, but the cost to the various objectors, well over $3 million, would have forced them to the wall and overwhelmed any question of justice had not an extraordinary coalition of valley people organized to fight for it. Private and public money flowed into the war chest. The state legislature created a special tax district comprising the whole valley, and in what amounted to the six poorest counties in the state 45 percent of the voters turned out for a special election (more than ever voted in general elections) and voted twenty to one for a property tax that raised another half a million dollars. By the time the trial began the following October in Alamosa, the principal town in the southern end of the valley, virtually every registered vehicle bore a STOP AWDI bumper sticker.

"The feeling has gotten so extreme that you begin to wonder what would happen if you didn't go along," Karen Whitten complained. "The main organization, Citizens for San Luis Valley Water, publishes the names of people who made private contributions to the defense, and everyone notices who is on that list."

The list of "joint objectors" officially filing to stop AWDI eventually included about 150 names, many of them associations or units of government, from the Wagners and Tim Lovato at the north end of the valley to the Spanish town of La Jara in the south. Among all the familiar ranching and farming names, the list embraced the Haidakhandi Universal Ashram, the State Engineer, the Spiritual Life Institute, the Travelers Insurance Company, a Japanese-owned bison ranch, the Columbine Telephone Company, a clothing-optional hot spring, the United States of America (for the Fish and Wildlife Service *and* the Bureau of Reclamation), and an ardent eccentric named D. Robin Hood, who lived in a shack not far from Donnie and Karen and who specialized in conspiracy theories. Savory never imagined a more diverse collection.

On the sparkling harvest morning of October 15, before the opening of the trial, they rallied some 200 strong on the steps of the Alamosa Town Hall. The American Legion color guard brought banners, and a troop of Boy Scouts, the Stars and Stripes stitched crookedly on their shoulders, cavorted around to keep warm while waiting to lead the parade past the courthouse. Two enormous Belgian geldings arrived pulling a wagon full of hay and sacks of Valley Fresh Carrots. A leather-faced gent with drooping mustaches and battered straw hat waved a sign that said in crayon, "Sin agua es disastro para el *valle.*" Everybody wore jeans and pounded newcomers on the back.

To the right of the microphones a 10-by-20-foot mural by a group of local painters depicted the composite wealth of the valley being sold out to men in fedoras wielding telephones and fistfuls of cash. The previous spring, a delegation including George Whitten had unveiled this work of art under the dome of the capitol in Denver, and it had spent the summer touring county fairs as a fund-raiser. "We the people of the San Luis Valley pledge to nurture and protect our resources and promote justice and human dignity," it said.

Dale Wiescamp, a local farm machinery salesman, took the

podium and warmed up the crowd with jokes, thanked them for coming, praised their solidarity, and introduced Pat Caverly, a dark, statuesque woman who swept onto the stage in her long gingham dress looking for all the world like Joan Baez.

"My name is Pat Caverly, and I'm a Sikanju, which means the Burnt Thigh People of the Lakota Nation," she said. "I'm honored to be here with you today, but I knew sooner or later you'd all be Indians."

Cheers.

"This has been happening to Indian people since colonization. We have suffered for this and we have been killed for this. This continues today, not only in this valley, but globally to indigenous people everywhere. These people who will be here today in this courthouse must consider the seventh generation, because there may not be anything left for our seventh generation."

Cheers.

"Today, when I was coming in here from Crestone, who would be in the car in front of us but the good ole AWDI boys. As the sun was coming over these sacred mountains, I thought, 'Are they seeing the same thing that I'm seeing today and that I saw yesterday and that I'll see tomorrow?

"'Do they see the same colors that I see, the chalk, the blue, the indigo?' Actually I think they saw green." More cheers. "I said a little prayer for them, because I know deep down inside that they're my brothers and sisters, too."

Next came homegrown country music man Don Richmond, who by actually making a living as a musician in Alamosa gave witness to both his own genius and the culture of the town. Dale held the mike up to Don's big acoustic five-string while the crowd belted out "God Bless America" and choruses of a Richmond original called "Land of Little Rain" that had played frequently through the summer on local station KRZY:

Some of us have taken only what we need.
Some of us have seen the need turned into greed.
Some of us would sell our future down the drain,
Washed down by water from the land of little rain.

Chorus:

Save the water. Love the land.
Our sons and daughters need our hand
To turn the wheel, to shape a plan,
To save the water for our land.
Some of us have said that they have found what's best,
Not only for themselves but for all the rest.
So take the cranes and cottonwoods, the amber waves of grain.
We'll live on dust and money in the land of little rain.

Chorus.

For we must learn to live together on this earth,
For it is our mother, the land that gave us birth,
And should the mother lose, the children cannot gain,
Be they in the city or the land of little rain.

By now the Boy Scouts were beginning to get obstreperous in the warming day, but they had to wait for the benediction by Father Pat Valdez.

Although he radiated the cherubic innocence of a choirboy, Father Pat knew his politics. Aiming to "crack the power structure of the valley," a fairly militant Spanish faction in the town of Center to the north had actually bought into a joint venture with AWDI for a communal farm and ranch. If other Spanish leaders like Father Pat had not eventually weighed in against them, the Stop AWDI campaign would have taken a nasty racial turn.

His name was Patrick, but he was de facto patron saint of San Luis, the oldest town in Colorado, incorporated 1854. He grew up nearby in La Jara, went to seminary in Denver, and joined an order called the Theotine Fathers that worked in Denver's inner city. He burned out quickly there, however, so they posted him back to San Luis, which had long since degenerated into a few streets of derelict adobes held together with food stamps. In about five years, Father Pat had turned it into a center of Spanish cultural revival, an artist colony, an architectural museum, and a mecca for tourists and pilgrims, humming year-round with fiestas and processions.

If Father Pat didn't like AWDI, neither did God. He prayed for family and community and asked for blessings on "our farmers, our ranchers, and the environmentalists" and that the "bonds and relationships be strengthened that have been initiated by realization of the value of our water."

Then the crowd marched off past the courthouse led by the Legionnaires, Dale Wiescamp, and the Scouts singing about the purple mountains' majesty above the fruited plain while small children waved to passers-by from the hay wagon.

Very little of this festive atmosphere penetrated the courthouse. The trial took place in a low-ceilinged upstairs room as large as the parish hall of a midsized church, which it resembled for all the masonite tables and folding chairs. A riser across one end elevated the desk of District 3 Water Judge Robert Ogburn only slightly above the bare linoleum. Before him at the general level the court reporter sat tensely at her machine from which the bickerings of two dozen lawyers and eighteen expert witnesses over 475 exhibits would lurch silently toward a cardboard box at her feet over the next six weeks.

A legal tracker sensitive to signs could easily distinguish the two sides. The AWDI team, eight or ten in number, occupied the tables to the right, the objectors to the left, looking, objectively speaking, more leftist. Five of them had beards, compared to one for AWDI, and the attorney representing Citizens for San Luis Valley Water, Dave Robbins, sported a red mustache as big as double dishmops. The objectors' suits also seemed to have a slightly browner shade—earth tones.

Most ominous were the cardboard file boxes stacked waist deep on the objectors' side and almost to the ceiling behind the AWDI team.

On rows of folding chairs across the back of the room, a few dozen local spectators came and went.

On the surface, the trial itself had, in the words of Judge Ogburn, "all the drama of drying paint." It consisted, for the most part, of endless recitations of computer-generated numbers pulled in bales from the file boxes. Nevertheless, the room tingled with the electricity that crackles around any championship match. In a region where per capita income hovered around $10,000 a year, much of it in food stamps, just to be in a room with people charging an aggregate flux of legal fees beyond $100 a minute was like attending a major league game, as the local newspaper put it. The tense atmosphere also came from the fear that the trial might not matter at all, that in a case like this justice had no reference point, that the law bound Judge Ogburn to decide on the basis of technical points that could not be proven and, even if they could be, had little bearing on the real questions.

The case itself was deceptively straightforward. AWDI asked for the right to pump 200,000 acre feet of water a year from beneath the valley floor by means of a 132 deep wells located within the boundaries of the old Baca Grande grant. The objectors argued that to do this would damage existing rights. Ambiguity arose from the fact that legal and hydrological reality parted company at this point.

In pretrial maneuvering, AWDI had in fact claimed that the two had no connection at all. The company could do whatever they damn pleased, they argued, because their rights originated in an unrestricted grant from the Spanish Crown in 1821. As this was recognized by the Treaty of Guadalupe Hidalgo following the Mexican-American War, neither state nor federal statutes applied.

Barring that, the company argued that its plan would not threaten existing rights. Nevertheless, this too involved some sophistry peculiar to Western water law.

Colorado recognized two kinds of groundwater, tributary and nontributary. Tributary groundwater was presumably connected to "flowing streams," meaning that pumping it would have a direct impact on those streams. An applicant filing a tributary claim had only to show that the stream system in question had extra water in it that had been unallocated theretofore. A tributary claim also presented the simplest technical challenge for AWDI. The valley had a lot of groundwater, and Colorado law tended to define "flowing stream" broadly, respecting the fact that for much of the year many Western rivers "flow" under what appears to be dry sand. On the negative side, a tributary right would be "junior" to other rights already granted in the system. This meant that if well levels or stream flows dropped enough to harm more senior rights holders, AWDI would have to shut down its pumps on the Baca or convince the water court that it was not to blame. Such a liability would make it more difficult for the company to negotiate contracts to deliver water to distant cities.

AWDI was ready to take this risk, however, because its engineers really believed that the impact on senior rights would not be so terrible. By the time evidence might prove otherwise, they would have the political and financial clout of cities grown dependent on their water. Then they could buy off or mitigate a lot of complaints or simply silence them with the threat of huge legal costs. A tributary right would put a foot in the door, in any case.

A "nontributary" claim argued that the water in question had no hydrological connection to any system in which rights had been previously adjudicated—that it was in effect a hydrological anomaly independent of the general drainage to the sea. The statute governing this definition reflected a long and bitter history of uncontrolled well drilling in the state. It said that in order to secure a nontributary right a claimant had to prove that his plan would affect "natural surface streams" less than 0.1 percent in 100 years. This was obviously difficult, but it had enormous advantages. To frustrate speculators, the law required the owner of tributary water to put it to "beneficial use" at once. The holders of a nontributary right could wait for the market to rise. Also, anyone claiming injury from their exercise of a nontributary right faced the expense of challenging the original judgment and all the evidence that supported it. Nobody could afford to think about that outside the federal government, and once many voters had tapped into the pipe, the case would arouse less enthusiasm there than an Indian land claim.

It might seem contradictory anywhere outside a Western water court, but AWDI claimed its water under *both* tributary and nontributary definitions, figuring perhaps that if the judge could not bring himself to grant the stronger nontributary claim he might find it expedient to grant the weaker right and the project could still proceed.

The engineers faced a similar task either way. They had to show minimal impact on "flowing streams," and how the court defined "flowing stream" could dramatically affect the difficulty of proving this. Just before the trial, AWDI dropped its tributary claim because none of its potential buyers would contract to put it to beneficial use before the right was secure.

This left the nontributary claim. AWDI would have to show that pumping 200,000 acre feet per year for a century would not take more than 0.1 percent from the flow of "natural surface streams"—in this case from the Rio Grande itself, among others. This somewhat arbitrary statutory threshold would have to stand in for all the questions actually on trial. Should a faceless consortium of private individuals, some of them foreigners, be allowed to buy at any price the right to skim immense profits in perpetuity off the export of the one resource that made self-sustaining life in the valley possible?

What power should private capital and markets have over major water policy decisions in the western United States?

Should cost/benefit analysis involve any costs or benefits that had no cash evaluation? The dust and money question.

What weight should the desires of 40,000 people in a marginal economy and a marginal environment have in the context of a whole state or a whole region? Should they be allowed to become the limiting factor in the growth of metropolitan Denver, already over 2 million?

Did anyone have a choice about the future, or was AWDI merely the chance agent of a fate that would as surely overtake the valley as European settlers had overwhelmed the Utes in the last century?

Ultimately, what kind of judicial reasoning could give answers to these questions?

AWDI lawyer Jack Ross well knew Judge Ogburn could adjust his interpretation of "flowing stream" and several other parameters to reflect his position on this subdocket, but he was not the sort for games.

A senior partner of Saunders, Snyder, Ross, and Dickson, he might have come out of central casting instead of Colorado's premier water law firm. The backlight from the east-facing windows flared off the polished pate of his bullet head and his coke-bottle glasses as he looked out at his audience and said in a dry and lugubrious voice, "May it please the court. This is an inquiry to determine whether water in a unique and enormous resource can be developed for the betterment of man or whether it must forever be locked up to serve the selfish whim of a few who refuse to accept inevitable change."

After spending a few minutes quantifying the immensity of the resource, he added, "In our search for reasons to understand why there has been no desire to settle or willingness to come to the conference table, we have come across again and again the fear of change. The fear of change occurring in relation to the way in which people live in this valley. We find that this fear of change is also reflected in the complaint that this applicant is not a homegrown company. That fear of change has been added to by a very serious xenophobia in the valley that has been institutionalized all the way to the statehouse.

"Why has that devotion, that fear of change, that fear of outsiders, had the impact it has? We find that it really has to be an almost religious devotion to the status quo."

And he went on to denounce wasteful irrigation practices in the valley.

To tee off like this in front of a hometown judge on such an emotionally charged case bespoke an arrogance as towering as the Sangre de Cristos, but of course Ross was right. Although valley people would have used different terms, they did fear change, and they worried a lot about what kind of change and for whose sake. Nevertheless, after Ross's opening statement, the case became the province of engineers. Ross himself did not appear again until the end of the trial.

That the law said the fate of the water claim depended on the effect rendered a century away recalled Pat Caverly's Indian concern for the seventh generation. Technically speaking, that posed one heck of a challenge, but one not unlike many challenges touching land and nature that science-as-we-practice-it is asked to take on, and all too often in the context of a trial where the parties clashed before science ever came into the picture.

The leaders of AWDI's large team of engineers, Robert Brogden and Isobel McGowan of Bishop, Brogden, and Associates, recognized the political minefield in their path, but they threw themselves into the work with the ingenuous optimism characteristic of their profession. Engineers work for money, but a role in opening a vast resource that could sustain the vigor of mighty cities far into the next millennium is why many people become engineers. Were hydrology music, the AWDI job would be a commission for a grand opera.

Both McGowan and Brogden were at the time on the ascending arc of mid-career, gray-haired but youthful and rooted in the generation that made the environment a cause.

Colorful prints of songbirds decorate Isobel's windowless office in one of Denver's anonymous brick and black glass office towers. "The model is valid in every way," she says. "No one should ever think that we are callous about destroying wetlands. We just wouldn't do this if we thought it would cause serious damage. There will be effects, sure, but that is the history of the valley. To hear the other side, you would think that all those canals and the 2,000 circles of center pivot irrigation had caused no changes at all."

Preliminary investigations convinced McGowan and Brogden that they could make the nontributary case by showing three things. First, they thought they could show that the general water table under the Baca Grande grant was not actually "in connection" with nearby surface streams. They proved to their own satisfaction that no groundwater was presently seeping into the principal water courses of the immediate vicinity and reasoned that future pumping could therefore not affect such seepage. Although seepage from groundwater demonstrably did contribute something to the flow of the Rio Grande and some lesser streams, they were 50 miles or more from the Baca. The distance would render the impact there negligible, and if anyone did challenge this, AWDI could easily mitigate any alleged damage by buying out an existing water right and leaving the water in the river.

Second, from various prior studies and satellite imagery of vegetation in the valley, they worked out that almost 90 percent of the 200,000 acre feet of water they would pump would scarcely affect the water balance in the valley at all because they would in fact "salvage" it from "nonbeneficial" plants such as chico and rabbit brush that sucked it up through deep taproots. Unlike grass, forbs, and lesser plants, which depend generally on moisture trapped by particles of mineral and organic matter in the upper layers of the soil, these so-called phreatotypes (from the Greek *phrear*, meaning "well") were known to tap directly into the water table by means of long taproots. Pumping that dropped the water table below the reach of these wasteful organisms would therefore represent mostly water that they would have pissed away into thin air otherwise. Science might dispute the meaning of "nonbeneficial," but the classification had a strong legal precedent. Chico and rabbit brush had never impeded a water claim before, and valleywide it appeared they were depriving beneficial users of 1.4 million acre feet a year. This allowed considerable margin for AWDI.

Still, rapid pumping from wells 2,500 feet deep would draw down the water table drastically in the immediate proximity of the pumps, and the effect might radiate out quite far unless water could move rapidly into the vacuum from elsewhere in the valley's vast subterranean reservoir. Fortune had solved this problem, however. A geologic fault zone ran right through the projected well field. A U.S. geological survey documented it, and they could actually see surface expressions of the faulting in their satellite pictures. This would allow water to flow freely up and down throughout the whole span between the surface and the bedrock below the valley. Thus, the great flux of snow melt that must be entering the water table at the roots of the Sangre de Cristos nearby could rush quickly into the void. Groundwater from farther out in the valley would then hardly have to move at all.

They did not worry over much anyway about the small amount of water beyond what they would salvage by cutting evapotranspiration from the nonbeneficial plants. In the context of such a dynamic system involving such immense quantities, the impact of the deficit spread over the vastness of the region shrank to insignificance. Nevertheless, just to cover any challenge, AWDI actually bought some well-adjudicated water rights from irrigated farms along the Rio Grande, so that if the court did quibble over a few acre feet they could offer to leave that previously used water in the river as mitigation.

To find out what would happen in a century of pumping, McGowan and Brogden constructed a model of the valley in the mind of a computer and pumped 200,000 acre feet of virtual water per virtual year for 100 years.

They built their model on a widely used program that treated the valley as a stack of square cells of varying depth and 2 miles on a side. Equations reflecting pressures, rates, of flow, and so forth governed how water would flow through the six faces of each block to or from its neighbors, and the computer's immense capacity for simple accounting kept track of where the water wound up.

The model had six layers extending down 18,000 feet to where the Sangre de Cristos on the eastern edge of the valley and the San Juan range rising to the Continental Divide to the west joined at the bottom of a colossal geological wrinkle under the valley. McGowan made her top layer of cells only 100 feet thick because of the widely held opinion that at about that depth a nearly waterproof layer of blue clay split the water table. Above the clay, in the so-called unconfined aquifer, water was understood to behave as in a sand-filled lake. Water in the confined aquifer below the clay, however, was under artesian pressure, although not nearly as much as in the days when the generation of Grandpa Whitten had first drilled into it. Water did pass back and forth through the clay layers, but opinions varied on how much or how fast.

The first time McGowan ran her model, the computer locked up after a few virtual decades. Fortunately, this was only a virtual glitch. Some of the top layer cells in the middle of the project had gone dry, and the program simply didn't know how to handle that. By making the top layer 500 feet thick, she created cells deep enough to stay in the system. Although this wiped out the model's distinction between the two aquifers, she could justify this on the grounds that water did pass between the two and arguably more freely than generally thought. She even had data from paired test wells near the project area—one deep, one shallow—in which water levels fluctuated in sync, indicating virtually no barrier at all between the levels.

Over the span of a century, a little delay in water getting from one level to the next would not matter. In any case, the model would still show what happened to the aggregate water level when AWDI fired up its pumps. It was what is known in the trade as an impact model. It showed how far the pumping would drop the water table in a given cell, everything else staying the same. Although extraordinarily sophisticated in structure, it performed a rather straightforward task—one variable, one effect. It did not predict what would actually happen to the water table as a result of all forces, only what share of any change the AWDI project would account for.

McGowan pegged the parameters to her data for the year 1970, when she had reason to believe conditions were average, and she adjusted the equations until the model tracked the actual changes that an extensive U.S. Geological Survey report had recorded through the rest of the decade. That period had seen an enormous increase in groundwater pumping due to the expansion of center pivot irrigation, and in theory a model calibrated to mirror what actually happened then would predict the results of other pumping scenarios.

When McGowan at last ran their model, they saw the depletion value for the Rio Grande rise gradually in a straight line into the next millennium, but in 100 years it did not top the graph line marking 0.1 percent. The project would fly.

Over the months leading up to the trial, the hydrologist Brogden verified his data as best he could. "We waded out in flowing streams to see if they were in connection," he said. "You drive a pipe down into the stream bed. If it is in connection with the water table, water will rise in the pipe. If the pipe goes dry, then the stream is losing water to the water table anyway and will not be affected if it drops. Whenever we could, we also checked wells near the streams. If you find water levels well below the bottom of the stream, it's hard to argue that groundwater has any influence on the stream."

Among the streams he checked he found Saguache Creek virtually dry downstream from the richly irrigated hay meadows west of the Gun Barrel and the thirty-one center pivot irrigation booms of the South Farm. "It basically ceases to exist as a stream at that point," he said. "If there's no water left in it anyway, there's no way the aquifer we're dealing with has anything to do with it."

To quantify evapotranspiration, he pored over the satellite pictures and made spot-checks on the ground. Because wetland plants yielded up water at a different rate from the chico and rabbit brush, each cell of the model had to have a custom-tailored value.

The work was as solid as Brogden and McGowan could make it. Their peers would defend it long after the trial. It was good enough to convince the AWDI board to take it to trial, and that was significant because despite the departure of Maurice Strong, the board still had some environmental conscience. It included William Ruckleshouse, a former director of the Environmental Protection Agency, and Richard Lamm. Lamm had won three terms as Colorado governor on the environmentalist vote and meant to run for the Senate, and on the strength of the engineering study he would publicly praise AWDI as an environmentally and economically worthy solution to the state's urban thirst.

From conception to conclusion, the study conformed to an intellectual tradition quite as deeply rooted in the minds of the community as the alleged religious devotion to the status quo of the valley objectors. It rested on the hypothesis that water in large quantity could be salvaged from evapotranspiration, and honoring the rigor of the scientific method, it tested the hypothesis by controlling the variables and observing what happened in reality, albeit virtual. If willingness to accept the result as clean objective truth did not amount to religious devotion to a venerable principle, it certainly came close. To Robert Brogden and Isobel McGowan it would at least justify action on a Jovian scale.

They drew strength from an optimistic faith. They saw life as a succession of discrete problems, of which water supply was one. A drawdown of the Rio Grande would be another, should it happen despite their calculations. They did not doubt their ability to handle whatever came, and they did not fear that a herd might suddenly turn and come at them down the side of some virtual Antora any more than good Christians fear witchcraft.

In the bright clean offices of Bishop, Brogden, and Associates, Inc., Robert Brogden can sketch with practiced hand on a felt pen board the funnel shape representing the pattern of dewatering produced by a 2,500-foot well, letting its spreading top overlap the top of a shallower funnel representing a typical irrigation well.

"AWDI will in fact dry up some wetland," he said. (In the trial he did not deny the probable elimination of 26,000 acres of it.) "But there are wetlands throughout the valley, and almost everyone who pumps affects some of them and not others, and seldom is a single party responsible for a given case.

"Anyway, the wetland that AWDI might impact is not natural to start with. There wasn't any before irrigation canals diverted water out into the valley from the Rio Grande."

"Wetland is not even supposed to be a legal issue," added McGowan. And she was right. Take some big yellow machines and drain and fill a half-acre of it, and the National Wetlands Act prescribes penalties that would make bigger outfits than AWDI blink, but the law does not acknowledge even the virtual reality of a well that pumps water out from under a nearby wetland.

"It makes no sense, but that's how it is," said Brogden. "We did our job within the rules as they exist."

Not very holistic, but it was the way scientific land management worked in the real world.

11

Sharma

After opening so dramatically with parades and rhetoric, the AWDI trial rapidly took its place among the small-town routines of Alamosa. While morning mists still rose from the streets, the company's champions would arrive in their van from over the mountains to meet the objectors' team trickling in from local motels. Both groups, their stomachs acid from too much restaurant coffee, would exchange cold pleasantries and clomp up the narrow stairs to the upper room, there to unlimber their attache cases on the Masonite tables and take up their ritual combat before the judge.

Throughout the day, curious potato farmers and ranchers in town for spare parts, bankers returning from lunch, grocery shoppers, journalists, and others who just wanted a place to sit down for a while dropped in to listen and whisper gossip in the back of the room. Judge Ogburn looked down upon them with laconic detachment, his robe unbuttoned, a toothpick often in his mouth, and his feet often upon his desk. Keenly aware of the theatrical dimension, he drew in his audience with wry asides.

"Don't you see what they're doing," he quipped once during the cross-examination of one of the endless stream of expert witnesses. "These guys have made their colleagues out to be idiots and now the attorneys for the other guys are now trying to make *them* look like idiots."

For the most part, Karen and Donnie followed the trial in the the Center *Post Dispatch* and the Alamosa *Courier*, both unabashedly partisan in their demonization of the water company team. George, through the Water Conservancy District Board, tapped into another grapevine. Also, his wife Jane's brother, Allen Davey, was an expert witness as head of one of the valley's two hydraulic engineering firms. Like most others in the valley, however, they formed their own opinions from their intuitions about the land.

"There is no way they can prove that water rights will not be affected by the pumping," said Donnie. "These aquifers are so complicated, no one understands them, and we've been trying for a hundred years. Someone might start up a pump four or five sections away, and your well loses its head while wells in between are unaffected. There's no way they can claim to know for sure what pulling out 200,000 acre feet a year will do."

The main engineers for AWDI, Robert Brogden and Isobel McGowan, realized they were in trouble as soon as the cross-examination began. Dave Robbins, the opposition attorney of the Great Red Moustache, and his colleagues on the side of the objectors aimed their questions to reveal the elegant structure of the AWDI case, and especially McGowan's computer model, as gross oversimplifications. How could they be sure about the rate of flow through blocks of their model many cubic miles in volume? How could they pick one value for evapotranspiration (ET) in a block 4 square miles in area? In their model, why did they wipe out the distinction between the shallow, unconfined aquifer, and the deep, confined aquifer?

The two engineers met these attacks with surprised annoyance. The rules of combat forbid them to say what they really thought. They were engineers, not lawyers, and they had justified the project as well as could possibly be done. Such picking at minutiae in their work ignored the elegance of its overall structure and denied the basis on which centuries, millennia, of hydrological feats had risen. Of course you could not account for every detail, but if you could not simplify, you could not act.

True, some of the greatest monuments to the craft had not delivered unalloyed bounty. The vast irrigation works of Babylon had eventually filled with salt and silt, but after enabling what brilliance! And the Aswan Dam. Of course, it wiped out the eastern Mediterranean fishery that the nutrient-laden waters of the untamed Nile had once fed and ended the seasonal floods that had kept Egyptian agricultural land fertile for 8,000 years, but it put 2 million acres into year-round production and generated 2.1 billion watts of power in a country that had no oil. Closer to home, no one would consider unbuilding any of the waterworks of the West no matter how dubious their original justification. Justification collected on them after the fact like tumbleweed against a fence. People found uses for them, if not always the intended people or the intended uses. They became accepted and necessary, including the most controversial swindles, such as the Los Angeles Aqueduct, which dried up the Owens Valley, the Garrison Dam on the Missouri, which destroyed what was left of two Indian tribes and more good land than it would bring into production, or even the Central Arizona Project, which pumped water out of the Colorado River at an expense no Arizona irrigation farmer could afford.

Sure, these projects had changed the script, but life would go on and make the best of whatever, and who could say what would have happened otherwise? Engineers committed to a grand project do not, cannot, reflect on the possibility of an absolute mistake except perhaps in terms of the work itself—the collapse of the Quebec Bridge or the Teton Dam or the Chernobyl disaster. They know they cannot begin to know all the consequences a century ahead.

Principles give an act its ethical dimension. To use natural resources efficiently is a principle. To encourage economic growth is a principle. To respect the environment is too, of course, but above these stands the principle of balance. Most gain causes pain, and the principled man in an imperfect world has a duty to strike the fairest trade-off. These principles had been applied, and a society that remained true to them would be borne forward by forces as powerful as any in the natural world.

If Savory's line of thought had ever come up on their screens, Brogden and McGowan would have found his rejection of trade-offs naive, his criteria for reaching a consensus on goals utopian, and his order of decision making backward.

The law's literal insistence on perfection on every point, symbolized by the need to show that AWDI would affect the Rio Grande less than 0.1 percent in a 100 years, struck them as hypocritical and corrupting of the proper role of science. Like the objectors, they knew courts could and often did apply such language selectively in response to political pressure and that scientists often fell in line. They could not explain otherwise why some of the other experts called by their own side hedged on supporting conclusions about evapotranspiration and aquifer characteristics that came out of their own research. The unscientific objections that referred to threats to the Valley Way of Life they simply found atavistic.

"For [Conservancy District Engineer] Allen Davey to testify that lower Saguache Creek was a flowing stream because he had hunted muskrats in it was beside the point," groused Brogden later. "It certainly isn't now, and isn't likely to ever be again, even without AWDI."

Davey also vehemently disputed Brogden's opinion on the unnatural origin of the valley's wetlands. He could tell how his great-grandfather, the English-born blacksmith who fled west to escape the Civil War draft, had settled by a place called Russell Springs, which then flowed so fast it never froze, and how it fed the vast alkali marsh that eventually became the Russell Lakes State Wildlife Refuge, although now perhaps only with the help of irrigation runoff.

That Davey could speak as a fellow engineer as well as a muskrat hunter made his testimony particularly damaging, but it still fell into the category of picking away at facts and technicalities. According to Davey, Saguache Creek had once been a flowing stream by any definition and without doubt connected to the aquifer. Brogden believed in a different past and found it irrelevant anyway, and he rejected the broad definition of flowing stream that credited water moving out of sight under the sand.

Quite possibly the judge could have decided the case without ever considering the deeper assumptions of the AWDI argument at all because the law allowed him to limit his decision to rather narrow questions of fact. The broad case got made, however, in the last week of the trial. Although in the court record it read as just another recitation of boring numbers relating to Isobel McGowan's computer model, even the most casual drop-in spectator recognized at once that this testimony laid an ax to the root of the case. It came from a man who had hardly ever seen the valley until he appeared in court. Nevertheless, he managed the remarkable feat of destroying the distinction between the "scientific" legal arguments and the subjective question of what vision they represented. He did this not by directly attacking data as right or wrong but by peeling away data to expose the principles and assumptions that gave it meaning beyond the arithmetic sum of the numbers.

He did this in a way curiously parallel to Allan Savory's holism, to which, however, it owed nothing.

Devraj Sharma looked into the soul of science, and what he saw there differed somewhat from the common faith. The very name of his firm—"Principia Mathematica"—stood out among the various "Associates," "Incorporateds," "Esquires," and "Doctors" on the list of experts and lawyers in the trial. Sharma had taken the name from the title of the foundation work of symbolic logic, written by Alfred North Whitehead and Bertrand Russell in the decade before World War I, knowing that Russell had taken it from Isaac Newton. Anyone who gave that name to a commercial enterprise, one might guess, had thought about the propositions of those men, about the power of logic, and about what it is and is not possible to know.

At the time of the AWDI trial, Principia Mathematica occupied several hundred square feet of commercial space not far from Brogden and Associates in an equally modern, equally sterile brick and glass office building. Only a hint of Hindu in the reception area decor distinguished the place at all. Sharma himself, however, was different. He was short, slight, dark, and modest in dress and gesture, but his eyes had a quality of innocence and wonder that only truly creative people retain past the age of thirteen. In conversation, they would widen in delight at nuances unforeseen by the speaker even when that was himself.

Sharma was born in India in 1943. His ultraconservative father served the Raj as a native army officer with a Crown commission. His mother was a Fabian socialist who at the time of her arranged marriage at age seventeen edited an important newspaper, having stepped in when her father went to jail for opposing British rule. The electricity running through such a marriage, Devraj claimed, gave him extraordinary impetus and encouragement to seek and achieve excellence.

As his father rose toward his general's stars, the family moved frequently. By the time Devraj graduated from high school, which he managed in half the time it takes most of us, he had attended eleven different schools in eight languages and several alphabets.

"I discovered as a child you have three options," he would explain later. "Either you learn how to box, and I was never very good in the English public school culture that existed in India. You could run very fast away from trouble, and I was no good at that. Or you could learn to say 'Don't beat me. I'll do your homework' in a dozen different languages."

A passion for science and mathematics had animated him from the beginning, so after his A-level exams he went to a college of engineering, the glamour choice in his rapidly industrializing country. There, however, he gravitated to the most arcane subject of the mechanical engineering curriculum, fluid dynamics. He did well and sought a master's degree at the recently established Indian Institute of Technology in Kanpur.

"And thereby hangs a tale!" His eyes widen at the thought of his early fascination. "There I narrowed my focus even more, because this was basically an American operation, established by USAID, and Americans tend toward extreme specialization. So for me, fluid dynamics became computational fluid dynamics."

The awe in his voice conjures up an enchanted castle out of Grimm.

"I was attracted because the most difficult problems in fluid dynamics involved solving equations that until the advent of digital computers it was thought were impossible to solve. It wasn't even known quite what the barrier was, and no one then could conceive of a tool that would enable us to approach it.

"But there had developed in the 1920s and 1930s a branch of mathematics called numerical mathematics where people started to depart from the advanced mathematics of the differential equations kind into the mathematics where you tried to solve problems numerically. What that simply means is you posed the problem in such a way that you operate instead of in algebra and equations based on algebra, more and more on simply arithmetic operations. I was fascinated by the promise of these theories, which were then advancing quite independently of their application to computer science, which was quite new at the time.

"I decided that I wanted to pursue this field, computational fluid dynamics, in a school that would take me as far as I could go and as fast, so I accepted a scholarship from the Imperial College of Science and Technology in London, where there was one professor who I knew was perhaps the best in the field anywhere in the world at that time. His name was D. B. Spalding. People who knew him very well called him Brian."

Sharma's stipend allowed him barely one hot meal a day, but what matter. He ate it in a cafeteria crawling with Nobel laureates where casual conversation engaged the *Principia Mathematica* at the deepest level.

Fluid dynamics, the study of flows and the characteristics of turbulence, and the numerical analysis Sharma had chosen to try to describe them, were the first areas of physics and mathematics to venture into the area broadly known as chaos. The revolutionary nature of this step is difficult to comprehend. It meant letting go of the ideal of a transcendental rigor extending all the way back to Euclid in order to explore the boundary between the knowable and the unknowable. It meant no longer using equations and theorems to define static, linear order but as descriptors of dynamic interlinked relationships, which, when iterated and fed back into each other, produced degrees of order as fantastically random as snowflakes. This would eventually stretch the very idea of mathematics into aspects of nature that up to then only artists presumed to interpret—the arrangement of leaves, the flocking of blackbirds, even perhaps the dynamics of a herd of cattle forced up a mountain.

At the Imperial College in the 1960s, however, Sharma cut his teeth not on driven cattle but on predicting the critical conditions under which air forced into a jet engine would break from a smooth, predictable stream into a chaotic turbulence that stalled the compressors. Sharma's doctoral thesis, accepted in 1969, presented "a three-dimensional mathematical model of rectangular sectioned diffusers," a generic way of describing the vastly more complex events inside a jet intake that happened to be not round but square, as in, say, the Concorde or the F-15.

Mathematically, this meant exploring the limits of numbers. How would a small imperfection, say, the rounding off of an irrational number, influence the outcome of a calculation that went round and round a few million times in a computer? Or, taken the other way, how much could you say with numbers about complexities beyond the power of numbers to describe in detail, and how would you know whether what you said was right?

Such questions had philosophical roots in diverse places, besides the *Principia.* Yet, just as the holism of Jan Smuts gave a subliminal pattern to Allan Savory's early thinking about biology, the rigor of logic had lighted the pathways of physics and math that had attracted Sharma. Unlike Smuts, the biologist, who saw creation as a hierarchy of "wholes," which had qualities that could not be deduced from their parts, Russell and Whitehead, being mathematicians, had looked for rules to do just that, to extrapolate greater truth from hard facts, and vice versa. That's what logic was, the mechanics of meaning.

In many ways, of course, the work of the two men did not fulfill all their hopes for it. Logic never quite reduced all the conundrums of metaphysics to hard-wired deductions from atomic elements. Deriving "good" and "bad" scientifically proved difficult, even for Russell. Although he meticulously reasoned out his often infuriating positions on every moral issue of the century, he had to transcend the *Principia* to do it.

Yet, if logic couldn't answer all questions, it could nevertheless show precisely which ones it shouldn't attempt. It could find the point where logic broke down. In its proper domain, it could trace the effects of a false premise through to a warped conclusion or break down a grand conclusion to its feet of clay. Paradoxically, perhaps only the mechanical precision of the discipline allowed appreciation of the complexity that lay beyond it.

The linguistic philosophy that grew out of Russell's work addressed paradoxes and anomalies that had mathematical parallels in the fields that intrigued young Devraj. If a barber shaves all those who shave themselves, does he shave himself? And what if he shaves all those who *don't* shave themselves? Conversations in the Imperial College cafeteria, however, dwelt less often on parallels in flesh and blood.

At this point, Sharma poses the fingertips of his two hands together before him in a gesture of a fabulist reaching the corner of his plot, and continues, "And it so happened that I applied for a research grant without knowing what its goal was. It was in the year 1971, and the subject was computational fluid mechanics in a very restrictive field called blast physics, which promised to lead to a tenured position at the Imperial College.

"And the subject was"—his eyes widen again—" 'The Impact of Semi-Molten Projectiles on Soft Surfaces.' " Another generic description. "Not to put too fine a point on it, the semi-molten projectiles were plastic shrapnel, and the soft surfaces were . . . human flesh. You see, it so happens that conventional metal shrapnel leave the ground at an angle between 18 and 21 degrees, so anyone who throws himself flat and covers his head in time is safe. Molten plastic, however, skims the ground at six to eight degrees. You get the drift.

"Turning down a major grant after winning it meant leaving the Imperial College. It was something that was 'not done.' My colleagues, including Dr. Spalding, did not understand. Having spent my whole life up to that point in academic environments, I hardly understood myself. But I decided to leave the academic world altogether and set out with the desire to turn what skills I possessed to a field that had not yet developed, which was computational fluid dynamics in the environmental field. I wanted to do something of beneficial practical use for a change, and I had the idealistic notion that all of my theoretical knowledge could improve efficiency and save money in certain areas of engineering that up to then had developed largely by trial and error."

On one of his first jobs, for a multinational engineering firm, he designed for a German power plant the first cooling towers that used air instead of water, thus freeing a small city from perpetual fog in summer and rime ice all winter. But his new path did not lead straight to virtue. Not long afterward, his employers transfered him to Denver, which was then entering a period of speculative boom in oil shale development, and then within a few months sent him to Iran.

The Shah wanted to build a 4,800-megawatt nuclear generating station (well over twice the wattage of the Aswan Dam) near Isfahan, on the edge of the desert. The site had no water, so the four 1,200-megawatt units would need air cooling.

"Air cooling takes roughly one thousand times the surface area required in the normal wet cooling towers, and this was not cool, damp Germany but one of the hottest, driest places in the world," says Sharma. "I determined that each of the four units would require four active towers and a spare, each 600 meters in diameter and 900 meters tall."

It takes a minute for the numbers to sink in. The world's tallest skyscraper, the Sears tower in Chicago, could lie on its side at the bottom of each tower with 500 feet to spare. Eighty copies of the Sears tower stacked in two 1,400-foot bundles would still fall 50 feet short of filling one cooler, and the project would require twenty.

Sharma grins at the memory of standing before the Shah of Shahs himself to explain this. "Reza Pahlavi was not a very likable man but an enormously powerful personality. He wasn't like his father, a shadow Shah. He had vision, money, and a kind of drive. He told us to proceed. I only tell this by way of saying that, contrary to the warnings of my professors, there was no lack of challenge outside their academic laboratories."

Only a few months later, Ayatollah Khomeini's Revolutionary Guards surrounded the Iranian offices of Sharma's employer, but Sharma escaped back to Denver. Before long, he went into business for himself.

"It had crystalized in my mind that I wanted to work on practical applications, and I had realized that good science, small amounts of money to pursue the science, and terrible deadlines are not always mutually exclusive. You might say the abstract reasoning of the Brahmin mind became coupled to the pragmatic, American, problem-solving attitude."

He sensed a niche for an outfit that could offer extremely sophisticated, state-of-the-art analysis of technical problems involving fluid flow. Furthermore, he realized that he had the theoretical skill to offer at reasonable cost the kind of data crunching normally available only in the most lavishly funded government and university labs. "Having studied in Britain helped," he explains. "Because they did not have the unlimited hardware of richer American labs, they had to develop software approaches that have put them far ahead in many areas." But he did not stint on hardware.

While most engineering firms were upgrading their hardware to personal computers based on 486 chips, he was writing software for a system of four multi-tasking work station networks that gave each the power of a super computer. He could reconstruct the mathematics of a model the size of the one Robert Brogden and Isobel McGowan put together from the data it produced. He could then run it for a hundred years in a matter of minutes. He could deliver vast extrapolations and interpolations of this data that would take their machines weeks to grind through.

In a major water suit between the states of Colorado and Kansas, the Kansas engineers took seven years making a model for the Arkansas Valley covering the twenty years between 1965 and 1985 in one-year stages. In a few months Sharma made one that accounted for data going back to 1940 in five-day stages.

"Fundamentally I noticed that when people say, 'This is the best,' the restriction is usually the machine or the tools they use, but everyone knows that this is an unnecessary restriction. It is bad science."

In the case of the AWDI model, however, he went a little further. Other scientific witnesses had merely questioned data and pointed out mistakes. Sharma's testimony questioned the whole manner in which the water company had invoked scientific authority. Resuming his storyteller's tone, he continues.

"I undertook to discover the assumptions on which the AWDI model was based and then demonstrate the effect of those assumptions on the outcome. I discovered that the AWDI model was concocted." He pauses. "It was concocted hoping that nobody else would be able to take it apart and say, 'This doesn't make sense.' It was concocted to avoid raising certain issues at all, for instance, wetlands."

The Alamosa *Courier* carried the headline, "Sharma Shreds AWDI Computer Model," and in five days on the stand he did just that.

Electronic models have always had a checkered history. The most enormous and sophisticated economic models, even though used to support financial decisions of global moment, have more often made famous economists look foolish. The interaction of equations representing such abstractions as consumer attitudes and harvest conditions, even if they could represent such forces precisely, produces oscillations far too random to be much use. Likewise, early hopes that super-computed models of the atmosphere could predict weather well enough to render it controllable foundered on the same thresholds of chaos that had fascinated Sharma. Groundwater models had a better reputation, but the record contained few on the scale of the San Luis Valley.

The first electronic model of valley water was constructed in the mid-1960s by a U.S. Geological Survey team before digital computers could shovel around gigabytes of information. The leader, Philip Emery, was also one of the first to explore the question of evapotranspiration, although he did not then consider it as a new source of income.

"We actually constructed the valley in three dimensions on sheets of pegboard at a horizontal scale of one half-inch to the mile," recalls Emery. "We divided the valley into cells extending down to about three thousand feet. For transmissivity, the resistance to free flow from one cell to the next, you soldered a resistor of however many ohms you needed into the wire. If you wanted a stream, you just ran a wire and connected it to different node points. The water was the current itself."

Dynamic effects, like the bend of the water table around a pumping well, would appear in the green eye of an oscilloscope and be recorded with a Polaroid snapshot.

"It was very elegant in its way, and very close to what the digital models can do now," says Emery. "You could manipulate it in the same way. Only if you wanted to change something basic like the transmissivity, you had to go in and physically change resistors. Now, of course, you just punch in a different number. That's good, of course, but the danger in the digital model is that scientists have so much flexibility that they can play games with it until they get the answer they want, which is not to say nice things about fellow scientists, but one can do that."

Emery could not tinker with the model itself so easily, but the basic rule of all computer simulations, "garbage in, garbage out," still applied. The only value Emery could measure with some accuracy was the average flow of the Rio Grande out of the valley because it had been monitored for years by automated gauging stations as part of the international compact governing its use. This he set at 500,000 acre feet per year. Inflow from the streams off the mountain was harder to measure, but he had data to support an educated guess of 1.5 million acre feet. The remaining factors in the balance were more tenuous.

Evapotranspiration presented a double challenge. Agronomists had extensive data on field crops, which Emery worked out to roughly 1 million acre feet. Virtually no data existed on wild land. To estimate that he had transplanted a number of common plants—chico, rabbit brush, and snakeweed—into big tubs and logged the water it took to keep the artificial water table in the containers constant. By extrapolating these numbers over vast reaches of land dominated by these plant communities, he concluded that another million acre feet left the valley through evapotranspiration.

The rest of the water needed to balance inflow and outflow would come largely from precipitation. A million acre feet would balance the equation of water entering and leaving the valley, but granting an official average of 8 inches a year, the valley's 5.25 million acres received not 1 million but nearly 3.5 million acre feet. Certain studies indicated that the dry air actually did snatch back over two thirds of it before it could enter Emery's equation, but who really knew? Much to the dismay of the lawyers for AWDI, Emery would testify in the trial that anyone who claimed accuracy within better than 50 percent on any of these figures was pushing it.

Brogden and McGowan set the water loss from wild land at 1.4 million acre feet, which threw Emery's water budget out of balance. There must be, they said, at least 400,000 acre feet entering the system underground and unseen from the roots of the mountain ranges on both side of the valley. They did not invent this idea. Others had estimated as much as 700,000 acre feet, but introducing a totally arbitrary fudge factor into a balance sheet makes all its terms fudgeable. Tinker with any term, say, stream flows or evapotranspiration, and charge the difference to the deep inflow, which is unknowable.

The AWDI engineers argued persuasively, however, that this problem did not destroy the strength of their model. As an "impact model" it only presumed to show the effect of AWDI pumping on *any* background.

The strategy divided the scientific question in two. It presented the water budget of the valley as a grand and well-understood resource and portrayed what people did to it as another matter altogether. Against the vastness of the resource and all the ways others exploited it, their model showed AWDI's project would have little impact.

Sharma attacked this whole premise. If changing one term of the equation also happened to affect the background relationships, as was likely, he argued, then the system became "nonlinear," like a weather system, and predictable only within broad parameters of chaos. The linear impact model, he said, assumed a simple causal chain that did not exist. A model pegged to a system in constant flux that did not even consider all of the background forces could not pretend to give accurate projections.

Also, Brogden and McGowan had chosen 1970 as an "equilibrium" year in which the water budget balanced perfectly and evapotranspiration equaled recharge. They had used that data to calibrate the impact of their project. However, said Sharma, no one had any idea whether it had been in equilibrium. In fact, although the presumed water budget had to balance over the very long term, it probably never did in any given year except by random chance, given the erratic climate and the human demands on it. Water tables fluctuated as imbalances shifted back and forth. Drought or frost or rain changed the demands of plants. Irrigation practices changed. If 1970 had been a wet year, and considerable evidence convinced Sharma it was, then recharge exceeded loss, and pumping would have less effect on the system.

Sharma also demonstrated the extreme volatility of the evapotranspiration salvage estimate. It came out of a quotient of at least seven elements—the makeup of the plant community, the percent of ground covered, the maximum potential evapotranspiration, the change in evapotranspiration as the water table drops, the end point where the plant dies, a seasonal factor, and the actual change in water level.

In his reconstruction of the AWDI model, Sharma discovered that Brogden and McGowan had told their computer that plants covered 100 percent of the ground and neglected to tell it that growth (and water demand) nearly stopped in winter. He also found that they had asked their model to calculate water table changes of less than 2 feet over many of the model's 2-mile square cells, a mathematical and topographical impossibility because even the valley was not that flat. As the seven factors were multiplied together to compute the amount of water saving, small variations compounded each other geometrically. Even a 10 percent change in ground cover meant 50,000–75,000 acre feet of water, which, times the seasonal error times crude analysis of the plant communities times inaccurate predictions of the water table made the game a crap shoot.

His voice rises at the thought of it. "You can tell the judge, 'Look, this is what we think within thirty percent or so,' but they said, 'This is it! We know!' And that's wrong."

Brogden and McGowan had argued that to handle a computational bug they had made the top layer of their model 500 feet thick instead of 100 feet.

Sharma lowers his voice in sadness. "A travesty of science!" The maneuver, he said, wiped out the distinction between the surface aquifer and the artesian water below. This, he demonstrated, vastly narrowed the region of artesian wells affected by the pumping. It also allowed the company's computer to assume that water could move freely down from the root zone of plants as their 2,500-foot wells pumped it out and that the suspected underground inflow from the mountains could rush quickly into the space.

These flows also depended on the presence of a geologic fault zone over a 200-square-mile area, for which Brogden had produced extensive evidence. This would allow easier flows all the way down to 18,000 feet. Sharma did not deny its existence but testified that for the model to perform the way it did, the water would have to flow 100,000–1 million times more easily throughout the fault zone than it did elsewhere.

Finally, when it came down to the Rio Grande, it was only a matter of algebra. In order for the Great River not to lose more than 0.1 percent of its flow after 100 years of pumping, its bed could not "leak" very much water into the sands below. Sharma discovered that Brogden had programmed in a rate of leakage so low that the EPA would have accepted it for the lining of a sewer pond. When he changed the value only a slight amount and turned on the virtual pumps, the line showing the loss to the river went quickly off the graph.

Sharma testified a full week, but the AWDI cross-examination lasted only three hours. It did not shake him on a single point, though, granted, the questions came from lawyers, not engineers, which left Brogden and McGowan without the last word.

On the last day, after hearing five hours of final arguments, Judge Ogburn granted a short recess. When his court reconvened late in the afternoon he astounded everyone by delivering his decision right then. His scorn was terrible for this case, "conceived as a twinkle in the eye of a multimillionaire."

He found that the water was in fact "tributary." Pumping it would indeed harm others' rights. To claim otherwise, he said, was "a smokescreen." The argument, which he referred to allegorically as "Little Non-Trib," was "an ill-conceived, misshapen, and stillborn child. I pronounce him dead," he said.

Amid mutterings and snapping of briefcases, the losers dispersed while the winners indulged in cheers and high fives. They would celebrate far into the night at a local watering hole.

When Ogburn issued his full opinion of the AWDI claim, which followed closely the brief filed by the objectors, he razed it to the ground and sowed the ruins with literary acerbities:

From Lewis Carroll: "If it was so, it might be; and if it were so, it would be; but as it isn't, it ain't. That's logic."

From Twain: "There is something fascinating about science. One gets such wholesale returns of conjecture out of such a trifling investment in fact."

From eighteenth-century Irish playwright Charles Macklin: "The law is a sort of hocus-pocus science."

He applied a broad definition of a flowing stream that included Saguache Creek and several others. He accepted all of Sharma's testimony in laying waste Brogden and McGowan's model. He ridiculed their estimates of evapotranspiration. He found that the Rio Grande would leak too much of itself into emptied sands.

Moreover, the record showed that Ogburn wrote opinions that stuck. He stood in line for a State Supreme Court judgeship, a mainstream judge, and in fact, although AWDI attempted appeals all the way to the U.S. Supreme Court, they failed at every level. If any judgment should have established a precedent, Ogburn's should have, but enormous claims based on evapotranspiration continued to proceed throughout the West. The city of Las Vegas alone filed for the right to pump over 800,000 acre feet of water to its booming suburbs from beneath the southern third of Nevada, most of it, a gift from "nonessential plants."

Robert Brogden and Isobel McGowan, stung by the loss, picked back over the bones of the case in search of arguments they might have made. They found a few. There were discrepancies in their opponents' data about leakage of the Rio Grande. They could have made a better case for choosing 1970 as a base year. Mostly, however, they re-convinced themselves that they had not fudged their assumptions, that Sharma, not being a hydrologist, did not understand the assumptions they had made about the faulting, evapotranspiration, and so on. They were right about their impact model.

Again, the real unfairness, they felt, lay in the law itself—all those unrealistic definitions of flowing stream and the impossibility of ever really proving that a stream that varied 50 percent from year to year would not drop less than 0.1 percent in a century. Later, at a meeting of hydrologists, Brogden presented a bitter paper about this, which he ended with a brace of aphorisms of his own including:

> An Expert's Lament: On a day-to-day basis, legal standards are of little use; only after the trial are they applied with certainty.
>
> Padlock's Paradox: Never argue with a fool, the court might not know who is the fool.
>
> The Attorney's First Law of Debate: Anything is possible if you don't know what you're talking about.

Judge Ogburn put his postgame commentary in a paper before an American Bar Association conference in which he elaborated on his Mark Twain quote:

"Computer modeling is not an exact science," he wrote, "even though it comes packaged with a lot of bells and whistles and other technological trappings. If the underlying assumptions are inaccurate, incomplete, or just plain wrong, then the computer model and the expert are not going to fare very well. Some lawyers think they can dazzle a jury with expert testimony, and sometimes they can. A judge who has been around for a while, though, usually takes a more jaundiced, skeptical point of view. But that's the lawyer's problem, not mine."

Further down he remarked, "A lawyer's first duty is not to bore the judge."

Privately he said, "Academic experts have become a plague on the judicial system. There's one for everything. In one case I was asked to hear a 'lawyer expert.' So many scientific experts have prostituted themselves. The scientific method means nothing. It's so obvious that most start out with the pitch, 'Where do you want to go? Tell us the bottom line, and we'll justify it.' Sharma, however, was the real thing. He did run that model through a shredding machine. He utterly decimated it, and he did it in such clear language that everyone in the room understood."

Then he added, "On the other hand AWDI's opening statement in the case was right. The issue wasn't only water. The community that fought them is xenophobic, but what's wrong with a little xenophobia? We all do it in our day-to-day living. We do it in the context of family, school, and even in the organization of our courts. Is it wrong that an outsider must come to terms with the community in which he does business? I would so much rather see these things mediated. The adversarial process does not do them justice."

Sharma got his moment for public reflection at a conference in Denver of wetlands scientists. He wound up on a panel with the lawyer, Dave Robbins, engineer Brogden, and a lawyer sympathetic to the AWDI case. The moderator announced that they would discuss how it happened that AWDI, despite well-researched evidence and an extremely sound computer model, had still lost.

Robbins, a lawyer who wore his social conscience openly, flew into a rage and denounced the opposition as thieves and charlatans living off the backs of the poor, but said nothing about wetlands.

The other lawyer made a snide retort about any attorney complaining of parasitism, but went on to say that, indeed, AWDI's experts had put forth an excellent case in favor of progress, but water and wetlands had mattered little in the outcome. The real question had been who owned the resource, and whether it should be sold, especially by foreigners.

Brogden followed and used his time to explain why, in spite of everything, exploiting groundwater involved less red tape, politics, and legal obstacles than surface water. At the very end, he projected a slide showing a map of the San Luis Valley and remarked that the only thing he and his opponents agreed on was where it was in Colorado.

"Even his map was wrong in the way it defined the limits of the valley," says Sharma, "but it astonished me that at this wetlands conference no one so far had talked about wetlands. I proceeded to show what I had done with their model and showed some foundational fallacies. I agreed that at some stage of our life groundwater needs to be developed, and then it needs to be well managed, but the model hadn't shown a well-managed approach. Whether such a thing can be shown with models is another question, though I believe it can be.

"Finally, I simply said to them, too, 'This model was concocted. It did not address certain issues at all, such as wetlands. What about wetlands, since that was supposed to be the focus of the conference? The question remains, even if you are biased in advance, how did you address these questions, and if you didn't, why didn't you?'

"Well, no one really had an answer to that. The answer at the trial was, 'We didn't need to. That wasn't the burden of proof on us.' I still don't think they realize the implications of what they did. That's what frightens me about scientific work that is done in justification of a legal position. In reality, as opposed to the law, all the issues count."

When, as expected, AWDI appealed Judge Ogburn's decision, speculation raged as to what it would do next. (The first appeal, to the State Supreme Court, would take nearly two years.) Through the whole summer of 1992, rumors circulated that the company would declare bankruptcy to avoid court costs and reappear in a new form to file another claim. Some said it would simply buy up existing water rights and dry up the valley that way.

But except for the rumors, the Great Water War was over, at least for the moment. In one of his last acts before leaving office at the end of 1992, Colorado senator Tim Wirth tacked a clause onto an omnibus water bill in Congress that effectively killed the project forever. It barred any groundwater development in the San Luis Valley that would damage wildlife (read: wetlands), the Great Sand Dunes National Monument, or "other federal projects." To everyone's astonishment the codicil stayed in the bill right through to President Bush's signature on practically the last day of the 1992 Congressional session.

It was a rare outcome in the convoluted history of natural resource exploitation in the American West, rarer still because the farmers, ranchers, and environmentalists who mounted the defense of the valley had seldom stood on the same side of any issue. Locally, at least, the fight had made all of them appreciate the vitality and diversity of their desert. They had thought beyond packinghouse and sale barn and the weather, thought about flights of cranes, the racket of migration through the marshes, thought about the fate of "nonbeneficial" plants and the benefits wrought by people they hadn't thought about before, thought of their valley as a whole piece, indeed more wonderful than its parts, and grander than any computer could simulate.

"Sure, we thought about a whole lot," said Donnie. "I wouldn't bet money that we learned anything. And we still don't know how to manage this place ourselves."

But valley people never rhapsodized overmuch about anything. "After all, the water is still there and still worth as much as ever," said George Whitten. "You wait. Someone will think up another way to take it."

And both brothers were right.

12

Monitoring

Late June. The Sangre de Cristos, in May still set off against the azure sky by white sheets of ice, now fade into it in the flat light of the solstice. Across the valley on Antora the alpine grasses are breaking out leaf like clipper ships making sail for the 100-day dash between frosts. Down on Tracy, however, the green flush of May has hardened off into summer. As in all the American Southwest, June is the driest, stillest month, a parched caesura after the adolescent outbursts of spring storms.

A good June heats the land enough to suck water all the way from the Pacific and blow it up into cooling towers of thundercloud, fantastic cumulo-nimbi flattened off like anvils against the stratosphere. The energy shed by vapor condensing in these roiling columns yields monsoon storms of thermonuclear power later in the summer. June itself, however, is a time to take stock—between branding and the drive to summer range, between planting and the first hay cut. June. Pale blue days follow each other in anonymous succession, and consequences that can't be seen take shape in silence.

At the end of the month, the two factions of the Tracy Common Grazing Association would turn out their stock on the allotment. The Whittens and Jim Coleman would start their cattle out in the newly fenced demonstration area in the north end, the others on open range to the south. In anticipation of that, Royce Wheeler set out one morning up the Gun Barrel, intent on taking the measure of the ecological health of the demonstration area so that he could respond to whatever developed on the basis of science rather than conjecture.

Compared to the AWDI trial and its stacks of data and computer printouts, this event aroused no widespread interest, but it did raise many of the same questions about the way science is applied to treatment of the land. What information was useful? What assumptions governed its interpretation? What could you really tell from it? Why did you need to know?

The BLM had recently transfered Royce's old colleague, Fran Ackley, to the office that handled the adoption of wild horses, so Royce had recruited a freelance biologist, Dennis Lamb, to help in the assessment.

Like Ackley, Dennis had wandered out of a Midwestern city, Davenport, Iowa, in his case, fallen in love with the West, and eventually worked his way through graduate school at Colorado State to qualify himself to make a living out of his love for nature. He had about him something of the orphaned look of any single man whose domestic interests begin and end with a can opener and a toothbrush. At six and a half feet, he lurched about with all the grace of a folding mason's rule, the resemblance becoming startling whenever he kneeled for specimens. Royce liked Dennis a lot, though, and felt a bit guilty for having never found a way to hire him full time, although this had spared him the burden of the young biologist's broken heart. The gothic melancholy of Dennis's love life could make the long shared drives required by the work somewhat trying.

As arranged, Dennis had gotten himself to Tracy by his own wheels, and Royce could see him from the distance folded over the hood of his pickup peering into the foothills through binoculars. He was a bird watcher. He was also a fine field biologist.

Monitoring range condition is one of the most tedious, undramatic, and thankless tasks of land management. It takes hours; it rarely yields conclusive results; and controversy over techniques and criteria have spawned so many methods over the years that data are seldom comparable over space or time. This, of course, defeats half the reason for gathering data in the first place, but ultimately all future policy, all present management decisions, and all recrimination over past failures get thrashed out and justified by numbers, because numbers, once transcribed into scholarly documents from the ambiguity of dirt and grass and wind, acquire runic authority as the language of science.

Every state university has published numerous monitoring procedures. State and federal land management bureaucracies have never set and stuck to internal norms, not to mention interagency standards. In 1989, the National Academy of Sciences finally commissioned a task force of range scientists and environmentalists to propose universal criteria and definitions, but by summer of 1992 they were still a year away from publishing. One task force member, Range Science professor George Ruyle of the University of Arizona, went so far as to say, "People use assessments of range condition to justify all kinds of political agendas, but the bigger the area, the less they tell you, and national aggregates are basically meaningless."

The sources of dispute lay in profound differences in point of view and conception of how range ecology worked and a large degree of institutional momentum. Cow people looked at bulk forage production. Ecologists measured the makeup of the plant community. Some procedures considered erosion and soil condition. Others didn't. And no one agreed on definitions of good and bad because every nuance of slope, soil, climate, and hydrology created unique potential at every site. In fact, argument raged over the potential of *any* site.

The intellectual roots of this situation went back to the theories of one Frederic Clements, who made the University of Nebraska a world center for the new discipline of ecology around the turn of the century. Clements's idea that plant communities developed through predictable stages of succession toward a stable "climax" community dominated academic thinking well into the 1950s and remains enshrined in high school curricula and agency technical manuals down to the present. The theory describes elegantly what actually seems to happen in stable, well-watered climates. Textbooks typically cite the New England beaver pond that fills with debris, becomes a rush bog, then a willow thicket, and finally dries out and turns into a hardwood forest full of sugar maples, the stable "climax" that doesn't change.

In more arid and erratic climates, where in fact Clements did a good deal of his work, the heirs of that tradition liked to compare measurements to undisturbed "relict" sites, such as the tops of mesas and box canyons where livestock or even wild grazers had never been, but they argued a lot over the role of disturbances, including fire, which was often a "natural" disturbance. The practical truth that livestock caused the most general and manageable disturbance led to monitoring methods that attempted to document the impact on Clements's predicted succession by counting "indicator species." Grazing under conventional management usually does cause certain erect bunch grasses, particularly cool season grasses, to decrease. Some prostrate turf grasses usually increase, and particular weeds may invade.

To the practical business of advising or regulating cattlemen, the exact nature of the climax community didn't matter. If invaders invaded or if increasers increased and decreasers decreased too much, then there were obviously too many cows. Scientists, too, began to discover so many factors that destabilized Clements's ideal community or seemed to produce quite different stable states that they quit talking about it. Disturbances such as droughts, fires, and insect plagues were more the rule than the exception, and relict sites yielded no common base line and rarely showed the diversity and vitality expected in a true climax community. The climax idea remained alive as a political concept, however, as environmentalists took up the cause of restoring "pristine conditions."

The best descriptions of "pristine" were of course gleaned from the records of the early pioneers, so they had reason to assume that removing their descendants and their stock and farms would reverse the decline. Range scientists argued with conviction that even if there were such a thing as "pristine condition," most damaged sites could not begin to restore themselves to it on a human time scale. Operating generally from land grant colleges that served a livestock industry indisposed to wait, they judged ranges by the forage production they could force out of them with the technology at their disposal, and their research reflected that. A "mechanical school" of range science developed on the theory that plant communities at least as stable and perhaps more productive could be established by main force.

Royce Wheeler had come up through this school and had sent squadrons of bulldozers and spray rigs forth to clear invading brush and suppress noxious weeds, but he had stayed in the Bureau of Land Management longer than the benefits had lasted, and he suspected that the long-term profit had gone mostly to the makers of the equipment.

The holistic idea intrigued him because it preserved the possibility of *management*, to which life had called him. He liked the thought that he might envision a "landscape" that was not mechanically produced, that the bruised community of plants required the conscious effort of animals and men to come fully to life, and that he would have a part in it.

According to the holistic canon, managing anything complex, not to mention land, people, and animals, required monitoring in a particularly focused way. Whereas most monitoring, particularly in government agencies, was done after the fact to prove somebody's plan right or wrong and to justify the consequences, a truly holistic manager would assume that if his plan wasn't wrong to start with, inscrutable nature would render it so sooner or later. Therefore he would monitor not to justify his plan but to change it as often as necessary to insure success.

Royce was curious to see whether this could in fact be done, but he also needed an objective way to measure whatever the demonstration area might demonstrate, because he did work for a government agency, and he would be judged.

Dennis Lamb groaned through his drooping mustache when he saw the Center for Holistic Resource Management logo on Royce's aluminum clipboard. He preferred it when Royce hired him to work on a game count or a biological inventory project anyway, but assessing range condition according to Allan Savory's biological monitoring form was unusual punishment.

Like most other range-monitoring techniques, this one required making transects of random samples along a line extending out from a permanent marker. Savory recommended selecting the points by tossing a dart backward over the left shoulder. There were seven types of information to log about each of 100 sample points:

Ground cover: Did the dart hit bare ground, rock, or litter?
Canopy: Did taller grass, weed, bush, or tree shelter the point?
Capping: Was the soil crusted over and, if so, to what degree?
Living organisms: Was there any sign of animal life within a foot or so?
Plant type: Was the nearest perennial plant grass, forb, bush, or tree?

Habitat: Did the nearest plants reflect arid, waterlogged, or moderate conditions?
Erosion: What kind and how bad?

Then there were five questions to answer about the perennial plant nearest to the dart:

How far away was it?
Was it a species that grew most vigorously in the cool or the warm season?
How old did it appear to be?
Was it overgrazed, overrested, or healthy?
What species was it?

This worked out to 1,200 observations per transect, and Royce had hoped to make two or three before the end of the day.

Unlike more traditional methods of monitoring rangeland, this procedure would not tell him anything concrete about how much forage the Tracy allotment would produce that summer. Its exhaustive observations did not include the almost ritual "clip," in which the professional range conservationist clipped, dried, and weighed a sample of the forage, computed the tons of dry matter available, and determined a stocking rate for the season. George and Donnie and Jim Coleman could gauge the latter pretty well from experience, and the evidence would mount quickly if they estimated wrong. As to whether the Tracy was in good, fair, or poor condition, well, according to legend, Grandpa Whitten had described a landscape of grass that could hide a sheep, which made a nice goal for conversation.

Properly tallied and analyzed, the transect data should, however, catch small but critical changes in the four basic ecosystem processes so that one would know whether things were getting better or worse in relation to the legend of deep grass on Tracy.

"I don't think doing a transect will be too bad," said Royce. "This place is pretty much blue grama grass all over. We're not talking about a lot of biodiversity."

"Yes," said Dennis, "and look at it. It really has seeded out this year. I wonder how long it's been since it did that."

It was the sort of detail a good field man would notice, and once made aware of the millions of slender culms all flashing seed heads like flags in the morning sun, Royce could almost imagine what real high grass would look like. The love life of grama grass was hard to fathom. Like all perennial grasses, each plant produced only one specialized seed stalk, or culm. It might do so early, late, or not at all and apparently did so more out of whim than need. One almost needed a hand lens to see the minute grains. Blue grama accomplished the serious business of propagation mostly by unromantic rhizomes that pushed out from the roots, extending its durable mats where less adaptable species persisted in growing erect and getting killed off. A season of prodigious seed production like the present one might hold the promise of a great flush of fresh seedlings somewhere down the road (the seeds had the intelligence to wait years for perfect conditions), but neither Royce nor Dennis had ever seen it happen.

It seldom did happen with any of the perennial grasses, in fact. It was an irony typical of creation that the durable grasses that hung in through good years and bad very often came from seeds as ephemeral as dust. Even when some rare combination of moisture and temperature persuaded them to germinate, they couldn't survive a day in the sun if capped soil kept their frail first root from striking a hold.

Annual grasses have adopted a fundamentally different strategy. Every branch grows a seed head as quickly as possible, and they all fling out gobs of bona fide grain, often aggressively sharp in form and packing enough energy to keep pushing out a root for a long time. The annual brome grass most common on Tracy bore the common name "cheat grass" because it sprouted so robustly in the spring, but by the time the summer got hot withered into useless purple wisps full of seeds that could actually pierce the lip of a lamb and cause a nasty infection. Annuals, too, know enough to pass on bad years, however. If they do not find the signs auspicious, they may not sprout—another case of nature's use of the hair trigger, an ineffable threshold between green and brown that becomes critical whenever rangeland loses the diversity of its more reliable perennials. Country dominated by annuals will periodically go through a summer bare as a parking lot.

The two men reflected some on this and also on the fact that for reasons not well understood in warmer climes—the Mediterranean, Southern California, parts of Arizona and Africa—vast stretches of land had lost their perennial grasses altogether under livestock grazing. Now classified as "annual ranges," they were considered good when they had grass and bad when they didn't. Because annual plants die whether grazed or not, most stockmen figured grazing strategy didn't matter much.

That perennial bunch grasses had ever predominated on such ranges had almost faded from memory. Some speculated that they never could return because in years when the annuals chose en masse not to grow, any perennials that had managed to make a start lay exposed to concentrated attack from animals. That nearly all of the annual species that now prevailed over so much of New World grazing land came, like cheat grass, from abroad, caused some to blame the plants themselves. In Africa, however, the shift to annual grasses during the same period involved only natives.

Royce and Dennis drove on toward the foothills looking for a suitable place to start. This involved more discussion than either of them expected because, as homogeneous as the gray-green flats appeared, they weren't quite. Russian thistle (known locally as tumbleweed), leafy goosefoot, salt bush, and a short gray-green shrub called winterfat outcropped here and there for no apparent reason, and it was tempting to put the transect marker in a place that would assure some variety. In the end, however, they picked the most ordinary site they could find, right out in the middle of the flats between the foothills and the boundary fence, a place utterly homogeneous to the casual eye.

They drove a steel fence post into the ground to mark the spot for all future years and took snapshots of it with Antora in the background. Royce noted on his clipboard that then and in future years the measurements would be taken toward the big mountain. The fence post, by serving as back scratcher for cows, a perch for birds, and so on, could itself influence the ecology of its neighborhood, so a few paces away, where they could easily find it, the men drove another permanent marker almost down to ground level. This they photographed straight down to record what the ground looked like. Then they began their 100 samples.

Official procedure called for selecting the first point by facing the marker with ones back to Antora and throwing the dart over the shoulder to foil any urge to bias the study by aiming at an interesting plant. From that point the transect would progress by ninety-nine more tosses toward the mountain. Royce found darts a bit Mickey Mouse, so he had brought an artifact from a previous sampling method, a steel frame one yard square welded to a handle of rusty re-bar extending up to his waist.

With eyes turned to the sky to honor the principle of random selection, he took seven great goose steps and dropped the frame against his right foot. The top left corner of the frame was his random point. Thump! Dennis folded down with the clipboard to look. The corner had landed on a piece of rock, under a tuft of grama ("canopy," on the form). The surrounding soil was capped over with a crust 1 inch thick. Other living organisms were represented by a shiny black stink beetle. The nearest perennial plant was blue grama, abbreviated "bogr" for *Bouteloua gracilis.* It was 2 inches from the point, mature, and "warm season" in growth habit as opposed to "cool season." Its form was matted. That the plant itself and the rock appeared to rest on short pedestals where wind and water had swept away a half-inch of soil rated a mark for erosion.

Thump! Next point. The corner of the frame landed on a mat of grama, but it was dead and rapidly disintegrating. Was this "organic litter" or "dead grass"? A discussion ensued. They decided to call it litter but note their convention on the form. Three inches again to mature bogr mat, no canopy, a couple of dried prairie dog turds for animal sign, heavily capped soil, pedestals. This time a small weed thrust up between the sample point and the live grama. Dennis identified it as the local lamb's quarters—goosefoot, *Chenopodium fremonti,* highly edible. It was also historic, having been named for the famous explorer and naturalist John Fremont, who passed that very spot in December 1848 at the head of an expedition that was soon after reduced to cannibalism in a nearby canyon. As an annual plant, however, it counted only for a check mark on the monitoring form. Only perennials got named because they represented stability.

Thump! Another point, and so on, again and again until Dennis's mind wandered and he began to make oblique references to his "non-job-related preoccupation," and the day grew warm. For all the tedium, the intent was ambitious, and there was no other obvious way to go about it because, in theory at least, the fortune of the land was inscribed in the top millimeter of soil.

The close attention to the soil surface, the amount covered by litter or plants, the hardness of the crust, and the kind of erosion should indicate the land's readiness to respond to rain. A broken soil crust well covered with litter would mean that a much higher percentage of precipitation actually got into the system. The condition of the litter, old grass, and dung, if there was any, would give evidence of whether nutrients were cycling through the organic life of the soil or were locked up in dead matter desiccating on the surface.

The distance between plants and particularly the proportions of seedlings, mature, and senescent plants would indicate whether the community was expanding, declining, or maintaining itself. Because most range plants respond to overgrazing by growing prostrate or hiding their leaves in stubble or prickers, and because overrested grasses tend to become senescent, the form of the sampled plants reflected the impact of the current grazing management far better than a mere count of indicator species. The soundness of management would show up also in a shift in the mix of cool and warm season species. Cool season plants, important for increasing the length of the grazing season, typically suffer most from overgrazing because they green up first in the spring. The presence of other living organisms would indicate the extent and vitality of the community the place supported, although outbreaks of ants, grasshoppers, or other creatures would show its instability.

Together, all these observations would show whether or not the plant and animal community represented by the transect was likely to increase in complexity, stability, and fertility or degrade. Royce, of course, hoped that in five or ten years he could look back in his files and say, "Hmm, as a result of our program, perennial species increased from three to sixteen, including four cool season grasses and several mesophytes [plants adapted to exploit better soil moisture], lusty broad-leafed bunch grasses, which made a lot of forage out of sunlight, western wheat grass, and prairie bluestem. Bare ground decreased from 85 percent to 40 percent." On the other hand, he knew the real reason for taking these particular measurements was to be able to say at the end of day what was wrong now and what had to be done to fix it so all those grama seeds might in fact germinate, plant spacings close up, and the living community become more vigorous.

Step, step, step, step, step, step, step, thump. Bare ground. Soil capped by a crust sealed with greenish algae. Inch and a half to the nearest plant—*Bouteloua gracilis*, once again. Dennis noted a pair of horned larks launching up from the gray-green grama turf a ways off, their relationship beautifully uncomplicated. Even Royce began to wonder whether they could take enough transects by the end of the day to cover the variety of discrete communities and possible management differences on the allotment. At best, he and Dennis could do North Tracy—one demonstration area on one allotment. He wondered whether there were a better way.

Other approaches to taking the pulse of the land have in fact come out of the relatively recent engagement of disciplines such as meteorology and physics with questions traditionally addressed by range scientists. The sources of this interest range from the threat of global warming to the challenge that new environmental laws raise to development projects like AWDI. This dignifying of the subject with implications far more terrible than the mere production of livestock has diverted a torrent of money and talent (like that of Devraj Sharma, Robert Brogden, and Isobel McGowan) into the study of natural systems and has inspired a host of new ideas and expectations.

Ever since the 1930s, when aerial photography became common in survey work, foresters, agricultural experts, and range managers have used it in a variety of ways. The explosion of information from satellites and a broad range of computer analysis techniques in the 1970s and 1980s, however, created a whole academic discipline and associated industry that came to be called "remote sensing," which promised to give anyone the power to call up by the tap of a computer key information about any point on the globe that would have once required the labor of a Dennis Lamb on his hands and knees.

Billions of dollars soon flowed into the development of satellite and aircraft-borne cameras for studying natural resources, and quick early returns kept enthusiasm high. It became possible, for example, to track the progress of the Soviet wheat crop virtually day to day by subtle changes in its color. An agronomist in Manhattan, Kansas, could tell an individual farmer in Dodge City to irrigate his milo (sorghum) without ever visiting the farm. And this information wasn't just available to big labs, grain monopolies, and the CIA. For ridiculously low cost, anyone could get mail order negatives, prints, or computer tapes of spectral data for any point on the globe for any time of year and pay for them on a credit card.

Furthermore, digitalizing the information allowed computers to search vast amounts of data for similarities and differences that the eye could never find. The analyst in Minneapolis could find a diseased section of durum wheat in North Dakota and ask his computer to show him any areas of Ukraine that had the same spectral "signature" of infrared and visible wavelengths. Then he could bet a few hundred thousand dollars on grain futures without losing much sleep.

The implications of remote sensing for desert research were obvious from the beginning, and worldwide concern about the prospect of global warming and climate change assured its application beyond simple crop forecasting. Scientists suspected that arid land probably played an important role in global weather systems because it represented vast areas characterized by extreme heating and cooling, and being marginal, it would provide the most sensitive evidence of change. In any case, they expected to discover numerous instructive scenarios for civilizations facing the prospect of radical climate shifts.

The techniques developed for croplands, however, did not work so well on "wild" land. For starters, the diversity of vegetation and chaotic landforms made extrapolation over wide areas risky, and the varied response of wild species to seasons and weather undermined generalizations over time. Satellites "see" the ground in chunks called pixels, and the sharpest pixels readily available for natural resource work (from the French SPOT, "Système Pour l'Observation de la Terre") still missed detail less than 20 meters square. Systems in the works will do better, and airplanes are still used to gather more detail, but every doubling of the resolution squares the amount of digital information required to record the picture. Even computers far beyond the power of those available to most researchers will slow down and choke on it at some point. The difficulties and difference of perspective came together in the very evapotranspiration problem that came up in the AWDI trial.

Range scientists, including the holistic school, look at the water cycle and the energy flow largely from the viewpoint of the plants and animals (including land-dependent people) with which they work, instinctively gathering data like Royce and Dennis, on their hands and knees. The physicists and meteorologists concerned with global climate, however, begin their observations from space, often working from theories and computer models that they try to adjust and calibrate with data from the ground only later in the process.

Although no one has yet constructed a global weather model good enough to yield long-range predictions of any use to farmers or ski resort operators, various attempts have revealed the sensitivity of the atmosphere to phenomena previously considered insignificant. They demonstrated, among other things, the very important role of clouds in weather. Clouds, it turned out, were not just puffy white things. They were massive solar energy devices. The evaporation of water put energy into storage, and its condensation into clouds gave it back. A monsoon wind, for example, could ship more BTUs cross-country than a 6,000-ton coal train.

This revelation forced the modelers to check out what happened to the entire energy flow if they looked at the water cycle as an energy transfer system instead of just moving water. What happened, for instance, to water that fell as rain? The portion of it that dried up or went back into a vaporous state through the transpiration of plants must also then affect the energy system and, if so, then clouds, temperatures, and climates. If satellites that covered the whole Earth every few days could pin down this factor, then their simulations of currents rising and falling over the continents and oceans of the world might look more like what really happened. They might discover whether deserts didn't perhaps exacerbate desert conditions or vice versa. Then, who knew? They might even expand the envelope of reliable prediction. Yet doing this demanded enormous technical finesse.

Given the many research teams that sprang up around the world to meet the challenge, it was not surprising that one had a toe in the valley. A tourist driving east across the valley toward the Great Sand Dunes National Monument between 1985 and 1987 might have deduced this fact from a piece of dynamic modern sculpture that protruded above the chico not far off the road. Atop a slender aluminum stand, two delicate semaphore arms swiveled about continually to face the wind, and every few seconds they flip-flopped, one up, one down, to the accompaniment of a whirring anemometer, an evapotranspiration measuring device designed by a young engineer named Dave Stannard.

Stannard himself was an engineer trained in hydrology and fluid mechanics, another urban refugee who after college left Connecticut for the open space of the West. He had turned to evapotranspiration when his specialties began to lead toward a career in solving nuclear waste storage problems. He worked out of a windowless cubicle in the U.S. Geological Survey complex in Denver decorated with an Escher study of waves and numerous photos of prairie and mountain, including the San Luis Valley. His assignment there had been to gather base line data for that other water scheme, the federal government's Closed Basin Project, which undertook to pump San Luis Valley groundwater into the Rio Grande so that enough of it would reach Mexico to satisfy U.S. treaty obligations. Presumably his findings would make it possible to tell whether lowering the water table really did balance against reduced water loss from plants. However, the work drew him into the much larger inquiry into climate change, because knowing how much water returned to the atmosphere would tell how much energy went into storage.

In the late summer of 1990, a group of thirty scientists from the USGS, NASA, the Los Alamos National Laboratories, the Jet Propulsion Lab, the Agricultural Research Service, the Soviet Academy of Sciences, two French government labs, and a brace of American universities gathered in a 50-square-mile area called Walnut Gulch surrounding Tombstone, Arizona, to try to gather the pieces of the puzzle. The project, called Monsoon 90, picked the place and season because it promised an extreme example of transfer and release of energy and might tell them what happened next. How quickly and how thoroughly, for instance, did the water of one storm go back into service as energy storage when the sun came out, and what effect did that have on subsequent weather locally or elsewhere? The project had at its disposal nearly unlimited money and equipment and an air force consisting of a DC-8, a C-130, and two smaller planes, all crammed with cameras and radiometers.

Stannard's evapotranspiration rig typified the high-tech sophistication of the campaign. Including recording devices, it cost about $10,000 and measured the humidity and temperature differences between the lower and the upper arms of the semaphore. Because no two devices could possibly be calibrated precisely enough to allow comparison of such minute differences, the arms flip-flopped to cancel out errors. The amount of energy absorbed by the evaporation of water (and the amount of water evaporated) could be sweated out of a simple equation. The total radiant energy from the sun equaled the amount of energy reflected directly back as radiation plus the amount that went to warm the soil plus the amount that warmed the air directly plus the amount that went into the evaporation of water.

The net radiation and the heating of the soil could be measured directly, and Stannard's contraption took care of the rest, but useful results required correction factors that made the whole process messy. The speed with which heat and vapor ascended past the rotating arms depended on turbulence, for example, which in turn came out of an equation relating wind speed to a "surface roughness coefficient" derived from the size and spacing of plants. More difficulties arose in the extrapolation of the results over wide areas of different vegetation and topography and over extended periods of time.

Other instruments, equally refined, complemented Stannard's work in Walnut Gulch. One used the distortion of small beams of radiation and sound waves to measure the heat and humidity differences of ascending and descending currents of air ten times a second. A raindrop hitting one of these delicate sensors did about $90 worth of damage.

All through the summer of 1990, the group gathered data simultaneously from different altitudes ranging from the various satellites to the high- and low-flying airplanes to phalanxes of graduate students carrying yokes of radiometers through the brush on foot. Researchers from dozens of institutions would spend the next five years or more pawing through it electronically in search of correlations with the "pure" information supplied by instruments such as Stannard's.

How closely could you estimate evapotranspiration, for instance, if you knew the surface temperature, soil reflectivity, density of vegetation, slope of the land, and its direction? Satellites could give a crude opinion on such things by means of some ingenious data manipulation. A measure of leaf area called the Normalized Difference Vegetation Index, for example, came out of the ratio between red light, which chlorophyll absorbs ravenously, and the neighboring band of infrared, which it strongly reflects.

"The problem is the statistical noise and factors that can't be measured," says Stannard. "Dust, pollution, and heat waves in the atmosphere distort some wavelengths more than others. The amount of shadow changes with the sun's angle. It's hard to tell the height of plants or the roughness of the surface. Space modules can't measure the wind or the air temperature at all.

"People continually develop equations for new variables and look for patterns of distortion that will enable them to make corrections, but there are so many feedbacks that make the calculations go chaotic. That may even be the case with the relatively simple estimation of evapotranspiration. We can take measurements from a given situation, but it is very difficult to predict what will happen if the situation changes because of the feedbacks. More biomass (vegetation) will generally mean greater evapotranspiration losses, but by changing soil texture, creating shade, depositing litter, slowing raindrops, etc., it can also increase infiltration of rainfall and slow other losses, so you might well get a net gain instead of a loss.

"Similarly, we know that greenhouse gases should increase air temperature, but if that increases plant growth and evapotranspiration, which increases cloud cover, which blocks sunlight and increases snowfall, you could get a new ice age. We don't know any of these things yet. We're a long way from the image you get in the press that one more multimillion-dollar satellite will give us all the answers.

"Just correlating all the data from the different sources so the computer knows it all relates to the same spot on the ground is enormously time consuming even for a well-defined research area like Walnut Gulch. Doing it on a world scale is still a long way off."

In the summer of 1992, the NASA aircraft were all off in Africa flying transects over the Sahel, but Walnut Gulch still occupied Monsoon 90 team members at the Agricultural Research Service lab on the north edge of Tucson. In this sere outcrop of World War II vintage prefabs with swamp coolers dripping out the windows, Stannard's colleague, Susan Moran, pored over images of the study area on a computer screen until her eyes ached.

Moran, a sandy-haired woman in her twenties who goes to work in khaki shorts and sandals, was a low-level technician with a biological research group at Grand Canyon National Park when she saw a lecture on remote sensing by a man from the Center for Arid Lands Studies at the University of Arizona.

"I was hooked," she recalls. "I said to myself, this is the way to really see what is happening on this planet," and she was soon steeped in differential equations and a Ph.D. thesis on satellite measurements of evapotranspiration from cropland. She had concluded that it could be done, but she had had to admit that anomalies in the data—she called it "noise"—made the measurements untrustworthy, and the wild land in Walnut Gulch presented a much more formidable challenge. That the satellites and the computer nevertheless let her "see" so much more with the naked eye than she could boil down to useful numbers kept her at her terminal, maddening as it was.

On her computer screen, the Normalized Difference Vegetation Index over Walnut Gulch showed as a mottled red stain laced by a white dendritic filigree. In real space, these were sand washes coming off the Dragoon Mountains, where the Apache chief Cochise once made his stronghold. She could see the flush of regrowth where a fire had cleaned head-tall sacaton grass out of a bottom land and the ruler-straight mark of a fence that separated one rancher's management strategy from another's. But she could not say yet what these and other anomalies meant in the big picture.

"We're working on it," she says. "We're exploring ways to sort out the impact of bushes and annual grass on the data," and by telling the computer to enhance invisible differences of shading, she turns the mottled red into patterns of brilliant yellows and blues, each some different combination of soil, moisture, and plant life. If she compared this to the same view of another season or year, what story would it tell?

Susan Moran brings up another image. It's still Walnut Gulch, but the washes recede into the background and other patterns dominate. "This is after a rain," she explains. "We're also investigating relationships between soil moisture, soil brightness, and soil type. There is something called the Universal Soil Loss Equation, which computes erosion from six factors, some of which we can get from remote sensing, but all that, too, was developed for croplands and cultivation practices. There are so many factors we haven't begun to think about yet, like algal crusts on soil and litter that piles against the brush and dams the runoff. The modelers tend to say, 'Never mind, just give us a number,' but the field people know what the data are worth and don't want to give it up before they're ready."

The idea of a systematic nature that can be figured out and predicted nevertheless pervades the persistently military atmosphere of the old barracks. In the hallways, big wall charts display the basic statistics of the global warming theory—atmospheric levels of greenhouse gases and chlorofluorocarbons and temperature statistics by hemisphere. Computer-generated images of mountain ranges and ubiquitous prints of satellite views of Earth convey a sense of scale in which the human factor seems to shrink to naught, but that of course is not the case in Walnut Gulch any more than on the Tracy Common.

Another member of the research team, Dave Goodrich, sidles up for a look at Moran's screen. "Even if we get our energy relationships, we have very little idea of what is going on out there ecologically," he says. "We're still at the stage of learning how to see what's there. We haven't begun trying to tell by remote sensing how it might be changing. The whole place was grazed off and the scrub oak and juniper cut down for fuel and pit props by the miners in Tombstone in the nineteenth century. It's never come back, and brush has invaded a lot of it in spite of chemical control and chaining. We've put in exclosures to see what happened when livestock was kept out, but nothing changed. We think rabbits wiped out any grass that came in, but we don't really know."

Not just people or cows mattered, but rabbits. Millions of them could be out there gnawing away at all that red normalized difference vegetation. Being seminocturnal and rather smaller than a 20-meter SPOT pixel, they don't show up in pictures. No one knows how to factor them in, or whether (as Savory would likely conclude) the lack of grass reflected the lack of heavy animal impact to break soil crusts and recycle minerals. Next year, perhaps it would be grasshoppers.

Truly remote deserts, of course, present even greater difficulties, and satellites' all-seeing eyes have revealed more fascinating phenomena than they come close to explaining. In that very year, 1992, for example, a paper originating at Texas Tech by one of the foremost scholars of deserts, Harold Dregne, threw the whole presumption of an advancing Sahara into question. Expanding on work by a Swedish scholar, he found that space photos of the vegetation index between 1980 and 1990 showed the southern frontier of the Sahara moving so radically back and forth from north to south from one year to the next that he concluded the matter would take another half-century to settle. Even around settlements and water holes, the desert turned green when it rained. When it didn't, it didn't. However, satellite technology is simply too young to show a major aspect of desertification that everyone Dregne's age actually living in the Sahel has witnessed—the massive shift from perennial to annual grasses. The loss has been so rapid and so complete over such wide areas that the difficulty of finding enough good perennial grass to thatch a traditional hut has become a cause of social crisis even in areas where the land looks green and rainfall averages out to twenty inches a year.

One of Susan Moran's former professors at the University of Arizona sees the problem philosophically. Stuart Marsh spends a lot of his time working on Drought Early Warning Systems at the Center for Arid Lands Studies. There he taps away at his computer terminal organizing multicolored images of Senegal into what the trade calls a GIS, for "geographic information system."

"Modeling will never live up to our hopes for it," he says. "Life is far too complicated, but you can see an awful lot by standing back and looking at it from new perspectives. I'm trying to develop a user-friendly system that will allow a government clerk in Africa to assimilate all kinds of information at once.

"There are correlations between the socioeconomic indicators and environmental ones that we are only beginning to consider. If you compared this year's flood on the Senegal River to last year's and overlaid it with data from a spreadsheet showing grain prices in local markets or the location of highly supported schools, or plantings of cash crops (as opposed to subsistence crops), perhaps you might learn something about how vulnerable the area was to famine.

"Just as Susan Moran is trying to do with the energy balance, the challenge is always to find a way to get the most detailed information you can out of what is, really, very crude data. You do this by looking for interactions and correlations or mathematical transformations that will reveal a pattern in data that look random. We're not very good yet, but we're getting better all the time."

Step, step, step, step, step, step, step, thump. The one hundredth random point. A direct hit on a live blue grama clump. Warm season grass, mature, soil-capped, no sign of animal life, but as the two men straightened creakily to their feet, they saw two long-legged birds take wing in middle distance and zigzag low over the grama. The two brown bars over their white breasts reminded Royce of the markings of pronghorn antelope.

"Killdeer," said Royce. "Must be a nesting pair."

"Guess so," said Dennis.

The transect was almost as static as it statistically could be. Ninety-six times the nearest perennial plant was blue grama. Four small sprigs of winterfat accounted for the rest. Of annuals, four small lamb's quarters sprouts and one tumbleweed. The soil surface remained generally crusted over and sealed against the penetration of water or roots. Not one new perennial seedling registered anywhere in the tally, but the corner of the frame hit dead grama mats fourteen times. It hit rock or bare ground forty-four times, lichens and other litter twenty-one times, and live grama twenty-one times. The fact that every bit of the grama grew in its matted form indicated that it had been grazed, but it showed no sign of dying from this.

Royce and Dennis might as well have made their survey by satellite. Nothing about the soil surface showed any sign of past or potential change—no masses of decomposing litter, no disturbance of the crust, no flush of new growth. If they had had to present an academic paper on the subject, they could only have argued that the land had reached some level of subclimax at which it would likely stay unless something radical happened to it. Because of all the bare ground and the low growth habit of grama, it wouldn't even carry a fire.

Royce wanted to take at least one more transect before the day wore out, but he and Dennis drove around inconclusively for so long that they lost the chance to actually measure another 100 points. Before agency quitting time they hammered in a marker near the dry wash bed where the main water tank stood but left the work for another day. They chose the place because it would surely get some animal impact and the soil and vegetation was different. It contained blue-green clumps of western wheat grass and some purple bee flowers.

"If any place will change, this will," said Royce. The big rusty water tank sat in what passed for a glade in the arid context of Tracy, but one could see by the way the rabbit brush and snakeweed petered out within fifty yards of it that something had already made an impact on the place. As they drove away toward the cattle guard, another long-legged bird flew up ahead of the pickup and skimmed off a ways on dextrous wings.

" 'Nother killdeer," said Royce.

"No," said Dennis. "That's an upland plover. A rare bird around here, and he's all alone."

13

The Theoretical Question Redux

Dennis Lamb and Royce Wheeler spoke little as they drove down off Tracy, the wings of the lonesome upland plover flashing ahead of them in the westering sun, the green government pickup waddling over the grama mat. Dennis was lost in the arguments of his non-job-related preoccupation, Royce preoccupied by regret for having taken only one transect. It all added up to the same thing, however, a vague existential angst that fate might have already decreed that nothing would ever get better but would hold them responsible anyway.

They were up against the Big Question once again. Can people work any long-term good for their efforts, or are we just lemmings with delusions of self-importance?

One way or another, of course, nearly everyone else in the system also felt called to do something to it or about it, from the AWDI engineers concerned about delivering water to sustain the growth of cities to the politicians at the environmental conference in Rio to the plover scouting for a mate. The impulse to make things better kept the remote sensing crowd bent over the satellite images on their terminals, the atmospheric modelers trying to psyche out global changes, and the makers of geographic information systems correlating ever more data to figure out what was really going on. If you could understand, maybe you could make things better—if you knew what "better" was.

And around them all, the election campaigns of the summer of 1992 had produced no end of voices presuming the wisdom and power to improve everything: "Improve, grow the economy, create jobs, invest in progress, the free enterprise system, restore hope, vote for me!" Even in the Saguache County Commissioner's race, "Robert Philleo, the Progressive Candidate" attacked the status quo for failing to advance the common weal. True, some members of the status quo questioned Philleo's background. He was a scholar of social psychology and organizational behavior, who had retired to Crestone from the American University Department of International Relations—which was normal enough—but rumors circulated that his wife's mongrel, because of its markings, was the reincarnation of a failed Dalai Lama. But no matter, in Crestone all recycling was progress. Among the academic disciplines, both ecology and economics have had mixed success at defining progress scientifically.

Ecologists use the word "succession" to sum up the result of the irrepressible impulse of living things to progress, grow, and better their condition, and of all the terms in the jargon, none discomforts them more. In fact, nobody completely understands its implications, and this ambiguity raises particularly inconvenient questions in deserts, where conditions are erratic, constraints severe, and any sort of progress tenuous.

Royce, for instance, had reason to wonder whether succession could ever overcome the stagnation evident in his transect, and no doubt Dennis had parallel doubts about his emotional wasteland. Although they had faith, past experience could have supported an argument that succession did not exist at all and things generally got worse instead of better anyway. Succession implies paradox. The spirit to progress may be irrepressible, but material consumption at least cannot go on indefinitely in a finite world. The whole discipline of ecology rests on the assumption that the ecosystem is closed. If succession does exist, how does it operate, and where does it fit into a world of limits?

The first scholar of rangeland, Frederic Clements, drew no philosophical conclusions about succession when he introduced the word in 1916. He used it to describe the obvious fact that plant communities developed by stages, each stage creating the conditions required by the following stage. All living things act on their environment, he observed, in effect creating new environments. Many species, from beavers to bacteria, appear to do this in a totally self-serving way, but their very success invariably opens niches for other species. By doing their own thing, these in turn open yet more niches, and so on down to the politicians mouthing slogans. That's succession.

Thus, lichens that could survive on bare rock would begin to reduce it to soil less hospitable to lichens than to small annuals, which would form yet more soil and shelter for perennials, and so on toward ever greater substance and complexity until some limiting factor such as climate stopped the process. Clements hypothesized that the resulting "climax community" would use energy, water, and minerals to maximum possible efficiency and would remain stable forever unless struck by catastrophe.

Clements's production-minded successors came to lose patience with this elegant theory, however, when they found only dubious examples of stable climax and an enormous variety of stages. Also, they observed that catastrophes were endemic, particularly in semi-arid environments. They did to Clements what Lenin did to Marx, who said climax communism would rise naturally out of the last stages of capitalism. If scientific argument foretold what should happen, why wait? they argued. Why dwell on distracting anomalies if one could develop direct, scientific ways to make the system perform according to plan? Let the vanguard of the proletariat pick a likely climax and enforce it.

The concept of succession itself, however, remains powerful, precisely because it describes why this approach has seldom succeeded.

Succession is what happens because life, stubbornly and consistently, runs counter to entropy, building, creating, and bettering itself wherever the chance exists. Poets grasp the significance of this more easily than scientists because the latter insist on measurements, and the essence of life is quality, not strictly quantifiable, even with transects of 100 random points.

Robert Frost observed a wave breaking backward on a flowing stream in "West Running Brook":

> And it is time, strength, tone, light, life, and love—
> And even substance lapsing unsubstantial;
> The universal cataract of death
> That spends to nothingness—and unresisted,
> Save by some strange resistance in itself,

Not just a swerving, but a throwing back,
As if regret were in it and were sacred.
It has this throwing backward on itself
So that the fall of most of it is always
Raising a little, sending up a little.
Our life runs down in sending up the clock.
The brook runs down in sending up our life.
The sun runs down in sending up the brook.
And there is something sending up the sun.
It is this backward motion toward the source,
Against the stream, that most we see ourselves in,
The tribute of the current to the source.
It is from this in nature we are from.
It is most us.

Not just a swerving, but a throwing back. Thus weeds invade the plowed field. People fall in love and build even as they age. The lichen breaks down the mother rock to living soil. On the flood of entropy, some force explained by neither physics nor chemistry throws back this wave of creativity. It is as undeniable as gravity. It is fragile but infinitely patient, and it screws up plans that do not respect it. It might yield on one front while flanking on another. It can remain latent for centuries but does not fail.

Succession is a much subtler process than even Clements himself imagined and far more interesting than mere tooth-and-claw survival of the fittest. If a creature's fitness often depends on its context as much as its strength, and if its context changes according to its success, then definitions get shaky. Thus tumbleweeds, cited in the textbooks as "hardy pioneers" of barren land, aren't hardy enough to compete after healthy perennial grass takes hold. Nor does head-to-head competition alone account for the development of communities. Cooperation (symbiosis, in biology) plays its part, as well as the fact that the "success" of one species or individual frequently creates opportunity for predators, and predators cannot survive if too successful.

Although the original dogma still survives in many textbooks, Clements's critics correctly pointed out that the force of life seldom drives succession forward in the linear progression to climax that he predicted. Moreover, some catastrophes fall very far outside nature's presumed Plan—the Industrial Revolution, for example, or the human introduction of exotic organisms into habitats where they run amok. Could succession respond according to the classical theory? Many have said no, succession really was out of date now, and made a further case for campaigns of eradication or preservation. The deep ecologists, on the other hand, say, Just wait.

Small wonder, though, that Clements's extrapolation on his brilliant insight was simplistic. When he published in 1916, few scientists or mathematicians would have suggested any other pattern or even dignified what actually happens with the word "order," had they managed to see it. The most advanced mathematicians of the time had hardly begun speculating about the infinite domain of "nonlinear" equations—those self-generating skeins of relationships and feedback loops that so fascinated the young Devraj Sharma because they were thought to be insoluble due to the fact that they slide into chaos. Succession is not only "nonlinear." It is at least partly "stochastic" as well, which makes it an order of order derived directly from chaos. "Stochastic" is a bit of postmodern jargon that describes a system that organizes itself not by relationships definable by equations of any kind but by random chance. Scientists of the old school find this hard to accept. In particular, ecologists, sociologists, and economists, long committed to bringing mathematical rigor to their "soft" disciplines, have resisted the idea far longer than the mathematicians and physicists who first recognized the elegance of chance.

Examples of stochastic order abound in nature, from the infinite variety of symmetrical snowflakes to the braided delta of the Nile to the vein structure of a leaf. Take a piece of graph paper and draw a line that advances straight ahead two squares for every coin landing heads and turns oblique right two squares for every tail, and the line makes a stochastic series of loops, random and full of anomalies, but of similar size and as easy to distinguish from other stochastic patterns as a pea vine is from kudzu. The only way to influence a stochastic pattern is to change the odds or the rules of play. Whole communities develop according to rules and odds, too, which also assert a pattern over time, because life never stops flipping the coin. Human enterprise can and often does impose change but often unwittingly distorts the underlying odds in ways that subvert the enterprise itself. Thus, poisoning pests vastly increases the survival odds for resistant strains, and resting rangeland to restore it can destroy the chances of new seeds sprouting. All too often, attempts to impose or preserve a particular "climax" community create conditions guaranteed to produce something else, as many totalitarian politicians have discovered.

So frequently and so ingeniously has nature reacted thus to so much human endeavor that it would seem in fact to have an intelligent campaign of opposition. The conflict, however, stems from our failure to recognize the power of succession.

Succession will attack anything overblown and monotonous. The plague of grasshoppers it sends into the grain crop today it may destroy with a swarm of gulls tomorrow. The Army Corps of Engineers can channelize a stream, but meanders, a good example of stochastic order, will start forming at once, and one day a beaver will show up. "If the whole world were to be paved over with asphalt, one day a crack would appear in the asphalt; and in that crack, grass would grow," wrote the Russian writer Ilya Ehrenburg in reference to Leninist politics, but he might have meant shopping malls. Similarly, most modern agriculture involves forcing back succession to the point of an annual monoculture on plowed ground, a forced infestation that we defend against relentless diversity by killing bugs and weeds.

Succession abhors simplicity. Life favors more species, if often fewer numbers of each species in any community. It tends to elaborate the food chain so that the energy flow (entropy) passes through the maximum number of organisms. It seeks to make the most of material, too, assembling fantastic compounds from simple elements, adding quality to quantity wherever it can, and passing it through the system again and again. This dynamic wealth, created as, in Robert Frost's words, the sun runs down in sending up the brook, is the only kind of wealth ecology recognizes—ecological capital, "solar dollars," in Savory's lingo. Individual species and communities may rise and fall, but the general thrust never shifts toward simplicity or sterility except under pressure, and never permanently. According to the classic theory, diversity also produces stability because population swings and infestations can assume drastic proportions when a community has only a few species to begin with. Agricultural monocultures, especially, amount to super-niches for outbreaks of other species. A single pest can devastate vast areas planted to genetically identical seed. Wealthy human communities dependent on a single crop or industry can turn to ghost towns in a year, as Bonanza and other boomtowns of the valley did when the price of silver fell. A community that carries its eggs in many baskets has more resources and possibilities and less exposure to disaster, according to the theory.

Stability is the wrong word, however. Some low successional monocultures, like the grama grass on Tracy, are remarkably stable, and other remarkably complex communities can topple like a house of cards at the gain or loss of one species, often a predator. Succession tends toward "health," not stability. Is the couch potato likely to enjoy better health than the athlete? In terms of his knee ligaments, yes. In terms of his heart, no.

Stagnation may be stable, but it isn't health. But health, like Robert Frost's eccentric wave, isn't easily measured. It has a measurable diversity factor, an efficiency factor, a biomass factor, a resiliency factor, and a degree of dynamism, but as many possibilities as poetry. Maybe the poetry of brittle environments is haiku. Changing a few words can make it rich or poor. Jungles enjoy a bigger vocabulary but not greater genius.

Through succession, energy and raw material acquire the intangible value of quality, to which there is no absolute limit or definition. In that dimension, "growth" can perhaps indeed go on forever.

It's a pity that economists, whose theories have progressed across similar territory without coming so far, seldom talk to biologists. Economists confronted their version of the big questions of ecology over a century before Clements. Thomas Robert Malthus foresaw that human striving would someday crash into the finite capacity of the ecosystem, although he did not use the word, and his contemporary Adam Smith saw in the dynamics of a free economy an "invisible hand" that created new wealth by a process nearly indistinguishable from succession. Smith's conception of capital was extraordinarily radical at the time. Up to then wealth was considered finite, measurable in gold, and only to be obtained by taking it from someone else. Capital was dynamic. Thanks to the market, it could be invested to make more of itself.

Ecology and economics might easily have fused, but they didn't. Smith's heirs ignored his thoughts about the limits of his ideas, including his prediction that once a nation had acquired "its full complement of riches" growth would stop, and his somewhat Marxist fears that untempered economic ambition might reduce the labor force to a level "as stupid and ignorant as it is possible to become." They became obsessed by the invisible hand.

Juiced up by a dash of jargon about the survival of the fittest borrowed from Darwin (a biologist!), Smith's ideas justified the cutthroat capitalism and imperialism of the nineteenth century that gave Karl Marx such cause for thought. Marx reasoned that a system that reduced people to the level of draft animals would unleash social forces strong enough to change it—succession as radical as any described by Clements. Unfortunately, Marx also shared Clements's nineteenth-century belief in a clockwork world. He, too, missed the whole truth for failing to appreciate the random diversity of life, and economics has developed along other lines of thought.

Some form of Darwinized Smith, albeit tempered by John Maynard Keynes and others, now rules in all major schools of economics and major economic councils and institutions around the world, and it has diverged even further from the science of ecology. This "neoclassical" model has dropped Malthus because, they say, technology and the vast untapped resources of the oceans, Siberia, and even distant planets ensure unlimited supplies of raw material and energy for what might as well be forever. And since everyone knows the human appetite for goods to be insatiable, nothing really matters except ensuring that growth as measured by the production and consumption of goods and energy expands indefinitely.

An ecologist would indeed call this the lemming conclusion, but if you want a "hard" science in the Newtonian tradition, you have to quantify all the factors, and in matters of quality that can't be done. No one has even found a way to measure the value of unmined coal, because it depends on the future quality of life and technology and even on the impact of its own exploitation on the quality of other things. Experts on energy flow have tried to approach that problem by quantifying the amount of waste heat (entropy, again) that economic activity produces and how much the ecosystem can stand. They warn that it might not even let the Chinese enjoy an American density of cars and air conditioning. Quite apart from the greenhouse gases released in generating the power, the waste heat alone could have more dramatic consequences than the monsoon . . . they think. However, it's a safe bet that no economist even remotely close to economic policy or development strategy in Asia or North America honors their calculations as much more than "soft" curiosities. People consumed by the relationship of GDP (gross domestic product) to M1 (money supply) to interest rates to productivity ratios to unemployment to tariffs to taxes don't chase the dollar worth of butterflies. It's too hard.

Reflecting on such questions, American economic historian Robert Heilbroner wrote in his *Inquiry into the Human Prospect* in 1972, "Therefore the outlook is for what we may call 'convulsive change'—change forced upon us by external events rather than by conscious choice, by catastrophe rather than by calculation. As with Malthus's much derided but all too prescient forecasts, nature will provide the checks, if foresight and 'morality' do not."

At the U.N. Conference on the Environment and Development in Rio, the difficulty of reconciling these two themes absorbed hours of debate. Economics ministers talked of "growth." Environmentalists talked of doom. Diplomats, skilled in oxymorons, called for "sustainable development," but no one offered an existing example.

"The present economic system is simply not adequate," said development tycoon and conference chairman Maurice Strong in his closing remarks to the conference. "This doesn't mean it needs to be scrapped, but it needs to be radically revised to bring it into tune with eco-realities. We need to move to a real eco-nomic system."

Better quality. Moral growth. Richer diversity. Increased efficiency. Cleaner air. Freer spaces. More love. "The backward motion toward the source, against the stream." The promise of succession in a finite world.

Of course, men like Royce Wheeler and Dennis Lamb and even Allan Savory didn't hang such metaphors on the problems of Tracy. They merely hoped to get succession moving again. Savory reviewed the monitoring report by Wheeler and Lamb and conjectured that land that stagnant would not awaken without animal impact, a dust-raising stampede on a scale the Whitten and Coleman cows in the demonstration area would not likely deliver. Maybe it would never happen until the civilization collapsed and a pack of wolves chased elk through there again.

Royce was afraid of that. He had never studied mainstream economics, but he had seen what the doctrine of unlimited resources did to land, and he wanted to think he had a role in succession.

14

Generations

After his sons took over the ranch, George Whitten, Sr., and his wife, Grace, had turned the big old two-story white farmhouse under the cottonwoods where they had raised their children over to George, Jr., and built a small one-story place a quarter-mile away. It perched like a guest cottage on the corner of the property and faced away toward Antora over the Rio Grande Canal and the empty levels of the Tracy allotment but gave the elder Whittens a window still on the younger generation. One morning shortly before the Whitten brothers moved their herd to Tracy, George, Sr., set off with George, Jr., toward Donnie's place to deliver some parts he had picked up in town to repair an old hay rake. He looked forward to seeing his sons together. It had hurt him considerably that they had not kept the ranch together as a working partnership. His vision of succession had the imperial cast of his grandfather's generation, a "big piece of country," as Westerners say, where his family would reign in stability and wealth forever.

He nevertheless still counted it a blessing to have two sons raising children on the land. It amused him that the geriatric bunch rake they were about to fix had survived the division of the empire as common property *because* it was obsolete. George, Sr., did not share his sons' enthusiasm for Holistic Resource Management, but he enjoyed the fact that his old-fangled rake served better and cheaper than modern wind rowers and swathers to create the hay piles that both sons now used in winter. A few bolts would give it the mechanical equivalent of a hip replacement and keep it going well into the next generation.

George, Sr., knew how miragelike visions of empire were. After his own father died, he, his brother Donald and his sister Virginia had carried on as a partnership, but that, too, had eventually come apart, and not just because the Whitten line carried some ornery genes. Life moved on. He accepted the remorselessness of change with as much amazement as regret.

He admitted that progress promised him and his wife a quality of old age their own parents had never contemplated. They had already managed to retire from winter altogether. They spent it now in a trailer court in Yuma, Arizona, square dancing through the evenings without a care for frigid nights in the lambing pens or March storms that blasted across the level, piling tumbleweeds against his fences and burying them under sand. Overall progress, though, was not so easy to measure. Even the hard economic data looked unconvincing.

During his seventy-five years, the population of the United States had grown one and a half times, and world population had tripled. Colorado was five times more crowded and metropolitan Denver eight times bigger. Economic activity had picked up phenomenal speed as the U.S. gross domestic product doubled six times and the power of a single dollar halved itself three times. World energy consumption had quintupled to nearly 9 million megawatt years, of which the United States accounted for a third. Roads were paved. Vehicles air conditioned. And leisure had become an industry, not only in Yuma, but even in the valley itself, where retirees, tourists, hunters, and the spiritual seekers of Crestone spent welcome amounts of money.

Yet in relative terms, the valley had not progressed much at all. Not counting the Bonanza silver mining boom of the 1880s, the population of Saguache County had peaked in about 1929 and then declined in every census until 1980. In 1990 it counted 4,619 residents, 19 fewer than in 1920, although the accuracy was questionable in both cases. At least half a dozen settlements had actually disappeared, along with post offices, newspapers, and a couple of railroads. Its per capita income, half of Denver's, was next to worst in the state at $11,000, including welfare. (Costilla County at the south end of the valley took the prize.) In constant dollars, its per capita income had actually dropped 12 percent since 1980. "If they closed our office, half the county would move out tomorrow," the state social services officers in Saguache liked to say. But this was not unusual. The population and relative prosperity of thirty of Colorado's sixty-three counties peaked before World War II, and a couple more before 1960.

Much of the dynamism of the old days had come from mining, which had petered out slowly but not completely since the turn of the century, but the fact was, something similar had happened worldwide during the same time. The population of the countryside from Saguache County to the Sahel had become markedly old. The invisible hand swept young people into the towns. Denver had boomed, but Calcutta, Dakar, São Paulo, Mexico City, Los Angeles, and a thousand others had grown even faster from people pouring off the land, and it wasn't obvious from the ten o'clock news that quality of life was improving in any of those places. Denise Whitten, George, Jr.'s daughter, high school honor graduate and star of the 4-H club, had moved that very year to Denver to find work and be with her boyfriend.

Still, it was possible not to worry about this while you had machinery to fix. From Donnie's place, George, Sr., rode with his two sons in Donnie's four-wheel-drive Dodge out to where the tines of the rake arched like the rib cage of an ancient reptile above the chico at the edge of the irrigated hay ground.

The rake had failed where it folded for towing on the highway. The repairs only amounted to some jacking, tugging, and banging. Anyone watching from a distance would have recognized a father and his sons. They shared hand gestures and the slightly rolling gait of short, well-muscled men, and although time had bent and dried George, Sr., a little, the square dancing had preserved a certain quickness that obviously ran in the blood.

As they worked, he glanced west toward the ridges of the San Juans receding into the blue and remarked, "By this time of year we would be moving up there. And you know I wouldn't mind packing me an old burro and doing that again."

He had been the sheep man among the three Whitten partners of his generation, and the move to summer range had set the rhythm of his youth.

"Why not?" said Donnie.

"I might surprise you," said his father. "But I don't know anyone else who's up to it. It can snow and get nastier 'n Hell up there in June, but it's a crime, all that grass going to waste now."

Both sons acknowledged that it was, but he looked at them

sharply. "That talk of overgrazing's so much malarkey," he said. "What the government really wants is to make the country a big playpen for 'recreationists.' " He spat out the word. "They've already got more power than we do."

Again, his sons agreed, even though both belonged to the Sierra Club and George, Jr., competed in trail bike races against recreationists from all over the West. Still, like everyone they knew who still lived from the land, they saw those who could only know it through recreation as exiles to be pitied, if not scorned. They also recognized that their father made some of the remarks he did because he pitied them a little for their progress.

It was so whenever he mentioned going up in the San Juans. George, Jr., actually had his own half-memories of the old sheep drives—blurry like an immigrant child's image of the Old Country. His recollection of riding in a wagon behind a team through high grass came from that. But the story was not just of sheep.

"I grew up with sheep," George, Sr., liked to say. "My dad didn't. After he bought his first herd in 1915, he went back to the same man for some more, and the fellow told him, 'Hell, I already sold you the worst stock I had.' That's how it was starting out. He learned. I grew up with a second band financed by old Gordon Gotthelf out of Saguache. Gotthelf ran the bank and ran about 5,000 sheep himself in an operation he put together by foreclosing on homesteaders and Mexicans, but we managed to hold onto ours. What the boys have now is from that stock, but of course it's been bred up to something very different now."

It was different. It counted for something in Saguache County in 1935 to wean a 75-pound lamb. Donnie reckoned on 90. A 70 percent lamb crop had satisfied his dad, who culled a ewe that bore twins because she couldn't keep either of them strong enough to survive a trail drive. Nowadays a herd had to wean nearly 150 percent to begin to pay.

"What you have now is good, of course," said the elder Whitten, "but our ewes were strong and as well-muscled as deer, and yours wouldn't last a day where ours went."

It was a line that his sons had heard often enough, and they took no offense. This old life that reeked of sweat, boiled coffee, and damp wool had a quality to it that, they knew, "recreationists" would pay a lot for. In fact, their neighbor Ken Schmittel's son and daughter-in-law made a living packing dudes into the high country all summer.

"We'd set out from here with three or four burros, two horses, two Mexicans, and me," said George, Sr. "One of the burros carried three fifty-pound sacks of salt. The others carried our camp. A lot of the route went above timberline, so we would pack firewood on the horses. I had enough Spanish to get along, but the conversation wasn't all that deep anyway.

"By the time you got to the first camp on the South Tracy, you were tired as a damn dog. Everybody got stronger after that. From there you went into the foothills. In two days you came over into Sanderson Gulch, where old man Mosier had a wheelbarrow gold mine. You only made three miles or so a day, and you had to let the herd spread out as it moved, so they could eat. That took some skill, but of course the Forest Service didn't like it. They thought you should move fast and stay on the trail, but if you did that you ended the day with hungry sheep, and you'd stay up all night herding them.

"Six days out you got to Carnero Creek, which sometimes flowed pretty good, so pushing them across was a hell of time, but the next day you got to the La Garita corrals. That was a Forest Service deal, and there used to be a shearing plant there with a big one-cylinder diesel engine that we later salvaged and used over here. That's where the bands all came together and waited for the rangers to count them through."

The scene was pure Western Bruegel, the canyon low hung by the smoke of campfires and ringing from the bellows of animals and men, the one-lung engine that drove the shearing machinery and inside the shed the racket of clippers. All through the 1920s, and 1930s, over 100,000 sheep went onto the public land along the La Garita Stock Driveway every summer. Separated by a quarter mile or less, the nearly endless succession of bands would begin their march simultaneously at the sun's first ray to avoid the chaos of a mixup, and on they went for the better part of a month deeper and deeper into the high country along the Continental Divide, the bands peeling off one by one to their designated summer allotments as the column passed. George ticked off the route by the Spanish names: Cerro del Castor

(Beaver Mountain), Rincon Quemado (Burnt Cove, which was burnt over), Bole Alto (High Peak, 12,944 feet).

The Stock Driveway, it was said, had once been a main Indian trail over the Divide to the southwest, and potsherds and arrowheads turned up all along it. From the ridges high above the boomtown of Creede, the trail dropped down a rock slide "steeper'n Hell" past giant gargoyles of volcanic tuff, now protected as Wheeler Geologic Area.

"I learned about liquor one Fourth of July when we left the sheep there and slipped down into Creede for the celebration. We had to set up for a day with the sheep to sober up. I was just a kid and sicker'n Hell on wine."

Around Creede, the miners had stripped the evergreen forest right up to timberline, and "quakies," aspen, the "hardy invader" of clear cuts, had come in thick. Succession. "You had to scout ahead on a horse to see where the next band was. Through Rat Creek and West Willow Creek it got so rough you had to stay on the trail. That was hard on the sheep, but then you came up on Snow Mesa and you could slow down to let them fill up. That is one beautiful place, just level country up on top of the world."

Snow Mesa, Mesa de Nieves, is unique in the Western world, about 50 square miles of tundra over 12,000 feet above the sea: springy turf laced by secret veins of glassy water, calf deep in sedgy green and carpeted in bloom all summer—yellow alpine avens and wallflowers, blue forget-me-nots, sky pilots, and gentian, and splashes of red paintbrush.

"At the end of that was Spring Creek Pass, where Dad resupplied us with his truck. If we'd lost a day he'd be madder'n Hell."

By July 10, the band reached the Whitten allotment, where George and the other herders lived on beans through August, looked out for coyotes and bears ("A bear could knock down a whole bunch at once"), and conversed in Spanglish.

They only needed about fifteen days coming back. The lambs were strong by then, and the route downhill through the white-trunked quakies now was shimmering in gold.

"In September you could get caught by snow and that was just awful." Just awful enough to make a man equally glad that he'd had to face it and prayerful that he'd never have to again.

A week or so after they got back to the valley floor and weaned off the lambs, they drove them, 700–800 in a band, to the railroad in Moffat.

According to Donnie's Aunt Virginia, between 1910 and 1940 more livestock was shipped on the narrow gauge at Moffat than from any rail station in the country. "The herds camped out on the flat around there for miles. You could count them by the clouds of dust coming in from every direction."

Now, Donnie and Karen sold their lambs, the twins that weaned at 90 pounds, without such pageantry to specialty buyers, organic meat brokers who air-freighted the best cuts as far as New York City, no doubt to be eaten by recreationists.

"I'd like to have seen those times," said Donnie.

"Maybe," said his dad, "but it's over. We had to give up after 1969 because there weren't any more herders willing to do the work. After the Forest Service cut us back to one thousand head, you couldn't afford to pay much anyhow. You could hire wetbacks that knew sheep, but they didn't know the country. People thought the sheepherder was a stupid cuss, but for what he did, he was a true professional."

The Whittens' herders had all come from a family with the curiously parallel name of White that had lived next door.

"Gaspar White had a little sheepdog named Chico who was so smart he could do anything," remembered George, Jr. "With just hand gestures they could send him what seemed like miles to move a bunch of sheep."

George, Jr., had communicated so fluently with the White boys, Eddie, Dickie, and Roger, that when he entered first grade in Center he spent a week in the segregated class where the teacher smacked his knuckles with a ruler for uttering a Spanish word. "Those were my buddies," he says. "Things didn't get polarized until much later, when Cesar Chavez came to Center and tried to organize the field workers. "I can't speak Spanish any more," he adds, "but I still dream in it sometimes."

He is reminded frequently of those days by a ding in the kitchen wall of his parents' old house, which is now his. A .22 round lodged there after passing through Dickie White's right eye and out the back of his head.

"He was just messing around with the gun, but it did affect him. After that he tended to be moody and quick-tempered."

"They were as ornery a bunch as ever was," said George, Sr. "You had to kiss ass a lot to get 'em to do anything. But they were *real* professionals, and they knew the whole rope of the sheep business. When they wouldn't do it anymore, we were finished, but I don't say I blame them. It's a hard life, away from women, away from booze, and those boys were sharp enough to see there wasn't much future in it." Succession.

One of the White boys' uncles, Frank White, Jr., published a small history of the nearby community of La Garita from where they all hailed. George, Sr., treasures a copy as a kind of relic because it is the only record of those times, so recently lost, out of which everything else followed.

"Of course, it's the Mexican point of view," he says, "but it tells it like it was, and I can see how they might feel a little bitter."

The White family saw as much succession as the Whittens. Despite the name, they were in fact Spanish and of the old Southwestern stock. Frank did not call himself Mexican. "Somos puros (We are pure)," he would explain from his home in Denver. His grandfather, José Adolpho White, was born in El Rito, New Mexico, in 1878, after his mother, Soledad Trujillo, allowed a love-struck but elderly (he had soldiered in suppressing the Taos Rebellion of 1847) Anglo carpenter named Jim White to marry her. According to Frank, Great-grandmother Soledad had done this only to give a name to her unborn child, José, whom she gave upon birth to a cousin in Del Norte, Colorado.

José was a prodigy. Before his voice changed, he hired out as a bookkeeper to two other El Rito men, Damacio Espinoza and Susano Trujillo, who in 1858 had helped found the settlement of La Garita. By the age of sixteen he had bought and stocked his own ranch in Carnero Canyon and the two men made him a full partner. By the time he died, well up in his nineties, he had 3,000 sheep and a major block of stock in the bank of Del Norte.

La Garita, at the mouth of Carnero, was by then a thriving community with a church and convent, organized festivals and civic groups, including several *penitente* societies, those passionate vestiges of medieval Spanish culture that survived only at its most distant edge in the

New World. Small *ranchos* lined Carnero Creek and La Garita Canyon far back into the foothills, and the Whites were local aristocrats.

The Whittens' sheep operation did not end because the descendants of José Adolpho became too proud to hire out to an Anglo but because the whole community of La Garita and the White family stake there simply disintegrated. An unwinding of succession. Like the mining camps of Bonanza and Creede and the railroad town of Moffat and half of Saguache itself, La Garita and its people succumbed in the same changing of the times.

Frank, Jr.'s book tells how La Garita grew and died. The people, the Whites excepted, by and large failed to file properly for water rights under Anglo law and thus lost them to a handful of land developers downstream. The same thing happened to the grazing rights. When the open range on the national forest was quantified, broken into official allotments, and leased, most went to the bigger outfits, most of which were Anglo. "After that," says Frank, Jr., "the people could aspire to nothing more than subsistence farming on 'stolen' water and a couple of cows. They eked out the balance of a living cutting pit props and railroad ties off the public land"—that, too, not strictly legal—"and by herding, field work, and stints in the various mines that lasted up into the 1930s."

Then, piece by piece, the diversity of possibility, meager as it was, fell away. The mines closed. The wood market died. The seasonal field work fell more and more to labor contractors, who hired *braceros* straight out of Mexico. At some point, the whole could not sustain itself.

"For La Garita, the big change was the end of the mines," says Frank White, Jr. "The wood business allowed people to live independently on their own land."

This was another illustration of a complex succession. The old sheep business depended as much on the bits and pieces thrown up by the larger economy as it did on grass. It required young people who needed experience, surplus uncles and cousins, people in transition in a community that had succeeded far enough to provide many niches. No matter how much grass grew in the high country, the La Garita stock drives couldn't survive progress that left no place for manual labor generally. But the Whites' case was a little more straightforward.

"We *were* an ornery bunch," says Frank White. "José and his wife died without wills, and their children [that was Melia, Soledad, Lupe, Gaspar, Frank, John, Locario, Arthur, Jake, Trinidad, and Joe] fought over the estate instead of managing it. The only ones who gained were the lawyers. When it was over, what was left was sold for about a third of its value."

That happened in 1958, exactly 100 years after the founding of the settlement. The young people drifted away to Center, Del Norte, Alamosa, Denver, California, and beyond. Gaspar and his wife retired to Center and died in the conflagration of their mobile home. Dickie White showed up at a Center High School reunion a few years back, still moody but apparently doing well, but the Whitten brothers have lost track of their old playmates. La Garita no longer even has a zip code, and no Whites live there.

Frank White, Jr., a gentle man of middle age, still speaks English with the strong accent of the valley's first Europeans, although he works now for a Denver radio station. Now and then he makes the six-hour drive to Carnero Canyon to pick over the ruins of his past. He knows of Indian petroglyphs and has mapped and named by family many vague rectangles of rock and adobe out in the sage that once were houses surrounded by beans and chilies.

"They're so small, and the country is so dry and so rough, it just amazes me that anyone tried to live there," says Frank White.

When the hay rake was fixed, the three Whitten men rode back to Donnie's house for iced tea, a concrete benefit of progress into the age of rural electrification and iceboxes. They talked some about a local family named Santistevan who had tried to revive the old sheep cycle. They had gotten one of many vacated Forest Service permits, bought a big band of sheep, and hired some migrant hands.

"They were crazy," said George, Sr. "Once the knowledge is gone you can't get it back just like that. They didn't even have a dog that knew anything. When they went through here, you knew they were looking for trouble. And they found it."

In fact, they never even got to the Forest Service boundary before the whole thing fell apart. They didn't even negotiate all the fenced-up country on the valley floor with any grace, forgetting how much forage and water a huge band of sheep would require from private land.

Soon sheep were scattered from La Garita to Saguache. Every coyote within 100 miles came in and feasted, and little backyard sheep operations suddenly became popular throughout the county. Hardly anything survived the disaster.

"A few Spanish operators in the south end of the valley still do it," observed George, Jr. But at that moment they were sorely pressed. The Gulf War against Iraq had recently knocked the bottom out of wool prices. By some weird economic twist, the Fertile Crescent, birthplace millennia ago of the sheep industry, no longer produced enough to clothe Saddam Hussein's army for winter campaigns against the Kurds, so he had bought American wool.

In 1988, most of the La Garita Stock Driveway had become part of the Colorado Trail, a magnet for backpackers, recreationists. If George, Sr., did take a burro back up the La Garita Stock Driveway, he knew he would find Snow Mesa as beautiful as ever, but different. From his own wish to go there again, he could understand why people who toiled fifty weeks of the year under fluorescent lights would brave blisters and freak storms just to see it once. That was what they meant by quality of life, but why wasn't it worth the while of a wetback herder to enter that country on infinitely more challenging terms? Intuition told him that the same progress that had created one class had destroyed the other, but he found the irony of that too bizarre to articulate.

"Well, it's just a shame to think of all that grass up there going to waste," was all there was to say.

After he and George, Jr., left, Donnie and Karen went out to check their own sheep and move the wire that forced them, in the absence of a skilled herder, to graze holistically. As always they looked at grass, weeds, chico, and animal signs as they went.

"Damn if it doesn't feel better here," said Donnie, and he stamped on the ground and skipped a little to demonstrate. "The ground just feels a lot more healthy. Can't you tell?"

"Looks pretty good," said Karen. "And look at those cow pies. I think they really are breaking down much faster than they used to." She liked to see him enthusiastic. "I wonder how many other couples get excited about manure," she added. But it really was important to them. A better mineral cycle, a sign of the health of the land, of its wealth of life, that once they would not have noticed but now delighted them because it showed how small acts really could ripple through the long and funky food chain that supported them.

Like most ranchers, they had once dosed their animals with IVOMEC to kill intestinal parasites until they read that this also sterilized the dung and made it nearly indestructible. IVOMEC was the third best-selling product of the pharmaceutical giant Merck & Co. and had become an unquestioned staple in livestock operations and aid programs worldwide. No one questioned that, but here was a little succession of nearly invisible creatures that turned cow shit into fertilizer, and when the animals kept moving and did not graze over their own dung, they seemed to suffer little from parasites.

"And see, there's more of that vetch," said Donnie. Indeed, above the pale sward of desert grass a dark green, viny plant with the teardrop leaves of a legume outcropped thickly around the chico.

Years back, in the days before ecological arguments complicated anybody's idea of stock raising, their Uncle Donald had bought the seed from a curious old man who used to appear every summer in an old green van that he also lived in. He mostly sold alfalfa seed. There wasn't much hybrid alfalfa then, but the original desert stock (*Al falfa* is "best forage" in Arabic) had evolved over a century into Montana Common, Kansas Common, Arizona Common, and some derived from Turkestan, Cossack, Ladak, African, Nomad, and other strains that weren't common. The old man sold Colorado Common, and nobody knew exactly where he got it, but it liked Saguache Creek water.

"Try this vetch seed, too," the old man had said. "It's damn good feed and will spread by itself." Uncle Donald had thrown a few handfuls around the irrigation pump and out into his threadbare pasture and forgotten about them. A few years later, he died himself.

George and Donnie certainly did not have vetch in mind when they returned from Allan Savory's holistic seminar in 1985 all full of zeal for doubling their production. They had taken so seriously his message that succession on brittle rangeland required animal impact that that very summer they decided not to put their herd on Tracy and took in 500 extra cattle on a lease arrangement besides. They got the impact, all right.

"You'd be amazed what one thousand animals in a small area will do if you throw a flake of hay in there. We followed the book and never left them in one place long enough to overgraze, but we hammered the hell out of everything," recalls Donnie. And they lost money. The stock gained a pound and a half a day, but they had promised the owner of the extra cattle more and had to return most of his fee.

But then the following spring, out of nowhere, Uncle Donald's vetch had appeared, and year by year it slowly spread. The botanist from the Soil Conservation Service could tell them no more about it than that it was indeed vetch, a nitrogen-fixing legume. It convinced them that even if they didn't know how to profit by it yet, old Savory did know what he was talking about.

"The sad part is," said Donnie, "as far as succession goes, virtually all our real progress goes back to that one season, and we've never done anything quite that daring since. Now that we're two operations, it's even harder.

"It's like everywhere else. The problem is the people. If we could work together and use all our animals in one bunch, we might get somewhere. Up on Tracy I think we're going to do okay in the bottom land back up in the foothills and around the water points, but out there on the flat where all the grama is we'd have to have one thousand head and a herder and all the rest of it to make some impact, but that's a long way off. Right now the water wouldn't support it anyway."

They walked on in silence, looking at the ground for signs of change, for a new plant, for anything green invading where bare ground still persisted.

"I wonder," said Donnie after a while. "If we're doing better with the land than Dad did, and we're producing as much with half the land, why do you suppose we are not producing four times as much on twice the land? Is that progress?"

15

Stockman's Water

Water dries up in arid country but controversy over it, never. The AWDI fight woke valley residents up to the stakes and to the possibility of some new order, but the complexity of actually establishing one became all too rapidly apparent. If the invisible hand of succession were indeed destined to lead the people out of bondage, they would still probably wander long in the desert, and strange prophets would be called.

The first reminder of this came in the spring of 1992 in the form of a notice in the Center *Post Dispatch* of a community meeting to be held in the Moffat High School gymnasium in which one Gary Boyce of Crestone intended to discuss a new enterprise called Stockman's Water Company and to lay to rest certain rumors circulating about his relationship to American Water Development, Inc.

"Old Gary's always up to something," said Donnie, when he read the notice of the Moffat meeting. "You just never know what to expect." A few years older than the Whitten brothers, Boyce grew up on his grandfather's ranch just south of the old Whitten house near La Garita. Back in the fightin' time of their late teens, he had even run briefly with the same gang as George and Donnie, although being older and more interested in the sister of another member than bashing faces, he had tended to avoid violence.

"He raced motorcycles, and you can still see scars on the foothills where he used to train, and he used to drive around in these muscle cars, a souped-up Pontiac Trans Am and a one-seater racing car that he said was a Lotus Ford, and there were others that he kept in that big old white barn of his granddad's," Donnie recalled. "It amazed us that his parents were that generous, when most of us were on foot."

Then one day a number of men in uniform appeared and seized the cars, and Boyce.

Valley people don't forget such things, but they realize that almost anything can happen when the fury of youth boils over the meager diversions of life in a place like La Garita, and in Gary the fire burned fiercely. Not long after the car incident, a story circulated in Saguache County that Gary and his best friend, despairing of ever breaking through to a higher plane of existence by any conventional means, had pooled their money, a few thousand dollars, and set off to Vail, where they had never been, vowing to seduce and marry movie stars—and both had succeeded!

Several elaborate versions of this story hardened into legend, however, when Boyce surfaced some years later in Crestone at the side of a beautiful woman of means fifteen years his senior, although his own tale was somewhat different. In fact, Gary was at heart a cowboy and horseman, not a skier. He had drifted east and, drawn by the scent of oiled leather, manure, and money, had fetched up against the hunting and racing set of Southern Pines, North Carolina, which, after twenty years of it, his woman of destiny was finding as oppressive as he had found La Garita.

Joanne Schenck was indeed a movie princess of sorts, the daughter of Nick "The General" Schenck, who had presided over Loews and MGM through the great golden age of Hollywood. She was also one of the sanest, most genuine, and unpretentious women that ever walked into Crestone. She was intelligent and vital, her open, timeless face at once put people at ease when Gary introduced her as Mrs. Boyce, and she genuinely loved her new home.

"I would never think of going back," she often said. "I once spent eight months in Africa, and the wildness and power of those landscapes affected me deeply. It never occurred to me that there were such places here, but this is just as grand, and in the same way. I can't think I'll ever leave."

As for the fine horses, the steeplechasers and grand prix jumpers and the private racetrack she once owned—"I love horses, of course, but cattle are the main thing for us now. It suits the land."

It was Gary who continued to walk as a stranger in his own country, the mere grandeur of which he found insufficient and unfulfilling.

Flash and modesty blend subtly in Western fashion. Ordinary jeans and a snap-button shirt set an image that boots and hat costing perhaps hundreds of dollars project onto a much grander screen. On top of that, Gary's trademark was a red silk choker, and under his yoked cord jacket he packed a gun. No one else in the whole valley dressed even remotely like that, although all understood the iconography of the ensemble perfectly. Gary dressed what he meant to be, what he meant the whole valley to be, the prosperous rancher who draws from his own property not only substance but independence and a dash of romance and danger on top.

He and Joanne bought 5,000 acres that they called Rancho Rosado near Crestone on the periphery of the great Baca land grant, and besides ample corrals and sheds (painted red), they built a high-ceilinged residence of massive adobe with halls wide enough to U-turn a truck in and paved in subheated flagstone. There, in the company of an extremely loyal Rotweiler, they withdrew behind a high fence set about with motion-activated spotlights. Aside from faithful attendance at services at the Trappist monastery, Joanne went little into Crestone society. And Gary, as dark, trim, and taciturn as a Western hero should be, went about the country attending farm sales, meetings, and gatherings of all kinds but speaking seldom to anyone. Almost at once, however, the Boyces began a series of ambitious experiments in ranching—fine horses, "super cows" that produced embryos for transplanting and mass production, and purebred bulls of various kinds—but nothing panned out very well.

"His heart isn't in it," observed Donnie. "His mind's too restless." Like others, Donnie began to speculate that the Boyces might have another agenda, and this suspicion blew into the wildest kind of rumors when Boyce opened and then abruptly closed a newspaper called *The Needles,* a name that evoked both a muckraking spirit and the grandeur of the Crestone Needles that rose behind the town.

For seven issues in 1990, a staff recruited among the underemployed intellectuals of Crestone produced a series of scathing investigative articles on AWDI and its backers, supplemented by cartoons drawn by Boyce himself as "El Gato" (The Tomcat). Then, with issue no. 8 halfway through production, he called the staff together and pulled the plug without any explanation whatever. It was just over. He said there would be no discussion, and for two years no mention of *The Needles* passed his lips. One of his writers, a Crestone lady who had left Merrill Lynch for the valley "as the place I want to be if the planet goes belly up, which I think it will," had complained just prior about a series of phone threats and break-ins, which gave credence to a rumor that a hit squad of Maurice Strong's lawyers and thugs had "turned" Gary somehow at a rendezvous in a Denver motel. No shred of evidence existed for this allegation, and Boyce, who vehemently denied it, probably would have shot someone had an attempt been made, but in the fevered atmosphere surrounding AWDI the very worst rumors had become the most believable.

The hope of getting the real scoop drew more people to the Moffat H.S. gym than a varsity basketball game, including most of the regular sports fans plus bearded Father William McNamara from the monastery, a Tibetan in saffron, a black motorcyclist in dreadlocks, and some Forest Service men in uniform. The Whittens, including Aunt Virginia, came in force, and both Denver newspapers were represented. Joanne Boyce took her seat in the middle of the front row, and all the Samsonite chairs creaked in unison as Gary ascended the low stage and began to speak.

He continued for the better part of an hour and a half without notes in clear, well-ordered phrases, and nothing he said was expected. After remarking, only half in jest, that as his topic would be water he hoped weapons had been checked at the door, he began.

"Okay, friends, neighbors, and concerned citizens. First off I've a few introductions to make here this evening. Stockman's Water Company. I don't have any billionaires or any senators or governors or ex-governors, but that doesn't bother me a whole lot. I can do a lot better than that.

"Right here in the front row is the best friend I have in this world, my wife Joanne. I think most of you know me. I've had the privilege of being born and raised in the San Luis Valley. It's a great place to grow up. Especially a great place if you can be a little boy, especially if you are a little boy and you are also the Cisco Kid. I think everybody knew I was the Cisco Kid. I was born in Del Norte. I grew up in Monte Vista. Spent my summers on my grandfather's ranch up in La Garita. Rode around on my old paint horse.

"It was great being the Cisco Kid, but that was then. Now I'm a man. I'm a mature person. I'm now Zorro. But I'm Gary Boyce, of course. I'm a Saguache County rancher and recently the founder of Stockman's Water Company. Tonight I'd like to talk a bit about why I formed this company, and just a little bit about what I mean to do."

In obvious reference to Maurice Strong, he added, "I'm not going to be driving around the countryside like some Jehovah's Witness saying I'm going to save the world. Saguache County's number one foreign resident is gone to save the planet, so don't worry about it. In any case I'd like to start off by taking care of some old business. Why did I close *The Needles* newspaper?"

The chairs creaked again. Boyce explained how he had formed the paper in attempt to "deal with environmental issues from a rancher's point of view" but had come around to the AWDI scheme as the great unaddressed issue of the region.

"So, like I say, we had a good issue. We came out spurring, and I think we hooked them pretty good at every jump."

However, down the road he foresaw they would have to take on other issues.

"Well, the staff got out there and began probing for the soft spots, testing the waters, as it were. And a few people got nervous about that. By this time, they were very much aware of how I ran the paper. They were very much aware of the great blade that El Gato had, that he had clipped a few people to make sure the blood ran red. They began to speculate on where we were headed next.

"At this time I had some people approach me. They were people whom I highly respected, people who had known me since my boyhood. And they said we think we have an idea of what you're thinking about next, which is okay, because some issues need to be discussed. But at this time nobody really knew what we were about, and they didn't really know if I was Zorro or, as they said, a loose cannon rolling around the deck waiting to crash into the mast, and they said there are some issues around that we agree need to be talked about, but now is not an opportune time to do this. Now we need to stand shoulder to shoulder to show strong opposition against the water plan. And I agreed.

"I got the staff together and started to lay out our agenda, but it wasn't going to work. Not with the people I had pulled together, not when the boss had gone out and done the very thing I had said I would fire them for even thinking about. It wasn't going to work.

"Well, it came down to some choices. One, just come out and lay it on the line and say, Listen, there are some things we can't talk about. And we could simply turn *The Needles* into the *Mediocre Times.* But that was unacceptable.

"We had another choice, go back on my word. That wasn't acceptable either. I didn't want it said some day that it was El Gato and *The Needles* that broke down and lost the war [against AWDI].

"I closed the paper. That was it. I didn't tell the staff. I didn't tell anyone. So you see, it's not a very exciting story. Not a story of intrigue. It's a sad tale. I wasn't threatened. No one bought me off. Everything I did, I did to myself."

But of course it was exciting, chiefly because he hadn't revealed enough to make clear what he meant. What other powerful individuals had come to him? What other issue had he thought to raise that could have split the valley? More than that, nobody could imagine Boyce's motive for wanting to stir up anything else—this neighbor's kid who had escaped from his humble birthright only to return from the ends of the earth with everything that should satisfy a man for the rest of his life, who lived in a fortress, who packed a gun and a Clint Eastwood stare but had not made his own land pay. His former staffers in the audience gasped in disbelief because they, being Crestone immigrants more attuned to politically correct crusades, were least able to imagine a local issue as gripping as AWDI.

As he spoke, the tight-wound frustration of his youth crept into Boyce's short Clint Eastwood phrases, which thumbed the keen edge between plaint and sarcasm. In truth, the people who did not understand him then did not understand him now. They could not believe that the former Cisco Kid, now Zorro, might really want to do a bright and shining thing for the place that despite all his rage meant more to him than any place on earth. A new creaking of the chairs telegraphed unease in the audience. The ex-broker lady, whose best AWDI piece had vanished in the closing, ground her teeth audibly. And Boyce slowly and cryptically gave shape to his new campaign.

"A big part of the war is behind us," he continued. "We've got to keep our eye on American Water Development, sure. However, we're past the point where they're going to divide and conquer.

"You see in the media where farmers and ranchers are just that, one word, farmers-and-ranchers. Well, in many cases that's true. They're tied to the land. There are many similarities. Some do both, ranch and farm, but I must admit I've never met a true rancher who was much of a farmer. And on the other side of the coin, I don't know if there was ever a good farmer who was dumb enough to even try ranching.

"Well, now it is time for us, the citizens, the residents of the valley, to do a little dividing and conquering of our own. I certainly would like to do a little dividing. I'd like to divide the clear-thinking and the open-minded from the short-sighted and the biased. I would especially like to divide the young and sincere from the disingenuous and hypocritical. I would like to divide the vested interests from the freeloaders and charlatans. You bet."

Ranchers-and-farmers. Aha. There was a theme all right. The broker lady didn't get it yet, but for most of the rest it was just a matter of seeing what new twist Boyce might give to the old story—nomad and peasant, Cain and Abel.

"Just last winter a friend of mine died—lived down in Monte Vista—by the name of Jack Crooks, one of my dad's old hunting buddies. When I was a little boy, Jack taught me many things about hunting, fishing. Taught me how to pack a mule. Taught me how to set up a camp in the high country. Helped me a lot about the important things. Dad and I went down to Jack's funeral, and naturally we didn't turn down a chance to visit with old friends down in that part of the San Luis Valley—farmers. And quite naturally we wound up talking about the water.

"One of our old friends said, 'Gary, I'd like to thank you and your neighbors up there for standing by us in the fight for the water.' Then we talked a little more, and it became very clear to me that when we talked about water, we were not talking about my water and his water. We were talking about his water and the water on the farm next door.

"Now I was raised down there, and I understand that he did not mean anything malicious by this. He was not being facetious. It was simply a perception, and easily understood if you stop to think about it. You drive through the farming country, and you see the water coming from these sprinklers, and you see the potatoes planted below them. However, when you drive through the ranching country, you don't necessarily drive by a rancher who is out there with a garden hose watering down his cows. It's a little different.

"But this was not the first time that I had heard this conversation. I think the first time was about thirty-seven years ago. I was about seven or eight. We lived out in the middle of the farming district, and during the winter a lot of the farmers would come to my mom's kitchen for coffee first thing in the morning, and they talked about water.

"Along about then, 1954 and 1955, it was very dry in the valley. The farmers were running their pumps twenty-four hours a day, taking all the water out of the river they were entitled to, maybe a smidgeon more. And there was other water. If you left that part of the valley and went up through Saguache County to the ranching district, you could see water spread out across the meadows. In some ways this disturbed them, that their crops were on the verge of burning up, and yet up there in Saguache County you had a bunch of archaic saddle bums that now called themselves ranchers running water all over God's creation growing grass to feed a bunch of cows. They realized that that water was probably more productive growing crops.

"I told my grandpa, 'Great Uncle Kelsie says all you Saguache ranchers are a bunch of water wasters.' And, well, he didn't always agree with his brother, but he explained that Mother Nature created this valley with different parts, and everybody simply had to do the best with what they had to work with.

"Well, the farmers, depending on water the way they do, gave this a lot of thought and developed a very ingenious plan. You see, we measure the water at Del Norte and we don't measure it again until we get down just north of the New Mexico state line. So it's simple. We simply go into Del Norte and borrow a little extra water, and then we go over here in the Closed Basin and dig a little ditch, and we pay it back just south of Alamosa. Borrow it in Rio Grande County and pay it back in Saguache County. I've been trying to use [a plan like that] at the bank. I take the loan, and they get the neighbors to pay it back.

"But that's not exactly how the Closed Basin Project works. It is working on some things that are beneficial to us, to the rancher. We've had some problems taken care of, we ranchers, problems we never knew we had. I guess we've had 'em here in Saguache County for a number of years. One big problem, it seems we've had evapotranspiration, right here in River City. A beautiful word, evapotranspiration.

"It reminds me of an old story out of Texas. They had a big malaria epidemic in this town, and a group of cowboys came riding in off the range. Probably hadn't been to town for a month or two. The judge went and stopped them in the street, said, 'Listen fellas, I gotta warn you. We got a lot of trouble with malaria.' Now these were Texas boys, and that made 'em fighting mad. So the leader answered, said, 'We're behind you, Judge. We see any Malarians, we'll run 'em out of the country.'

"Well, what we're working on here is evapotranspirators. But some of us ranchers got together and got to studying up on this deal. We're way ahead of those Texas boys. And we found out about this evapotranspiration. And we come to find out it's not as bad as malaria. In fact, it's just part of what Mother Nature uses as one of her tools. It's part of the natural chain of events, like growing brush and salt grass and wheat grass, sand grass. Grass. Like the stuff that cows eat, and the deer and the elk and the antelope.

"Evapotranspiration is a process that, as these big spring storms begin to blow, helps keep the dirt out of your boots, and out of your eyes, your nose, and your ears. Evapotranspiration is part of the process of moisture going up into the atmosphere, moving over above these mountains, condensing, falling back to earth as precipitation, forming streams and going back down onto our ranches. A pretty good deal for an old cow. Kinda hard for an old cow to get along without this process. Like the deer, the elk, and the antelope. If you kill the grass, create a situation where the grass won't grow, you not only damage the grass-eating creatures, you kill the fish. It sounds kind of crazy doesn't it, but that's the way it works. It's all tied together. One big circle.

"All you have to do to look at what's happening is take a saddle horse and ride off from the edge of this town to the southwest toward Center and Del Norte, and you'll ride out through a lot of brush country. However, you start wondering why this is all brush. You keep running across these old hay corrals, little squares and rectangles fenced in with rusty barbed wire. You don't necessarily have to ride out there. Just go into Moffat and talk to some of the old hay contractors, Kenneth Biggs, Charlie Bunker, Ralph Mitchel. They'll tell you about the hay corrals. There was hay all over that country. By the end of summer, they had so many stacks of hay out there it looked like a forest.

"Because the old-timers weren't a bunch of fools, they didn't go out and build hay corrals in a brush patch. There used to be hay meadows. And the reason there aren't hay meadows any longer is water. Where'd the water go? Good question. We know where it didn't go. It didn't just off and evapotranspirate up into the old atmosphere and disappear. It's being used in other places.

"However, not everything that's happened in that situation has been harmful. Just drive down into the farming district. It's a lot different down there now from when I was a kid. If you drive down there, you can see a lot of new houses with cars and pickups in the driveways, even motorcycles, motorboats, motor homes. You see a lot of new buildings—potato storage, potato processing. You see a lot of machinery. Tractors, big green John Deere tractors. They don't even haul the machinery out to be repaired anymore. A lot of these guys have their own shops with all the special tools. They've done a good job. It looks great. They have a lot to be proud of.

"Well, you drive through the Saguache County ranching district, things look a little different. That's what I'm concerned about. You don't see many new houses out in the ranching district in Saguache County. Most of the ranchers are living in the houses their folks lived in or their grandparents. That new car or pickup is an exception. There's hardly been a new barn or cow shed built in Saguache County in the last fifty to sixty years. Any tractor under ten years old is new.

"It's like my grandpa said, you have to do the best you can with what you have. You have to work with Mother Nature. But we've designed the plumbing, waterworks, the canals, the ditches, the laterals, the reservoirs, the Closed Basin Project. We've done a good job. The only beef I have with it is that in installing the plumbing we installed most of the spigots down in Rio Grande County, and most of the drains in Saguache County. But maybe that's the way it has to be.

"You've heard Judge Ogburn say, 'What's sauce for the goose is sauce for the gander.' However, every time we decide water policy in the San Luis Valley, Rio Grande County takes the gander and the sauce. The Saguache County rancher gets the goose."

At this point, the monk in the front row handed Boyce a card from which he read, "Do not forget to cuss the government! Signed, Father William McNamara." And everyone laughed for the first time.

"Father William didn't want to say that, of course," said Boyce. "However, I do know he spends a lot of time praying for the souls of politicians. And I will talk about them.

"You always hear politicians speak when you go to any water conference or water seminar, but you don't ever listen to them. It's the time to go the the men's room or get a cup of coffee, 'cause you already know what they're going to say. 'In the West,' says the politician, 'water runs uphill toward money.'

"Lord, I wish I had an acre foot of water for every time I've heard that. Of course it does. But what the politician would really like to say is that water runs uphill toward votes. Wouldn't that be great, to have the politician out there measuring cubic feet per second, gallons per minute, acre feet per annum? And wouldn't it be great if these politicians measured our water exactly the way they keep their checkbooks? Wouldn't that be great? Sure, turn the water over to the politicians. Let 'em tanker it in pork barrels from Mexico to Canada, from the Rocky Mountains to California. It'd be just great.

"There are a lot of folks who might want to vote on water. What about Denver, Boulder, Aurora, Colorado Springs, Castle Rock, those developments along the Front Range? Well, I don't have to tell you how that's going to turn out. I got a friend who lives over on the Front Range. He and his brother own a big ranch out east of Castle Rock, prime development land. They own a heavy equipment dealership in Aurora. They and some others own a bank in the Denver suburbs. I talk about water to him.

"He laughs. Says, 'Hey, that's great. Have a big water fight over in the San Luis Valley. Tie up the water tight as you can, 'cause one day we're going to need it over here, and when we need it, we're gonna come and get it.'

"He believes that, and his brother believes it, and most of their neighbors believe it. It's not off the wall at all. Every working day of the year in the United States of America the government condemns some property, the land, the house, the barn, a right of way, and sometimes water. They don't do it for the benefit of the few. Ostensibly it's for the benefit of the many, meaning several million people on the

Front Range are going to be more important than several thousand, and right now the cheapest water in the State of Colorado is right here in Saguache County.

"Because this is how it works. You get a notice. Your water has been condemned, or your property. Then the government sends an agent over. You're going to get fair market value. The government arrives here with a little list called a use list. I keep one right here in my pocket.

"He's gonna pay you a visit and talk about these uses. First on the list, 'historical use.' Have you been keeping proper records, or have you maybe been a little lax? Who's to say that you use this water the same as your granddaddy used the water? Well, maybe you might have to give up a little water to the state.

"So let's look at the next use, 'beneficial use.' Do you use your water all the time, put it to beneficial use? Aw yeah, always do. How do you know? How about that little old junior water right down in the bottom that sometimes runs and sometimes doesn't? Do you get any benefit from that? Well, maybe you do, maybe you don't. If you don't maybe you'll give a little water to the state.

"Now let's talk about 'expanded use.' Here you are doing your best to operate in the framework of historical use, but maybe you've gone too far and used a little more than you're supposed to, historically. Well, you might have to give some water to the state.

"Now here comes the real kicker. You're probably fed up by this time too. You're saying okay, this is enough. I've got this amount of water, and I water this amount of land, pure and simple. But you just thought it was pure and simple because we now have 'consumptive use.' It's not you who decides how much water it takes to grow a bale of hay. The government knows how much water it takes to grow a bale of hay, although you may disagree. The government agents are going to tell you about this little bill they have here in Colorado, the Colorado Pouring Water down a Rat Hole Bill. If you've been doing that, plan to give a little water to the state.

"So you started off the day thinking you had a big barrel of water. The government agent might wind up just handing you a milk pail. But don't take your milk pail of water and walk off just yet, 'cause we ain't done yet. We've got one more use. So far we haven't established how much that pail of water is worth.

"So now we get down to the big use, 'highest and best use,' a term you'll like to use. Right now the Saguache County rancher's highest and best use of his water is in direct proportion to what it takes to produce a bale of hay. You might get a lawyer to niggle around and get that agent to consider that it might be worth a little more after you run that bale through a cow, but it wouldn't be much.

"You can say, 'Hey, listen, we've seen that this water's worth a lot of money. Cities are willing to pay a lot of money for this water.' Then the agent is going to look at you and get that little gleam in his eye and inform you, 'That's good, but you don't have any way to get that water to the cities. All you can do is grow hay. You're in the Closed Basin, and you're locked out of the water market.'

"Now our friends down in Rio Grande County are a little more fortunate. They might go through the same wringer, the same list of uses, and they might come out with a pail of water, but their water is going to be worth more for the simple reason that it is used for growing potatoes. A sack of potatoes from time to time is worth more than a bale of hay.

"They start higher, but that farmer, fortunately, has an ace in the hole. He's going to take that agent down to the courthouse and talk to the judge. He'll say, 'Your Honor, it's true, I'm using the water for growing potatoes, but that's my option, it's my choice. However, should I or my children or my grandchildren wish to take that water to a higher and better use, we could do it first thing tomorrow. We'd simply leave it in the river, and down there in Albuquerque or El Paso, that water's worth whatever those city people want to pay for it, even though they might simply use it for recreation.'

"That government agent is going to come right back up here to Saguache County to the cheap water.

"Now after dealing with American Water Development for several years, when someone mentions water development, a lot of people might want to run outside and throw up. But stop and think about it. There's not a farm or a ranch in the entire San Luis Valley, not one, that is not part of water development. That's what we've been doing for the past seventy-five years, developing our water.

"That's what we've done. We've probably developed all of it, developed more than we should have. Some people want to go into the confined aquifer and develop that water. However, last year, down at the courthouse, we learned one thing about the confined aquifer. From all the experts, all the witnesses, all the engineers from both sides we learned one thing, and that one thing is, we don't know anything about the confined aquifer, so we don't want to mess with it.

"We have developed our water, and what we do with this water in the future is going to make a big difference in all respects for the Saguache County rancher. It's possibly going to make the difference between survival and extinction.

"It's hard to get a loan in Saguache County. Everything's going up, costs are going up, prices are going up, taxes are going up, insurance is going up, grain's going up, everything but the price of beef. It's probably gone up as much as it's going to go. I'm willing to guess that right now the beef market is probably the best it's going to be.

"Lotta talk about red meat. Lotta talk about cows messing up the environment. The meat market's going to soften. It's not a rosy picture for the Saguache County rancher. Right now with the beef market the best it's ever been, possibly the best it's ever going to be, things are still marginal for the family-owned cow-calf operation. When the beef market backs up, it's going to be less than marginal. At that point, the Saguache County rancher is going to be left with two choices.

"One. He can go out and plow up the grassland and go to farming, but I don't think that's going to work too well. The reason they're grasslands is that years ago someone figured out they shouldn't be farming these grasslands.

"Second choice, we start selling off these ranches piecemeal. Well, if you have a rancher who's been maybe the third, fourth, fifth generation ranching this ranch, and he can't make it, I promise you no one's going to come in here and buy that ranch and turn that thing around and make it work for him.

"I know some of you folks, especially up in Crestone, might be thinking, 'Hey, this might do some good. Get all those ranchers out of the road. Do some other things with those grasslands. How about a 'Buffalo Common.'

"I want to tell you. When you lose these ranches, you're going to lose more than just a herd of cows. I want you to know this, especially you that don't live on these ranches. When these big winds begin to blow and the dust clouds roll across the valley, that does not come from these ranches. When you see those airplanes out there flying around this summer spraying insecticides, pesticides, herbicides, you don't see them flying around over these ranches. It's not the rancher that has to go out and pour tons and tons of chemicals on the earth that possibly sink down into the water table and streams and rivers.

"So where are we now? Well, we could join some others, pass a law, get some lawyers, tie this thing up in court. Well, I guess I'd say that'd be great, if I were a lawyer. Big money-backed city slickers on one side. Taxpayers on the other side. Lawyers in the middle, heck yeah. Let's argue. Let's argue till the world looks level, or at least until somebody runs out of money.

"But there is another way, the way we've been making it work in America ever since we founded the country.

"Let's go head to head. Let's compete. Like I say, we've developed our water. It's ready to go. We know the quality of our water. Any business that has the quality and the price advantage has the overall advantage. It's also true that those that can't compete fail. This is what I'm talking about—Stockman's Water Company. It's not your conventional style of water company. See, generally a company goes out to an owner, and they buy options on that water right, then they go out and find a market for it. And when they find a market, they come back and exercise the option.

"This is a different deal. Stockman's Water Company goes out and *sells* (to people who have water rights) an option (to market some of their water through the company). For a token fee, you buy an option. You hold title to the water. The company finds a market for the water. It comes back and gets together with the people who hold options and discusses what's on the table. If you don't want in, you have that option, too. The choice is yours."

Saguache County ranchers could sell their water in two ways, Boyce explained. They could get an agreement to send it south into the Rio Grande through the same canal that the Closed Basin Project used to send its groundwater there. Not to worry that the legislation authorizing the project expressly forbade this. Water runs toward money, and votes. Or, as AWDI had proposed, they could pipe it north into the Arkansas River drainage. Nothing could be more simple.

"Now, I know, people will say, 'Hey, that's makin' money off the water. We've already been through that. Maybe that's going to offend a lot of people's sensibility. And maybe the rancher's going to go out here and make a *lot* of money. That never offended my sensibility. A lot of these people who are offended about somebody making money are the same people who aren't offended when it's time to get a grant from the taxpayer. Maybe they'd open their eyes and be reasonable, too."

A titter ran through the crowd. Boyce hadn't connected. The murmuring threw up words like "sellout," "another scam," "*Needles.*" Boyce looked a little deflated, paused, and continued, nevertheless. The tone of bitterness and nostalgia that comes from an unrequited passion rose slightly in his voice.

"Now, how far will I go with this? A lot of this country has meant a great deal to me. I guess everybody knows that I don't have to brand cows for a living. My heart brands cows for a living. However, twenty years ago, when I left the San Luis Valley, I didn't have a future. I had so little money, it was tantamount to having no money at all. I went to the East Coast. I went to England and made a little. In fact, I became a wealthy person. I became a wealthy man, and I married a wealthy woman. We moved back to Colorado. I bought a piece of the ranch where my grandfather ran sheep when I was a little boy.

"It took me nine years and eight separate land transactions to put that ranch back together. It hasn't been easy. It's been worthwhile. It took five years to build my house. That's been worthwhile. That's what we're about, the ranch. Joanne and I don't have any limousines. We don't spend our money on airplanes or yachts or boats. We don't have a condominium in Aspen. We don't take day trips abroad. We could care less about that. When we take a vacation, we take our mules and go to the mountains.

"If you go to look around the ranch where we live, along with the streams and the cottonwood groves, you'll see piñons and junipers, hay fields and pastures that run clear up to the national forest. It's nice and quiet, nice and beautiful. There are a lot of deer, a lot of elk, a lot of antelope, a lot of wildlife. It's all there for one reason, because a stream runs through that ranch.

"Now if there is anyone here who thinks that I would not do anything in my power to keep anything from happening to what Joanne and I have put together there, they don't know Gary Boyce. They don't know me at all. Well, it's not anything I want to change. It's more what I want to keep. The best way to protect my ranch is to help my neighbor protect his.

"That doesn't mean that in the future, when the warlords again beat the drums for the water war, that somebody who's faithful won't run down and prostrate themselves at the feet of the great Rio Grande Water God"—by which he meant the Rio Grande Water Conservancy District Board—"those of us that are left. We'll be there to defend the valley's water like we were before! However, in the meantime, you might want to listen to another drumbeat. Then again, maybe we don't want to hear any drumbeats at all. Maybe, just maybe, it might be nice if we couldn't just stop and see if we can't listen to our heartbeat. It sort of makes you think.

"For a closing, I want to tell you that I came here to tell you what was on my mind. I'm not here tonight to answer a bunch of questions. I'm not going to answer *any* questions. I'm going to start answering questions tomorrow. Those of you who wish to get hold of me, you can't call me at home, not because I have an unlisted number, I just don't have a telephone. But you can call me at my office at Rancho Rosada, and as soon as the telephone company gets around to it, at Stockman's Water Company. It'll be a new listing. If anyone wants to talk, we'll talk.

"Another thing I'd like to point out is that Joanne and I very much value our privacy. And I think you can respect that. Don't come dropping by the house to talk about the water. I'm happy to have people come by the house. I just want to know when you're coming. If you arrive uninvited it upsets me, and it upsets Joanne's puppy."

At this reference to the Rotweiler, open laughter broke out. Gary stiffened noticeably, then gentled his voice.

"I'll give you an idea of how I work day to day. First thing in the morning I go down to the corrals and take care of the horses and my mules. Check the water. Saddle a horse and ride down through my ranch. If I don't have a sick cow, I ride over to my neighbor, Henry Lamb. Henry and I go through our ritual of drinking coffee and cussing the government. I get to the office around ten or ten thirty. I'd be happy to talk to any of you then. I'd like to thank you very much for turning out tonight and hearing me through. I appreciate it. Thanks a lot. Good night."

And he got down off the stage, took Joanne on his arm, and walked out as the din of controversy breaking out among his audience echoed in the gym.

"Well *that* was sure different," said George Whitten. "If old Gary's going to make that thing fly, he's going to need more trust than he's got. He shouldn't have walked off."

George's Aunt Virginia, more cynical about human nature, said, "Don't listen to what people say. There're a lot of hard-pressed people in this county who'd never admit it but would cut any kind of deal they could get away with. I think Mr. Boyce will have a lot of visitors, even if they don't park their pickups where the rest of us can see them from the road."

In the weeks that followed, the valley's paranoia quotient rose measurably. All transfers of land or rights became an instant source of rumor. Was Boyce involved? Did the purchaser look like a rancher, farmer, or water speculator? This did not abate when Boyce proved his seriousness by hiring a high-profile water expert, one Jeris Danielson, who had been recently fired as Colorado State Engineer for suggesting the sale of Colorado water to California.

Such reactions weren't surprising, but the fact remained that Gary Boyce, for all his sentiment, had not clearly conveyed his purpose, which was more subtle than his speech and had an intriguing logic. To those few who did call Rancho Rosado and talk he would gladly explain.

His purpose was not, in fact, to sell large amounts of water but to establish the fact that water could be sold, thus vastly increasing its value and thus the wealth in assets of the people who owned it so that they could get credit as in the old days when rising land values kept agriculture alive. The idea of landowners contracting to deliver water while retaining ownership of the water right was also novel. But more important yet, it would only take one water sale to make all the water worth defending. Boyce was not alone in believing that the farmers of Rio Grande County had in fact been stealing water for years. Pumping levels had dropped, intermittent ditches and streams had become more so. However, it cost too much to prove that the center pivots of

Rio Grande County or even the Closed Basin Project, which allowed them to pump, had caused this, but if water became worth $5,000 an acre foot. . . .

"People might even look into why for years they hadn't been able to exercise that junior ditch right."

The audience murmured. Because in Western water law the oldest claims got to divert water first, so-called junior rights got nothing in time of shortage, which had become nearly all the time. Indeed, Virginia Whitten had said, "Sure, I've got water rights on Saguache Creek I'd be glad to sell as long as I wasn't liable when no actual water came with them."

Said Boyce, "For years we ranchers have been like someone with a pile of rocks in his yard who never minded much if his neighbor hauled one off now and then. You can bet that attitude would change mighty quick the first time someone sold a few for half a million dollars. Under this plan, a rancher could sell some water through the company and use the cash flow to stay in business. He wouldn't have to sacrifice the whole show. I'm a free enterprise man. I don't believe anyone should ranch on the public land. That's a subsidy any way you look at it, but I believe we should have full advantage of the capital we own."

It was an interesting read on the relationship between city and country. If Texas ranches survived on the strength of their oil wells, why not Saguache County ranchers who could ride out every morning through herds of cattle and antelope because they made the ranch pay by selling water?

There was the trace of something extremely revolutionary in the idea, which Boyce did not quite articulate, although he came close. If it could be shown that the fate of great desert cities still depended, as the lost cities of the past had depended, on the environmental health of their watersheds as well as the engineering works that brought them water, and if ranchers could show that this health depended on hoofed grazing animals, then they could indeed cut deals that would keep them in business forever. They could market water as a *crop*, not just a severable piece of real estate.

Boyce, on the most conspicuous circumstantial evidence, saw potato farmers and urban sprawl as the source of the water crisis. Yet, among the environmental strengths of ranching (no plowing, fewer chemicals), he did not see the actual capture of water through creative stewardship of animals. That was, of course, a possibility that the Whitten brothers and Royce Wheeler brought up often in their discussions about the Tracy allotment and their own land, but it probably wouldn't have done Gary Boyce much good to mention it. It was still by a long shot too different to throw up against the conventional wisdom that all cows were bad.

In any case, only since the AWDI trial had the ranchers and environmentalists in the Moffat gym begun to appreciate how intricate the connections between geology, law, economics, ecology, and practice actually were. Most just went out into the night determined to hang on tighter to what they had and wait for much better proof that Boyce wasn't up to some trick.

Donnie and Karen felt confirmed in their decision to get an independent engineer to keep a log on the production of their own wells. George decided that the next meeting of his Water Conservancy District Board should take place in Saguache instead of Rio Grande County so that they could start hearing from ranchers.

Then, when word swept the county that the South Farm, that sprawling speculative complex of center pivots next to where Saguache Creek disappeared, was about to sell, and when Gary Boyce was seen poring over plat books in the foyer of the Saguache County Courthouse, everyone foresaw another horrendous plot.

16

South Farm

Belying its name, South Farm was the only major irrigation project in the north end of the valley—eight square-mile sections where Saguache Creek crossed the Gun Barrel just south of Saguache town. From up on the slopes of Alexander, its 31 quarters of center pivot irrigation made a brave green polka dot pattern on the desert, but when the South Farm switched on the pumps serving its 200-foot wells, lower Saguache Creek disappeared into the sand no matter how much water Lovato had left in it. Shallow wells for miles around went dry as well.

Worst of all, South Farm was less farm than financial casuistry. According to the great leather-bound land book in the Assessor's Office, a document reconstructed amid some controversy after the courthouse burned in 1916, the core patch of salt bush and chico had belonged to the ubiquitous Gotthelf Investment Company of Isaac Gotthelf of the Bank of Saguache. However, on the breakup of Gotthelf holdings in 1951, the land passed through a broker to Newhall Land and Farming Company. Newhall, a California company built on citrus groves, truck farms, and cattle, has since made billions by transferring its agricultural water rights from the country to the suburbs of Los Angeles and building subdivisions, but in the 1950s it saw profit in the valley. In one gulp, Newhall also bought not only the future site of South Farm but also the 100,000-acre Baca grant and considerable other ranch land.

In those days, the faith was already strong that irrigation and fertilizer could turn deserts into gold, and cheap oil and high prices made large-scale pumping from deep wells feasible for the first time in history. On the South Farm property, Newhall drilled into the water table beneath the barren chico, planted grain, vegetables, and potatoes, and lost money continuously until 1963, when they sold out. The next owners, another absentee land company speculating on rising farm prices, lost money until 1966 before passing the place to the Arizona-Colorado Cattle Company, which also speculated on the Baca. They ran in the red until 1977. Then the South Farm fell into the hands of a real visionary.

A few years prior, a man named Ted Cook had arrived in the valley from the Midwest on the wings of the discovery that the recently developed center pivot irrigation technology had once again rewritten the rules on desert development. By eliminating the need for costly and time-consuming land leveling and ditch construction, you could make a first-class farm anywhere by just punching down a well and hauling in some pipe. The profit, however, came not from turning sunlight into food but in increasing the assessed value of the land by several hundred percent. Thanks to a rapidly inflating bubble in farm prices, this generated a capital gain that Cook leveraged again and again with dazzling results. Far out in the chico northeast of Center, he built an imperial palace so huge that when an army of creditors sacked and pillaged his empire five years later, it took them seven years to find a potato farmer rich enough to buy it.

At the height of the bubble, Cook bought South Farm because it came cheap, not because it fit his formula. That was a mistake. It was already a bad farm, and borrowing more money to buy center pivot sprinklers didn't change that. In 1984, after Cook fled the valley, South Farm became the property of Wells Fargo Bank. They ate losses for four years before swapping it in a consolidation of other Cook debts to the Travelers Insurance Company, which was still losing money on South Farm in the summer of 1992. And now someone else apparently wanted to buy it. After forty years of continuous disaster, why, if not for the water?

Gary Boyce had argued that if Saguache ranchers had the choice of selling their water for the same price that the farmers could, then the market would induce them to defend it and sell only enough to give their cattle business a healthy margin. This oblique way of making ranching viable had a definite appeal, but for it to work, people had to trust Gary Boyce personally, which many didn't, and the price incentive couldn't reward speculating or selling out completely. Boyce could not offer any guarantee against this temptation, as an urban economy totally unrelated to farming or ranching set the price.

On the other hand, as George put it, "Old Gary had drawn the line in the dirt between the farmers and the ranchers, and that really got a lot of guys upset. There were folks up here who didn't even know who was on the Conservancy Board or what the rules and statutes were. Suddenly they had a lot of questions. And a lot of those guys down in the farming district got really nervous, especially those that didn't have rights to surface water from the ditches. They're all pumping water out of the ground, and if someday it comes to strict regulation, they'll be last in line."

Consequently, George's Rio Grande Water Conservancy District Board meeting drew an even larger crowd to the Moffat High School gymnasium than Boyce had a few weeks earlier. Amazingly, in a community where water gossip dominated more conversation than football, cars, politics, or prime-time TV, the board had never before held an open public meeting and never any meeting at all in Saguache County.

Gary and Joanne sat in the front row as George said that the time was fast approaching when everything was going to be codified, quantified, and enforced, legislatively if not in court, but that the haphazard squabbles of the past had left such a mess that sorting things out would require the utmost goodwill and patience. Almost everyone in the room had a question, but the Boyces said nothing.

Not long afterward, in the spirit of codifying, quantifying, and enforcing, George and Donnie's Aunt Virginia called a meeting of Saguache Creek water right holders. She proposed to resolve once and for all the suspicion that the people of upper Saguache Creek, those west of the Gun Barrel, were taking more than their share and thus keeping rights holders on lower Saguache Creek from seeing any water at all. The gathering was a thinly veiled rebellion against the district water commissioner, the resourceful Tim Lovato, and had the hallmarks of a coup plot.

The meeting took place at night in the cavernous gloom of Saguache's ill-lit courthouse. Donnie and Virginia presided from the judge's dais, and certain people, notably Lovato himself, were conspicuously absent. A great deal was said in code by way of arcane references and innuendo, but ultimately nothing got decided. It just didn't seem worthwhile opening another box of grief when a creature far thirstier than Lovato was sucking up Saguache water—South Farm. The possible sale of the South Farm was discouraging hydropolitical news because it symbolized for both farmers and ranchers all that was irrational and implacable about modern agriculture itself, which was supposedly their industry.

When Boyce had invoked the ancient tribal animus between shepherd and plowman, he had not neglected to indicate how economics and technology had turned up the heat. In Colorado, as elsewhere, conflict often assumed a tribal character. The Utes, the Spanish, the Cowboys, the Miners, the Farmers, the Speculators all fell back on custom and culture when under the duress of advancing modernity.

George Whitten avoided inflammatory statements in his Conservancy Board meeting but said later, "The farming district down there really has been sort of living off the backs of the ranching area. All the groundwater for all that country east of Center comes from up here, and in fact the water table is going down there every day."

The ancient wrangle was institutionalized in the doctrine of allocating water "to the highest beneficial use," which Boyce had warned of as the cities' trump card. Everybody knew that in America suburban development and golf courses came ahead of anything in agriculture and that farms came well ahead of range-fed livestock. "I don't know how well we'd fare in a court of law," George admitted candidly after warning his neighbors that their water would be codified and quantified. "We've let this thing go on so long without asserting our priority rights, and those potato farmers have put that well water to such beneficial use, that their efficiency per dollar really is quite a bit more."

Yet South Farm, which had lost money continuously for four decades, was definitely not efficient, and in terms of deep ecology perhaps no irrigation was. Indeed, clear back to Babylon all societies based on irrigation have without exception subsidized it heavily, whether through inflation, grants, incentives, bankruptcies, taxes, or forced labor. Irrigated land, an environment totally synthesized for maximum production, long ago became as unquestioned an artifact of high civilization as taxes and credit. Mere cost seldom mattered, and the power of this assumption to shape landscape was well documented in the earliest financial history of San Luis Valley water.

Most of the major irrigation ditches, hundreds of miles of them, were dug between 1874 and 1890 by joint stock ditch companies that virtually without exception went bankrupt at least once. Typically they crashed several times, breaking waves of credulous investors from La Garita to Amsterdam. Their losses thus subsidized the valley's first plumbing system just as generously as unquestioning federal taxpayers later would donate the Closed Basin Project, which Gary Boyce criticized for pumping Saguache County groundwater into the Rio Grande and thus allowing Colorado farmers to consume water without worrying about hurting rights down river on which Albuquerque, El Paso, Juarez, Matamoros, Laredo, Brownsville, and a few others depended for growth. It was not a question of making valley agriculture sustainable but of sustaining it so that money could be made elsewhere—in construction, manufacturing, land speculation.

The prospectuses for the old ditch companies, like the feasibility studies for federal dams in California and foreign aid irrigation works in Africa or AWDI or the Closed Basin Project, all presented scientifically rigorous cost/benefit analysis. However, ordinary accounting methods can never determine whether such schemes will "pay" in a world context any more than they can prove that Versailles or the Great Pyramid or a nuclear submarine has "paid." Such things get built because certain people for a vast and often conflicting set of reasons think they ought to exist. Indeed, after the investment has been written off, they often do benefit someone, and no one remembers who bore the costs or whether *their* vision mattered much.

In the end, valley farmers had followed the star of high-production, capital-intensive, industrialized agriculture with relative success. They had produced a landscape of fanatical order and refined it continuously. From a speeding pickup, the rows of potatoes and other vegetables in Rio Grande and southern Saguache counties flash past the window more regular than bar codes in a supermarket. The quarter-mile circles watered by the ever-revolving sprinkler booms make a pattern clearly visible from space. Potatoes, barley, barley, potatoes, alfalfa, a quarter here and there of lettuce, carrots, or onions, and then again potatoes, barley. At harvest, ragged lines of laborers from the hungry villages of Mexico and the Spanish settlements of the valley itself work the table vegetables. Otherwise, humans move among the crops encased in the occasional spray rig or tractor cab. In getting from seed time to harvest, valley farm managers take on weather, soil condition, and pests the way the skipper of a nuclear carrier takes on the Atlantic—with skill, energy, and realism, but not much humility. They care about productivity. The original center pivots of the early 1970s revolutionized the efficiency of labor, and they get better every year. Where once the pumps had to deliver up to 90 pounds per square inch and 30 percent of the water dried up without touching a plant, they now work at 20 pounds and get 95 percent of the water to the plants through artful hoses that sweep the ground. And yet, the best science cannot promise how long the soil and water can support even that.

It was ironic but not surprising that the world's biggest center pivot systems were built not by valley farmers but by a self-styled ex-nomad, Libya's Muamar Qadafy, who thought a "modern" state required nothing less. Not too long after he came to power in 1969, ambitious American engineers sold him a brace of computer-controlled center pivot booms 3 miles long. It bothered no one that to stay ahead of the Saharan evaporation rate the outer end of these booms had to wheel itself nearly 20 miles a day and mount a battery of water cannon worthy of the Los Angeles Fire Department. Libya has oil to pay for such things. It mattered more that one glitch, say, a shot bearing on one of the rolling towers, could and often did hold up the contraption long enough for 28 square miles of grain to die of thirst. When that project fell short of expectations, Qadafy commissioned a $25 billion scheme to pump fossil groundwater from Libya's southern desert to farms on the coast through two 350-mile pipelines, each carrying half again the flow of the Rio Grande. It was the largest construction project undertaken anywhere, in all history up to then, designed and managed despite a near state of war between Libya and the United States by the firm of Brown and Root of Houston, Texas (through their London office).

The rationale, of course, was to invest oil revenue in something that would sustain the country after the oil ran out, but at the planned scale, the pumping requires burning massive amounts of oil instead of selling it and the water may actually run out before the oil, almost certainly drying up the ancient oases and seeps that gave the desert culture its character and sustained its fragile life.

Eccentric dictators have no monopoly on subsidies of this scale. The Soviets caused one of the world's worst environmental disasters when they built the Karakum Canal to grow cotton in Kazakhstan and dried up the Aral Sea. The World Bank largely financed the destruction of Sudan, for decades pouring good money after bad into agriculture schemes intended to "modernize" the Sudanese economy. They did not respond to (in fact, could not even see) the social or environmental consequences because such matters had no definition in their understanding of "economic" development. That story deserves telling because it covers the same period as the South Farm and was just then in the news because large numbers of Sudanese were killing each other and over a million had recently starved to death. American newspapers routinely characterized Sudan's sorrows as a tribal/religious war, fundamentalist Muslim Arabs beating up on black Christian and animist tribes. That did describe the combatants, but development projects not unlike South Farm caused the war.

The world's largest irrigated farm (2.1 million acres) is in Sudan between the Blue Nile and the White. It is an expansion of the British Gezira scheme that made Sudan a major cotton exporter before independence in 1956. Nevertheless, it had already soaked up several hundred million dollars in World Bank and petrodollar loans by the mid-1960s when another scheme, the 450,000-acre New Halfa project, designed to turn nomads into cotton farmers, opened on another Nile tributary. Within a decade, the dam supplying Halfa had lost a full half of its capacity because of silt rolling down off the degraded grazing land above it, and crops grew on only a third of the project. But the World Bank saw nothing and in 1983 underwrote Rahad I, which "subjugated" another 325,000 acres with electric pumps on the Blue Nile at a cost of $400 million. Since the money for Rahad ran out before the fields were leveled and the heavy clay soil could not handle furrow irrigation anyhow, that rapidly become a wasteland, too.

Sudan still grows a quarter-billion dollars' worth of cotton annually on projects that still function, but they spend half the gross for imported fertilizer and pesticides alone, and the net does not even pay the interest on the outstanding loans.

Irrigation took precedence, but the drive to industrialize agriculture did not spare the pastoral sector. To pacify the herding tribes, foreign aid agencies poured hundreds of millions into the rangeland economy. They drilled thousands of wells for livestock and strung barbed wire across the grassland to make the nomads into Texas ranchers. When the grassland ecology collapsed in the mid-1980s, hundreds of thousands of cattle, sheep, and goats died, but the program lived. Since then, half a dozen schemes have compounded the damage by forcibly settling displaced people on farms *without* irrigation on land too brittle to farm at all.

When the World Bank realized that their cotton projects could never pay back a national debt half again as big as Sudan's GDP, they imposed a draconian austerity program. The militant anti-Western Muslim party seized power, and the southern tribes revolted. But the imposition of Islamic law simply finished their tolerance for distant governments where they had no voice. They were already fighting mad after three decades of irrigation projects, model villages, fenced ranches, tree plantations, and of course wells had ridden roughshod over an ancient land tenure system that had served them well. The usurpations of property by the right of eminent domain that Gary Boyce warned of hardly compare.

The leader of the black Christian and animist tribes of southern Sudan, John Garang, actually comes from the north and holds a Ph.D. in agricultural economics from Iowa State University. The radicalizing experience of his life was the eviction of his family from land flooded by the backwaters of the Aswan High Dam. He fought the government until, as part of a truce agreement in 1972, he and some fellow rebel officers agreed to go the United States for an education at the expense of the U.S. State Department.

While Garang studied in Iowa, his country launched its most ambitious development project yet, the Jonglai Canal. At a cost of half a billion dollars, this would drain the famous Marshes of Sudd in the southeast corner of the country and send the water 200 miles up into the Nile for the benefit of the irrigation schemes in northern Sudan and Egypt. In 1981, Garang turned in his thesis on the impact of the canal, went back home, and within six months ran off the French construction crews and blew up the head gates, beginning a second round of warfare that promised to last to the end of the millennium.

According to one of Garang's former comrades-in-arms, John Lueth, who married and settled down as a professional accountant in Ames, Iowa, "Of course the fight is now religious and racial, but it has everything to do with resources and resource policy. The government is in the hands of the Arab north, but it is under two great pressures—to produce cotton for export and to deliver water to the Egyptians, whose population has grown so much. John Garang's home was once a broad forested valley where the Nile cut through the desert. It had monkeys, lions, and every kind of life imaginable, but all that was inundated by Lake Nasser. There is nothing left now but the desert. Nothing. The people were promised new homes in 'model villages,' but of course most never saw anything of the kind.

"John successfully stopped the Jonglai Canal, but not before enough of the embankment was built to impede the seasonal overflow of the Nile that replenished the marshes and provided water and grazing for vast wild and domestic herds. I went there for my own research in 1981 and saw thousands upon thousands of animals that had come to the former water pools and simply died there in heaps. Thirst-crazed wild animals came right into the villages, into houses, begging for water.

"But that was only part of the story. Here in Iowa, nobody understood what we were talking about. Our professors were very old style. They could not imagine that their idea of 'development' could have such terrible consequences, so we learned what we could and tried to keep them happy. And now, look at my country. It's almost beyond hope."

The South Farm did not represent anything as life threatening as the development projects in Sudan, largely because the valley had seen its most violent era of development before the age of automatic weapons. Yet, the mistrust of cultures, the new technology, the falling water table, and the inscrutability of the financial powers that ruled in absentia had put the valley society and hydrology under terrific strain in the same way.

Relationships had changed among farmers nearly as much as between farmers and ranchers. Light sandy soil where ditch water would not run to the end of a furrow produced bumper crops under the gentle sprinklers. Thus, wasteland far from the old ditches suddenly became valuable, and in the euphoria of expansion, the ancient doctrine of "first in time, first in right" had not been enforced on wells, so enterprising farmers just drilled into the water table and pumped. Old power declined and new fortunes rose overnight.

Boyce had made his case against the established farmers of Rio Grande County, where the senior ditches left the river; however, from the mid-1970s to the mid-1980s, the real revolution had taken place in Alamosa County to the southeast of Center and in southern Saguache County itself, which had up to then been ranch country. There, barley planting nearly doubled to 64,000 acres. Potato planting tripled to 32,000, almost all of it new ground. Barley productivity rose from 60 bushels per acre to 90, potatoes from 240 sacks (cwt.) to 340 an acre, but this new productivity came at the expense of the old.

As George Whitten explained, "It might have cost you $1,200 a quarter [160 acres] to exercise your senior ditch right, but the water came down the ditch all at once, so you had to store it. As long as the water table was pretty high to begin with, it paid to do that by running the excess into a pit. It would seep into the ground and raise the water table some more, and it cost little to pump it out as you needed it. Then suddenly in and around and amongst the old rights holders people appeared who paid nothing. They just pumped. A lot of people simply stopped exercising their ditch rights rather than put expensive water into the ground for their neighbors to pump out. They drilled their own deep wells."

Throughout the 1970s, the rapid drop of the water table precipitated no end of lawsuits and squabbles, which led to a moratorium on deep wells in 1981 and on shallow wells in 1989 and caused the clamor for the Closed Basin Project to take the pressure off, but matters had not stabilized much by the time Gary Boyce threw out his challenge in the Moffat gym, and in George's meeting that followed it became clear that matters could only get worse unless slack could be found somewhere. All eyes turned to the South Farm, which pumped enormous amounts of water but had never made a profit. Even counting numerous local rumors of generous returns on crops purposely allowed to wither for the benefit of crop insurance, only a Sudanese government official could have found promise in the books of this gem of American agricultural capitalism.

If somehow the South Farm could be eliminated, its wells shut down, then many Saguache County ranchers, including George, Donnie, and their Aunt Virginia, might be able to use Saguache Creek, not to mention a good number of wells. If that happened, they would talk less about regulating farm wells farther south. On the other hand, selling South Farm water for export, through Boyce or some other enterprise, would open a breach that would almost certainly precipitate another major water grab. What other value could the place have?

"The problem," said George, "is the soil. It's just adobe. There isn't any biological capital there at all. It's just real tight dark black stuff when you turn it over. It doesn't absorb water."

His family knew it well because one year long before it became investment property they had tried to grow alfalfa on a couple of quarters there. Putting money into it, he thought, was insane. The "tight dark stuff" is black alkali, another curious curse of deserts, generally exacerbated by irrigation. It is a condition that sometimes develops on ground rendered salty by the upward flow of water toward the sun (remember the P/PET). In patches throughout the valley, the salt actually covers the ground like snow, but in most cases, if the direction of flow is reversed through some combination of drainage, mulch, and flooding, the salt will leach out, and the soil becomes fertile.

Sometimes, however, overexposure to sodium can force the silica particles of clay to collect sodium atoms where they might otherwise have hooked onto calcium, potassium, or other less radical elements. A touch of water there does a world of hurt. Washing the buffering salts away allows the clay to swap a sodium atom for one of the hydrogen atoms in a water molecule, turning the moisture into sodium hydroxide (NaOH), also known as lye or caustic soda. In paper mills, NaOH reduces mighty logs to pulp. In soil, it tears apart organic matter and reduces clay to an impermeable bricklike state. The only remedies are either overwhelming amounts of organic material or costly compounds of sulfur and calcium.

"With chemicals, they can force soil to perform in a way that would take years and years to build up to with manure crops and animals," said George, "but when all your fertility and tilth has to come out of a bin at the co-op in Monte Vista every year, it isn't cheap. That's what most farming seems to be these days, but the South Farm is in a class by itself. It's real desert."

The situation was well known outside the ranching district, and not long after the Conservancy Board meeting in Moffat one of the valley's more successful potato farmers convened a secret meeting to plot the sacrifice of South Farm for the good of all.

Bill Kopfman was a modern farmer's farmer, a proud conservative but ready to risk money, common of speech but shrewd, stout but strong. He lived in a rather grand house of his own south of Center in the old farm district of Rio Grande County, which he pronounced Ryo Grand in the manner of Texans who don't acknowledge the Spanish origin of anything. He was also president of the Ryo Grand Water Users Association, which existed to protect ditch rights *and* well rights, and he and his son Lynn were heavily invested in the latter.

About seventeen people attended Kopfman's meeting, including the officers of the Water Users Association, a number of other substantial farmers, both Whitten brothers, officials of the Bureau of Land Management, the U.S. Fish and Wildlife Service, and the president of the Bank of Monte Vista, which was the only bank in the valley that had navigated the agricultural credit mania of the late 1970s with reputation intact. When all had poured coffee and settled in on the ranch modern furniture of the spacious living room, Kopfman opened the meeting.

After some preliminaries he said, "I think everyone here is concerned with water, but the thing you want to remember, and I was told this by a very dear dear friend who's passed away now, but he told it to me when we were talking about the AWDI case. 'Billy,' he said, 'I want to tell you that whenever you kill a snake, there's always five more that stick their heads out, so it will always be a continuing war to watch and safeguard your water rights, and I'm sure there'll be more come along all the time.' And money's what does this, and it seems like the history of destroying agricultural water is that the need for money and the weakness of agriculture being able to organize and protect their water have worked hand in hand. So that the money will buy the water after they split the water users up."

Then he outlined a plan so ingeniously conceived to unite the water users that for a moment conversation stopped. He first pointed out that in the interest of diversity the Bureau of Land Management had some time before established the Blanca Wildlife Habitat Area in what had been ephemeral lakes northeast of Alamosa on public land just outside the center pivot country. To sustain sporting amounts of trout, bass, and blue gill, not to mention water birds, they were pumping large amounts of water out of the ground. However, a court decision had recently declared this pumping illegal, as even the federal government had to obey the state ban on new wells. The BLM would have to buy water rights.

Why couldn't it in fact buy the South Farm water rights and transfer them 50 miles to their wildlife habitat? Thus alienating the water from the land would make the latter next to worthless, and civic-minded ranchers and farmers could afford to buy it. They could more than get their money back by selling the thirty-two center pivots, especially if they got a tax break by tying up the land with some kind of conservation easement. The Fish and Wildlife Service would certainly guarantee government support for this, as it was known that the director of the refuge in Monte Vista wanted dispersed feeding areas for ducks, geese, and sandhill cranes.

The idea was brilliant. It would exploit the public's enthusiasm for the environment to buy some slack in the tug of war between the farmers and ranchers. Saguache Creek would run again. The pressure to codify, quantify, and enforce all the groundwater pumping in the main center pivot area would relax. And at least some water would be sequestered forever from exporters. No one dissented.

Only the BLM could not guarantee the money, so the assembled company would have to sign a note from the Bank of Monte Vista for $1.6 million.

"We have to move fast," warned Kopfman. "I understand there is another buyer."

Who would sign? It was like the call to join a secret society.

"For some of them, it was no big deal," recalled Donnie, "but for us it was. I'd never been in Kopfman's house, and I looked around the room and thought, 'Can I trust these guys? What common interests do we really have?' Bill had the paper right there, and one after another people went up and signed. George did, but I didn't. I felt terrible about it, but I couldn't do it without thinking and talking it over with Karen." That was perhaps why, when it appeared a few days later that it might take several fiscal years for the BLM to get the money, Donnie volunteered to go to John and Carol Wagner.

Donnie had no hard knowledge of their wherewithal except that they did things like go to Paris for Thanksgiving, and when spring was long in coming and dust storms boiled off the South Farm and a day of calving on their land down on the valley floor turned their hair brown with grit, they might decide between Sunday night and Monday morning to check on their condo and yacht in Florida, from which they would return in a week's time, refreshed and tan.

Donnie knew, though, that Carol had kept a sharp eye on all the politics of Saguache Creek. She had attended the night meetings at the courthouse and taken notes and could be counted on to have figured the stakes exactly. John himself would be in good spirits. After weeks of harassing his cows through aspen thicket and willow break, he finally had them up on the shoulder of Antora happily fattening on the tundra among herds of elk. He was now devoting his spare time to ripping out old fences built by his predecessors, the Woodards, "so this place won't look so much like a goddam ranch."

Donnie thought of the horses on the road and times John had gone around his ranch flinging open all the gates just to give his animals and neighbors a creative dose of *real* chaos. He found John as usual, surrounded by his 500 pounds of dogs and ready to offer a friendly glass of Glenlivet.

Donnie had never asked anybody for money in his life, certainly not $1.6 million. It took him most of a glass to get around to the point. He watched Carol set her jaw as he spoke.

"I don't trust any of those guys," she said.

It was important to both John and Carol that they not be looked on as fair marks to be left holding any sort of bag. The Whittens notwithstanding, they could cite some nasty parallels between the breakdown of honor in the bond market and valley attitudes toward newcomers.

"We've already got too much land," said John, "and I don't know anything about center pivots. To get our money back, we'd have to unload them in a market they know like the back of their hand, and they'd crucify us."

But it was clear they were in. They knew money like Donnie knew cattle. They could think of it not just as something to make more of but as the most versatile of tools. The challenge gave them a little of the old bond market adrenalin rush.

"I'll contact our lawyer," said John, "and see what we can work out."

So, in another series of clandestine meetings in Monte Vista, an arrangement was worked out, and the Travelers Insurance Company, through the agency of Colorado's premier broker of agricultural real estate, Hall and Hall, was offered $1.6 million for the South Farm. It was even impressed on Michael Hall himself that Travelers stood to make some public relations capital by accepting. It would end on a positive note a continuous history of financing agriculture in the valley that went back over a century. There was even a Travelers Ditch.

The offer was made, and then everyone waited. It was in the days that followed that Gary Boyce, armed and dressed immaculately in his yoked tweed jacket, silk choker, and boots, was seen poring over the great land books in the foyer of the Saguache County Courthouse, and a tremor ran around the north end of the valley that perhaps he was the mystery buyer of the South Farm, and if so, how long until the next full-scale water war? And there was another Gary, Gary Hill, whose name was also mentioned, since he actually had made a killing up north on the Arkansas River by selling his ranch water to a Denver suburb and had used it to buy a foreclosed ranch on upper Saguache Creek.

However, word soon spread up from the farming district that the mystery bidder was not a conspicuous villain at all but a soybean farmer named Myron Smith from Medina, Ohio. Moreover, he already owned several quarters of good potato ground in the new country east of Center, which he had farmed in partnership with a long established local family named Corzine.

New rumors quickly spread that since Medina lay within commuting distance of both Cleveland and Akron, someone was once again leveraging suburban real estate values to grab a big piece of the valley. But certainly Travelers would not sell to him, not given the enormous hydropolitical benefits of the alternative.

But of course they did. A spokesperson for Hall and Hall said merely, "Our obligation is make the most prudent choice financially for our client, in this case, Travelers. We were not authorized to consider other factors. Although the San Luis Valley group nominally offered more, we felt the other bid was more reliable."

Myron Smith announced that young Todd Corzine would manage his new property and put the entire 8 square miles into alfalfa. This would integrate with the Corzine's cattle operations, Smith said, but nobody quite believed him.

During the AWDI fight, an Indian speaking to a rally of valley farmers had said, "I knew sooner or later you'd all be Indians," and that's how almost everyone felt—like the tribes of southern Sudan.

"That's not only far more alfalfa than the Corzines need, it's enough to kill the market in the whole valley," said Donnie, when he heard the news. "Also, to do alfalfa, he'll have to pump more water than the South Farm has taken in forty years. It's the worst possible scenario."

At the Farmer's Buffet restaurant in Center, where potato farmers eat at red Formica tables when stopping over in town, Bill Kopfman tried to appear philosophical. "Oh, it'll come up for sale again, for sure," he said to a court of his peers. "I don't think there's any way that ground can be farmed and make a profit. It's tough, it's real hard, and it's hard to farm good ground, and it's a hell of a lot harder to farm ground like that. With no debt, it may cash flow this year, and it may again next, but there will be a lot of years when it won't."

But Myron Smith himself rebuffed any challenge of his true motives. "I don't know anything about speculating in land or water, and I wouldn't do it if I did," he said. "I'm a farmer first, last, and forever. I'm also good at what I do, and I've operated in that valley long enough to know what I bought. It'll pay all right. But I can't tell you why Travelers sold to me. I'd had my bid into them for over a year and never heard a word. Then one day they called me and said it was mine. I never heard of another offer."

Both George and Donnie took it hard but with resignation. "It would have shown that we really can work together and make rational decisions about the whole valley, but I guess it isn't that easy," said Donnie.

"It makes everything that much harder," said George. "When I last saw Bill Kopfman he said he hoped I could 'keep my people in line' up here in the ranching district, and *that's* sure harder every day. You know I wonder sometimes that we've sat up here in the ranching district since about 1950, when all this high energy petrochemical agriculture began, predicting that it had to break down somewhere, and we've sat up here and let it all go by. I sure have to shake my head sometimes, if what we're doing is right or if we're just fools."

17

Tracy Again

By early August people were saying, as they said every year, that the weather sure was different. This time, however, it actually was. The rest of Colorado had enjoyed the mildest of winters, but the San Luis Valley had recorded its coldest in history. For the better part of January and February, the mercury had fluctuated between –40° and 0°. When it finally thawed, grown men were seen to splash in puddles in the streets of Alamosa just to celebrate the sight of liquid water. Then spring came calm and damp without any of the wind and dust that often made it the hardest season to bear.

It had rained also in June, and the monsoon came on so strong in July that alfalfa farmers became quite neurotic. In principle they liked rain, but to hold its color and nutritional value and escape mildew, hay must dry quickly and evenly from about 75 percent water to 15 percent. The only help for soaked windrows is to turn them constantly with a rake until they dry. Untended, they bleach white on top, advertising to every passer-by that some farmer or foreman got caught out. The victims got teased like losing poker players.

Some were tempted to look for signs of divine justice. George Whitten's pickup got nicely dimpled by one hailstorm that laid a swath of ice 3 inches deep but only 300 yards wide across the Tracy, but he had the satisfaction of seeing it slash on across the South Farm and shatter some of the Travelers Insurance Company grain and peas. Another storm took out thirteen of Kopfman's fifteen circles of barley.

By August, people talked as if they lived in Seattle, but there was a reason. Meteorologists put the blame on dust from the eruption of

Mt. Pinatubo in the Philippines, which blocked sunlight, caused familiar pressure zones to act strangely, and dampened the hue and cry over global warming as well as the alfalfa, but there was a local twist, too. The record winter, the scientists said, had resulted from a deep and seamless snow that turned the valley into a giant mirror that reflected solar energy back into the thin air so effectively that the land simply never could warm up. And the coldest of the air settled into the sump near Alamosa, where it simply got colder.

At the worst of it, a trucker might enter the valley from the east over La Veta Pass at 9,400 feet with his elbow out the window and within 10 miles feel the temperature drop 40 degrees. Stopping 20 miles beyond that at Alamosa (7,500 feet), his hands would stick to the gas pump and the snot freeze on the end of his nose, but 30 miles beyond at Del Norte (7,950 feet) he would have to fight melting slush on the road.

Such phenomena gave some practical authority to the preoccupations of the atmospheric scientists and their arcane measurements of energy fluxes. If a little volcano dust from the back side of the planet and snow could make such drastic local changes, then smog, sandstorms, and the increased reflectivity of desertified lands might indeed produce . . . well . . . who knew, but something.

Changes of great significance might even occur in the demonstration area on Tracy, but it was proving a lot of work. Because Donnie had to spend so much time chasing the Wagners' cattle up on Antora, most of this fell to Karen and to George's family. The temporary fences that kept the herd bunched and regulated the time the animals spent on the various divisions of land occupied them greatly because in this first year they often had to adjust fence lines in response to what the stock actually did. Did the cows get to the whole enclosed area? Did they form trails on steep slopes? They also had to monitor to see what got eaten, how fast, and how fast it regrew, so they would know when to move.

And there were occasional water problems. About a quarter mile from the big storage tank on the demonstration area, the restored pipeline served another watering trough made of surplus bomb containers fitted with a toilet float valve. Before the fencing, when cattle roamed at will over the whole allotment, a small group of cows would have colonized this resource while others established territories around other water points on the allotment, but a problem developed when the whole herd occupied a section that contained two water points. They preferred the smaller because it required less walking. Unfortunately, without a storage tank, the smaller water point could not satisfy many cows at once. Those who felt cheated went after the toilet float and repeatedly broke it. Once they pulled the pipe off its connection so the water ran out on the ground.

Karen tied up the float with baling string to force the animals to walk over the hill to the main tank, but they continued to badger the float until they made it drip, and then out of inertia or plain bovine pride they would stand around sniffing at the trickle all day without eating or ever getting a decent drink. The margin of the cattle business lies in such details.

A thirsty calf can shrink 1–2 pounds a day and a cow or bull 6–8 pounds, which at $.75 or $1.00 a pound gets very expensive. So on Wednesday when Karen drove up on the Tracy with Clint and Sarah bouncing in the back of the pickup, she ground her teeth and growled at the sight of half a dozen cows and their calves staring at the valve that they had once again caused to leak. When she skidded to a stop, Clint and Sarah swarmed out of the truck bed and with shouts and chips of rock sent the cows shuffling off toward the main tank. Next year, she would just cap the pipe, but the incident caused her to consider once more that cows, like people, too often applied what brains they had to the wrong problem.

What did wild things do that only had seeps and trickles to drink from? Of course, they didn't worry about selling their offspring by weight at the end of the season, although sometimes, as in Sudan, they hung around inadequate water too long and died. Almost certainly, the water strategies of animals involved a fairly sophisticated combination of learned behavior and reasoning power that took into account distance, quantity, predators, climate, and the politics of territory.

By the time George and his son Kirk arrived, Karen had picked out a route for the next fence that ran 2 miles south from the tank up a ridge to the top of Alexander.

It was one of George's favorite hunting spots because when frost brought the elk down out of the high country they liked to graze mornings on the east-facing slope, and when he approached they would move down into the gulch on the west side, and he could gain the ridge top and set up to make his shot as they climbed the next ridge over. "I've often stood up here after getting my elk and watched the Texans in their Land Cruisers burning up the Tracy road to get up on the Forest Service land without suspecting that the game was here," he said.

In a normal year, the Colorado Division of Wildlife logged about 4,000 elk and deer hunters into that half of Saguache County alone. They killed about 200 deer and 600 elk, leaving 2,000 or 3,000 of each.

Temporary electric fencing does not demand the heavy drudgery of barbed wire—the thorny coils, heavy posts, digging, fence stretchers that snap back in your face, and staples—but it's a hassle nonetheless. The medium is one strand of "polywire," a plastic string the thickness of binder's twine with strands of foil woven into it that comes on 1,000-foot spools. This strand is looped along molded plastic posts about a yard long that have hooks for the wire at a choice of heights and a steel spike on bottom. A big plastic prong at the root of this spike supposedly allows the fence builder to stomp posts into the ground without breaking stride, but along the rocky rib of Alexander, they would not stand without plentiful oaths, prayers, and little stacks of rocks. As George and Karen ran short of posts, they zigzagged the wire among sage and cliff rose bushes. The sun had already swung around into the southwest by the time they reached the top of Alexander and tied off the polywire around a dark volcanic boulder, but when Karen went back down and hooked it to a live section of permanent fence, George's volt meter registered nothing. Somewhere the foil strands had broken, which meant another 1,500-foot climb to discover and fix.

And yet, after all that, from a resting place high up on Alexander, the world looked beautiful and beautifully alive and beautifully of one piece. They could see their children cavorting among the rocks and their cattle eating and the chrome-wheeled grain trucks rolling down the Gun Barrel toward the barley harvest and where Saguache Creek ran out of water and how the dry bed of it, outlined in pale chico, snaked out across the great valley, pooled here and there by the inky shadows of cotton cumuli. And 60 miles off against the Sangre de Cristos—the pale smudge of the Great Sand Dunes, where the prevailing southwesterlies dropped their burden before leaving the valley over El Paso de las Moscas, the Pass of Flies.

The wind was visible. Monsoon clouds advancing like siege towers from the west over the Continental Divide sent little gusts that flashed light off blades of fescue sprouting in the rocks; and from Antora, already shrouded in extravagant nimbus, came a mutter of thunder.

"That's Donnie throwing rocks at John Wagner's cows," said Karen, but she was mistaken. The dust plume of Donnie's pickup was peeling off the Tracy road toward them. Now they could identify his and Clint's motorcycles in the back.

On foot, Donnie climbed toward them rapidly, full of the slightly annoying enthusiasm of those who arrive after the job's done, although he and Clint had in fact put in a full morning hauling minerals up beyond Antora's 12,000-foot timberline.

"It's working," he said, gesturing down toward the tank. "There's wheat grass, everything. It's coming back so strong, that's going to be the best place."

And sure enough, looking down on the water tank from up on the ridge, the effects of all the moving of fences and cattle appeared quite remarkable. Where the divisions of the demonstration area came together at the tank like slices of pizza, the one that the cows were about to leave after five days appeared beaten nearly down to the white sand and richly topped with cow pies. But the green was obviously returning to sections grazed earlier, and the first section already looked nearly as good as the ungrazed area still ahead. True, the effect did not extend far out into the grama, but no one could doubt the trend, and it defied common wisdom altogether.

Throughout the arid world, water holes (for domestic stock) are sacrifice areas, the mother of desertification, and a powerful argument against the indiscriminate drilling of wells in the name of economic development. The destruction of plant life around an African village and its well or a windmill and tank on a West Texas cattle spread is usually absolute, and a trained eye can trace the degradation outward for a mile or more. This happens for the obvious reason that many animals visit these water points every day and loiter, compacting soil and overgrazing any plant that dares grow.

On the other hand, animals transport large amounts of fertility from the edges of their range toward their water point in the form of manure, so it is also logical to assume that if grazing were timed so as not to kill plants, they would exploit this fact and grow lusher and faster in the predicted sacrifice zone than anywhere else. Even the trampling of all those hooves changed from a liability to an asset through the manipulation of time. A dog walking back and forth over the same spot every day will make a packed pathway over time. A thousand bison stamping round may pack the ground also, but if they leave quickly, a living soil laced by growing roots will recover quickly, and the stamping itself grinds organic matter into the dirt and roughens the surface, slowing runoff.

In their study of Allan Savory's unorthodox grazing theories, Donnie and George had visited ranches in Utah and eastern Colorado where water points had indeed become the most productive sites on the range. Greener, denser grass was easily visible half a mile from the water, but they hadn't really expected to see this on their own land in one season. Unfortunately, they could find no effect at all on the grama turf beyond the immediate area of the tank.

"It's the animal impact," said Donnie. "That's what does it, but there's no way we'll ever get it out away from the water with the small herd and the water resources we have to work with."

George shrugged. "As usual we'll go broke doing good. Talking about animal impact. Look at our cows. They can't even walk. How are they going to gain weight?"

This, too, was something different. Jim Coleman's dry heifers that had only themselves to feed had thrived on the demonstration area, but the Whittens' cows that had to feed a calf at side had walked themselves footsore when they got into sections that forced them up into the rocks. They were harvesting areas that cattle had seldom gotten to before, but they were paying for it in energy and wear and tear.

"When you see cows lying down chewing cud in the middle of the day like they're supposed to, it's always Jim's heifers," said Karen. "Ours are working. I don't know when they settle down. They probably get their rumination done in their sleep."

Donnie opined that over time they should get fit enough to handle it, and if they didn't they still had over a month to go, and for most of that they would be back on easier ground, but his brother did not take the cue.

The two brothers sat on opposite banks of a little stream of rivalry that flowed down between them from their youth, and George sometimes sat on the side of those who scratched their chins and said, "Well . . . and maybe not."

"At least it benefits us psychologically to think we're doing something and using our brains," he admitted, "but aside from the water tank, it's sure hard to say we're getting back what we put into it. You listen to old Savory a while, and you think it's easy, but we really don't know shit, and neither does he. Why should you believe our little herd can make enough difference on this much land to ever benefit us?"

Actually, part of his distress came from remembering that he had invited the Agriculture Committee of the Colorado Sierra Club (whose urban recreationist membership generally embraced the slogan "Cattle Free by '93") to visit Tracy to see that in fact Cattle Could Save the West. His own participation in the Sierra Club shocked most of his fellow ranchers, and he often felt the membership, too, alternately Regarded with Suspicion his boots and hat or approached him with the extravagant delicacy accorded to black Mormons. So he had founded the Agriculture Committee to promote intercourse between two groups that spoke continually about the "health of the land" but found themselves separated, he believed, mostly by language and symbols. He needed, soon, concrete evidence that a profession which inspired the purchase of Marlboro cigarettes also held the key to good stewardship.

The Sierra Clubbers had seized on "riparian" habitat as symbolic of all the evils of cattle. Donnie had had to look up "riparian" the previous summer after accepting an invitation to join a panel at the annual meeting of the Colorado Riparian Association. He had discovered that it came from the Latin word for stream and in environmentalist jargon referred to the catastrophic destruction of streamside habitat by loitering cattle throughout the West. The scoured bed of Tracy Creek that cut through North Tracy would have made a good poster child for the Riparian Association, although the stream had died so long ago that neither Whitten brother had given its habitat much thought.

Representing the "progressive rancher" on the association panel,

Donnie had enlivened the debate by taking the unexpected position that although the direct impact of loitering cattle on riparian zones might be severe, the more serious damage came from the destruction of whole watersheds by misguided grazing practices. That, he said, produced flash flooding and washouts, scoured banks, lowered water tables, and made small streams intermittent. Simply fencing off stream banks and mucking around with the stream proper could only bring superficial improvement.

Now he and George had to show what progressive ranchers did about this, and after some discussion they decided that the demonstration area, after less than a season, didn't show enough, especially since it did not encompass the main channel of Tracy Creek. The only possibility was the small square of Whitten private land that surrounded the spring at the head of the pipe. For several years now, they had tried to treat it as one division of a holistic grazing plan by putting the whole North Tracy contingent of cattle in there, not just their own, for several days each season.

Eventually everyone piled into one pickup to go check it out, as they hadn't really taken a good look since the beginning of the summer. Just beyond the cattle guard, however, an enormous yellow bull lay in the road without any sign that he cared to move.

"It's gotta be Glen Alexander's," said Karen, and when they eased close enough to see the brand, even the kids standing up behind the cab whooped because it was, and they leaped to the attack with the enthusiasm of herd dogs and drove it out.

George groaned, "Well, so much for stopping overgrazing in our riparian zone. The sonofabitch has probably been there a month."

A single bull could make a difference. According to Allan Savory's understanding of overgrazing as a function of time, rather than numbers, one big animal could severely overgraze a lot of plants if allowed to hang out in one place, such as the Whittens' private riparian zone. "It's probably an accident," said Karen, "but you guys are all thinking, 'It's those Alexanders!' Shame on you."

Glen Alexander was a lifelong friend and one of the more supportive members of the Tracy Common Grazing Association. His roots in the valley went nearly as deep as theirs. In most things that mattered regarding the larger world, they would almost certainly agree. If Glen ever needed help, they would turn out, day or night, to give it, as they knew he would help them, and they would never say he had willfully put the bull on their land. Yet such a small incident could remind them of divisions etched into land as tangibly as the eroded stream channel.

"Yeah, you're right," said Donnie. "Glen's okay. It's just that in this place nothing ever quite gets forgotten, or learned either. I guess that's why we're so ornery."

Glen Alexander's grandfather had in fact been as ornery as any of the frontier people of his time. He had appeared out of Kansas in 1910, having swapped a used-up piece of ground there for a plot in a new irrigation project in the valley, sight unseen. Not a little embittered when that inevitably failed (the ditch company had not delivered), he homesteaded a rough piece of ground at the head of Tracy Canyon and proceeded to bolster his living rounding up and selling wild horses, which by then had filled in for the elk, deer, and antelope that the miners, loggers, and subsistence farmers had wiped out.

As Glen himself phrased it, "We rounded up and sold anything that wasn't branded, *most* of which belonged to nobody." One day the Alexander boys, wielding logging chains, fell upon George and Donald Whitten, father and uncle of today's progressive ranchers, drove them out of a meadow they were irrigating, and kept it. The land books had burned in the courthouse fire of 1916. The aura of wildness about this clan that made its stand at the head of Tracy Canyon had proven more durable than a paper record. It had survived three generations, going on four.

"So we dig that up when we see Glen's bull?" said Karen.

"Yeah, sorta. We shouldn't, but it's there. Grandpa Whitten hated violence, so he backed off, but our grandma never would forgive them at all. And they were experts at scattering little bunches of cattle out over their land and the BLM land and *our* land in such a way that they could never be counted."

But Karen pushed, "And, of course neither Grandpa Whitten, nor your Aunt Virginia, nor your Uncle Donald and your father ever did anything like *that!* Not *one* of them *ever* tried to put one over on the Forest Service."

"Well. . . . That was different."

About that time Glen himself came flying up the road in a pickup whose dilapidations thundered on the gravel like a tin roof in hail and sailed over the cattle guard in one climactic tintinnabulation. Everyone gave a neighborly wave, and he flashed his snaggled grin, raised a forefinger, and vanished up the road.

"Hello, Glen!" cried Karen, then muttered to her menfolk, "Country neighbors and their skeletons."

Glen was on his way to see his mother, who in her high eighties still kept the Alexander flame, living stubbornly by herself without running water or power on a remnant of the old homestead, seeing nobody and scorning the world.

Then George pointed out that there should be a fence line contrast between the Whitten land and where Glen's cattle hang out all the time. So everyone looked, but the differences between the two sides of the fence, if there were any, weren't startling. Glen's side had a big patch of kochia weed, a ragweedlike annual that somehow got to Tracy from Asia and often kicks off succession on bare ground. Donnie said he thought he could see a difference in the rabbit brush along the road. Ranchers detest this knee-high gray-green shrub and often attack it with poisons and machinery because nothing eats it. Most will say that it pushes out grass and, being nearly immortal, keeps it out. In fact, its niche expands when something else kills the grass.

But, yes, the Whitten rabbit brush had suffered. Something as heavy as a cow had broken a lot of it, and it was getting stiff competition from fescue and wheat grass. Further up on the slope, any differences between Alexander and Whitten land would have required a transect complete with darts, measuring tape, and statistical analysis to determine.

Donnie: "It's the hoof impact again that makes the difference, more than the grazing. You can see the benefit in places like this by the creek and in the corners of pastures where the stock bunch up, but it's nearly impossible to get the effect on enough land."

The three adults looked last at the creek itself, their showcase riparian area, which so long ago had turned into dry wash. They did not find much damage from the bull. Hip-deep sacaton grass carpeted the wash bottom, and masses of yellow clover and clumps of purple bee plant bloomed out of every ledge on the banks. In their lives they had never seen anything but sand in the wash bottom, and now they ran their hands through the waving green as if caressing a pet.

It would have been gratifying for the verdure to stop at the fence, but it didn't, of course. Glen, too, had sacaton heading out in panicles and lots of yellow clover. The wet summer had had some effect. But the dynamics of stream restoration are subtle, and both Donnie and George felt they had something to show the Sierra Club and a lot to think about themselves.

The characteristic wrecked riparian zone has nothing growing on the banks, which become vertical from constant undercutting by flash floods. Also, since the water table of the flood plain cannot rise above the level of the wash bottom, the deep cutting eventually dries up the root zones of water-loving plants just as surely as excessive ground-water pumping would. Traditional Soil Conservation Service strategy calls for countering this by building check dams to slow the current and raise the water table and by dumping wrecked cars in the curves where the current slams against the banks. More recently they have provided millions for sloping the banks with bulldozers and building barbed wire rip-rap structures in the wash bottoms to catch debris and slow the current. The expense aside, the success record of this approach is dismal.

Naturally rooted plants of any kind do a much better job of slowing currents and if thick enough will catch enough silt over time to raise the bottom of a wash. The more meanders a stream can develop, the less steeply it drops and the slower it flows. A herd of cattle can also break down a vertical bank into a shape where plants can take root and stabilize it. The trick, of course, is to time the cattle so the plants survive as well as germinate and are tallest when most likely to face a silt-laden current. Ideally, the lush condition of the surrounding hills would make devastating floods rare, and the Whitten quarter couldn't show much progress on that yet, but the stream banks did show signs of softening, promising the return of gentle meanders, and the visiting ecologists would see that the grazing plan would assure that the new perennial sacaton and wheat grass would survive.

"It would be nice to think that Glen's side looks as good as it does because we slowed the current down," said George. "Now all we have to do is get the grama grass to grow leaf."

Animal impact. Perhaps wolves or hunters could make the elk herd stampede and bring back grass that could tame the water cycle above the creek. Horse thieves might have once driven a occasional herd of mustangs into the canyon to sort and break and brand. Only cigarette ad cowboys stampeded their cattle. Cows have delicate emotions. Fear and stress cause them to lose weight and produce gamy beef, even if they don't run. On the other hand, they can cavort like mad out of joy or desire without ill effect. Some ranchers have successfully induced herd effect out on the range by throwing out rock salt or sweetened cottonseed cake or even the occasional bale of alfalfa on weed patches, bare ground, or stream banks where they wanted to advance succession. The animals trample as furiously and happily as kids under a piñata, but it is still difficult to have any impact on a large area without a herd of a thousand or so, and George and Donnie had yet to try this. Maybe they would this year. But they also had fences to fix back on their deeded land. They still had the hay to cut in the meadows. The 4-H fair in Monte Vista was almost upon them. The Wagners' cows needed gathering off the mountain. Maybe they wouldn't until next year.

They all drove back out through the demonstration area to check the tank one more time. A small group of mothers and calves moved stiffly away from the pickup as they approached. "Damn, look at that," said George.

"They'll be all right," said Donnie. "Remember the time we held them too long on a pasture at the home place and they all turned yellow from the alkali."

"I'd rather not."

While they talked, a magnificent pronghorn buck and the little harem he had begun to gather came down out of the rocks across Tracy and moved obliquely toward them at a soft trot. Moving briskly over the gravel road they leapt nonchalantly over the main electric fence and continued on toward the shoulder of Alexander, leaping first one polywire and then another before disappearing among the rocks.

But pronghorn antelope don't leap fences. It is a fact so certain that Indian hunting parties across the whole Southwest used to drive them into corrals hardly a yard high and shoot them point-blank. In winter, if snow covers the holes where they customarily slide under fences on their knees, even a blizzard won't force them over it. They commonly crowd against the wire and die, even if it is only a barbless electric strand without a charge. Pronghorn antelope, the fastest runners on earth, don't jump, not because they can't. They just don't.

"Well, *that's* different," said George.

And Donnie felt a twinge of regret. For years he had put his name in the Division of Wildlife drawing for an antelope license, and only the week before the notice had come that this was his year. But maybe he wouldn't shoot this buck. Original thinking was so hard and original thinkers so rare.

18

Lamm

Two events dominated the second week of August, the valley-wide 4-H Fair coming up at the Monte Vista Rodeo Grounds on the weekend and the statewide primary elections on Tuesday. Both events in their way measured the health and prospects of that heterodox community of land and people that was the valley and tested its connection to the world beyond.

More than any other institution, 4-H symbolizes rural America's struggle for cultural survival. Nothing else focuses so clearly on binding the young to the land by Head, Heart, Hands, and Health. Losing the young is a fear known in rural cultures everywhere, although it may take different forms. It is said that of the 3.1 billion people working on the farm and rangelands of the globe today, 2 billion would pour into the world's slums tomorrow if agriculture became as labor unintensive as it has become in the United States. The implications of this are complex enough, but people pour off the land for other reasons, too: because the land is worn out, because old age and ancestral property rights must be supported by the city wages of countless children, because of bigger welfare checks and more choices, even if riskier ones. Somewhere in this panic, this picking up and kissing good-bye, this striking out to seek fortune, is part of the great crisis of progress and succession. How can it be that the world's population is exploding while everywhere, even where the land is statistically filling up, people's hearts are full of loss?

4-H touches that. It embraces everybody, Spanish and Anglo, rancher and farmer, Protestant and Catholic, and it goes far beyond learning the diseases of sheep or the canning of apples. There are essay and public speaking contests, photography and model airplane projects, foreign exchanges, and public service work. Living on the land is not just a matter of raising something to sell at a profit. Children must see that the world that comes to them through the satellite dish in the backyard is no more challenging than the one they can make for themselves and that they can enjoy the thrill of both, even while living out on the flats between Saguache and Moffat. The contest is often touch and go, but 4-H tries hard.

Thus, Karen Whitten spent less time during primary election week thinking about the fate of distant politicians than about how to transport carloads of model rockets, curious bits of pottery, photo displays, journals, and painfully magic-markered title cards to Monte Vista. And that paled beside the logistics of relocating the usual menagerie of fat lambs, goats, rabbits, chickens, guinea pigs, and geese of her small charges along with the requisite feed and bedding.

For several days she found little time for sleep and subsisted almost entirely on cold nachos and pop sold by other volunteer parents and kids at the fairgrounds, but frequently amid the swirl of small bodies rushing about and the calls for help she found herself reflecting long on the extraordinary scope of her responsibility. Here she was, an average farm wife, thrust equally into veterinary work, art, and astrophysics. What did you say to an astrophysicist whose life's work, lovingly assembled out of balsa, cardboard tubes, and gobs of Elmer's glue, had hopped 6 feet in the air and demolished itself by whipping dangerously through the chico like a mad thing? You persuaded the young scientist that he could advance his own knowledge and still get a ribbon at the fair by artfully exhibiting the wreckage and writing a good report about what went wrong. That's what you did.

All those birds and vases and piggy banks and coasters and figurines of fantastic animals that you took for firing to the struggling ceramic artist in Saguache (whose son was the struggling astrophysicist) and which turned unexpected colors, slumped, cracked, or outright exploded in the kiln? You commiserated and cajoled and pointed out that they came out beautiful anyway, even though different. And you thanked God that the 4-H gave out so many ribbons and acknowledgments that every kid who tried hard would get one, even if it wasn't a ticket to the State Fair in Pueblo.

In every community, people threw themselves into the fair with a double zeal—to affirm one kind of life and defy another. The members of the Tracy Common Grazing Association greeted each other without reference to their differences. Danny Temple contributed to the raffle a piñon pine properly harvested from the public land and balled for landscaping. "And besides that," said Karen, "when we all get back home, and I catch up on my sleep, I'll remember that I got a kick out of it."

Meanwhile, on Tuesday before the fair, a thin but noticeable trickle of people trooped up the cottonwood-shaded steps of the old yellow brick courthouse in Saguache, and in chalk-scented school buildings of Moffat and Center similar flows of citizenry augmented the usual traffic of grade mothers and parents summoned for disciplinary conferences. These people voted, and at least one item, the choice of a Democrat to run for Senate, was important in the same way the fair was important.

Unfortunately, all Whittens were Republicans. For all their environmentalism and distrust of George Bush, a valley rancher had to be a lot more radical than that to register the family name in the party of Big Government, the Spanish radicals in Center, and urban welfare activists. Like many other Republicans, however, Donnie and Karen watched the Democratic race with great interest because, Donnie said, when the big election day came around in November, "I might be ornery enough to vote for a Democrat. I'd just find it hard to be one."

In fact, this time around, the ranchers, the farmers, the Spanish radicals, the old Spanish conservatives, the Crestone liberals, old-timers and newcomers, rich and poor throughout the whole valley had a strong interest in the defeat of one Democratic candidate, former state governor, Dick Lamm, and no interest at all in the unopposed Republican, a suburban Denver real estate developer whose strident Ayn Rand rhetoric stretched to embrace rich subsidies for beltways, the new Denver International Airport, and urban water projects, but no help of any kind for agriculture or rural Colorado.

Richard D. Lamm was an interesting case. In the late 1960s, he had appeared out of Wisconsin via Berkeley Law School to lead a whole genus of brainy idealists who overran Colorado politics on the extraordinary platform of slowing economic growth. They had spread like spurge and actually passed a *constitutional amendment* (!) barring the state from hosting the 1976 Winter Olympics on the grounds that it would touch off a "Californication" of cozy, small-town Denver, increase pollution, and upset the harmonious relationship of town and country that the state's suddenly significant number of hikers, skiers, hunters, and trout fishermen (recreationists) had come to cherish. The movement briefly took over the whole state legislature and launched several other young upstarts toward national fame, including Senator Gary Hart, who later ran for president, and Representative Pat Schroeder, who became the best-known woman in Congress.

Unfortunately for Lamm, just as he made it to governor in 1974, the Arab oil embargo set off the biggest speculative bubble Colorado had seen since the Cripple Creek gold strike of 1891. The state went growth crazy over oil shale, and the Republicans, richly backed by development money, soon reconquered the legislature and deadlocked everything Lamm undertook. Then, when oil collapsed in the early 1980s and the state's economy un-grew, leaving Denver's new forest of skyscrapers half empty and half paid for, the word "growth" became the mantra of salvation, even for Lamm, who hung on as governor until 1986. He retired undefeated as a candidate, but the state population had grown by 50 percent since he entered politics, most of it in unplanned, unrestricted, underserved, underfinanced tracts that had turned Denver into a typical overtaxed, overstressed American metropolis with a smog problem and a crime problem, rush hour jams, and a shopping district full of empty stores and cheap parking lots.

For the next six years, Lamm pondered the art of government as head of Denver University's Center for Public Policy and Contemporary Issues and published massively in scholarly journals. By 1992 he felt called to try governing again.

His chance came when incumbent Senator Tim Wirth, a patrician liberal of considerable national stature, denounced Congress as vacuous, mean-spirited, and incompetent and decided not to run. Under normal circumstances, Wirth's mantle should have slipped easily onto Lamm's shoulders because the men were friends and both powerful personalities of great intellect and common values. However, two other candidates threw hats in the ring, and all three campaigned as viciously and nastily as only people outraged by a challenge to divine right can. Lamm, who had good reason to think he had the longest and most noteworthy record, came on heaviest.

Of the other two candidates, one was a woman from Boulder named Josie Heath, the high-minded, articulate wife of a millionaire. She was politically correct in every way, but her money and the mere fact that many Colorado voters of both parties referred to her high-tech, university hometown as the People's Republic of Boulder, and appraised its politicians accordingly, made her an automatic lightweight.

The third candidate was U.S. representative Ben Nighthorse Campbell, whose background differed from Lamm's in every way possible. He had grown up in orphanages and foster homes in the small towns of Northern California because his mother, a tubercular Portuguese immigrant, couldn't take care of him. His father, who was part Indian, drank himself to death. Campbell himself was a self-described juvenile delinquent. He dropped out of high school. He lived now in the southwestern Colorado town of Ignacio on the Ute reservation. He had also bootstrapped himself through college after a stint in the Air Force, studied in Japan, competed on the 1964 Olympic judo team, become a silversmith of national stature in the craft, and bought a ranch. He had served two terms in the Colorado House and three in Washington, where he had fixed his reputation by disarming a mugger with his bare hands and driving to work on an enormous Harley with his ponytail flying. On the wall of his office hung the knife his great-grandfather had wielded on the winning side at the Battle of Little Bighorn and a 72-feather Northern Cheyenne headdress, which he wore proudly in parades whenever he could, including one for the Rose Bowl and the Rio Grande County Fair.

Campbell did not expound knowingly on public policy and contemporary issues as Lamm did, but he was smart, honest, and for all his flamboyance a wise listener whose skill as a peacemaker among dogmatic partisans people found refreshing.

Valley people had reason enough to distrust Lamm after he joined the board of AWDI, at a compensation of $10,000 a year, although he said he only did it to give the water development enterprise an environmental conscience. Every subgroup had its private grievance against him, however. The Spanish detested him for saying publicly that uneducated, unmotivated Mexican immigrants blighted our future and that those already here should not crow about discrimination until they learned English, got an education, and shaped up their dysfunctional family life. That he said this before the Denver Rotary Club seemed to them racist on its face.

He infuriated the elderly for saying the country spent too much on them, especially for health care, and that when the time came a lot of them should reflect on "their duty to die" rather than expect to be kept alive at great expense. The farmers didn't like him because he would tax fuel to cut pollution. Ranchers feared he would raise grazing fees. Besides that, he was one of the most culturally urban men ever to win the governorship. He never even wore boots. Lamm's most passionate issue, the slowing of world population growth through government policies of the strongest kind, outraged Catholics and conservative Protestants. Knowing that he had nothing to gain from the few thousand voters in the valley, Lamm didn't campaign there even once, but at least once a voice from the valley challenged him.

It happened three weeks before the primary, when the Lamm campaign announced with great fanfare that he was to receive the endorsement of the League of Conservation Voters in a Laying on of Hands ceremony featuring league president and former Arizona governor Bruce Babbitt and population scholars Paul and Anne Erlich, coiners of the phrase "population bomb."

The news release inevitably landed in the offices of Citizens for San Luis Valley Water in a back room of radio station KRZA in Alamosa. In its heyday, the CSLVW, backed by donations from individuals throughout the valley, had coordinated the campaign against AWDI, raised funds for the lawyers, printed the bumper stickers and window posters, produced the art exhibits and songs, ferried lobbyists to the capital, and published a highly researched newsletter called *Valley Voice.* Its activity had waned with the defeat of the water project, but its two minimum wage employees still carried on to fight lesser threats to the valley's resources until the money should run out.

The thought of Lamm winning the endorsement of a mainline conservation organization so infuriated the voice of *Valley Voice,* a gangling, open-hearted man named Gary Theimer, that he decided at once to attend the ceremony and embarrass the governor by making him defend AWDI in front of Babbitt and the state's environmentalist establishment. Then it occurred to him that he probably couldn't get in without a suit and tie, neither of which he could remember owning.

Also, his car was down to three operative cylinders. On a hunch, he called a freelance writer friend who had worn ties in a former career and owned a car that could climb the three 10,000-foot passes between Crestone and Denver, even though it had only one working door handle. He also called the Campbell headquarters, where the young volunteer on duty said he might be able to arrange some pickets and make an anonymous call to the press about a spontaneous protest.

Theimer was yet another Midwesterner trapped by a Rocky Mountain High addiction. Now in his early thirties, he had missed most of college while engaged alternately as a ski bum and a carpenter in the condominium boom that consumed the Roaring Fork Valley below Aspen during the 1980s. Then one day he had simply rolled up his tools and flogged his car over 12,000-foot Independence Pass and put well-thatched head and calloused hands at the service of Citizens for San Luis Valley Water with or without pay.

"I had always said that someday I would be a journalist, and suddenly it struck me that I had enjoyed these mountains for an awful long time, and it was about time to give something back."

Within no time he became the most reliable source of background on the legal, financial, and technical intricacies of AWDI for a steady trickle of reporters from the national press.

Gary and his friend got to the Campbell headquarters in Denver about 90 minutes before the open bar reception for Lamm was to begin in the Beethoven Room of the Executive Tower Inn. While Gary's friend and Campbell volunteers got down on their hands and knees and applied magic markers to blank picket signs, Gary rushed around to a one-hour dry cleaner to get the dog hair removed from his shirt. "If your only shirt with a collar is black cotton, don't live with a chow," he said.

The Executive Tower Inn was not the major downtown convention hotel. It had clean rooms and good service, but it fronted on a side street and had no lobby. It was the kind of place a team of auditors might stay in when in town for a week, or a troop of affluent Korean Boy Scouts, who indeed had added their note of khaki to the conservation voters waiting for the elevator when the two valley men arrived.

"Oh hell, there's no sense picketing this place," said Theimer, when he saw it. "No one walks past here but winos. I might as well attend," and he deftly slipped his picket sign behind one of the concrete planters by the door and squared his shoulders—too late. Halfway to the elevator, a short man in a polyester sports coat appeared out of a side door, blocked Theimer's path with outstretched arms, and threatened to call the police.

"I know your kind," he said. "We have some important people here today, and we don't have to put up with you."

There ensued a confused moment when it developed that Theimer had reserved one place at the reception in his own name and intended to pay for it by check. After some taut conversations over the house phones, the security man escorted the two men all the way up to the Beethoven Room on the third floor so Theimer could sign in and pay. He left the blazer-clad freelancer to blend into the company but escorted Theimer back down, ejected him, and called the police.

Despite the promises of the Campbell people, the only other picket to show up was a smashingly turned out paralegal from the water law firm of Hill and Robbins, which was lucky, because she recited the picketing ordinance verbatim to the hotel man and the cop. Then she took Gary to a blue-collar bar and bought him a margarita while the show got under way in the Beethoven Room.

The Beethoven Room was a windowless alcove big enough for fifteen rows of stackable chairs in two ranks of four with an aisle between, and on each chair sat an information packet about the Candidate. In the thoroughfare between there and the elevator, the state's environmental establishment and a scattering of Korean Scouts had gathered to sip Chablis and Budweiser (Coors being a Republican beer) from plastic cups and grazed on broccoli and carrot cuts dipped in something white.

The space was full of former Lamm staffers, the top state officers of Audubon, the Sierra Club, the Colorado Environmental Coalition, Planned Parenthood, and Boulder Open Space, all white and healthy and gathered in little knots, the biggest around Lamm himself, whose trademark coif of hair, as white as a styrofoam bike helmet, stood out above the crowd. The women wore kilts or cocktail dresses. The men tended toward tweed and chinos with a remnant of crease. They were not the sort one saw much in the valley, even in Crestone, but they were talking about AWDI. By the time the company had assembled and State Representative Ruth Wright of Boulder began the introductions, a trace of actual tension had crept into the room.

At sixty-two, Wright shed the energy of a young forty and although hard pressed as leader of the Democratic minority in Colorado's deeply Republican House of Representatives, she was perhaps the most respected legislator of either party. She sat between Paul and Anne Erlich behind a table placed across the dais. The two former governors, Lamm and Babbitt, faced each other from opposite ends.

Paul Erlich rose to speak first. He and Anne had stopped off on their way to a conference in Sweden from their summer post at the Rocky Mountain Biological Laboratory in the resort town of Crested Butte. They had met while studying entomology at the University of Kansas in the mid-1950s and had since made a name for themselves at Stanford, where Paul became a professor of population studies and she became director of the university's Center for Conservation Biology. Their knowledge of insects, when joined to a deep social consciousness, found its expression in their work on human population dynamics and publication of their two most famous works, *The Population Bomb,* in 1968, and *The Population Explosion,* in 1990. They knew how infestations worked and how they often ended and translated the scenario into human terms.

Now, bending his rangy frame over the mike and flailing hands the size of ping-pong paddles that shot a foot beyond his sleeves, Paul began by saying, "Anne and I weren't pessimistic enough in 1968. We maybe didn't get it right on a catastrophic rise in basic commodity prices, but we did warn that strange viruses turn up in conditions of overcrowding, and sure enough, now we've got AIDS."

He said they had warned of ecological limits and degradation but hadn't dreamed of anything as dire as acid rain, rain forest destruction, global warming, or loss of the ozone layer.

"Now," he said, "we've got to get rid of George Bush and elect Dick Lamm, because he understands about population."

Anne Erlich, as round, blond, and placid as her husband was angular, dark, and passionate, reminded everyone that the United States had embarrassed itself by ignoring the international call for environmental action that came out of Maurice Strong's environmental summit in Rio and that electing Dick Lamm would help restore our national honor.

Then Babbitt spoke. Babbitt, within the year to become U.S. secretary of the interior, was Western gentry. His family had owned a half-million-acre ranch for nearly a century. He had studied geophysics in England and law at Harvard and served nine years as governor of Arizona, during which time Phoenix had doubled in population for the fourth time since World War II. He had more experience in the politics of urban growth, real estate, and water than even Lamm. He was even then helping rural counties in southern Nevada fight an enormous evapotranspiration salvage claim by the booming city of Las Vegas.

Babbitt credited Lamm with "planting the environmental ethic" in the political culture of the West and went on to repeat the new wisdom that since the economics of the world were becoming global even as its politics were becoming tribal, a new senator would have to define issues in global terms but address them at the local level rather than as national or even state problems, and he and the league thought Lamm understood that.

When Lamm rose to acknowledge the acclaim, he said that he took pride in his ability to recognize gaps in his knowledge and seek out the best minds he could for advice, but it pleased him equally to demonstrate that one could succeed in politics by taking stands on issues like population and environment that were intellectually honest rather than merely popular. He wanted protection for Colorado's environment, a national energy policy that addressed global warming, an industrial policy that would solve environmental problems, and, above all, population control, without which nothing else mattered. A recent visit to Calcutta had reminded him once again what the world was coming to. World Bank loans and other foreign aid should be tied to a country's success in cutting population growth, and we should put big money into supplying RU-486 abortion pills and other birth control aids worldwide to help. We should develop the less developed countries, too, so that like us they will want fewer kids, and we must insure strong economic growth for ourselves so we can pay for it all.

The applause was polite. Lamm's arguments, delivered with all the conviction of an extension agent declaiming on weeds, made perfect sense. The Third World would overwhelm us, directly through immigration or indirectly through environmental havoc, if someone didn't act soon, and he was ready.

Then came the questions.

"How," asked an elder gentleman from the Audubon Society, "do you talk on one hand about environmental responsibility and on the other promise economic growth?"

Lamm had just published an article in the *Annals* of the American Academy of Political and Social Sciences in which he speculated on what would happen if China succeeded in putting hydrofluorocarbon refrigerators in 300 million households by the year 2000.

"That's a problem," said Lamm. "I do have a conflict between my two passions, economic growth and population control, except that I don't believe all growth has to damage resources. Beyond that, I don't *have* a good answer."

Erlich did, though. "Growth has to go on in poor countries through modification of the rich countries," he interjected. "We've got to cure economists of the idea that growth is the cure for everything. Even biologists are only beginning to think about that."

A woman asked how population control could be made to appear less racist, and Anne Erlich said she was hopeful that minorities could be educated to see the trade-off between birthrate and economic power.

The lawyer for the Sierra Club asked why Lamm didn't nail his opponent, Ben Nighthorse Campbell, for supporting the Animas and La Plata River Dam Project that the U.S. Bureau of Reclamation was building in the southwest corner of the state despite enormous evidence that it could never pay for itself.

"Good question," said Lamm, while explaining that both he and Campbell *had* to support Animas–La Plata because it was key to settling an Indian water claim. In 1880, when the Army herded the Ute Indians onto their reservations in exchange for the western half of Colorado, the government had promised to make them irrigation farmers, and the only way to honor that commitment now without damage to all the rights and uses that had been granted to non-Indians since was to build these dams.

How about the water in the San Luis Valley, and did the League of

Conservation Voters consider that? The question was inevitable. The information packets rustled audibly, and Babbitt answered first.

"The first observation one can make about these things is that there is no presumptive right or wrong about them," he said. "It depends on your point of view. The second is that this is an intensely fact-specific subject. Every case is unique and extremely complex. And thirdly, you have to ask what are the alternatives. I'm satisfied that Dick really gave those things a lot of thought."

Then Lamm spoke, first pointing out that, his board stipend notwithstanding, he had no financial stake in San Luis Valley water and had come on the board of AWDI at the invitation of two renowned environmentalists, Maurice Strong and the former director of the Environmental Protection Agency, William Ruckleshouse. "But really this is a matter of principle," he said. "I am not an ordinary politician. I've come a long way by not changing my position for political gain, and I really did see AWDI as an alternative to building another big dam on the South Platte River to supply the growth of Denver and the other metropolitan areas."

But was it right that such a vast and vital resource as water should be controlled and exploited for private profit by an absentee corporation that had exhibited only the most cynical interest in the people of the San Luis Valley? Didn't the unprecedented coalition of people that had arisen to block it demonstrate exactly the kind of local environmental concern that Babbitt had mentioned? Did it surprise Lamm that these people who had never allied for any cause in nearly two centuries might feel bitter that he saw no value in their common stand now?

"Of course, I see their point," said Lamm. "But the development of natural resources through private capital is the wave of the future. It's the way it's happening everywhere, even in England. Governments don't have the money anymore. The only thing you can do is try to see there is some conscience in it."

"What a sellout! What a slime ball!" fumed Gary Theimer as he listened to his friend's account on the drive back to the valley. But of course, as Babbitt had said, opinions depended on one's point of view. By all common standards, Lamm had the perfect environmental platform. His information packets documented his commitment to old growth timber, no loss of wetlands, enforcement of U.S. environmental standards abroad, no drilling in the Alaska wildlife refuge, tougher exhaust standards, mandatory recyling, a carbon tax, equal rights for women worldwide, and a host of more arcane issues. Anyone without strong emotions about San Luis Valley groundwater would find that he stood on the accepted green side of every single problem except one. Contrary to the ranchers' image of him, he actually opposed raising grazing fees on public land.

But even many conservation voters had left the endorsement ceremony with doubt. "He won't make it," the Sierra Club lawyer had said on leaving. Lamm had come over a little too hard-edged, a little too smug about what progress meant, a bit too likely, perhaps, to treat all problems as weed problems. He understood something about population, sure, but perhaps not quite enough about people.

By the time the fat lamb judging took place at the 4-H fair, Colorado voters had handed in their verdict on Richard D. Lamm. He won 36 percent of Democratic voters statewide but only 8 percent in the valley. He won pluralities in only eight counties, all but one around metro Denver, where high densities of brainy middle-aged liberals like himself abided. Ben Nighthorse Campbell, Harley and all, was on his way to the Senate, which he would win by ten points statewide and two to one in the valley over the Republican real estate developer.

Donnie's oldest son Nathan's entry in the fat lamb contest met defeat, too, but for different reasons. The competition was divided into ten classes according to the lamb's weight. The lambs that he and the other nine contestants led by the neck around the sawdust-covered show ring that Friday afternoon all weighed between 117 and 120 pounds—class 6 of ten classes. He thought it had done rather well for a lamb, having gained a better than average three quarters of a pound per day for the nine weeks or so he had hand-fed it and cared for it. He had also groomed it to a snowy luster and taught it to stand for the judge with its feet spread and its nose in the air, although sometimes it didn't.

It was nevertheless different. The overwhelming percentage of lambs in all classes and seven out of ten in class 6 were Suffolks or Suffolk crosses, meat animals from the biggest and fastest-gaining of all breeds, but notably unhardy. Nathan's was listed as a Hampshire, but that was not strictly true. It was a Whitten sheep of unique ancestry. The crowd of parents and club leaders leaned forward on the aluminum bleachers as the judge called the contestants into a show line. He was a portly, red-haired man who glanced nervously at his clipboard through thick, wire-rimmed glasses. One after another he checked the entries for conformation and "cutability," feeling their rib cages, flanks, and loins for excess fat and gauging the weight of muscle between hock and stifle joint, examining their teeth and eyes. Nathan had some difficulty keeping his charge standing during this operation, but it was soon over, and murmuring in the crowd stopped as the judge stood up, fingered his red mustache, and picked up the microphone.

"This here is a fine lamb," he said, gesturing to a large purebred Suffolk exhibited by a radiant boy named Dominic Valdez from Conejos County. "You can see it has a long straight back, long, well-muscled legs all around, very little excess fat over the ribs and loins. You'll get a yield grade on that carcass of of one or two. A truly fine lamb."

Dominic looked pleased and left with his lamb for the officials' table to pick up his blue ribbon.

The judged proceeded to the second place, Jamie Morris of Alamosa, a little extra fat, the front legs not quite so widely spaced or well filled. And so it went—Landon Jackson, Amanda Horton, Louis Sanchez. Each lamb a little less perfect, until Nathan Whitten stood alone with his Hampshire cross-something looking out through the open doors of the show barn as if imagining himself out there somewhere blazing through the chico on his motorcycle.

"Now this one has some problems," the judge was saying. "Notice how short the back is, and the belly line here is not straight. Also, as you can see, these hind quarters are not what they ought to be. But of course, that's why we're all here, so we can learn. Well. Are we ready for class number 7?"

Nathan led off his lamb with the expression of someone who had wasted a beautiful summer day doing housework.

Karen hardly had time to speak to him. She had Danny Temple's son Beau and Amanda Hazard to hustle into the show ring. But Donnie was vocal in his disgust. "What do they think anybody's going to learn out of that?" he fumed. "That you can take some fancy, overbred animal and feed it in a way that no commercial animal is ever fed and make it grow to fit some model of conformation that has nothing to do with real production under real conditions. When 4-H has come to that, it's sold out. It's just getting kids hooked on the same old addiction that is destroying us. That's not learning. That's . . ."

"It's okay, Dad," said Nathan in a comforting voice.

Nevertheless, that evening, when the prize lambs were auctioned off and the bankers and equipment dealers and potato merchants of Monte Vista and Alamosa bid up the prices to reward the valley's youth, and when Amanda Hazard sold her 122-pound Suffolk cross lamb for $3.25 a pound, Nathan did consider how far the money would have gone in his mail-order motorcycle accessories catalog, had it been him.

19

Xenophobia

One afternoon in early August, Darrell Plane turned off the Gun Barrel onto County Road X, which leads from Saguache to Moffat, and noticed a sprinkling of yellow flowers in the pasture to his left, causing him to break hard. Certain plants had a profile, a way of standing among their peers that set off alarms in his mind like the silhouette of a long-dreaded assassin.

He eased himself through the barbed wire and Russian olive bushes and set out across the rough meadow grass to have a look, but he already knew what he would find. Adorning 3-foot stalks richly draped in narrow leaves, the delicate greenish yellow blooms, really heart-shaped yellow bracts intricately lapped over each other, resembled nothing else in the valley. Without question, this was leafy spurge. A 20-acre patch had turned up near Moffat a few years back, but the absentee landowner had money to burn and had dutifully had it soaked with 2,4-D two or three times a summer. The valley's only other outbreaks were far to the south in Conejos County. According to Colorado law, however, leafy spurge had no right to exist anywhere. It was an outlaw plant, and Plane had a duty to report it, especially since he was, himself, chief weed control officer for Rio Grande County, which had enough other felonious flora on its docket without any imports from Saguache.

As Saguache County had up to then failed to hire a weed control officer, under the law, Plane immediately notified Larry Brown, the Colorado State University extension agent in Center, and Tracy Miller at the county Soil Conservation Service office. The latter at once called Tom Ouellette at the regional office in Alamosa, who took the news very seriously because he had just transferred to the valley from Montana, where leafy spurge had infested nearly 600,000 acres, at a cost of many millions.

Within a matter of days, the news came back to Jim Coleman, who owned the strip of land where the alien spurge had landed, that he had a problem which the law bound him to address or else the county would and slap a lien on his property for the expense. However, the SCS offered to organize a field tour of experts on the site to help him decide what to do.

From various industry publications, Jim knew that weed scientists assigned *Euphorbia esula* a desirability quotient somewhere between AIDS and cholera. It caused potentially fatal irritation in the mouth and digestive tract of any cow that ate it, although its mere presence, it was said, could keep cattle out of vast areas. Its explosive pods could throw seeds 15 feet, more in a good wind, and they remained viable for eight years or longer, even after passing through the gut of an animal such as a pronghorn; and the energy stored in a spurge plant's massive 14-foot-deep root system could send up new sprouts almost indefinitely. Chopping such roots only multiplied the stock. Furthermore, spurge eradication had a worse track record than the War on Drugs. Years of research by weed science departments at several major agriculture schools in the West had so far only uncovered ways to annoy it.

For Jim Coleman, this information was doubly or triply bad. For starters, he didn't have any money to spend on spurge. After surviving a century of booms and busts in the valley's ranch economy by prudent practice, the Coleman family had succumbed to the inflation craze that swept agriculture in the late 1970s and bought a great deal of land on credit that was now almost mortally negative.

Also, to support their grand designs, Jim and his brother Mel had founded a company called Coleman Natural Beef, which marketed organic beef at a premium. Now, after selling off huge chunks of even their ancestral land at deflated prices had not paid their debt, they depended more than ever on Coleman Natural Beef. However, the Colemans could not legally call their beef natural if it came from poisoned pastures.

And the world was watching. Small as they were, the Colemans had sent a shock wave through the whole beef industry by successfully pushing red meat in health food stores. The mighty National Cattlemen's Association had denounced them for treason because, they said, Coleman advertising mocked the millions going to promote "Real Food for Real People" as well as the bitter fight against the European import ban on meat from hormone-implanted herds.

This also affected both Whitten brothers because they sold their beef through Coleman and counted on their survival. Donnie and Karen felt particularly threatened because their land and the Wagners' ranches lay down ditch and down wind from Coleman's, and the prospect of either wall-to-wall spurge or a massive herbicide campaign would cost them dearly. So on a sun-washed Thursday in mid-August when Karen was off at a goat show, Donnie pulled into the long line of pickups forming along the border of Road X by Coleman's field to hear the prognosis.

Everybody knew everybody else, of course. All the local ranchers came and some farmers from the south, plus Dale Edwards from the Colorado State Extension office in Center, Darol Cox from the Forest Service, Jim Metz from the state's Rural Conservation and Development Office, and Soil Conservation Service agents from all over the state—sixty or more people wearing cowboy hats, billed caps advertising farm supplies, or uniform caps, according to habitat and niche. And there was Jim in his battered Stetson, friendly as always, greeting people with the air of someone who hopes that a big show of community support will help him over a hard place.

The people milled about in the field for a spell, fingering the cheerful yellow blossoms, pinching off leaves, and sniffing them—trying to gauge the personality of the spurge and imagine the point of view of a cow. Then they gathered, standing, around certain of the men who carried aluminum clipboards and heard speaker after speaker build an incontestable case for genocidal war against the spurge. The plant had apparently escaped from some Ukrainian wheat seed and first appeared in the West along a street in Fargo, North Dakota, in 1909. The infestation had doubled every decade since. It had now taken over a million acres in North Dakota besides the 600,000 in Montana, and over 100,000 in South Dakota. Minnesota, not being a cattle state, had allowed it to spread uncontrolled over a million acres, and it had now seriously invaded Nebraska and Wyoming. In North Dakota, a state-county-landowner cost-share program to control it was costing between $1.5 million and $2.5 million a year, and that didn't count campaigns mounted by the state highway and game and fish departments. Beyond that, the Agricultural Economics Department at North Dakota State figured that in 1992 the spurge would cost the two Dakotas, Montana, and Wyoming about $140 million in lost production and its fallout, and this figure would grow at about 4 percent a year in real dollars indefinitely, or at least until spurge covered the entire West.

According to research at North Dakota and Montana State, every year the spurge could develop its root system would take two to three years to kill back with Tordon (Picloram), the most powerful and persistent agent on the market that will kill broad-leafed plants and spare grass. Picloram screws up the metabolism of phosphorus. It also stays active for years and leaches into water tables. In virtually unmeasurable quantities it makes potato plants grow clusters of marble-size knots instead of real tubers. Since 1987, when DuPont had to pay several million dollars for potatoes cracked by one of its herbicides that wound up in the water table, Tordon's maker, DowElanco, has printed a message on every box disclaiming liability for damage in one particular place in the whole world, the San Luis Valley of Colorado.

That made it imperative to attack the spurge at once because the only weapon left was good old 2,4-D, which acts by overstimulating growth but breaks down quickly.

"The pressure on Jim to do something right then was about overwhelming," said Donnie later. "They had everything figured out and backed up by research. What could Jim, what could any of us, say to that? We were just little old cowboys who'd never seen the stuff before. What they said would scare you to death. There were even two commercial chemical companies that brought their spray rigs up from Monte Vista, loaded. They were bidding to come into the field and treat the problem right then."

Several farmers in the crowd made particularly impassioned appeals to get on with the spraying at once, and this carried particular weight because one of them was a young man named Michael Entz. Mike's father, State Representative Lewis Entz, had created the state weed law, and the two were partners in a potato and barley enterprise west of Center. They had strong feelings about ranchers because the powerful Colorado Cattlemen's Association had for years refused to endorse any weed law. Ranchers generally objected to the idea that weed officers might enter private property and charge for killing crop weeds like bind weed or jointed goat grass that made good forage and sometimes infested enormous areas. (The Cattlemen, of course, had long pressed the federal government to pay for campaigns on public lands against broom snakeweed, sage, Canadian thistle, and other rogue vegetables that affected them there.) The threat of a spurge invasion had played a major role in finally getting the Cattlemen to support Entz's legislation.

Although Entz's weed law campaign went almost unnoticed by the urban voter, farmers, chemical companies, and the Weed Science Department at Colorado State had lobbied hard. (Information requests to the Weed Science Department were answered with packets mailed from DowElanco and DuPont.) In 1990, the bill had passed, ordering counties to draw up weed control plans and granting broad powers to fund and enforce.

Aside from that, however, the Entzes had some standing in the valley, having settled there in 1919. At one time they had raised sheep, but they had made their fortune by understanding early that the sprinkler revolution made their land east of Center too dear for stock raising. Despite rather junior water rights, they worked hard and smart and produced 400 sacks of potatoes an acre, well above the valley average, with only 16 inches of water on seven of the cleanest quarters anyone ever saw. They kept outbuildings and sheds spic and span and whitewashed and the white gravel around them raked and their lawns as perfect as Astroturf and beds of petunias and asters well watered and fertilized. Even after rain, their vehicles appeared freshly waxed.

Regarding weeds, they lived by what they preached. Representative Entz carried a hand sprayer in his truck at all times and kept it loaded with Roundup (Glyphosate), which kills anything green, whether broad-leafed or grassy. Even far from home and dressed for legislation, he never hesitated to stop and crawl under a few strands of barbed wire to zap an alien invader that looked like the outrider of an outbreak.

In the legislature, Entz had warned suburban tax rebels that Col-

ould lose millions to Kansas in damage claims if they did not ie hordes of Dalmation toadflax already staging guerrilla incur- across the border. Kansas, like most Western states, had good weed laws, he said, and every right to start inspecting and even banning interstate cargos of Colorado hay and other crops.

Entz had secured the nonopposition of the state's powerful environmental lobby on the argument that most of these plants were not native and had no right to be here. "They are far more dangerous than industrial pollution because they expand on their own, and they make the land that we ultimately depend on to feed us as useless as desert. A plant like leafy spurge has shown that it will destroy wildlife habitat as surely as cattle range. Because in this country these exotic plants have no natural enemies, they will extend their impact without limit unless we human beings act to stop them. We have a duty to take responsibility." Indeed, of some 314 weeds listed in the 1992 edition of *Weeds of the West* published by the Western Society of Weed Science, 56 percent came from foreign shores.

The representative and his son Mike really did see themselves as true environmentalists and took pride in their personal record. In the corners of their fields where the center pivots could not reach commercial crops, they planted drought-tolerant grains and wild grasses for wildlife. In the last four rows of every hundred in his potato fields Mike sowed two to sorghum and two to corn. These he left uncut as a gesture against wind erosion, even though most farmers derided the practice as a 4 percent voluntary nuisance tax invented by the Soil Conservation Service. Valley winds carried so much soil off unprotected farm ground that every spring Mike's shelter belts trapped a ridge of dirt tall enough to foul heavy machinery. "But a man should do what's right and care for the land," he said, "and in principle my neighbor's topsoil shouldn't be a liability."

Against the scientific knowledge and political will and personal example of such people, Jim Coleman could say very little but scratch the back of his neck and say, "Well, I don't know. We'll have to think about this."

But weeds are not bound by scientific, political, or even economic conventions as much as created by them. Nothing tells where a civilization stands with nature better than its weeds. They are the divine fools of succession. They are botany giving the finger to society. ever disobeys laws, defies jurisdictions, degrades property valu ploits our honest toil, mutates beyond our attacks, or costs money is a weed because we make laws, survey jurisdictions, value property, toil, attack, and like money. Weeds fiendishly try our tolerance of diversity because one person's weed may make another's living.

In the legalese of Lewis Entz's weed bill:

> "Undesirable plant" means a plant species that is designated not desirable by this article, or the advisory commission. "Undesirable plant" includes an exotic plant, a noxious plant, or a weed.
>
> "Exotic plant" means a plant with one or more of the following characteristics: It colonizes disturbed habitats, is not a native member of the original plant community in which it is found, or is economically of little value.
>
> "Noxious plant" means a plant or parts thereof with one or more of the following characteristics: It is aggressive, is difficult to manage, is detrimental, is destructive, is poisonous, is a carrier of detrimental insects or diseases, is parasitic, or its direct or indirect effect is detrimental to the management of the ecosystem or the general welfare of humans.
>
> "Weed" means any plant that is not wanted.

Startlingly similar language appeared several years later in a bill that defined "disruptive" students, who could be legally expelled from Colorado public schools. No botany there at all.

Yet in neither case was succession so easily subjugated. By the time leafy spurge appeared on Jim Coleman's land, Representative Entz had long ago lost the battle against the particular weed that most affected him, a Levantine member of the mustard family called variously tall white top, broad-leaved pepper plant, or *Lepidium latifolium.* Although it dared not show itself much to the passing eye on Entz property, it showed in their financial statements for what they spent fighting it, and it surrounded them in such profusion in every borrow ditch and waste corner that no campaign that any county weed officer could ever afford would likely push it back. Out in the chico country east of the last center pivots, it covered 3 square miles solid where yet another land company had plowed out the ground and gone bust, leaving nobody at all to take responsibility. It cropped up here and there on Donnie and Karen's land, too, but since cattle ate it, they didn't care.

As Donnie stood in Jim Coleman's field listening to the experts preach against the spurge, he realized that before the service ended the congregation would be expected to testify, to witness as the Methodists put it, which was not something he did very spontaneously, even when he believed, which he didn't think he did.

No one else dissented until Donnie asked Tom Ouellette, the SCS man who had just come from Montana, "Up there, have they found that Tordon will actually kill this stuff?"

"No," said Ouellette, and he confessed that at the maximum authorized strength of 2 pounds per acre (6.6 *thousandths* of an ounce per square yard) even Tordon would slow down spurge for only a couple of years on most ground, and few ranchers could afford to treat many acres at that rate anyway. The preferred dose, he said, was an annual cocktail of half a pound Tordon and a pound of 2,4-D per acre, which would roll back some of the damage in about four years but wouldn't actually kill out the spurge, and of course they couldn't use Tordon in the valley.

From there the arguments went something like this:

So you would have to keep doing that, wouldn't you?

Well, you never get rid of it, but you can slow the spread and put off the enormous cost of doing it later.

And there was nothing that ate spurge, no biological control?

Not yet. They had imported a certain flea beetle from the motherland of spurge that seemed to be reproducing and ate the seed head, but that wasn't enough because the plant also spread from the roots. They also had a hawk moth whose larva ate stems and leaves but hadn't adapted as well.

But sheep and goats did eat spurge?

Yes, and in fact repeated grazing would weaken it and did figure in a new philosophy of weed control called integrated pest management, IPM, which, they said, was more holistic. It amounted to engaging a variety of tools, each in its most efficient way.

According to Tracy Miller, the SCS man from Center, "Some of the best control has in fact been achieved by sheeping it off and then applying herbicide just before it goes dormant, so it carries the herbicide along with the nutrients it transfers to the roots for winter storage. But if you don't do it right, you just make the plant mad, and then it sprouts like crazy."

But when you got right down to it, herbicides, even full-strength Tordon, did not cure the problem, had in fact not even slowed it down much on the northern Plains, so why start it? Why risk the organic beef business? Why kill off all the *other* broad-leaved plants, many of which made good forage? Why not try sheep? Why not see what a different grazing regime might do? As a matter of fact, Karen Whitten had 200 sheep and Donnie was pretty sure she would volunteer for the job.

Well, that was sure all right with Jim Coleman. Ultimately, the extension agent and the SCS men saw some professional credit in overseeing a "scientific study" to settle the question.

"We'll be very interested to see what happens," said Tracy Miller. "We'll monitor, and if it doesn't work, we'll probably have to spray."

Karen would work with Jim on a plan. Jim made a point of thanking people personally for coming and promised to keep them posted. Donnie had scored by extracting the admission that Tordon had not saved Montana, so his neighbors were spared his full Holistic Resource Management pitch, but if the others did not realize it, he knew that he and Karen now faced a much more subtle challenge than merely crowding their sheep onto the spurge with polywire.

Although the SCS might regard spurge as a "problem" to be isolated and solved, they sensed that perhaps that approach was itself the real problem. Certainly making sheep eat the spurge did not differ much from making the spurge eat Tordon. Nothing different in that thought model. You had a goal to produce something, so you pushed production and killed whatever got in the way in the quickest, cheapest, most efficient manner that research had discovered and politics allowed. Then you defended your decision, chemicals or sheep or whatever, until reality proved you right or wrong.

The whole matter looked rather different, however, if the goal was not eliminating spurge but building a healthy, diverse landscape that would support a family through the production of livestock. Then spurge, if it was a problem at all (one could after all raise sheep on it), was not a problem in itself but a figment of succession. Why did it choose to live in that community and what element of human management made the community so attractive? Although the experts argued vigorously that since leafy spurge had escaped into the New World from the Eurasian insects, nematodes, fungi, bacteria, and viruses that had coevolved to attack it, it now fell outside the law of succession, this was not strictly true.

Different species seldom compete head to head in nature. They may contend within niches. Once established they sometimes act to preserve their niche, and small differences may give one variety an advantage over another in micro-niches. However, tap-rooted plants like spurge, clover, dandelions, vetch, sage, salt bush, ragweed, tumbleweed, piñon pine, tall white top, toadflax, mesquite, thistles, sunflowers, and thousands of others do not compete *mano a mano* against grasses, which have a fibrous root system and an altogether different approach to life.

When looked at as a matter of succession, most stories of rogue plants taking over the world sound like the old myth that sheep and goats destroyed cattle country when in fact the misguided grazing of cattle destroyed the land for cattle, reducing it to a successional state where sheep and goats did better. If a tap-rooted plant invaded the grassland, then it happened because something else had happened to open a niche for it. The exact species of the invader didn't matter much. If not an exotic, then a native. If not spurge, then white top, ragweed, or goosefoot.

The law that defined plants that colonized disturbed habitats as "exotic" neglected to note that disturbed ground *always* gets colonized by something. Build a beltway and watch the shopping malls sprout, anchored by Sears or J.C. Penney's. Cut a road through the rain forest, and shanty towns will sprout within a week. Break 3 square miles of ground east of Center and you get solid white top, but it could have been spurge or kochia or native ragweed. Savory had broadened Donnie Whitten's opinion on this point by observing that he had looked at rangelands all over the world and found not one case without a local expert preaching the same *jihad*, verbatim, against some plant that had suddenly allied with the devil to destroy rangeland—mesquite in

Texas, dichrostachys, lantana, and acacia in Africa, jarilla in Argentina, guava in Hawaii.

But grassland, even in humid environments, only exists in dynamic circumstances. Without mowing, grazing, hoof impact, frost, or fire, succession moves toward tap-rooted plants. Afflicted areas always had one thing in common—grazing regimes that allowed animals to overgraze some plants and let others pass into senility, both treatments that opened niches for tap-rooted plants and favored unpalatable ones. Similarly, all arable lands subjected to the same crops and treatment year after year without exception develop weed and pest problems, just as certainly as all ditches, roadsides, and other "disturbed areas" are colonized by something—weeds, as defined by law.

Spraying the spurge did not pass any of the guidelines for a holistic remedy. It did intentional violence to the ecosystem as a whole by killing much beside the targeted plant. It did not address the cause of the infestation, the existence of a niche. It focused principally on killing adult plants instead of foiling the establishment of seedlings, which is the "weak link" in the life cycle of most plants. It committed expensive, dangerous, and nonrenewable wealth and energy to a never-ending consumption without building any durable capital asset. The same money could better promote a healthy diverse landscape capable of supporting a family if spent in other ways, they believed. On the other hand, "sheeping off the spurge," as the SCS agent put it, would obviously not work if the sheep overgrazed the grass along with the spurge. That would open new niches wider and faster than Tordon.

"If the sheep at least keep those yellow flowers out of sight, maybe people will just forget about it until we figure out what works," said Karen when she heard about the sheep, but when she and Donnie sat down later to really think about what they had committed to, they realized how little help they could expect.

Most of the vast research on spurge had focused on carrying out and justifying mechanical or chemical control methods because that *was* weed science and had been since the discovery of 2,4-D in 1944. Also, methods that required applications of patentable compounds in perpetuity made a lot of money, some of which went into research grants. Grants for research on flea beetles and hawk moths came almost exclusively from the U.S. Agriculture Research Service under pressure from environmentalists and desperate farmers because you could only sell a good bug once, and it paid no royalty on its offspring. Research on what Donnie and Karen wanted to do—"cultural control," in the jargon—had never progressed much beyond the "just sheep it off" stage because it had no sexy lab component, no hope of patentable discovery, and involved messy relationships with farmers and ranchers who had little time for scientific rigor.

"We don't even really know what sheep do to leafy spurge," said Donnie. "They may keep it out of sight, but sometimes plants like that respond by developing a root that simply never gives up. We don't know when it is most vulnerable or whether it matters to graze it at all. If you spread a bale of alfalfa on it, would a herd of cattle beat it down as effectively? Suppose you sprayed it with molasses, would sheep, or maybe something else, take it down faster?"

"And of course," said Karen, "they could be right. In five years or ten years, the spurge might put us all out of business."

They had really nothing to go on but the principle that managing for a single species almost always fails. It was a good principle, whether applied to preserving whooping cranes or eradicating leafy spurge, and it deserved some reflection in that year when election rhetoric overlaid stories of ethnic cleansing, riot, and famine on the evening news.

After supper, Karen poured tea sweetened with honey that ran from the spoon in a green-gold stream as clear as good Chablis. It came from the hives of George's brother-in-law, Everett Davey, whose honey house sat beside Road T on the way to Swede's Corners. In this place that did not allow many of its young to establish roots, he had found a niche in the buzzing chaos of borrow ditch and waste corner where the country could not afford to send a spray rig and the landowners didn't care.

The extraordinary clarity and sweetness of his trademark honey came from the tall sweet clover that grew as high as a man and made the Gun Barrel an avenue of gold all summer and bloomed on the recovering riparian habitat of Tracy Creek. Like the Whittens and the Colemans and the Entzes and the spurge and the cattle and the sheep and the barley and potatoes, and even the bees, it was of course exotic—another Old World creature that colonized disturbed places.

20

Ducks

The irony of Donnie Whitten's outburst over the overbred impracticality of the standard 4-H fat lamb did not escape him. What was it his father had said about the athletic woolies of the 1930s whose low fertility and stringy form would have broken any sheep outfit of the 1990s? Well, whether they had to scrounge through the high country of the Continental Divide or munch their way through level meadows partitioned by wire fences and 5,000-volt fence chargers from New Zealand, the point was to raise animals that fit the country.

The huge, soft, doe-eyed Suffolk, with its long straight back full of succulent grain-fed chops, did not.

For all that, however, neither Donnie nor Karen saw anything ironic in the notion of raising lobsters in their high desert. Ill-adapted was not the same thing as exotic. If leafy spurge and tall white top, and yellow sweet clover, and White Anglo-Saxon Protestants did all right in the valley, how could one discount foreign organisms a priori?

Quite recently a woman named Norma Milanovich had come to Crestone with the news that some "Arcturans" on a spaceship parked in the fifth dimension southeast of Albuquerque had ordered her to build a 450-foot pink granite pyramid topped with an obsidian as tall as Cheops's number beside the Nile. Thanks to a fortunate convergence of planetary energy lines, such a structure at the foot of the Sangre de Cristos (where AWDI had wanted to put its well field) would serve as a kind of lightning rod for benign cosmic vibrations, she said, and that alone could keep the accumulated sins of modern civilization from throwing the Earth off its axis with hellish consequences. She hoped to begin soon, as time was short, although she hadn't quite raised all the money.

But that was not perhaps any stranger than the great windowless concrete bulk of the Rakhra Mushroom Farm that rose from the plain north of Alamosa. The exotic element there was not the gloomy structure itself or the Brahmin family that owned it or the incongruity of raising mushrooms in a desert (it did consume two semi loads of barley straw a day) but that its profitability depended on virtual slave labor provided by three little villages from the province of Huehuetenango, Guatemala. Mayan Indians, direct heirs of real pyramid builders who spoke only their ancient tongue, had found a niche in the reeking dank vaults of Rakhra when right-wing terror and the terminal erosion of their mountainside milpas cut them adrift like spoors on the winds of modern civilization.

Just up the road from Rakhra a local visionary named Earnie New grew quinoa, an exotic Incan grain from the highlands of Bolivia that was given to him by a Colorado State University researcher who was later murdered by guerrillas while collecting more. New sold quinoa to health stores for $2 a pound, but it was in fact a chest-high domesticated variety of lamb's quarters, so close to the *Chenopodium fremontii* that grew wild in the valley that hybridized versions grew in the waste corners of New's center pivot.

In any case, raising lobsters was not any stranger than raising alligators, according to the example of the SLV alligator and tilapia farm, where the big grinning lizards multiplied happily in some corrugated steel sheds out near the Great Sand Dunes National Monument, thanks to warm artesian well water. After all, alligator hides made high-end cowboy boots.

"Well," said Karen, "we've always got to be raising something. Growing things is sort of what we do, so when we're not working hard enough or see an empty niche somewhere, we can't help looking around for something else to take care of."

Succession at the level of heart, mind, and pocketbook.

"The extension agent down in Center has been talking up aquaculture to such an extent that you couldn't help but get curious," said Donnie. "Besides, there've been trout farms here and there around the valley for years, and these tilapia fish seem to be doing okay, the only trouble being that you either have to process fish or ship them live in water, which costs a bundle. Then we heard about Australian red claw freshwater lobsters, and they sounded ideal. They live four days out of water. They're not cannibalistic. They're so valuable, it would actually pay to air freight them full grown from Australia to Denver and sell them to the resort that a Japanese businessman runs out near the Sand Dunes.

"Growing them here could be a hell of a deal. And they claim (who knows how they do it, maybe eating algae in the tanks) that these things can turn 11 ounces of feed into a pound of lobster. They're so efficient they eat and recycle their outgrown shells."

Donnie released the first shipment from Down Under into an irrigation ditch served by a well that flowed a constant 73° year round. They scuttled in as merrily as any native crawfish and almost immediately back out.

"We learned later that Australian red claws have an extraordinary homing ability, and they meant to walk back to Australia. We had to put them in tanks after all, and even then for the longest time they tried to rip up the plastic covers and head south. We also discovered they get nervous prostration without something to hide under during the day."

The prospects of fish farming in the desert in large measure arose, of course, out of the desertification of the sea. The list of collapsed wild fisheries documents a tragedy of the commons matching anything seen on land—the Grand Banks cod, the North Sea herring, the Atlantic salmon runs, the Pacific salmon runs, the anchovies off Chile and Peru, the Russian sturgeon, the oysters of Chesapeake Bay, the sardines and flounder of West Africa, the Gulf shrimp, the once teaming banks from Taiwan to Kamchatka, to name a few. Whales. Whole seas lost, the Aral, the Caspian, the Black, the Baltic, the Sea of Cortez, even the Mediterranean. So it pays now to do things like dike-off mile after mile of mangrove swamps that once sent their rich spawn into the Caribbean and turn them into shrimp farms.

A flow of clean, warm water having become as rare as it has, aquaculture has become big business, and if lobsters would pay in the San Luis Valley, why not? Donnie ran lobster farming through all the relevant tests of the Holistic Thought Model: It respected the whole ecosystem; although he and Karen would buy feed, they would not consume much nonrenewable energy or wealth; the enterprise promised to return a high gross margin without adding much at all to overhead; it did not offend society and culture.

None of this was directly on Donnie's mind on the fresh late summer morning when he and Nathan set off down the Gun Barrel toward the Monte Vista Wildlife Refuge, but that experience, too, would give him cause to reflect on whether it mattered much that life, including his own, was "natural" or contrived, or whether life was life because its evolution created altogether different categories of its own, of which modern civilization was merely one.

The occasion, an open house and tour hosted by the refuge, fell into the category of social and political events that keep ideas and contacts circulating in far-flung rural communities. Karen had taken Clint, Sarah, and a pair of her prize earless La Mancha goats to compete in a stock show beyond Denver on the eastern plains of Colorado. They weren't exactly range goats, either, but Karen enjoyed caring for them, and they provided great cheese.

Having set off immediately after chores, Donnie and Nathan stopped at the High Country Steak House on the main street of Monte Vista and breakfasted extravagantly on long stacks of pancakes. Above them on the walls of the renovated frontier building Remington-style prints reminded them of the savor of Western life. Fierce cowboys dying at the hands of even fiercer hordes of Indians. Terrified pack mules shying over cliffs at the sight of the slavering grizzly. Roping horses getting dumped sideways by the panicked longhorn. Runaway chuck wagons with the wheels flying off.

The refuge lay a few miles on south down the arrow-straight road past meadows freshly shorn of the last hay cut of summer. Blackbirds that had recently begun to congregate again in flocks darkened scraggly cottonwoods by dry ditches. A small flight of pintails, newly bright and airworthy after the summer's molt, and a darkly flapping heron heralded their approach to water, although they could not see it. Nathan tracked them with an imaginary shotgun.

By the time they turned into the yard of the maintenance shed, where the tour was to begin, a number of other pickups had already arrived and a group of familiar faces were standing about with coffee cups—ranchers in Stetsons; Kirk Cunningham of the Sierra Club in his funny little straw hat; the University of Colorado geography professor Bill Riebsame and John Wagner, both without hats, both smiling and gesticulating; Carol Wagner in earnest discussion, no doubt more practical. And glad-handing among them all and looking a little like Smokey Bear in his uniform was the refuge manager, Steve Berlinger.

The venue, surrounded as it was by a dense cordon of Russian olives, had no organic connection to the refuge itself, which was at best hard for the visitor to grasp as a coherent entity. The olives and low willow thickets allowed few grand vistas across the level land, so that one sensed rather than saw the presence of wilder creatures in the offing.

The Monte Vista Wildlife Refuge had a reputation for being, acre for acre, the most prolific source of ducklings in the lower forty-eight states and perhaps in all of North America. It was also the principal pit stop for the 20,000 sandhill cranes that migrated between Gray's Lake Refuge in Idaho and the Bosque del Apache Refuge on the lower Rio Grande in New Mexico. It was the oldest national refuge in Colorado, established in 1953, at a time when a restored and generously minded nation began to find enough slack in its budget to spend significantly on wildlife.

Monte Vista is part of a system of federal refuges actually begun in 1940 on the basis of ideas promoted by the great naturalist Aldo Leopold. In 1933, in a seminal work called simply *Game Management,* Leopold had outlined how a network of protected habitats might function to let wild creatures thrive in the interstices of a domesticated economy as the cranes did, hopping between very small, protected sites. Monte Vista, however, was not altogether what Leopold had in mind.

"A game refuge is an area closed to hunting in order that its excess population may flow out and restock surrounding areas," he wrote. But a few lines later he added the qualification, "No area is properly called a refuge, however, which is not surrounded by range suitable for the species in question."

Monte Vista did indeed produce a lot of ducks, but no one gave much thought to surrounding ranges. Indeed, in the minds of many, the refuge existed to eliminate the need to. To compensate for the lost and expected-to-be lost natural wetlands of the San Luis Valley, Monte Vista had turned 14,000 acres of waterlogged ground into largely synthetic duck habitat. Rectangular ponds excavated by large yellow machines and filled from pumped wells grew lush coverts of Baltic rush descended from the marsh flora of East Prussia, and irrigated fields of barley provided food. The warm pumped groundwater did not even freeze over in winter, which made the refuge as attractive as a ski resort with a heated pool.

Life wasn't getting any easier for wildlife in the valley. Small changes had big consequences, like the move to short straw barley, which left stubble too short to hide a pheasant. In the ranching district, overgrazing and the loss of flowing springs and wetland had altered habitat on a grand scale.

When massive plowing out of prairie potholes in the northern Great Plains sent duck numbers into a steep decline in the late 1970s and 1980s, a refuge that could accommodate 10,000–15,000 nesting pairs acquired new importance. As flowing surface water in streams like Saguache Creek withered, so little water remained ice free past Thanksgiving that the refuge became critical to wintering birds as well. Spring Creek, a stream that passed through the refuge itself, went dry in 1965, thanks in no small measure to the refuge's own pumps. Before long, 95 percent of the water birds that stayed over in the valley crowded into Monte Vista. In the winter of 1987, 30,000 ducks stopped there, and the slum conditions left 15,000 of them dead from avian cholera.

Within the U.S. Fish and Wildlife Service, this was considered unfortunate but not a sign of intrinsic dysfunction. Various remedies such as feeding grain laced with antibiotics were discussed but never pursued. Fairly large numbers of wintering ducks *always* died on the refuge.

Nevertheless, at least one man in the service didn't need this example to conclude that the refuge philosophy was dragging anchor. Through most of the 1980s, Steve Berlinger had held the position of land management specialist for Region 6 of the agency, covering eight states from Utah, Colorado, and Kansas north to Canada. The job carried considerable prestige but unfortunately very little power. The land management specialist could advise, but refuge managers did what they pleased, and the degree to which they seemed to lurch from one crisis to the next appalled Berlinger.

Far from complementing the habitat of surrounding ranches and farms, most refuges, he found, were isolated and locked in destructive dispute with neighboring landowners, another situation that the agency had come to accept as fatalistically as cholera. After all, weren't the goals of modern production agriculture and wildlife preservation fundamentally opposed?

Berlinger, however, was psychologically incapable of accepting conventional wisdom. His grandfather had tried to accommodate himself to a homogenized society by knocking an "I" off his surname, but the Berlingeri gene for passionate argument had survived in Steve. He had developed its full potential growing up in the utterly urban environment of northwest Denver. Yet, he often said, the only truly painful aspect of growing up in the Italian neighborhood was that he and his brother Ben could see the Rockies without ever being able to go there.

"Somehow we always knew we would get out and find careers in the country," says Steve. "I didn't grow up as a farmer or a cowboy or a wildlifer with all those prejudices. I just wanted to get outdoors and enjoy the whole thing. Anyway, you know how it is with us Italians. We're ornery sonsabitches. We get emotional, and you can't tell us what to do."

Both Berlinger brothers went to Colorado State. Ben graduated into the Soil Conservation Service and Steve into the U.S. Fish and Wildlife Service. At some point, both of them ran into Allan Savory and became even bigger nuisances to their respective bureaucracies than they had been by nature. Steve, by far the more confrontational, began challenging his managers to test their use of herbicides through the Holistic Model and hold "goal-setting" sessions with farmers whose wheat fields were leaching nitrates into the duck marshes. His superiors heaved a sigh of relief when, in 1990, he voluntarily jumped off his mainline career track in the regional office and applied for an opening as manager at Monte Vista.

"I was tired of being a consultant," he said. "As a manager, you can really do stuff."

Now, after two and a half years, he stood surrounded by four or five dozen farmers, ranchers, and sundry others who had come to hear him explain.

"This is our management plan," he began, waving a sheaf of papers in one fist. "It begins with a description of the whole thing we try to manage. It is not the refuge but the whole darned San Luis Valley. We're concerned with all of it.

"Our mission statement reads, 'Monte Vista NWR will be intensively managed, including the use of technology and agronomy, as well as ecologically sound management practices to attain biologically diverse and healthy ecosystems,' but those ecosystems don't stop at our boundary. We've taken down the fences, literally pulled out the wire. We have a responsibility to get involved in everything.

"Sounds pretty bland, but actually it's pretty revolutionary. It means I never agreed to run a duck factory. We all know that single species management is a dead end, but for a long time that's what this place was all about. What I found when I got here would have done justice to Frank Perdue. I refuse to do that. I'm after health, which means health of everything—ducks, cranes, hawks, eagles, ranchers, farmers, people. I'm not interested in species."

Once warmed up, Berlinger talked so long and ardently that half the time allotted for touring the refuge in the big yellow school bus he had commandeered for the occasion evaporated with the morning mists. He had done stuff.

The minute he had got hands on the operating levers of the refuge, he had telephoned the head of the Rio Grande Water Conservancy District and asked for help on the cholera. He wanted permission to ask well owners to let artesian water flow so ditches and recharge pits would stay open all winter. In return, he would cut pumping on the refuge. The request was unprecedented. It broke a lot of rules and would take months to balance out and tie down with formal agreements, but under the force of Steve's description of thousands of birds rotting in plastic bags, the official agreed to act at once and handle the paperwork later.

He crisscrossed the valley, knocking on doors and speaking at every public gathering that would give him the floor for ten minutes, and eventually he involved over a hundred landowners in providing water or leaving stubble and even unharvested grain for his birds.

Then, with most of its wells shut down, most of the refuge froze up when winter came, 40 percent of the ducks dispersed over the valley, and the cholera plague ended.

Berlinger stopped spraying mosquitoes, stopped using 2,4-D on the tall white top, and went before the Rio Grande County Weed Board to argue for using sheep and goats instead. He stopped shooting coyotes from airplanes ("Without coyotes, foxes and raccoons explode and raid far more duck nests"). He stopped the monocropping of barley that had come to demand doses of phosphates, nitrates, and pesticides no commercial farm could have afforded. Of 500 acres that had been planted to barley year after year without rotation, he replanted 300 to permanent vetch and native grass. To combat erosion, he did not plow the remaining 200 but drilled directly into the stubble a mix of barley and leguminous peas that provided nitrogen as well as feed. He pulled down the sheep fence around the boundary, and pronghorn antelope showed up the next day. He stopped using caterpillar tractors to clear snow from winter feeding grounds and let the elk move off the surrounding federal land and do it for him.

He ripped out miles of barbed wire that had divided the refuge into grazing management units and occasionally entangled a crane or a fawn and introduced single-strand electric and portable polywire. He conducted goal-setting meetings with landowners and discussed quality of life, production, and landscapes. He saved money.

Most radical of all, he reorganized a grazing regime that had followed a strict routine for over fifteen years.

According to the common wisdom, the sub-irrigated meadows and bogs critical to duck nesting would eventually choke themselves into stagnation or succeed into willow thicket unless periodically cleared or, in the case of the boggier places, dried. This was not far from Savory's observation that the vitality of grassland actually depended on grazing, but it had been pursued without much finesse.

Before Berlinger pulled out the barbed wire, the refuge had been cross-fenced into 19 mile-square blocks, and every year between the end of the growing season and snowfall a third of them were grazed flat. Anything left standing was often burned before growth started in the spring.

"Obviously, if you give a piece of ground exactly the same routine for fifteen years, you get extremely uniform communities, and above all I wanted diversity," Berlinger recalled. "Diversity of communities implies diversity of use. Geese like to graze in close-cropped pastures, and cranes roost in them. Pheasants, ibises, and some other birds like the thick cover you get from years of rest. And other species favor the grades in between. The cattle owners actually got quite excited about managing their herds to achieve this when they realized that I meant to use animals somewhere throughout most of the growing season, when forage is at its best. Hell, the refuge was spending money cutting hay and shipping all that organic matter and mineral value away. If stock ate it, we got the benefit of all that manure, and the ranchers paid *us* $7.50 per animal unit month besides."

By the time Berlinger fell silent, hardly any time remained for questions, although there were a few. Some of the stockmen wanted to know about the sheep and the noxious white top. And someone who knew the story said, "Tell about the elk."

It had happened in Berlinger's second autumn that at the first twang of archery season at the end of August word had spread rapidly through the elk herds on the surrounding public that the refuge was safe, and they came down from distant mountains long before the weather would have given them cause.

"By rifle season, we had hundreds," said Berlinger. "You can call an elk anything you like but dumb. But we couldn't afford that amount of grazing pressure on the refuge for that long. Unlike domestic stock, we couldn't control where elk went or how long they stayed, so the impact would have been severe and unplanned. And then there were the hunters. They were pissed off about the game being out of reach, and there are always some ready to poach on the refuge, which we weren't staffed to handle, so we had to harass the elk back out. Unfortunately, word spread among the hunters about that, so we wound up driving these poor animals literally into a firing squad lined up at the boundary. It was a massacre. It was the most disgusting display of bad sportsmanship I've ever seen.

"So last season I talked to the Bureau of Land Management. Imagine that! The Fish and Wildlife Service *never* talks to the BLM. They're not supposed to have anything to do with each other, for Chrissake. We're under different undersecretaries of the Interior Department, right? But it was so easy. They said, 'No problem! We know how to handle hunters!' And you wouldn't believe how they did it. They just closed that area to motorized vehicles—jeeps, four-wheelers, and that stuff—and it worked! This is modern times. Hunters don't walk or pack horses any more."

Laughter rippled among the ranchers. Those whose property abutted the public land had had similar experiences, both with elk that smashed through their fences and ripped up their haystacks after the start of hunting season and with motorized Texans who came roaring in after them. And they liked this guy who would say anything to anybody.

"In spite of that, the one thing I did discover," Berlinger was saying, "was that the overwhelming majority of people in this valley really do care about their wildlife. Maybe that's new. Maybe that came out of the whole AWDI fight. Maybe it was always there and nobody ever asked. I came here fearing people might laugh me out of the room, but it hasn't happened once. When I got invited to participate in that plan for the South Farm, I said to myself, 'Hey, this is how it's supposed to be.' "

For a minute nobody noticed a young man waving his hand to speak. He looked to be in his twenties and not a cowboy but tan from the outdoors, clean shaven, and not the cowboy's image of an Earth First! vegetarian, either, though in fact he was exactly that. He had hitched a ride down from Boulder with the Sierra Club representative, Kirk Cunningham of the funny straw hat, who chose this moment to step backward out of the circle into the shadow of the Russian olives. Cunningham was as diffident as Berlinger was outspoken. He worked as a chemist for the U.S. Geological Survey in the bowels of the Federal Center in Denver, but he lived in Boulder. He cultivated acquaintances on both extremes of environmental issues and got a wry pleasure out of bringing them together. "Constructive dialogue," he called it. "Very holistic." But it was also unpredictable.

The young man stepped forward and began to speak.

"I feel like I'm standing in the middle of the enemy, but somebody has to say this," he said with heat. "I'd like to know how you can even think about letting livestock on this refuge? I mean, you're letting private ranchers make money off a place that's supposed to be dedicated to wildlife. How can you begin to justify that? These ranchers standing around here don't look poor, and it isn't as if we need the beef. This country has more beef than it can use. The beef industry says it doesn't have enough market in this country, so they even want to export beef to Japan. There's no earthly reason why we need to put these . . . these . . . these *exotic creatures,* on something as sacred as a wildlife refuge so we can *export* beef to Japan! Now you all may think you have an answer to that, but it better be a good one."

The young man looked around and glared. Dead silence. "Well!!?"

Kirk Cunningham looked at his feet and blushed. One or two young men actually took a step forward, fists clenched, and Donnie found himself looking around to make sure that Danny Temple was not there.

Silence. Tension growing by the second. Then Berlinger's bellow.

"Oh Jesus! God! Help me! Let's get on the buses and see something. If I open my mouth, I'll just get myself in trouble. Where's Kirk? Where's Donnie? You guys are environmentalists. You handle this."

Closely followed by murderous glances, the compact stock grower and the lanky chemist cut their charge off from the crowd and got him onto the bus, and for the rest of the tour they kept him in check, although occasionally the phrases "exotic animal" and "just as a management tool" showed that the discussion was not dying down.

"I really thought he might get hurt," said Donnie later.

The tour itself was anticlimactic, as one might expect of a freeze-frame view through a dirty school bus window of something as patently dynamic as a wildlife refuge. It bored Nathan Whitten utterly. He'd seen cows confined by polywire before, although in fact there weren't many. Only occasional coots floated on the slack waters of the artificial lagoons. To really know what the place was worth, you would have to leave the tour road and stalk the willow thickets, stake out one of the lagoons at four in the morning, and see what happened at sunrise. You would have to watch it through a season or two. You would have to go out setting traps for the nest-raiding coons and skunks to really know what it took to raise a duckling. Despite the coyotes, Berlinger said he did trap coons and skunks because during nesting seasons those animals knew the refuge for the best dining within a hundred miles. The paradise effect, he had called it. Yet the ravens were smarter. They ate ducklings, too, but a hired gunner had only bagged two before every raven in the county knew what a 12-gauge looked like and stayed clear—or plundered out of sight. Even on a refuge with neat signs explaining different kinds of habitat, you couldn't see the interesting stuff, the moving and stalking and courting and rutting, from a school bus at eleven o'clock on an August morning.

A tour was not to see nature, though. It was for politics.

When the hot dogs and baked beans were getting passed out back at the starting place, Donnie and Kirk sidled over to Steve Berlinger and congratulated him.

"Oh shit," he said. "Who knows how long I can stay here. That fellow this morning was an idiot, but I've got guys with Ph.D.'s that are coming at me with scientific papers and saying the same thing. They're coming at me screaming about the duck count and exotic animals, and I'm thinking, 'What the hell's more exotic than a duck farm in the middle of a goddam desert?' And lemme tell ya, it's gonna get much much worse before it gets better. These guys are dead serious, and they don't want to hear any crap about holism."

Not long before, Berlinger had given his spiel and his tour to a delegation of specialists led by Gene Knoder of the Audubon Society. They were curious about his new grazing program, a "full-blown Savory system," as Knoder would refer to it later, "which everybody knows is based on very dubious science." At the time, Knoder was nearing retirement as manager of Audubon's Appleton-Whittell Research Ranch east of Tucson, which was the focus of a running battle over the impact of grazing on semi-arid desert environments. The Audubon property happened to abut a ranch managed by an equally passionate Savory disciple who had outraged both Knoder and the University of Arizona Range Science Department by tripling his livestock in the middle of a drought.

Once Knoder ran a journalist off the property for having written of being able to pull up moribund overrested bunch grass on the Audubon side of the fence, just as Savory had predicted. The unfortunate part of the controversy had been the total loss of perspective. The rancher had indeed achieved a remarkable restoration of the beaten up place he had inherited and had ample statistics to show reductions in bare ground and improved water sources and species diversity alongside his cattle production. But the rested Audubon land had proven interesting, also, and supported a quite different assemblage of creatures. And the so-called edge effect along the fence between the two properties created the most interesting ecological zone of all. Deer, for instance, regularly bedded down in the Audubon thickets but crossed over to the Jelks Ranch and fed among the cattle. The contrast made a better argument for diversity than dogma of any kind. Knoder, however, had fought too many wars with unreconstructed cattlemen to consider the possibility of a common interest.

"You can say all you want about livestock as a tool for habitat management," he grumbled. "But the minute the ranching crowd gets a vested interest in it, it's going to get abused. We're better off without them."

He and the other members of his group listened politely while Berlinger talked of water tables, diversity, the elk, the pronghorn, chemical-free management, taking down the barbed wire, ecosystem health.

"Berlinger's a fine fellow," said Knoder afterward, "but he has entirely misunderstood his mission. He's oriented now to grazing above all else. The proof is his allowing in sheep and goats. It is well known that they are far more destructive than cattle, and goats are more destructive than sheep. They graze much closer than cattle and sometimes even pull grass right out of the ground. In any case, exotic animals that were never part of that ecosystem have no business being there whatsoever.

"Besides that, Steve has cut the grain production unconscionably. He's dewatered impoundments to the point of disrupting colonies. He talks about the need for community support, but he's selling out. Those people will never honestly support the refuge, and the Wildlife Service has the mandate and the power to get along quite well without them."

Unfortunately for Berlinger, Knoder had come to Monte Vista armed with two scientific papers that proved beyond question that livestock grazing drastically reduced both duck nesting density and the success of any over-optimistic birds that did try to nest in the wake of cattle. The chief author of the studies, Dr. David R. Anderson, led the Colorado Cooperative Fish and Wildlife Research Unit at Colorado State University, which brought together the expertise and resources of CSU, the U.S. Fish and Wildlife Service, the Colorado Division of Wildlife, and the Wildlife Management Institute of Washington, D.C. The Research Unit had high standing in the field of wildlife management, and Anderson had long experience in waterfowl production and a particular interest in the impact of grazing.

"I've seen countless cases where waterfowl production declined in the presence of cattle," he said, "but until we came across the Monte Vista records, we could never document cause and effect in a rigorous way. They had a fifteen-year series of statistics for both ducks and cattle. It was an unprecedented opportunity. I don't know of a similar body of data anywhere."

The records for all 19 mile-square grazing units were not, of course, quite perfect. Also, each had unique potential. And external conditions such as weather had varied considerably from year to year, all of which Anderson's research team had to reduce to coefficients that functioned like golf handicaps to make all the years and units comparable. Then they averaged the handicaps into a constant and figured out coefficients for the terms that recognized grazing intensity (in animal unit months) and the years since the last grazing and adjusted them to make the equation fit the data.

The result was a series of upswooping curves reflecting the long-practiced cycle of three years of free growth without grazing or other human intervention followed by fall grazing and/or fire for each section of land. The ornate mathematics well became a scientific paper but were a great deal less scientific than the computer models of San Luis Valley aquifers, to say the least. The equation did fit the data admirably. Plug in grazing intensity in animal unit months per acre and the number of years since it occurred and you got something close to the measured number of duck nests. However, since the treatment of the land had been remarkably uniform, there were no control cases outside the data sample. Thus, using the equation to extrapolatate other cases had no rigor at all.

As predicted, in the season following grazing, nest density fell dramatically, but it grew at an accelerating rate in the following two seasons. Furthermore, the more severely you grazed off a section after the third summer, the lower nest density fell, and the less it recovered by the third season. A dramatic graph showed various scenarios. Plug in 1 animal unit month per acre and you got 347 nests per square mile the first year and and 508 the third. Plug 0 AUM per acre, and you got 610 nests the first year and 772 the third, and if you ran the equation to a fourth year, you got 914. After 2 AUM per acre, nests fell to 83 per section.

In reality, the land had been grazed between 1 and 1.8 AUM per acre, depending on how much forage there was. The criterion was to graze each section as heavily as required to clean it completely. Whatever didn't get grazed was burned in the spring. The graphics showing the impact of even heavier grazing thus meant nothing because the data already represented the absolute maximum. The case of zero grazing was equally unreal. Zero grazing from what base? From a factor added into the equation to make the equation fit the data. Nevertheless, in a formal monograph the numbers looked very damning.

Even worse, a similar regression analysis of nesting success showed that it dropped from nearly 64 percent in the extrapolated no-grazing case to as low as 46 percent in the first season after grazing.

"We showed that grazing affected duck nesting more seriously than we suspected and that the impact persisted much longer," said Anderson. "It was about as clear proof as you could get that cows and ducks don't mix."

In fact, as several peer reviewers and even some people on the team were quick to point out, the study showed nothing of the sort, even without mathematical casuistry.

"It doesn't take a doctorate to predict that if you take a square mile of ground, graze it hard from August through November, and maybe burn whatever's left, fewer ducks will nest there in the spring, which is all Anderson's study tells you, absolutely all," Berlinger fumed. "Furthermore, the grazing program they studied doesn't exist anymore. The timing is different, the size of the areas is different, the density of the herds is different, the recovery periods are different. Furthermore, they're all flexible, so we can respond to problems that inevitably will turn up. But some people see one cow and never ask where that cow goes, when, how long, or what it does. A cow is a cow, and it's bad."

But Anderson discounted that criticism and pointed out that Berlinger concentrated his cows into far more dense herds than the previous management ever had. It didn't seem to matter that Berlinger was actually grazing 25 percent fewer animal unit months, that he was going to rest some land more than three years to see what actually happened, that he grazed in small patches to create more diversity and "edge effect," that much of his severe grazing took place during the growing season and vegetation grew back before fall. It didn't matter that he was experimenting with elk and pronghorn as well as sheep, goats, and cattle.

It didn't even matter that the duck study had not tested the original justification for grazing, the revitalization of the grass and the suppression of brush, nor did it even speculate on the hypothesis that at some point too much cover might benefit predators or wildfires. As Knoder put it, "If a time came when you had to reduce the vegetation, there are other ways to do it besides livestock. Fire, or even mowing machines."

"And they talk about exotic animals," scoffed Berlinger. "What's more exotic than pumping water to raise ducks in a damn desert?"

"What can we do?" asked Donnie.

Berlinger shook his big smiling head. "Hell, Donnie, I don't know. I'm gonna keep doing what I'm doing. If it's the right thing, it'll come out right. I can't keep up with the politics of it. I just try to keep my mouth shut and stay out of trouble."

"Oh yeah, sure. But maybe we could write a letter or something. Maybe Kirk could write a letter?"

"I dunno," said Berlinger. "Wait till something happens. Maybe nothing will. Things are looking good this year, and next year it's going to really start moving."

Donnie and Nathan drove home by the back road through Center to avoid the predatory state cop who worked the Gun Barrel out of Monte Vista. As it happened occasionally in the valley, the late summer air lay absolutely still. It had rained not long before, so even in the alfalfa, the tireless center pivots stood still, and above them anomalous puffs of white cloud hung like tethered balloons.

They passed a field where ranks of lean dark men with razor-sharp knives cut lettuce, exotic workers out of California who lived in a camp in Center nicknamed El Borracho. They did not pull carrots or sack onions or sort potatoes. Lettuce cutters were proud.

Donnie and Nathan saw a man on a big green John Deere turn into his potato crop and turn on his spray rig—sulfuric acid to defoliate the plants so the mechanical harvesters could go to work without waiting for a freeze. Exotic elements. Donnie remembered hearing rabbits scream above the sound of the tractor the first year it was done, but now there weren't so many rabbits.

The barley had been cut, and the phone wires beside the straw-white fields were alive with mourning doves that made gleaning sorties into the stubble on whistling wings. They were fueling up to head south on the Tuesday after Labor Day, when the Colorado dove season opened.

Past Center, over the Farmer's Union Canal, past the airstrip where the crop dusters hunkered on the grass like robotic pterodactyls and where Mike Entz kept his stunt plane, over the Gibson Ditch at County Road G, where the farms ran out and the rangeland began. Beyond any other habitation they came upon the low buildings of the Meadow Ranch, where an absentee Japanese owner raised bison, partly for export. Exotic livestock. After years of being handled and fed like cattle without ever having seen a pack of wolves or a mounted Indian with a lance, they had become cattle. They lounged there now, cowlike, around feed troughs and salt blocks. They even smelled about the same.

Further on, they passed a half dozen pronghorn, a subdivision perhaps of the hundred headed herd that come winter would yard up on the Crestone golf course. Exotic behavior.

The road passed now through chico flats at a low point of the valley where streams ran out and died, and the ground was snowy with salt. An exotic place.

Finally, they dead-ended onto Country Road T by the home place of a grizzled old rancher named Larry Baker who was another exotic, a flaming liberal left-wing Democrat.

It was no small thing, what Steve Berlinger faced—trying to manage one piece of land in one corner of such a vast and eccentric place for the health of the whole of it. If it could be done at all, it would indeed happen in a way that grew out of apparently aimless diversity. And that was perhaps Leopold's hidden subtext, which Steve instinctively understood.

"A game refuge is an area closed to hunting in order that its excess population may flow out and restock surrounding areas," Leopold wrote. "No area is properly called a refuge, however, which is not surrounded by range suitable for the species in question."

But the species he had in mind wasn't really ducks. It was ideas, thoughts, connections, the ever-mutating DNA of survival. Wildlife was important because it was free to evolve and progress as it damn pleased, and it would stay important only as long as it remained so.

It did not need protection. That was backward. The modern world needed protection against the regimentation of the creative power of random nature. If living ideas were like living creatures, they did not come from the deductive logic of linear equations but out of the same irrepressible emergence of order out of free intercourse that put the stripe on the neck of the pintail and made the grass dependent on the grazier.

The learning that came from bison that acted like Herefords or ducks kept alive by medicated grain was not the same as that which came from having ducks whirring all over the valley all winter, or from Berlinger inviting himself to meetings and stumping for his wild ideas. It didn't much matter what was "exotic" in the system, the Baltic rushes, the rectangular lagoons, the Russian olives, the tall white top, the tall white humans, the sheep, the cows, as long as it all served the cause of freedom, as long as the idea of spontaneously diversifying evolution stayed alive, and perhaps the most vital examples of that occurred on the fine line where wild and tame met. The edge effect.

The legal papers didn't cross Steve Berlinger's desk until late October:

> The National Audubon Society, The Wilderness Society, Defenders of Wildlife, et al., Plaintiffs,
>
> v.
>
> Manual Lujan, Jr., Secretary of the Interior, John F. Turner, Director, U.S. Fish and Wildlife Service, Defendants.

The suit cited ten refuges for allowing secondary uses that violated their mandate as protectors of wildlife. Paragraph 74 of Count VII began:

> The Fish and Wildlife Service permits cattle owners to graze cattle on more than 6,000 acres of Monte Vista National Wildlife Refuge. In 1992, the agency permitted grazing by goats and sheep on 544 acres of the refuge for the first time.
>
> The Fish and Wildlife Service's grazing program on the refuge is causing serious damage to the refuge's habitat. Recent scientific research has found that grazing on the Monte Vista National Wildlife Refuge has significantly reduced the density and success of duck nests on the refuge for the past fifteen years. According to this research, expected nest density declined by 55 percent in the first nesting season after grazing at 1 animal unit month per acre, and remained depressed by at least 17 percent three years after grazing was terminated on some lands.

This, charged the suit, violated the National Wildlife Refuge System Administration Act, 16 U.S.C. section 668(d)(1)(A), the National Environmental Policy Act, 42 U.S.C. section 4332(2)(C), and applicable regulations of the Council on Environmental Quality and the Department of Interior. Such actions, it argued, were "arbitrary, capricious, an abuse of discretion, and otherwise not in accordance with law, in violation of the Administrative Procedure Act, 5 U.S.C. sections 701–706."

"Holy shit," said the refuge manager.

For good measure, he also received a flyer from the Audubon Society advertising the suit among its members, and this included the sentence: "A 1992 publication on long-term research at the Monte Vista refuge identified clear negative effects of grazing on the refuge's waterfowl nesting density and success. Despite this finding, the refuge has intensified its grazing program by supplementing cattle with sheep and goats."

Most of the Whittens' lobsters died that fall. Donnie and Karen could not figure out why. They sterilized the tanks to eliminate disease. They provided cover. They changed suppliers. They had the water tested, which turned up a part or two per billion of arsenic, but not likely enough to kill anything. They thought of homesickness. Still, one by one, the little creatures grew listless and checked out. Except for six, which grew vigorously and anticipated their daily feedings with claws raised and antennae waving. To create a healthy environment for a wild creature was no easy enterprise.

21

Finale

August arced over toward Labor Day and the summer played out from the top down. The noon sun still raised a healthy sweat on Donnie as he bunched hay with his antique rake on the valley floor, but up in the tundra on Antora, where frost could come in any month, it came regularly now, so the Wagners' cows began to drift down into the timber, down into the green gold aspen halls, where the frail grass made a misty carpet under the rippling shade. The aspens, "quakies," as people born in the Rockies call them, quaked more excitedly now as the long stems of the leaves stiffened at the end of their growth, and they gave the winds the impatient voice of migration, change, and vague foreboding.

An aspen grove is a single plant, a forest of identical clones shot up from a subterranean mat of interconnected roots. The world's largest single living organism is not a giant sequoia but some anonymous aspen grove colonizing a burned-over patch somewhere along the flanks and loins of the Rockies, and to go inside even a small one is to enter a genetic space created by multiple barbershop mirrors where all clues to direction vanish except for the slope of the ground. Come the witching cusp of autumn, and all the leaves, herdlike, turn golden and face death gloriously together. Yet even this united realm has its mavericks, one branch that's different and turns before all the others, announcing autumn with a flaming frond.

The cattle, generic bovines but independent-minded, came back down in slow marches day by day through the bright aspens and the dark firs, in among the great armored ponderosas, and at last to the fragrant piñon, juniper, and sage, down over the shoulder of Antora past the knob of Baxter Mountain down Phantom Creek, then over into Ford Creek and up past the old diggings at Spook City into Little Kerber Creek, past Lucky Boy Gulch, Columbia Gulch, Ute Creek, Standhorse Creek, Graveyard Gulch, and the Coleman Cutoff Trail to Kerber Creek itself just above the Wagners' home place. Along the way, they passed through three rusty Forest Service fences and numerous nameless side draws where the bulls and the more contrary cows cut out and hid.

Ahead lay the trials of weaning and weighing, culling, sorting, and shipping, and for many the feedlot and slaughterhouse, still they went down on the whole more willingly than they had gone up because they were going back toward the familiar and for the most part downhill. In one place, where a half-dozen cows turned aside to pleasure themselves lavishly in a swale of tall fibrous weeds with dentilated palmate leaves, a pale young man with a ponytail appeared suddenly out of the underbrush and drove them out with a volley of rocks and curses. For the most part, however, such lapses still required the *yip* and shout of Peggy and her dogs and often John or Chuck Wagner or Donnie brumming around on their knobby-tired dirt bikes. Somewhere in the middle of all this, Carol Wagner suggested that inasmuch as a lot of people were putting a lot of time into this work and all manner of sorting and loading lay ahead, everyone might profit from reviewing the Bud Williams videotape.

Bud Williams is a lanky old Oregon farm boy who has brought to the ancient art of handling livestock the seeds of a revolution as profound in its way as the one Allan Savory fomented in land management and curiously similar in its intellectual approach. Entirely outside the ken of university departments of animal husbandry, behavioral scientists, ethologists, and highly certificated engineers who designed farm equipment and feedlots, Williams has arrived at the point where ranchers, cowhands, and feedlot owners who have worked livestock all their lives will pay half a grand to attend a three-day seminar on how to gather animals from a pasture and put them through a chute.

Williams commands over $1,000 a day as a consultant. His six-hour video includes some blurry images of actual animals transposed from super-8 clips shot by his wife Eunice but is mostly the family camcorder's view from the back of a Holiday Inn conference room full of men in big hats who sometimes get up and block the camera while fetching coffee. It sells for $100 and communicates enough wisdom in the first 5 minutes to pay for itself ten times over in a day. By reputation, Williams could save a medium-sized feedlot several thousand dollars a month in vet and medicine bills alone just by imparting a healthier relationship between animals and people, and no corporate manager could fail to see the implications for situations involving merely people.

Profit margins in the livestock industry are to an amazing degree a function of stress, to which hunger, thirst, rough country, and harsh weather contribute only in part. Angry or scared animals get sicker, fight more, eat less, gain less, give less milk, wreck equipment, require more labor, and even taste worse if they die mad with their blood full of adrenalin. And all of that costs money, big money. Not a few dairies that sought Williams's counsel have seen costs plummet and milk production rise 20 percent or more, far in excess of the increase promised by the synthetic hormones that have raised such ethical, hygienic, and economic furor in the industry.

The prior winter, Donnie and the Wagners had sponsored a Bud Williams workshop and demonstration, one day at the Whittens', the next at the Wagners' place, but although Donnie and Karen spread the word among their neighbors, few came. The quorum that did gather around their kitchen table came from the other end of the valley, from the back side of the Sangre de Christos, from out on the eastern plains, from that scattering of congenital old radicals, innocent neophytes, people in crisis, and uncommon intellects that gave Savory his first audiences.

"Bud Williams was utterly amazing," said Donnie later. "We challenged him to bring in a little group of cattle that had hung out in the mountains, gone half wild, and then come down into the willows along Kerber Creek. I offered to help him out by taking down a section of fence, but he said no, he wouldn't need that. He started working them from half a mile a way and never got closer than 100 yards. He didn't seem to do much but walk around with his hands in his pockets. He was responding to signs that none of us would notice until he pointed them out, an ear twitching or a head swinging around. And darned if those cattle didn't come up out of the creek bottom, cross back over on a narrow bridge, jump over an irrigation ditch and go in through a gate as if he'd told them they were going to get fed. We all started to run up and shut the gate, but he said, no, we needn't hurry, because they had gone in because they wanted to and would stay until they had reason to leave. And darned if it didn't look that way."

"You don't have to work with your hands in your pockets," said Williams. "I say it's great to wave your arms around if it helps you. I just work that-a-way to show people that you don't *have* to do it. I haven't picked up a stick or a whip or a hot shot cattle prod in years, and I think I get the job done quicker. Whenever you're working animals, and you're working hard, you're doing something wrong."

Yet, despite this gospel that was so expensively bought and diligently attended, the spring drive up Antora had not been the only workday that left everyone exhausted. "We're a lot better than we used to be," said Donnie, "but sometimes you don't want to mess around. Sometimes things just need done." Nobody but Carol really wanted to watch the video again.

On the VCR, as in life, Williams comes on as a tall rangy man in jeans with sixty-plus years of weather in his face and grass-fed metaphor in his speech. He introduces himself as an "old country boy who grew up on a farm with cattle and sheep and dairy cattle and workhorses and hogs, and I never thought much about it until I got married and my wife wanted to live on a ranch.

"For her sake I got a job on a place, but it drove me nuts. I just couldn't stand the way they did, and they couldn't stand me. So finally I even quit. I said I wouldn't handle stock this-a-way, but they got interested in what I had to say, so I kept working at it, and that's how I got where I am today. I don't have a fancy education, but I'm a workaholic kind of fella, and I've spent my whole life learning these things."

Williams's insights derived most of all from a stubbornly childlike attitude that made him unashamed to inquire about simple truth. Did the Marlboro Man cowboy's ropes and whips and spurs serve him any better than the emperor's clothes? His unrepentant naiveté gave Williams remarkable powers of observation and the ability to see universal principles where others saw only annoying confusion that they tended to suppress.

Although animals obviously possess intelligence of unexplored complexity and sophistication, they usually apply it according to predictable preferences, he concluded, like people. They want to be with other animals. They'd rather go in the direction they're headed than change course. In a tight spot they want to go around you. And they haven't any patience at all. Most of all, though, they don't like pressure. In the course of his spiel, Williams implies often that most animals know that these principles apply equally to people and that this affords an opportunity for unstressful dialogue and mutual understanding.

In the animal context, though, pressure has a very specific meaning, according to Williams. He draws a narrow oval on the chalkboard representing the aerial profile of a cow and adds an arc extending out from either side to make a figure not unlike a stylized butterfly. "This out here," he says, pointing to the wings, "is what I call the flight zone. If you come inside that, the animal feels pressure, and he will move to take it off. This is what I mean when I talk about working an animal from the side. It's any time you can see its eye, and it can see you, and you work with this flight zone.

"You never pressure an animal from the rear. The thing is we expect to chase animals, but animals don't really want to be chased. If you really want to irritate somebody, just follow them around, just walk behind them. If they slow down, you slow down, if they speed up, you speed up. I guarantee you, they'll let you know what they feel about that. But you can increase or decrease the flight zone with the same animal or group of animals, and you can do it very quickly. If an animal responds to your pressure and starts moving, you can bring it out farther and farther. It took me a long time to figure this out.

"On the other hand, if you're working animals in a small pen, you're definitely going to be within their flight zone, so you've got to understand that it's important to be able to change that flight zone, so you're not inside of it as often, because the farther you are inside, the more they tend to either panic or fight.

"Say you're in this room. The walls start to come in. At some point you or anybody else will panic. But say you have a real good friend that you trust, and you know that when the walls get so far from you, they're gonna stop. When those walls get about there, you're going to get a little nervous about whether they're really going to stop, but if they stop like he said, Whew. After that they can come in that far without panicking you. Before, if you didn't know they was gonna stop there, you might have been in a real panic.

"Now, I'm not a real scientific person. I didn't get all this high-priced education. The only thing I did is I worked cattle. And what I find is that they're not afraid of those shocks you give them. I'm not even sure that they're thinking about that. What causes the panic in an animal when you work them is this pressure. They're brought in from a pasture. They're put into a corral. These walls are coming in. Then they are put into a smaller corral, and then a chute, and by then it's total panic. It wouldn't matter whether you gave a shot. It wouldn't matter what you did. Give 'em a piece of candy and they're still going to be scared to death.

"My theory is this, and I've worked elk. I've worked reindeer. I've worked fallow deer. I've worked wild cattle. I've worked gentle cattle. I've worked sheep. I've worked all these things. And this works. I teach that animal, 'Look, that wall is going to stop. And that wall *will* stop. Trust me, and I don't cheat.' I absolutely don't cheat, and they know I don't cheat. And when those walls stop here and they know they can trust me, they don't panic. When I put cattle into a chute, they want to go in there. They don't mind being in there, and they don't panic, and they don't mind coming back five minutes later or five days later or five months later. They don't remember that as a bad experience.

"It don't matter if we brand them. It don't matter if we dehorn them. It don't matter if we give them every shot known to man. They don't mind that. What they mind is that pressure. I've been in situations where we worked cattle every day and did things to them that there's no way by most people's standards they wouldn't have been afraid of, but they weren't, because we didn't do the damage panicking them before they got in there."

At about this point the video screen disintegrates into a static of snow and dark careening blotches, and it takes Williams' voice-over a minute to apologize for his wife's photography and for the viewer to realize that this is not a technical failure, that the snow really is snow, and the rocketing blobs are actually reindeer and men.

It is a herd of about 1,800 that have been herded across the tundra by helicopter and that an entire village of Eskimos has surrounded with an immense strip of burlap for the purpose of driving them through a 30-foot opening into a corral. And they are panicked. By the dozen they break over, under, and through the burlap. The line surges forward. The deer charge. People and animals sail through the air.

"Well, this is the way they were doing it. And of course they did get some of them through the gate, but Eunice was up on the fence a few hours later, and here's what the corral looked like."

What looks at first like a North Atlantic blizzard rolling past the lower porthole of a ship turns out to be a cauldron of deer packed so tight you can't see the ground and yet still stampeding around in a circle at a full tilt.

"Now you tell me what that does to an animal."

The audience knows. New stock arriving at a feed yard in that state of agitation may not eat or drink for a couple of days or even more, and the weight loss and disease rate among them can be terrible. Williams tells of a feed yard in Canada that was doctoring seventy-five animals a day and had stopped accepting young calves altogether because so many simply died. After the hands learned how to calm them down, the daily sick list dropped to four or five and the death loss to virtually zero.

The next time reindeer appear they are walking through an 8-foot gate like Rotarians going in to lunch, and the Eskimo herder doesn't even close the corral. The deer just stand there.

"I worked with them for eighteen hours," says Williams. "I taught them to take this pressure before I even headed them to the corral. The corral was nothing. They walked right in. They were not afraid of the corral. I just walked back and forth behind them. Speed is not important. You have to approach an animal so that he sees that you're going to go on by him. They are so sensitive. If an animal raised its head, I'd veer away. One step was enough, and that head would come down. It was four to five hours before I could get them to moving at a walk."

"And how big an area were you working in?" comes the question from the room.

"Oh, about 5 million acres," Williams answers without expression.

"Reindeer are a really quiet animal, one of the nicest I've ever worked with when you get them gentled down."

This is it. This is the secret. If you could walk nearly 2,000 reindeer out of 5 million acres without giving any one of them the jitters you could do anything. You could bring peace to the West Bank of the Jordon and cure lower back pain. You could dealienate youth so they face the inner city without drugs and violence and crowd into schoolrooms like aspiring Rotarians. You could turn the police force into a diaper service and prisons into mushroom farms. Bud Williams makes no such claims, but he does not put much distance between animals and people.

"Did you ever notice that when you sit down on a bench, everybody will move over a little bit—every single time? The first thing we've got to do is understand the animals a little better," he says. "The next thing is to understand the principles they operate under and the principles *we* operate under. *We* have to know ourselves a little better and what we're asking of the animal."

He explains how, as he did with the reindeer, you can start a herd moving by walking across behind them, not directly into their backsides but across at right angles to the way you want them to move, just brushing the after-edge of their flight zone but in a direction that they can see will take you on past. As the herd begins to move you make another pass a bit further on. As they move, he says, you can steer the leaders by extending your pass out farther on one side until it looks as if you *might* move to put pressure on them.

"You read the animals and they tell you when it's enough. When you're moving a group of cattle, they will tell you what you can do. There is no pat answer. Whenever you give a pat answer in anything dealing with animals you're going to get in trouble."

But there are these principles. You do not to drive into the back of the herd because the animals will turn so they can see you, and then they will try to go around you. You do not go up alongside because that will speed up the leaders, the ones most sensitive to pressure, and slow down the followers and string out the whole bunch.

"*But,*" he says, "when you start to teach somebody, you don't just say, this is how you do it. You've gotta understand what they don't understand. And there is one thing that people don't understand, and that is you don't go up the side. You go in a straight line across behind.

They just don't understand, and you can say it, and you can say it, and you can say it. You get on a ranch horse and he passes that rear cow and *he, too,* will turn and go straight at it. He's been trained just like a person to do that all his life. He can't go on by that animal. He just can't do it. There's probably not one person in this audience who can walk all the way across the first time without yielding to the temptation to drive in from behind.

"I've shown over and over how to do it, and then turned the job over to the people watching, and it will not be two minutes before there'll be a guy up one side and a guy up the other, and a bunch right in back whipping and spurring. It's hard to understand why that is so difficult. They'll say, 'Well, I had to turn them.'

"The fact is, walking straight across behind is not what we want to do. We *want* to go up there and turn them. Just going out to the side isn't enough for us. We want to go up there and push her over to show we can do it. And when we do that we create all these other problems, but we're happy because we did what we wanted."

Williams drops reindeer and takes up the most elementary task of all, moving cattle out of one pen and into another, which is normally done by walking around behind them and driving them toward the gate, which *will* work except that a certain number always cut back and have to be rounded up and driven again, and the last one usually gets ornery and has to be energetically hazed and tricked and spooked on through.

But there on the hazy old video stands Williams with his hands in his pockets, not at the back of the corral at all, but quite near the gate itself, and cows are placidly walking by him single file. Not only that, he clearly is controlling the flow precisely, letting some go on through and turning others back, quietly sorting calves away from their mothers and heifers from steers, a job that typically requires quick and forceful action amid horrendous bawling and scufflings and not uncommonly open rebellion and broken wire and smashed rails. And not only is Williams standing in the wrong place, his behavior is backward. He moves as if to block the gate and animals spurt through. He steps back, and they stop, but his movements are in fact so understated it takes a minute to figure out *what* he's doing. He is letting the cattle go around him, which he knows they want to do.

"We like to walk around things," he says. "Take anyone into a corral and they'll walk around and in behind. An animal wants to go around people. He wants to very very badly. If you stand at the back of the pen, he will try to go around you and away from the gate. Now if you stand at the other end with a little more space on the gate side to make it more attractive, I'll bet you any money I'll ever have that all the animals in that pen will go around you and out that gate. If you step toward their side or even make a motion, they'll go right on through to take that pressure off. If you step back, *you're* taking the pressure off, and they'll stop. If one's coming that you don't want, just step in a little sooner and he'll go around you on the other side and back with his buddies.

"He gets what he wanted. You got what you wanted. You didn't get to *do* what you wanted to do, which was to run around and chase him, but you got the result you wanted. It's kind of funny about that. We are so darned impatient. If I stand there, even if the animals are way down at the other end, I'll bet they'll move. An animal has no patience at all, but he's got more 'n us. And all you have to have is that much more than him, and you'll win ever' time. But the heck of it is, he's got just that much more 'n you, and you have to fight him all the time. We are so aggressive and demanding it's unbelievable. Boy we want that so and so, and we're going to get him if we have to mess up everything till the end of the day."

"Do you recommend any kind of fencing or handling facilities?" someone asks.

Williams shakes his head in a gesture of despair.

"Oh, all that stuff is wonderful and a lot of folks swear by it," he says, "but I've never built one foot of fence or told anybody to change one board on a corral, because I just never have seen the need. I know they'll tell you all these things. The corral should be curved. It shouldn't make much noise. The cattle should flow through so they go back in the direction they came from. And they have all these special gates. But the thing you get into is this. We're kind of strange in the way we go about things. We've taken something we do wrong, and we've built a facility to perpetuate it. We do a lot of that. I won't condemn the facilities totally, but I'll condemn the people who design them.

"I'm not being totally fair because they are forced to design what people want, and that's what *we* want. We *want* to stand at the back, and we *want* that middle animal to go in there. And that so-and-so is so damned stupid and ornery, so we want them to build us something so we can force it in there. Well, in the first place the animal isn't dumb. In the second place it isn't miserable. Then, we don't have to force it in there. So the basis for the whole thing is wrong. So we go to a bunch of people who we pick on a lot, these experts who probably don't really want to do it, and ask them to help us. The direction we're going I think is all wrong. And this is why I really don't have the easiest job in the world. You're dealing with a very intangible thing, which is why the universities won't touch it."

There was more. Williams, moving quietly alone, could gather wild cattle from pastures full of mesquite where they would hide and taunt and run lesser men to a lather. He could form up herds and lead them to graze densely and holistically without barbed wire or polywire or high-voltage chargers or any fences at all. He could persuade newly weaned calves to eat strange food. And all of it he did with his hands in his pockets and backwards to how most people would ever think to do it, counting on the animals to act as reliably and fairly as he did.

"You don't have to do like I do," he said. "But I wanted to show you that things can be done that-a-way. It does work, and it works good."

Yet when Carol watched the video or Donnie thought about those half-wild cattle merrily trotting over the bridge and into their pasture, they still doubted, even in their wish to believe.

"Sometimes you don't want to mess around. Sometimes things just need done," Donnie had said.

Carol Wagner knew the high cost of misplaced trust. "It's hard for me to let my guard down," Carol had said—about people, not cattle. "John and I moved to Saguache County to get away from the crap going on in the financial world, and there were people here who tried to pull more blatant ripoffs on us than any bond trader ever dared. I can't complain, because we Armenians can be worse than any of them. But think about us, for example. With our history, why should we trust anyone but our own? It's an instinct I have to struggle with."

Reality was at hand. The time came to sort, sell, and ship—to take the measure of land and animals and people in dollars and cents. The

Whittens' cows came in from Tracy, and the Wagners' down off Kerber Creek. The grass stopped growing, and when Karen and Donnie went out to do chores in the dark mornings now they wore gloves and heavy socks.

All in all, the numbers looked good for both herds. George and Donnie's calves from Tracy had recovered from their rocky start and topped 430 pounds—respectable for their race and age. When the vet, Martin Shellebarger, came around, he found 97 percent of their mother cows pregnant. "Even ten years ago we would have been happy with eighty-five percent," said Karen. The Wagner herd did nearly as well, considering their more random heritage and despite a few losses from altitude sickness, lightning, and just plain losses.

Trying their best to keep Bud Williams in mind, Donnie and Karen separated their calves from their mothers, although the chorus of filial dismay and maternal woe that followed kept them awake long into the night, and they rose a couple of times in the small hours to make sure that the fences held.

A few days later they cut out forty or so of the best heifers to build their herd and to replace cows they had lost or culled. The rest they had contracted to sell through Coleman Natural Beef, and these were loaded into trucks and taken to "finish" for a couple of months on organic grain at a feedlot in La Jara in the southern end of the valley before going to slaughter. The feedlot period before sale is a tradition that grew out of America's chronic overproduction of grain and most ranchers realize makes no ecological sense but feel pressured into it by fate. The purpose is no longer only to turn cheap subsidized grain into a pricier product but to get rid of any grass-fed yellowness in the fat, the American buyers having been conditioned to think yellow beef fat rancid. "Pretty crazy," Karen liked to point out, "since the same marketing geniuses have gotten producers to add artificial color to the same grain to *make* chicken fat yellow, so they can sell it as healthier than beef."

Jim Coleman's brother, Mel, still under pressure from the National Cattlemen's Association for marketing organic meat as healthier than any other, was at that moment trotting bucolic pictures of the valley around Tokyo, hoping the Japanese would buy Coleman Natural Beef as the uncorrupted essence of America. Karen and Donnie hoped for premium prices.

The shipping of the Wagner cattle followed a more traditional course. Many ranchers hedge their transactions and often speculate actively on the commodities exchanges, buying and selling options and contracts to lock in a good price or take advantage of some other region's drought or plague. John Wagner, however, champion that he was at the financial game, did not.

"Those bastards in the pits in Chicago will simply take you for all they're worth," he grumbled. "Out of the whole business, they have no ethics whatsoever. They know who's got to sell, who's got to buy, and the spread they take is just outrageous. No matter how volatile, I'd much rather trust the cash market."

He had negotiated to sell 220 410-pound steers to a buyer in Nebraska who would feed them all winter and sell them again in the spring as yearlings that would spend another summer on grass before being sold again and finished on grain the following fall. He got $1.06 a pound after discounting the weight by 2 percent for "shrink," the expected loss from stress and death in transport.

Of the heifers, some 200 big ones would be cut out to sell as "bred cattle" (pregnant) the following spring. They would spend the winter on regular feed in La Jara and be artificially inseminated there because quite likely they would not conceive under the stress of moving back to grass.

Heifers too small to breed (under 400 pounds) and any steers that didn't go to Nebraska would go to another feedlot at La Junta out on the eastern plains to be either finished for slaughter or sold as yearlings in spring.

"It's not an unusual strategy," said Donnie. "Calves may be born in Mexico, run as yearlings in Wyoming, and finish in Kansas, and somehow, even with the shrink and the haulage at two cents a mile, I guess it works out, even though it doesn't really make sense."

The day before the sorting, when a procession of great steel-sided semi trucks would arrive to set this scheme in motion, Donnie shut off water to the whole herd. It was a noteworthy gesture, as a great many cattlemen would have taken some pains to do the opposite. "Watered stock" originated as a cattle trader's term. Cornelius Vanderbilt, before he ever got into railroads, was famous for feeding his animals excessive salt to make them drink deeply before sale.

"My drying them up like that will probably make the buyer or the feedlot owner eight or nine bucks a head just by letting them drink after they weigh in, because they get paid for the gain. That's about 2 percent right there, but it's not worth it. If the cattle are full of water, working them in the corral gets so stinking and sloppy it's unbelievable, and of course the trucks get just terrible. If you're not actually selling the animals but just paying the feed yard to feed them for you, you'll probably lose anyway because of the ones that get sick standing in their own muck."

When the trucks arrived, they would not wait gracefully, so Donnie hired on two extra hands to help—the cowboy poet Peggy Godfrey and a moonlighting Forest Service worker named Sid Hall. Also, a neighbor named Gene Whitaker, who thought one of his calves might have gotten in with the Wagner cattle, showed up to help.

So much for Bud Williams. None of them had ever heard of him. They would sort mostly in the old way, which worked, and always had, although Donnie did use certain ideas like standing near the gate to move cows out of the bigger pens instead of pushing from behind.

Like most handling facilities, the Wagners' corrals consisted of several pens surrounded and in some cases divided by alleyways wide enough to drive a truck through. Standard operating procedure is to crowd whatever animals one wants to sort into one end of an alley and then let them go one at a time if possible. As they flee or are hazed along the narrow runway, someone manning a swinging gate either lets them pass or diverts them into a pen. Because the panicked animals tend to come fast, break away in groups or all together, charge the gate man, duck round the end of the gate, cut back to rejoin their buddies, and stampede back out of the sorting pen, this is a lively activity. The gate position demands lightning reflexes and judgment, and in the stupendous clamor of screaming calves and bawling mothers, human communication often fails badly. The first runthrough never goes perfectly, so the dance is played over again and again until the cut is complete.

After separating the calves from their mothers, the crew at the Wagners' had to cut out the contingents for Nebraska and La Jara and corral the remainder, each cut requiring a couple of passes. Finally, the animals had to be herded onto the scales in bunches of fifteen or twenty and pushed into the trucks. Ankle-deep cowshit would have indeed made it hell, but as it was, the mad activity, the din, the ruminant breath steaming in the frost, and the leaping back and forth to stop the rush of beasts put everyone in a good mood. One coffle of steers bursting toward the scales slammed John Wagner against the gray aspen poles of the fence, knocked out his breath, and kicked him hard in the shin for good measure, and it was hard to tell as he danced around on one foot in their wake if he grinned in pain or excitement.

Donnie had no time to consider animal sensitivities as the high-stakes challenge of sorting fell to him. As knots of shaggy, ice-bespangled beeves bore down upon him from John's end of the alley, he had about a tenth of a second to decide whether they were steer or heifer, more or less than 410 pounds, healthy or weak, well formed or scrubby, and signal in time for Sid or Peggy to jam over the gate or snatch it back in time to let something of less worth bound past. Hup, $500 this way. Hup, $400 that. Three hundred thousand or so sent one way or the other in a thrill of adrenalin.

In the middle of everything, there was only one island of calm, the brand inspector Tommy Moss. Moss, the prototype of the tall, strong, silent cowboy, was almost a legend, and his horse was better than he. It knew its work so perfectly and communicated with Moss at such a sophisticated level of telepathy that it needed no bridle beyond a single loop of rawhide around its nose for form's sake.

The two of them had to move among the calves jammed in the alleyways, count them, and make sure they all had the Wagners' Double Bar V on the left flank, but this was anything but simple given the swirling activity and the difficulty of seeing any brand at all, much less identifying it under a scruffy winter coat. Moss found Glen Whitaker's lost calf almost at once, but it was not the one Glen expected to find. Otherwise he moved quietly above the sea of furry backs making notes as his horse isolated groups of calves and then let them flow by in an orderly fashion—stepping forward, stepping back, gesturing with his nose, flipping an ear, subtly shifting a hip. The horse hadn't learned this dance from Bud Williams, of course. He just knew how and did it. When the operation fell behind and the waiting truck drivers began to pace up and down beside their rigs, Moss and his horse without being asked moved a whole alleyful and sent them down past the sorting gate trotting lightly in single file.

Carol and the buyer from Nebraska ran the scales. He loomed tall and rough cut beside her in his sheepskin rancher's coat and made notes with patronizing detachment. The scale itself was a pen that would take about twenty calves at a time. When the gates were shut, Carol would release the mechanism and watch the hand on the great wide meter swing up and settle. She and the buyer would record the weight and number, and the calves would go on down the alley to where the trucks backed up to the loading chute. There the drivers, fragrant young men in coveralls and armed with cattle prods, swore and jabbed until the animals disappeared into the booming maw of the truck, as many as sixty per load in two layers locked in by dung-encrusted panels. But sometimes calves would come tearing back out of the trucks and charge in among those coming onto the scale and small disputes arose over animals that might have gotten weighed twice and how many actually got on the truck, but Carol made her figures tally right. She left no room for disagreement. The sale would honor her weights, and the same number of animals that left Saguache County would be logged into the feed yards in La Jara and La Junta.

The last steer for Nebraska refused absolutely to board, which, of course, was why he was last. The truck man's shoulder against his backside, one hand twisting his tail, the other jabbing with the hot shot, he would mount the ramp halfway, then in a spasm of effort flatten the big man against the rough timbers of the chute and rocket backward into the little piece of alleyway between the scales and the truck.

Bud Williams had told an anecdote about that. Just try to pin that calf in the corner opposite the chute, he said, and watch where it goes when it gets by you. "But we don't think that-a-way. We've made up our mind we're gonna put them up that chute, and there's only one way to do it."

The truck man, Sid, John, Donnie, and Gene Whitaker formed behind the calf like a football linemen and cheered when the rolling steel door of the semi rattled down behind it. It was a lusty, growthy, 450-pound steer, better than the sales contract required. The buyer grinned broadly and shook Carol's hand and said he had enjoyed doing business with "you" folks.

"I think you should give me your check now," she said.

He paused and opened his mouth to say, "Well, ma'am, I'll just send that along, shortly," when he caught her eye and reached for his hip pocket instead.

He had said that to John last year, and shortly had not been so short, and his check had bounced. There, against the hood of his Cadillac, he wrote out one now for $91,223.47, and Carol filled in the blanks on a receipt she had pretyped in duplicate and gave him a copy. The brand inspector signed off on the load.

It was over. The year was over. After all the clamor and din, the corrals suddenly stood empty as the last truck blasted off down the county road toward Moffat, double black plumes of diesel smoke against the chilly rampart of the mountains. Suddenly the deep bass plaints of the 600 bereft mothers, answered now only by silence, sounded as unfulfilled as an anthem sung by half a choir. Peggy and Karen moved among them, standing on the back of the Whittens' flatbed putting down hay, popping open the bales with pocketknives, and peeling flakes of cured summer down off the sides of the old Dodge to leave a double dotted path of faded green on the yellow land as the truck idled along driverless in bottom gear.

The cows fell in behind, still bellowing intermittently; they would do so well into the following day. But at some point, children always leave. So they would snuffle and munch through another winter of wan days and long nights and drop new calves in the spring and stand for the bulls and go up the mountain and come back down. And someday they would die, either by lightning on the mountain or in an agony of labor or by the hand of some equally driven, underpaid wetback at the end of a killing chute, but that wouldn't happen this evening or tomorrow; and being animals, they didn't have much patience; and no one was pressuring them now; and they were hungry after all that; so they spread out in a long line behind the hay truck and ate.

The people also went home, exhausted but in spirits lightened by the thrill of vigorous work and success. "It wasn't quite the way we would have done it alone," Donnie admitted, "but when you have a lot of people in to help, you fall back into the old ways." But he had enjoyed it.

As Bud Williams would have said, most everyone there got what they wanted, even got to do what they wanted. Their work for the

Wagners would give Donnie and Karen enough extra to contemplate some trips outside the valley. Donnie could even spend money on his dream of getting a pilot's license without stealing from his children's college fund. Gross margin mattered somewhat less to the Wagners. They were flying to Paris with their two children for the Thanksgiving holidays, but coming out ahead would advance them in their own and the community's mind as serious ranchers, and they would if nothing bizarre happened at the feedlots.

Yet, those among them all who had seen Bud Williams put the wild cattle across that bridge at a hundred yards with his hands in his pockets, who had seen Allan Savory's slides of scoured rangelands coaxed back to health by a subtle understanding of nature, felt little pangs of guilt beneath the triumph. Could you really load cattle without a hot shot, given the situation? Could you really elect a president without attack ads and impossible promises, given the nature of the public? Was there ever really a time when you could just shake hands on a deal and leave it at that, given past experience?

Not long after the shipping of the Wagners' calves, Royce Wheeler came up from Alamosa for a wrap-up meeting of the Tracy Common Grazing Association. He brought his new range conservationist, a dazzling redheaded woman named Melissa Johnston who had just fled west from New England. Royce was upbeat about the future and keen on seeing his ideas flourish—the demonstration area, the cooperative, holistic restoration of the land. He could offer more plastic pipe. He would suggest a BLM-subsidized training course in holistic management at a motel in Monte Vista. He would hire someone from Savory's Center for HRM in Albuquerque to teach it, maybe Savory himself. The hard-core opposition would demure. He knew. Yet surely Jim Coleman and Eric Davey, and even Glen Alexander would go. And next year . . .

The Tracy meeting took place in a high-ceilinged room at the county courthouse. The foretaste of winter entered through the wavy antique window glass and rattling sash frames despite the exposed steam pipes and a hissing radiator cast with lion's feet and bas reliefs of ivy vines in a bygone era. His back to the heat, old John Davey nodded off in his chair. Above him on the wall, the Monte Vista Production Credit Association calendar, with its depiction of maddened longhorns flinging startled old-time cowboys and wrought-iron branding irons through the air, gave the only hint now of the kind of ranching he had seen.

For all the doubts and hours spent hauling polywire, the year had finished well. The areas of maximum impact around the tanks had grown back remarkably and promised to look even better come spring. The cattle on the demonstration area in the north had caught up and finished well. Although the grama flats had of course not changed visibly, the riparian areas did indeed look good. They could replan next year to avoid some of the problems of sore feet and lack of water. They might have wished for more heat in midsummer to push up warm season grasses, but you couldn't have everything. If the dissenters who had kept their stock in the southern half of the allotment were not impressed enough to join the experiment, they did not put it down.

Royce listened to it all and presented his case, but he did not push for fear of spooking his stock. Everyone dutifully wrote down tentative dates for the Savory school. If he had hoped for enthusiastic commitment, he was disappointed, but he left it at that. He wouldn't pressure. Surely come spring . . .

Afterward, George and Donnie went round to Packer's Place for a beer. Packer's was a Celtic bar set about with shamrocks and clan maps of the Emerald Isle. It had opened recently under the management of an amateur historian named John Callaghan who had wandered into Saguache from California, the first new businessman to hang out a sign on the otherwise boarded up main street in years. Callaghan had come, he said, because after retiring from the Marines he found he had viable roots nowhere else. He'd never seen Saguache before but claimed descent from the Jewish banker Isaac Gotthelf who had financed so much of the town's checkered past. He named his place after Saguache's most famous transient, Alfred Packer, who escaped from the Saguache jail in 1874 after his arrest for shooting and eating some of his buddies while snowbound in the wilderness of the time. This history and Callaghan himself made Packer's the most stimulating philosophical salon in Saguache.

As the level in the pitcher of Coors Gold dropped, the two brothers concluded that for all their efforts the world had not conspicuously improved. Desert still ground forward in the Sahel. Rapine and murder were still rampant in Armenia, Bosnia, Somalia, Sudan, Burma, Angola, Sri Lanka, Natal, the upper Amazon, and half a dozen other places, and drive-by shootings were now epidemic in Denver. Even in Saguache a few of the rowdier teenagers had spirited ninety-seven cases of beer off a truck that broke down one night on the Gun Barrel and hid them in the piñon trees above Tracy.

"They were pretty good boys, too," said Donnie, making unconscious comparison to their own youth. "Folks around here probably would have been kind of tickled by that if they hadn't gotten greedy and taken so darned many."

They did not know about Tracy.

"We don't have much right to push our ideas on the others," said George.

"The problem," said Donnie, "is too much history, too many personalities, too many other agendas. If it was just the land, it would be simple.

"And what does it take for a person to care about the land, really deeply care about it enough to risk something to look after it right? Do people not care, or just not know? Or do they care to know? How much can you pressure them before they cut back on you?"

The pitcher was half empty before they remembered to drink to the defeat of AWDI, to the new cooperation of environmentalists and producers that developed in the fight, to Steve Berlinger's work on the wildlife refuge, to the prospect of rationalizing Saguache Creek at last, to the sheep solution to the leafy spurge. There were events to celebrate because they might have happened but hadn't—no pink pyramid had risen yet over Crestone, Gary Boyce hadn't sold any water, and maybe nature herself was on the brink of proving them right about other things, too. The South Farm would fail. The industrial agriculture that had so powerfully invested in the south end of the county would have to face reality soon.

After all, they had survived another year. They had produced, organically no less, something of basic worth to human life, food, granting even popular concerns about red meat and yellow fat. They had wrung it from harsh and stingy land, if not without occasional lapses of faith. But they had left that land softer and more bountiful, if only marginally so. And they had diminished no one in doing that, except to the extent that the glittering, humming wheels of "progress" bound even them to a certain amount of bootless consumption. Altogether, maybe they had done something, maybe more than something in the vast ages of creation, that, multiplied by endless powers of ten so many small acts, small margins, minute gains or losses of water to the soil, atomic bits of wisdom, accretions of knowledge, might shape the Earth.

Donnie left George talking politics and Saguache County history with the rerooted barkeep and drove out of town into a desert night so clear and black he could look past the looming stars straight into heaven as his grandfather had about a century before. His way led past the cemetery, where so much of the flesh of that generation had come to rest, past Don Baker's private scrap yard, where much of its mechanical extension had followed, out County Road X past Coleman's corrals and the leafy spurge and the South Farm, down 50 Road past that ruined homesteader's place and its derelict willow trunks, past the slumped skeleton of that house that feller what's-his-name from Saguache left half-built years ago when his wife left him, past Everett Davey's beehives and the empty shack where an old hermit named Gordon LaMue died amid heaps of scavenged junk and an apparatus for eavesdropping on the party lines in half the county, toward a single distant square of light that was his own house.

As he pulled in among the familiar silhouettes of his own place, a lopsided moon swung up like some avatar over the Crestone Needles, and coyotes broke out yelling all over the valley. They would be courting and fighting and mating now, and the world should know that, at least in their desert, life went on, irreverent, lusting, snarling, exultant life. Coyotes make the most outrageous noise of any animal on earth, and Donnie thought it beautiful, although he hoped that Ralph the Great Pyrenees was listening well among his sheep. When Donnie came in he found Karen in good humor, still. She was making the month's supply of Whitten Coffee Concentrate and had set 2 pounds of Folger's best to steep for however long it took to render a liquor virulent enough to quicken life at chore time in sub-zero darkness.

"So, how'd it go?" she asked, putting some antelope chops in the microwave to reheat. "Am I glad I wasn't there?"

"Nope," said Donnie. "It was okay."

"Well, that's good," said Karen. "What's it going to be like next spring?"

"I don't know," said Donnie, "It's for sure going to be different."

Which was the one thing a person in Saguache County, or maybe anywhere, could say that was for sure always true.

Epilogue

I spent a year in the San Luis Valley to explore a thesis. I supposed that a fresh understanding of nature, as crystallized in Allan Savory's holism, Devraj Sharma's mathematics, or Bud Williams's cattle herding might indeed save the world from becoming desert. Such insight could save the world because average people of good heart like Donnie and Karen Whitten could put it to work today, anywhere, in decisions large or small. And their success would not depend on massive subsidy and high-tech support but on the elegance of the insight itself.

In addition, I believed that such an elegant conception of the life around us promised to give us the basis of a language capable of bridging the cultural and intellectual divisions that bedevil public discourse over our collective natural endowment.

On that sharp October day in 1992 when the Wagners shipped their cattle, I closed my notebooks and went home to write my story. For the people and places I wrote about, however, the story continued. Winter chapters followed—hunting season, bull sales, 4-H, politics, high school basketball, and driving home down the alphabet of county roads where Orion's belted sword guards heavens spangled brighter than Jacob's dream at Bethel.

Then spring came again and other seasons in their course while my manuscript, which took a year to write, would spend another two in a fitful editorial purgatory. I saw no justice in that, but God's mercy is subtle. I had picked my subjects and my year to make a point, willfully ignoring the humiliation that time often visits upon the scientist, ideologue, or journalist who impales one moment to prove a thesis while nature, careless nature, meanders on.

I, too, moved on to other things, and when I checked back in the fall of 1995, George Whitten gave me a long list of happenings in the San Luis Valley. The news was not completely bad. The water users of lower Saguache Creek had finally organized a strict enforcement of upstream diversions, and water ran farther out into the Valley than it had in years, despite the pumping of the South Farm. Much, however, had not turned out well.

- Acrimony in the Tracy Grazing Association had progressed to threats of violence. The allotment had been split to give Danny Temple his own piece. Only George Whitten continued to pursue the holistic demonstration, and Royce Wheeler of the BLM was seriously considering early retirement.
- After winning the fight against American Water Development, Inc., Valley activists had fallen into disunity. They had not responded when the enigmatic Gary Boyce and his wife had bought all the AWDI land and numerous additional water rights and launched another campaign to sell water out of state. The Boyces clearly hoped the Republican revolution in Congress would help. Colorado's new senator, Ben Campbell, had switched to the Republican party.
- The holistic director of the Alamosa–Monte Vista Wildlife Refuge, Steve Berlinger, had been downgraded to a desk job with orders not to meddle in the San Luis Valley. When noxious weeds broke forth after new regulations categorically excluded livestock, airplanes were called in to spray herbicide in the name of preserving a natural system.
- Cattle prices had fallen drastically, pushing practically all Valley ranches to the brink of insolvency, including the Whittens', despite all their holism, though their case was exacerbated because . . .

Donnie Whitten was living in a 600-square-foot rented cabin down-valley from Aspen with a married woman named Stacy from Miami. He had left Clint, Nathan, and Sarah and signed over to Karen the cattle, sheep, doublewide trailer, and his share of Grandpa Whitten's century-old ranch.

"Donnie's different now," said George.

I considered recalling my manuscript and destroying it, and probably would have had I not in the intervening time become much more sanguine about "proving" anything. After all, hadn't I actually set out to argue that the very insistence of science on linear proofs had blinded us to much of the brilliance of nature, the year-long research-project-plus-monograph being a caricature of our self-limitation.

Not long afterward my car broke down in the middle of the night not far from where Donnie now lived, and I met him in the local pancake joint for breakfast. His hair was longer, but he wore his old boots. He didn't dwell on the reorientation of his holistic goal. He told how the past winter the Wagners had invited him to accompany them to Florida so that with his new pilot's license they might rent a plane and island-hop around the Caribbean. In the space of two weeks, he had snorkeled off exclusive beaches, cruised on the Wagners's yacht, and seen martinis vanish by the quart at poolside condo parties. Among the fauna of this unfamiliar niche he had met the red-haired Stacy, whose husband spent the workweek at their other home in the New Jersey horse country tending his insurance business. Donnie had also flown to Haiti where bodies lay dead in the street in the daytime, and he lay awake all night listening to voodoo drumming outside in the dark and contrabandistas fighting in the next room. "I never imagined that a country could be that devastated," he said. "There's hardly a tree or a blade of grass left, and that Dominican Republic next door is so green you can't believe it coming from Colorado."

As I listened to him talk, it seemed to me that all these experiences had astounded Donnie equally, that for all he valued the diversity of plants and animals in the valleys and mountains of Colorado and all the wildness of it, the variety of life he'd seen on his trip had simply blown the fuses of his imagination. Meeting a bona fide Saguache County cowboy had evidently destabilized Stacy in the like degree. Two more casualties, perhaps of an oversimplified view of life.

"Ecological processes are not only more complex than we think," according to American soil scientist Michael Crofoot in reference to common dirt. "They are more complex than we can *ever* think." Surely the process—call it divine, call it evolution or succession—that raised us from the dust into our present humanity did not simplify matters by giving us free will as a bonus, as Donnie Whitten's story bears witness. Maybe a year in the San Luis Valley only reminds us again not to seek Euclidian logic in nature and certainly not in human nature. Grand insights like those of Copernicus, Adam Smith, Darwin, and perhaps even Savory may turn history down new paths, but common people animate history, and prediction there is ever Delphic, never determinate.

I still believe my thesis that true progress, progress not borrowed against the health of Earth, must come from individuals learning to do the right things at the margins, in the San Luis valleys of the world where the desert bares its teeth at our fabulous global economy. Thence must come the language that makes economy and ecology into one word that people at the center *and* the edges all understand. Since leaving the Valley, however, I've become much more philosophical about our human capacity for this. It became a very personal concern, as I spent most of 1995 in continual travel in western and southern Africa lecturing about Holistic Resource Management on the account of the World Bank and an alphabet soup of development agencies.

I can't say that I saw worse land degradation than I've seen in the American Southwest, but it is dramatic. It has happened recently. And it actually kills people. I met men younger than I (I'm fifty-one) who told of stealing meat from lions as teenage daredevils, where today's children ate meat only at funerals and had never seen a wild animal bigger than a hare. They remembered perennial grass growing taller than a man and streams full of crocodiles and hippos and walking the fifteen miles to market in the shade of trees. Now the trees were 95 percent gone. The streams ran four months out of twelve, and "grass poaching" had become a serious crime because people could not find thatch to maintain their huts.

In the wasted landscapes of Chad and Burkina Faso I found myself telling people who knew they might die if the rains didn't come next month that their real problem wasn't drought but ineffective rainfall resulting from a damaged water cycle. I would say through an interpreter in twice-broken French that they wasted their breath begging for a $5,000 well from an agency that had spent $10,000 to send this stranger among them. Instead, they should restore the landscape of their dreams by unleashing the creative power of natural succession.

I had no idea what to expect when I first delivered this bizarre gospel, but the foundation blocks of the ecosystem really were an idiom through which I could relate to people as far from myself in language, culture, and background as I might ever know. Once started, African villagers would fantasize about water and mineral cycles, energy flow, succession, and animal impact until all their dead rivers teamed again with crocodiles and hippopotamuses, and yet their enthusiasm burdened me more than rejection would have. If uncritical belief led to mistakes and disappointment, it would be my fault. That thought depressed me as much as the failure of the Whittens' marriage and the Tracy Common Grazing Association and Steve Berlinger's brave experiments.

I have gained some perspective on my dread, however. One can only do one's best and pray for forgiveness. Nature knows how to take care of itself, and by nature people are ornery, as they say in the San Luis Valley. Maybe the contrariness and individualism that makes us human is in some inscrutable way as necessary to progress as hope. Maybe the two are related.

While traveling about, I acquired the habit of asking recognized opinion-setters why they thought the land had gone to hell, and almost everyone answered in the same vein. A village chief cited the decay of tradition and morality. "The young people are not initiated. They do not make the sacrifices. Some follow other religions, and in the city you see women wearing pants. So of course it doesn't rain." The Assembly of God minister in the same district referred me to the Bible. "Without question we have entered the Last Days. It's all written out in Revelations." A climatologist, at an international conference in Tucson with the remarkable title "Desertification in DEVELOPED Countries: Why Can't We Control It," said, naturally, that more study was necessary, but climate change caused by global warming caused by industrial pollution was probably the main factor, plus, of course population growth.

It really didn't matter whom you asked. They all blamed forces so vast and abstract that nothing really could be done about them, not at least without a great deal more study. "If you respect these people," I would challenge my hungry audiences, "you should all give up. I could well be wrong. Maybe you should just get out of this place. Why spend the last of your energy preparing your fields in May, when the rain will probably *not* come in June?"

Stupid question. Fatalism, whether based on Revelations or Science or Tradition, is an affectation of people who have time to chat. People who must act *must* hope. People who hope must act, not always correctly but always creatively, and they will not let the world end in desert.

A Note on Sources

The books cited here include titles that were either direct sources of attitudes and opinions represented in *The Last Ranch* or that should be of interest to readers who want to follow up on them. By no means exhaustive, it is limited to books that might be found in a reasonably good library or that have good indexes and bibliographies. The categories are rather arbitrary, as most combine scientific, philosophical, and practical observations.

HOLISM *Holism* has become a very fuzzy word. Those who are philosophically inclined should go back to Jan Christian Smuts, *Holism and Evolution* (Highland, N.Y.: Gestalt Journal Press, 1996). Allan Savory's application of holism to land management is thoroughly discussed in very readable but rigorous form in *Holistic Resource Management* (Washington, D.C.: Island Press, 1988).

LAND AND PEOPLE Books in this category are extremely varied, but all combine an instinctively holistic point of view with acute observation and practical applications. Frederic Clements's seminal theory of succession is a good place to start. The most available publication is *Plant Succession and Indicators* (New York, Hafner Publishing Co., 1966), which combines two of Clements's most important early works. Of his later work, *Dynamics of Vegetation: Selections from the Writings of Frederic E. Clements*, edited by Clements's wife, Edith (New York, H. W. Wilson, 1949) shows his own refinement of his succession thesis and gives many examples of the nearly lost art of conducting scientific research by eclectic observation over long periods.

Even better in that vein is *Game Management* by Aldo Leopold (reissued by Madison, Wis., University of Wisconsin Press, 1986). It has the focus and rigor of a truly academic work and all the literary grace and breadth of his better known *Sand County Almanac.* A radical but practical view of farming is presented by Masanobu Fukuoka in *The One-Straw Revolution* (Emmaus, Pa., Rodale Press, 1978). On the livestock business I invite a quick read of *The Lasater Philosophy of Cattle Raising* by Laurence Lasater (Texas Western Press, University of Texas at El Paso, 1979), which is written by one of North America's most successful commercial stockmen for others in the business.

For contrast, read *Beyond Beef* by Jeremy Rifkin (New York, Dutton, 1992), which fulminates against all the evils of a cattle culture associated with people who haven't read Lasater or Savory. Wendell Berry's *The Gift of Good Land* (San Francisco, Sierra Club Books, 1977) is an eloquent critique of industrialized agriculture, as are most of Berry's other works. For anyone seeking affirmation of the intelligence of the plant kingdom, there is the best-seller *The Private Life of Plants* by David Attenborough (London, BBC Books, 1995)

DESERTIFICATION Difficult to find but well argued is *Desertification in the United States*, published by the Council on Environmental Quality (Washington, D.C., U.S. Government Printing Office, 1981). The book deals mostly with destructive farming, but the bibliography, dating from before Savory began promoting an alternative approach to management, is encyclopedic on the damage caused by uncontrolled, unholistic grazing. *Conquest of the Land through 7,000 Years* (USDA Soil Conservation Service, Agriculture Information Bulletin, no. 99) is a pamphlet of only twenty-nine pages and a classic. It chronicles the destruction of past civilizations through dysfunctional agriculture and the threat to ours. *Deserts on the March* by Paul Sears, published in 1935 and reissued in 1988 (Washington, D.C., Island Press, 1988), is also a classic and revolutionary for its day for citing very broad cultural and scientific attitudes as causes for ecologic disasters, symbolized by the Dust Bowl. *The Threatening Desert* by Alan Grainger (London, Earthscan Publications, 1990) describes the state of the art of desert control in Africa, much of which is either impractical or outright destructive from a holistic point of view, being high on technology, livestock reduction, and introduced species. *Drought Follows the Plow,* edited by Michael H. Glantz (New York, Cambridge University Press, 1994), documents the mega-effects of bad agriculture worldwide. *Only One Earth* by Lloyd Timberlake (New York, Sterling Publishing Co., 1987) gives a more hopeful view of local initiatives from around the world to counteract environmental degradation.

MATHEMATICS, ECONOMICS, AND SCIENCE One will never find better on chaos theory than the best-seller *Chaos* by James Gleick (New York, Viking, 1987), including its bibliography. *Complexity* by M. Mitchell Waldrop (New York, Simon & Schuster, 1992) extends the subject in important ways. A wise critique of mainstream economics is found in *21st Century Capitalism* by Robert Heilbroner (New York, W. W. Norton, 1993) and his *An Inquiry into the Human Prospect Looked at Again for the 1990s* (New York, W. W. Norton, 1991). One of the most intriguing and controversial alternatives is *Steady-State Economics*, written in 1977 by Herman Daly (reprinted by Island Press, Washington, D.C., 1991) and its sequel, *For the Common Good* (Boston, Beacon Press, 1989). Daly owes something of his outlook to another economist, the late Kenneth Boulding; see Boulding's *Human Betterment* (Beverly Hills, Calif., Sage Publications, 1985). For a provocative look at humanity and science, I like *So Human an Animal* by René Dubos (New York, Scribners, 1968). It fits well with *Gaia: A New Look at Life on Earth,* which James E. Lovelock published in 1979 (New York, Oxford University Press). Lovelock has collected extrapolations on his Gaia hypothesis in *The Ages of Gaia* (New York, W. W. Norton, 1988) and defends it well in a highly illustrated and rather technical book called *Healing Gaia: Practical Medicine for the Planet* (New York, Harmony Books, 1991).

THE AMERICAN WEST *Western Water Made Simple,* by the editors of the *High Country News* (Washington, D.C., Island Press, 1987), puts the water conflicts of the San Luis Valley into highly readable context, as does of course *Cadillac Desert* by Marc Reisner (New York, Viking, 1986). An engaging history of public lands in the West is *Lands of Brighter Destiny* by Elizabeth Darby Junkin (Golden, Colo., Fulcrum Press, 1986). Two rising historians/analysts of the West are Charles Wilkinson, *The Eagle Bird,* (New York, Pantheon, 1992) and *Crossing the Next Meridian* (Washington, D.C., Island Press, 1992); and Patricia Limerick, *The Legacy of Conquest: The Unbroken Past of the American West* (New York, W. W. Norton, 1987). Both writers take a sharp look at the development of a land ethic or lack of it and the role of outside economic forces and subsidies on the supposedly pioneering spirit of the region.

Index